ASVAB: POWER PRACTICE

LEARNINGEXPRESS®

NEW YORK

Library of Congress Cataloging-in-Publication Data:
ASVAB : power practice.—1st ed.
      p.   cm.
   ISBN-13: 978-1-57685-749-6 (pbk. : alk. paper)
   ISBN-10: 1-57685-749-2 (pbk. : alk. paper)   1. Armed Services Vocational Aptitude
Battery—Study guides.   I. LearningExpress (Organization)
   U408.5.A8465   2010
   355.0076—dc22

                                                              2010017564

Printed in the United States of America

9 8 7 6 5 4 3 2 1

First Edition

ISBN-10 1-57685-749-2
ISBN-13 978-1-57685-749-6

For information or to place an order, contact LearningExpress at:
   2 Rector Street
   26th Floor
   New York, NY 10006

Or visit us at:
   www.learnatest.com

CONTENTS

CONTRIBUTORS ▶

The following individuals contributed to the content of this book.

Gregory C. Benoit is a freelance writer and editor living in Rhode Island. He holds a BA in English from Connecticut College, and an MA in medieval literature from the University of Connecticut. He spent 12 years teaching college-level English, writing, and literature, and also worked for many years as a newspaper editor and freelance photographer.

Alec Durrell is a graduate of the University of North Carolina at Chapel Hill with a BS in chemistry. He is currently a doctoral candidate in inorganic chemistry at the California Institute of Technology.

CDR Bill Paisley is a former F-14 Tomcat radar intercept officer with 25 years' active and reserve service. He holds two undergraduate degrees in education and an MA in national security. He lives in northern Virginia and works as a modeling and simulation professional for the U.S. Navy.

Jason Rivera received his BS degree in chemical engineering from Cornell University and spent two years working in the pharmaceutical industry. For a few years after that he taught life science in private school and outdoor settings.

The editor would also like to especially thank **Alex Duym** for his invaluable assistance in the creation of the manuscript.

ABOUT *ASVAB:* POWER PRACTICE

LearningExpress understands the importance of achieving top scores on your ASVAB, and we strive to publish the most authentic and comprehensive ASVAB test preparation materials available today. Practice does indeed make perfect, and that's why we've created this book—composed of full-length ASVAB practice exams complete with detailed answer explanations, it offers recruits all the extra practice they need to get great scores. Whether used on its own or as a powerful companion to our other best-selling ASVAB preparation titles, *ASVAB: Power Practice* is the key to a top score and a brighter future.

CHAPTER 1

ABOUT THE ASVAB

CHAPTER SUMMARY

This chapter introduces the Armed Services Vocational Aptitude Battery (ASVAB), describes what is included on the test, and explains how this book can help you prepare and achieve maximum exam success.

The Armed Services Vocational Aptitude Battery (ASVAB) is a multiple-aptitude test taken by over 800,000 Americans every year. It is comprised of timed subtests in different subjects that measure the range of aptitudes necessary for military enlistment and job placement. A breakdown of these subtests—by test version—is shown in the table on pages 2–3, and a more detailed description of each subtest test appears later in this chapter.

The ASVAB, which was created by the United States Department of Defense in 1968 and adopted by all armed services by 1976, is used for two main purposes:

- **As a military recruiting tool.** The United States Department of Defense uses the ASVAB to determine the abilities of potential recruits, to gauge what they already know about certain subjects, to measure their general learning and vocational aptitude, and to predict performance in certain academic areas.
- **As a guide for high school and post–secondary school students.** The ASVAB helps students make decisions about their career paths, whether in the military or in another field.

ASVAB:
Paper and Pencil versus CAT

Individuals can expect to take a paper-and-pencil version of the ASVAB at their local high school or a neighboring school offering the test. The student version of the exam (offered to high school juniors and seniors) is often referred to as the *institutional* version; candidates for military enlistment take the *production* version.

Depending on where an enlistee takes the ASVAB, he or she will take either the computer version of the ASVAB, called the CAT-ASVAB, or the paper-and-pencil version. Candidates taking the ASVAB at a Military Entrance Processing Station (MEPS) will take the computer version, while candidates for enlistment taking the ASVAB at a reserve center or Mobile Examination Team (MET) site will take the paper-and-pencil version.

The paper-and-pencil version of the ASVAB consists of either eight subtests (if you're a student) or nine subtests (if you're a candidate for enlistment). The majority of military applicants, approximately 70%, take the CAT-ASVAB. The CAT-ASVAB is a computer-adaptive test, which means that the test adapts to your ability level. The computer will give you the first question, and, if you answer correctly, it gives you another question on the same subject—but one that is a bit harder than the first. The questions get harder as you progress, and after you answer a certain number of questions correctly the computer skips to the next subtest.

The following is additional information about the CAT-ASVAB:

- It consists of ten subtests—the Auto Information and Shop Information subtests are administered separately. However, the results are combined into one score (labeled AS).
- The test takes about $1\frac{1}{2}$ hours to complete.
- Each subtest must be completed within a certain timeframe. Most individuals complete the subtests within the time alloted.
- Once you have completed a subtest, you do not have to wait for everyone else to finish—you can move on to the next subtest.
- As you complete each subtest, the computer displays the number of items and amount of time remaining for that subtest in the lower right-hand corner of the screen.
- Once an answer has been submitted, you cannot review or change it.
- Test scores are available as soon as you complete the test.
- If you choose to take the CAT-ASVAB, you will be trained on answering test questions, using the computer keyboard and mouse, and getting help before starting the exam.
- The number of subtests, number of questions, and time limits for the CAT-ASVAB differ from the paper-and-pencil version in the following ways.

Please Note: If you are a recruit, chances are you're going to take the CAT-ASVAB. However, because this book is geared toward *power practice*, the six practice

NUMBERS OF ITEMS AND TESTING TIME FOR THE PAPER & PENCIL ASVAB		
SUBTEST	NUMBER OF QUESTIONS	TIME (MINUTES)
General Science (GS)	25	11
Arithmetic Reasoning (AR)	30	36
Word Knowledge (WK)	35	11
Paragraph Comprehension (PC)	15	13
Mathematics Knowledge (MK)	25	24

NUMBERS OF ITEMS AND TESTING TIME FOR THE PAPER & PENCIL ASVAB (continued)		
SUBTEST	NUMBER OF QUESTIONS	TIME (MINUTES)
Electronics Information (EI)	20	9
Auto and Shop Information (AS)	25	11
Mechanical Comprehension (MC)	25	19
Assembling Objects* (AO)	25	15
Institutional Version Totals	**200 Items**	**134 Minutes**
Production Version Totals	**225 Items**	**149 Minutes**

*The Assembling Objects (AO) subtest is not included institutional version of the ASVAB taken by high school students as part of the ASVAB Career Exploration Program.

NUMBER OF ITEMS AND TESTING TIME FOR THE CAT-ASVAB		
SUBTEST	NUMBER OF QUESTIONS	TIME (MINUTES)
General Science (GS)	16	8
Arithmetic Reasoning (AR)	16	39
Word Knowledge (WK)	16	8
Paragraph Comprehension (PC)	11	22
Mathematics Knowledge (MK)	16	20
Electronics Information (EI)	16	8
Auto Information (AI)	11	7
Shop Information (SI)	11	6
Mechanical Comprehension (MC)	16	20
Assembling Objects (AO)	16	16
Totals	**145 Items**	**154 Minutes**

tests found here follow the paper-and-pencil production specifications because of the higher number of questions.

The ASVAB Subtests

The following is a detailed description of each of the subtests on the ASVAB. Most sections of the ASVAB depend on your knowledge of the subject as covered in high school courses or other related reading. The two sections that do not depend on knowledge of the subjects in advance are the Paragraph Comprehension and Assembling Objects sections. For the Paragraph Comprehension questions, you will be able to find the answers using the information given in the paragraph provided. The Assembling Objects section tests your natural spatial aptitude skills.

Subtest 1: General Science

The General Science subtest consists of questions that are designed to measure your ability to recognize, apply, and analyze basic scientific principles in the areas of:

- **life science:** botany, zoology, anatomy and physiology, ecology
- **physical science:** force and motion, energy, fluids and gases, atomic structure, chemistry
- **earth and space science:** astronomy, geology, meteorology, oceanography

Subtest 2: Arithmetic Reasoning

The Arithmetic Reasoning subtest consists of word problems describing everyday life situations and is designed to measure your reasoning skills and understanding of:

- operations with whole numbers
- operations with fractions, decimals, and money
- ratio and proportion
- calculating interest and percentage
- measurement of perimeter, area, volume, time, and temperature

Subtest 3: Word Knowledge

The Word Knowledge subtest consists of questions that ask you to choose the correct definitions of verbs, nouns, adjectives, and adverbs. These questions come in two forms:

- words presented alone, with no context
- words presented in the context of a short sentence

Subtest 4: Paragraph Comprehension

The Paragraph Comprehension subtest consists of questions that are based on several short passages, written on a variety of topics. No prior knowledge of the subject is required—all the information you need to answer the questions will be found in the passage.

The questions in this subtest are designed to test the following abilities:

- **literal comprehension:** ability to identify stated facts, reworded facts, and sequence of events
- **implicit, inferential, or critical comprehension:** ability to draw conclusions, identify the main idea of a paragraph, determine the author's purpose, mood, or tone, and identify style and technique
- **comprehension of main idea or words in context:** ability to condense a paragraph into a single main idea, and determine the meaning of an unfamiliar word based on its context or usage

Subtest 5: Mathematics Knowledge

The Mathematics Knowledge subtest contains questions designed to measure your understanding and ability to recognize and apply mathematical concepts, principles, and procedures. The questions cover:

- **number theory:** factors, multiples, reciprocals, number properties, primes, and integers
- **numeration:** fractions, decimals, percentages, conversions, order of operations, exponents, rounding, roots, radicals, and signed numbers
- **algebraic operations and equations:** solving or determining equations, factoring, simplifying algebraic expressions, and converting sentences to equations
- **geometry and measurement:** coordinates, slope, Pythagorean theorem, angle measurement, properties of polygons and circles, perimeter, area, volume, and unit conversion
- **probability:** analyzing and determining probability

Subtest 6: Electronics Information

The Electronics Information subtest consists of 20 questions that are designed to measure basic knowledge of principles of electrical and electronics systems:

- electrical tools, symbols, devices, and materials
- electrical circuits

- electricity and electronic systems
- electrical current, voltage, conductivity, resistance, and grounding

Subtest 7: Auto and Shop Information

The Auto and Shop Information subtest includes questions on automotive repair and building construction. General shop practices are also included. The CAT-ASVAB splits these two subtests into separate subtests, but combines results into one score. The questions cover the following topics:

- automotive components
- automotive systems
- automotive tools
- automotive troubleshooting and repair
- shop tools
- building materials
- building and construction procedures

Subtest 8: Mechanical Comprehension

The Mechanical Comprehension subtest consists of problems—many of them illustrated—covering general mechanics, physical principles, and principles of simple machines such as gears, pulleys, levers, force, and fluid dynamics. Problems involving basic properties of materials are also included. The questions may test knowledge, application, and analysis of:

- **basic compound machines:** gears, cams, pistons, cranks, linkages, belts, and chains
- **simple machines:** levers, planes, pulleys, screws, wedges, wheels, and axles
- **mechanical motion:** friction, velocity, direction, acceleration, and centrifugal force
- **fluid dynamics:** hydraulic forces and compression
- **properties of materials:** weight, strength, expansion/contraction, absorption, and center of gravity
- **structural support**

Subtest 9: Assembling Objects

The Assembling Objects subtest consists of illustrated questions that test your ability to determine how an object should look when its parts are put together. These questions measure:

- general mechanics and physical principles
- aptitude for discerning spatial relations
- problem-solving abilities

Arranging to Take the ASVAB

Over 14,000 high schools across the United States offer the ASVAB. If you are in high school, ask your guidance counselor about taking the ASVAB. Many high schools offer the ASVAB at a specific time during the school year. If you missed your school's offering of the ASVAB, chances are a neighboring school will be offering it at another time during the school year.

If you're out of high school, go to the nearest recruiter of the branch of the armed services that you're interested in. There is no charge to take the ASVAB. Taking the exam doesn't obligate you to join the military, although you can probably expect a persuasive sales pitch about the opportunities available in the Army, Air Force, Navy, Marine Corps, and U.S. Coast Guard. The military service in charge of maintaining the administrative elements of the ASVAB is the Army, but all armed services use the information provided by taking the test. For more details about the ASVAB, visit the ASVAB website at www.goarmy.com.

What the ASVAB Means for You

If you're taking the ASVAB as a high school student with no intention of entering the military, the test can help you find out what things you're good at and what areas might be good career paths. Your ASVAB results can also help you decide whether or not to go to college or get training for a specialized career in an area such as electronics. Your scores may also show you areas that you have less aptitude for. Your guidance counselor can explain your score report and how best to use it.

Approximately 500,000 people each year take the ASVAB in order to enlist in the military. Your scores on certain subtests of the ASVAB help determine your eligibility. Furthermore, once you're enlisted your scores on various subtests help determine which jobs, or Military Occupational Specialties, you'll be allowed to train in. For example, if you want to learn how to be a computer operator, you need good scores in the Paragraph Comprehension, Word Knowledge, Mathematics Knowledge, General Science, and Mechanical Comprehension subtests. See Chapter 2 for more details on what your score means to your choice of military careers.

The bottom line is that you want to score well on the ASVAB if you're looking forward to a career in the armed forces, and this book is here to help.

Advice for Parents

As your son or daughter prepares for the transition to their next phase of life, there are a number of things you can do to help pave the way for a successful ASVAB experience and score. Chapter 3 of this book, "The LearningExpress Test Preparation System," provides valuable guidelines and suggestions for ways your child can prepare for this test. The nine-step process includes sections (such as "Straight Talk about the ASVAB" and "Conquer Test Anxiety") that will address concerns you or your child may have about this exam, while the section titled "Reach Your Peak Performance Zone" will provide valuable tips on how to perform best on test day.

The Internet can be a great source of ASVAB information and assistance as well. The ASVAB Career Exploration Program webpage, sponsored by the Department of Defense, is aimed at high school students and their parents and can be viewed at www.asvabprogram.com.

It's also important to remember that the ASVAB is not only for military recruits. It is offered at no cost to high school students across the nation and is a great tool for helping students determine their aptitude across a wide variety of technical, scientific, and social fields.

As a parent, your knowledge of your son or daughter's efforts and accomplishments over the years, coupled with your own experience, makes you an invaluable resource for your child. Being a positive and encouraging part of your child's ASVAB prep is a great way to help make his or her goals a reality.

The key to success in almost anything is preparation, and one of the very best ways to prepare for the ASVAB is to take each of the six practice tests in the book and measure how you're doing as you pass each milestone. There are a number of ways to use this book to help you achieve a top score, depending on what you are trying to achieve:

If You Purchased This Book as a Stand-Alone Practice

If you purchased this book on its own to get concentrated practice for test day, start off by taking the diagnostic test in Chapter 4 to get an idea how you might perform on the ASVAB if you were to sit for it today. When you are finished with the diagnostic, find your scores by using the information in Chapter 2 and then note what subtests you may need extra practice in. As you work your way through the book, be sure to note your progress in these and other areas. If your scores don't improve significantly as you work your way through the tests and you feel like you need to review particular subjects, we highly recommend purchasing our ASVAB review title *ASVAB, 4th Edition*. In addition to comprehensive review of all the subjects tested on the ASVAB, you'll get five more complete tests.

If You Purchased This Book in Conjunction with *ASVAB, 4th Edition*

If you've purchased this book in conjunction with one of our other ASVAB test prep titles such *ASVAB, 4th Edition*, we recommend that you read that book first to learn all about the ASVAB and the recruitment process and then use the review and practice tests to hone your skills. Armed with the knowledge you have gained from that book, you can determine your strengths and weaknesses and tailor the rest of your preparation accordingly. Use the six additional tests in *ASVAB: Power Practice* to solidify your preparation and track your progress, and then return to the review and practice chapters in *ASVAB, 4th Edition* as needed to ensure that you are focusing on the material that you need the most help in.

Remember, practice and preparation are the keys to doing well on this or any exam. This book will give you everything you need to score your best. Good luck!

THE SCORE YOU NEED FOR THE JOB YOU WANT

CHAPTER SUMMARY
To get the most out of this book, you need to know the score you need to get into the service branch of your choice, and the score you need to get the specialties that interest you. This chapter walks you step-by-step through the process of converting your scores on the practice tests in this book into the scores the military uses. Reading this chapter, you will also learn what scores you need for selected Military Occupational Specialties.

When you take the six practice tests in this book, you will want to know whether your scores measure up. You will also probably want to know what kinds of jobs or Military Occupational Specialties (MOSs), your score will enable you to select. You will need some patience here. There are several different kinds of composite scores you will need to compute from your raw scores on the individual parts of the ASVAB.

About Your Scores

Your first step is to convert the raw scores you got on your practice exam to the scores the military uses to compute the various composites—the composite score that says whether you can enlist, and the composite scores that show which MOSs you qualify for.

In the table on page 11, write your scores on ASVAB Diagnostic Test in the column that says "Raw Score" under Diagnostic Test. Your raw score is simply the number you got right on that subtest. For the raw score in the last blank, Verbal Equivalent, add together your raw scores on both the Word Knowledge (WK) and Paragraph Comprehension (PC) subtests.

Note that blanks are also provided for ASVAB Practice Test 1 through 5; you can fill in those blanks when you take those tests. This table will help you keep track of your improvement as you work through the practice tests in this book.

All the score conversions throughout this chapter are approximate. Different versions of the ASVAB vary in their score conversions, and your scores on the practice tests in this book will not be exactly the same as your score on the real ASVAB. Use the exams in this book to get an *approximate* idea of where you stand and how much you're improving.

Now you need to fill in the column on page 11 labeled "Scaled Score." On pages 12–13 is a table that shows you approximate correlations between raw scores and scaled scores for each subtest. On the left are raw scores. The other columns show the equivalent scaled score for each test. (Make sure you're using the column for the proper subtest! The subtests are labeled with the abbreviations shown in the left-hand column of the table on page 11.)

Do You Qualify?

Now that you have your scaled score for each subtest filled in on the table on page 11, you're ready for the next steps: finding out whether your score will get you in to the military and finding out which MOSs your scores may qualify you for. Remember to use only your scaled scores, not your raw scores, for these conversions.

The Armed Forces Qualifying Test (AFQT) Score

All five branches of the military compute your AFQT score—the one that determines whether you can enlist—in the same way. Only the Verbal Equivalent (which you determined by adding Word Knowledge and Paragraph Comprehension scores and then converting to a scaled score), Arithmetic Reasoning, and Mathematics Knowledge scaled scores count toward your AFQT. The military just wants to know whether you have basic reading and arithmetic skills. The score conversion goes like this:

$$2(VE) + AR + MK = AFQT$$

YOUR SCORES

SUBTEST	DIAGNOSTIC TEST		PRACTICE TEST 1		PRACTICE TEST 2		PRACTICE TEST 3		PRACTICE TEST 4		PRACTICE TEST 5	
	RAW SCORE	SCALED SCORE	RAW SCORE	SCALED SCORE	RAW SCORE	SCALED SCORE	RAW SCORE	SCALED SCORE	RAW SCORE	SCALED SCORE	RAW SCORE	SCALED SCORE
General Science (GS)												
Arithmetic Reasoning (AR)												
Word Knowledge (WK)												
Paragraph Comprehension (PC)												
Mathematics Knowledge (MK)												
Electronics Information (EI)												
Auto and Shop Information (AS)												
Mechanical Comprehension (MC)												
Verbal Equivalent (VE = WK + PC)												

Please note: Assembling Objects (AO) has been omitted from these tables because at the time of publication only the Navy uses the (AO) score.

RAW SCORE TO SCALED SCORE CONVERSION									
RAW	GS	AR	WK	PC	MK	EI	AS	MC	VE
0	20	26	20	20	27	26	28	27	20
1	21	26	20	20	27	29	30	28	20
2	23	28	20	20	28	31	31	29	20
3	25	29	22	23	30	33	33	31	20
4	27	31	23	26	32	35	35	32	20
5	28	32	24	30	33	38	36	33	20
6	30	33	25	33	35	40	38	35	20
7	32	35	27	36	37	42	40	37	21
8	34	36	28	39	38	44	41	38	22
9	36	37	29	42	40	47	43	40	23
10	38	39	30	45	42	49	45	42	24
11	40	40	32	48	43	51	47	44	25
12	42	42	33	51	45	53	48	46	26
13	44	43	34	54	47	56	50	48	27
14	46	44	35	58	48	58	52	50	27
15	48	46	36	61	50	60	53	52	28
16	50	47	38		52	63	55	54	29
17	52	48	39		53	65	57	56	30
18	54	50	40		55	67	58	58	31
19	56	51	41		56	69	60	60	32
20	58	53	43		58	72	62	62	33
21	60	54	44		60		63	65	34
22	62	55	45		61		65	67	35
23	64	57	46		63		67	69	36
24	65	58	47		65		68	71	37
25	67	59	49		66		70	72	37

Find the subtest you want to score in the column headings on top. Then, in the left column, find your raw score for that subtest. Follow the raw-score row to the right until you get to the proper subtest. That number is your scaled score for this subtest.

RAW	GS	AR	WK	PC	MK	EI	AS	MC	VE
26		61	50						38
27		62	51						39
28		63	52						40
29		65	54						41
30		66	55						42
31			56						43
32			57						44
33			58						45
34			60						46
35			61						47
36									48
37									48
38									49
39									50
40									51
41									52
42									53
43									54
44									55
45									56
46									57
47									58
48									58
49									59
50									60

RAW SCORE TO SCALED SCORE CONVERSION (continued)

Find the subtest you want to score in the column headings on top. Then, in the left column, find your raw score for that subtest. Follow the raw-score row to the right until you get to the proper subtest. That number is your scaled score for this subtest.

In other words, your AFQT (scaled score) is your Verbal Equivalent scaled score, doubled, added to your Arithmetic Reasoning and Mathematics Knowledge scaled scores. Fill in the blanks below to find your AFQT on the ASVAB Diagnostic Test.

VE score	_____ × 2 =	_____
AR score		_____
MK score	+	_____
AFQT (scaled score)		_____

Now use the table "AFQT Scaled Score to Percentile Conversion" on page 15. Look up the score you wrote in the blank for AFQT scaled score above, and next to it, you'll find your approximate percentile score.

If your AFQT on the Diagnostic Test isn't up to par, don't despair. You're using this book to help you improve your score, after all, and you've just gotten started. Remember, too, that your score on these practice exams may not be exactly the same as your score on the actual test.

On the other hand, a higher score makes you more attractive to recruiters, and depending on your score on individual subtests, it may qualify you for more of the occupational specialities you want.

Military Occupational Specialty Qualifying Scores

If your AFQT is high enough to get you in, the next thing your scores will be used for is to help determine which Military Occupational Specialities (MOSs) you qualify for. For this purpose, the branches of the military use composite scores—different from the AFQT—made up of scores on various subtests.

Each branch of the military has its own way of computing composites and its own classification system for the MOSs. The tables here use the Army's MOSs and composites. All the branches offer similar MOSs, and the composite scores required are also similar. So if you're considering another branch of the service, you can still use these tables to get a good idea of where you stand.

Turn to pages 16–19 to find a list of selected MOSs and the requirements for each job. If you're using the ASVAB for career guidance rather than for entrance into the military, pay special attention to the column labeled "Other Equivalent Civilian Occupations."

In the column "Minimum ASVAB Composite Score," you'll see which composite is used to determine whether you're qualified for a given MOS and the minimum score required on that composite. Go on to the section "Computing Your Composites" on page 20 to find out whether you match that minimum score.

AFQT SCALED SCORE TO PERCENTILE CONVERSION

SCALED SCORE	PERCENTILE	SCALED SCORE	PERCENTILE	SCALED SCORE	PERCENTILE
≤109	1	185	33	218	68
110–118	2	186	34	219	69
119–124	3	187–188	35	220–221	70
125–133	4	189	36	222	71
134–137	5	190	38	223	72
138–141	6	191	39	224	73
142–145	7	192	40	225	74
146–147	8	193	41	226	75
148–151	9	194	42	227	76
152–153	10	195	43	228	77
154–156	11	196	44	229	78
157	12	197	45	230	79
158–159	13	198	46	231	80
160	14	199	47	232	81
161–162	15	200	48	233–234	82
163–164	16	201	49	235	83
165–166	17	202	50	236	84
167	18	203	51	237–238	85
168–169	19	204	52	239	86
170	20	205	53	240	87
171	21	206	54	241–242	88
172–173	22	207	55	243	89
174	23	208	56	244–245	90
175	24	209	57	246	91
176–177	25	210	59	247–248	92
178	26	211	60	249–251	93
179	27	212	61	252–253	94
180	28	213	62	254–256	95
181	29	214	63	257–259	96
182	30	215	64	260–263	97
183	31	216	66	264–268	98
184	32	217	67	≥269	99

REQUIREMENTS FOR SELECTED MILITARY OCCUPATIONAL SPECIALITIES

MILITARY OCCUPATIONAL SPECIALITY	PHYSICAL DEMANDS	MINIMUM ASVAB COMPOSITE SCORE	REQUIREMENTS	OTHER EQUIVALENT CIVILIAN OCCUPATIONS
Infantryman*	very heavy	CO 90	red/green color discrimination, vision correctable to 20/20 in one eye and 20/100 in the other	none
Combat Engineer*	very heavy	CO 90	normal color vision	truck driver, construction worker, laborer, blaster, others
PATRIOT Missile Crewmember	moderately heavy	OF 100	red/green color discrimination, SECRET security clearance	none
M1 Armor (tank) Crewman*	very heavy	CO 90	normal color vision, vision correctable to 20/20 in one eye and 20/100 in the other, maximum height of 6'1"	none
Multimedia Illustrator	moderately heavy	ST 95, EL 95	normal color vision	illustrator, sign painter
PATRIOT System Repairer	medium	MM 105	normal color vision, SECRET security clearance	radar mechanic, electronics technician
Radio Repairer	heavy	EL 110	normal color vision, SECRET security clearance, one year of high school algebra and science	radio mechanic, electronics mechanic
Single Channel Radio Operator	very heavy	SC 100, EL 100	SECRET security clearance, ability to enunciate English, ability to type 25 WPM	radio operator, communications equipment operator, radio installer
Aviation Systems Repairer	moderately heavy	ST 115	normal color vision, TOP SECRET security clearance, completion of high school algebra course; certain restrictions on foreign ties	automatic equipment technician, radio repairer, teletypewriter installer
Psychological Operations Specialist	medium	ST 105	normal color vision, SECRET security clearance, minimum score on language test	editor, intelligence specialist

*As of the time of writing, this MOS is limited to male candidates.

REQUIREMENTS FOR SELECTED MILITARY OCCUPATIONAL SPECIALITIES *(continued)*

MILITARY OCCUPATIONAL SPECIALITY	PHYSICAL DEMANDS	MINIMUM ASVAB COMPOSITE SCORE	REQUIREMENTS	OTHER EQUIVALENT CIVILIAN OCCUPATIONS
Dental Laboratory Specialist	moderately heavy	GM 100, ST 95	normal color vision	dental laboratory technician
Fabric Repair Specialist	very heavy	GM 85	civilian acquired skills (i.e., prior training in fabric repair)	sewing machine operator, automobile upholsterer, tailor, canvas worker
Machinist	heavy	GM 100	normal color vision, visual acuity of 20/30 without correction, minimum score on other visual tests	machinist, welder, drop hammer operator
Broadcast Journalist	light	GT 110	ability to type 20 WPM, completion of at least two years of high school English, driver's license	announcer, continuity writer, reader, screen writer
Carpentry and Masonry Specialist	very heavy	GM 90	normal color vision, freedom from vertigo	carpenter, bricklayer, cement mason, stonemason, rigger, structural steel worker
Interior Electrician	heavy	EL 95	normal color vision	electrician
Ammunition Specialist	very heavy	ST 100	normal color vision, CONFIDENTIAL security clearance, not allergic to explosive components, not claustrophobic	accounting clerk, stock control supervisor, supply clerk, explosives operator
Crane Operator	very heavy	GM 90	red/green color discrimination, driver's license	crane operator, power shovel operator
Light-Wheel Vehicle Mechanic	very heavy	MM 90	normal color vision, equipment qualifications	automobile mechanic, diesel mechanic
UH-60 Helicopter Repairer	very heavy	MM 105	normal color vision, no history of alcohol or drug abuse	aircraft mechanic

REQUIREMENTS FOR SELECTED MILITARY OCCUPATIONAL SPECIALITIES (continued)

MILITARY OCCUPATIONAL SPECIALITY	PHYSICAL DEMANDS	MINIMUM ASVAB COMPOSITE SCORE	REQUIREMENTS	OTHER EQUIVALENT CIVILIAN OCCUPATIONS
Executive Administrative Assistant	not applicable	ST 105	SECRET security clearance, ability to type 35 WPM, minimum score on English test	stenographer, administrative assistant, secretary
Legal Specialist	light	CL 110	ability to type 35 WPM, no civil convictions	court clerk, law clerk
Administrative Specialist	medium	CL 95	ability to type 25 WPM	administrative assistant, clerk typist, office helper, mail clerk
Finance Specialist	light	CL 95	no record of dishonesty or moral turpitude	bookkeeper, cashier, payroll clerk
Information Systems Operator	moderately heavy	ST 100	normal color vision, SECRET security clearance	computer operator, data processing technician, coding clerk
Personnel Administration Specialist	medium	CL 95	ability to type 20 WPM	personnel clerk
Cartographer	light	ST 85	normal color vision, other visual tests	drafter, cartographic technician
Watercraft Operator	very heavy	MM 100	normal color vision, vision correctable to 20/20 in one eye and 20/40 in the other, prior training	boat operator, seaman
Motor Transport Operator	very heavy	OF 90	red/green color discrimination, driver's license	chauffeur, truck driver, dispatcher
Medical Specialist	moderately heavy	ST 95	normal color vision	medical assistant, first aid attendant, emergency medical technician, nurse's aide
Practical Nurse	medium	ST 95	normal color vision; ability to complete licensure training or already licensed	licensed practical nurse

REQUIREMENTS FOR SELECTED MILITARY OCCUPATIONAL SPECIALITIES (continued)

MILITARY OCCUPATIONAL SPECIALITY	PHYSICAL DEMANDS	MINIMUM ASVAB COMPOSITE SCORE	REQUIREMENTS	OTHER EQUIVALENT CIVILIAN OCCUPATIONS
Behavioral Science Specialist	light	ST 105		caseworker
Radiology Specialist	moderately heavy	ST 110		X-ray technician, radiologic technologist
Animal Care Specialist	moderately heavy	ST 95	normal color vision, completion of high school course in biology	animal health technician
Food Service Specialist	heavy	OF 90	normal color vision, driver's license, possess or be qualified for food handler's license	chef, cook, butcher, baker
Military Police	moderately heavy	ST 95	red/green color discrimination, minimum height 5'8" for males, 5'4" for females, CONFIDENTIAL security clearance, driver's license, no record of civilian convictions	police officer, guard
Intelligence Analyst	medium	ST 105	normal color vision, TOP SECRET security clearance, no record, certain restrictions on foreign ties	editor, intelligence specialist

Computing Your Composites

Maybe you looked at the table of MOSs and said, "Wow, I didn't know the Army had Animal Care Specialists!"—or Broadcast Journalists or Legal Specialists or whatever MOSs caught your eye. The Air Force, Navy, Marines, and Coast Guard have all these specialities, too. You might think, "I could go for Animal Care Specialist training, and then when I get out I could use my G. I. Bill money to go to veterinary school and become a vet. I could work as an assistant in a vet's office while I go to school. This is great! But what does this ST 95 score mean? Can I make it?"

This is absolutely the last score computation you'll have to do, but it's a complicated one. Stick with it, and be patient. Your future may depend on your performance on the ASVAB.

ST 95, like the other letter-number combinations in the "Minimum ASVAB Composite Score" column, is the composite score the Army uses to determine your eligibility for the given MOS. The composite scores used by the other branches of the service are similar, though not identical. Here's a key to the meaning of the composite scores listed in the MOS table:

- FA: Field Artillery
- OF: Operations and Food Handling
- ST: Skilled Technical
- GT: General Technical
- CL: Clerical
- GM: General Maintenance
- EL: Electronics Repair
- MM: Mechanical Maintenance
- SC: Surveillance/Communications
- CO: Combat

So, if you want to be an Animal Care Specialist, you need to know your ST, or Skilled Technical, composite score. (You'll also, of course, have to meet the other requirements listed in the MOS table. Check with your recruiter.)

Here's how to compute the composites. Look for the composite(s) for the MOS(s) you want in the list below. After the name of the composite is a list of the subtest scores you have to add together. Go back to the table on page 11, where you filled in your subtest scores, and get your scores on those subtests. (Remember to use your scaled scores, not your raw scores!) Adding them up gives you a sum called a Subtest Standard Score (SSS). When you have the SSS for the composite you want, turn to the table on pages 22–23. That table lists SSSs in the left column. Find the SSS you computed for the composite you want, and then follow the line to the right until you get to the composite you're looking for. That's your composite for this subtest, and you should write it in the blank next to the appropriate abbreviation. Now you can compare your composite score to the minimum requirement listed in the MOS table. You don't have to compute all the composite scores, just the ones that are required for the jobs you're interested in.

FA:	AR _____	+ MK _____	+ MC _____		= SSS_____	FA composite: _____
OF:	VE _____	+ AS _____	+ MC _____		= SSS_____	OF composite: _____
ST:	GS _____	+ VE _____	+ MC _____	+ MK _____	= SSS_____	ST composite: _____
GT:	VE _____	+ AR _____			= SSS_____	GT composite: _____
CL:	VE _____	+ AR _____	+ MK _____		= SSS_____	CL composite: _____
GM:	GS _____	+ AS _____	+ MK _____	+ EI _____	= SSS_____	GM composite: _____
EL:	GS _____	+ AR _____	+ MK _____	+ EI _____	= SSS_____	EL composite: _____
MM:	AS _____	+ MC _____	+ EI _____		= SSS_____	MM composite: _____
SC:	VE _____	+ AR _____	+ AS _____	+ MC _____	= SSS_____	SC composite: _____
CO:	AR _____	+ AS _____	+ MC _____		= SSS_____	CO composite: _____

Suppose you want to be an Animal Care Specialist. The composite score you need for this MOS is ST 95. So you look at the ST line and find you need to add your scores for VE, MK, MC, and GS. You go back to the table on page 11 and find your *scaled scores* (not raw scores) for these subtests. Let's say you did pretty well in Mechanical Comprehension and General Science, and not as well in Paragraph Comprehension and Word Knowledge (your Verbal Equivalent score) or Mathematics Knowledge. So you fill in line ST like this:

ST: GS __54__ + VE __41__ + MC __61__ + MK __38__ = SSS_____   ST composite: _____

Add up your four subtest scores to get the SSS:

ST: GS __54__ + VE __41__ + MC __61__ + MK __38__ = SSS __194__   ST composite: ___

Now go to the table on the next page. Find ST at the top of the table, and follow that column down until you get to the row for 190–194. You find that your ST composite score is in the range of 95–97; in fact, it's probably about 97, since your SSS is near the top of its range.

ST: GS __54__ + VE __41__ + MC __61__ + MK __38__ = SSS __194__   ST composite: __97__

Is your score good enough to get you Animal Care Specialist training? Well, maybe just. Since you're so close to the minimum of 95, you would want some insurance. Remember, your scores on the exams in this book are only an *approximation* of your scores on the real ASVAB. So you would want to study hard on the subtests that make up your chosen composite, in this case, Paragraph Comprehension, Word Knowledge, Mathematics Knowledge, Mechanical Comprehension, and General Science.

You can use this procedure to find the composite score for whatever job you want. If your score is well above the minimum required for the MOS you want, you don't have much to worry about, though you'll probably want to work through this book just to make sure. If your score is below the minimum required, you know where to concentrate your efforts as you prepare for your ASVAB.

SSS	FA	OF	ST	GT	CL	GM	EL	MM	SC	CO
STANDARD SUBTEST SCORE (SSS)										
TO COMPOSITE SCORE CONVERSION										
45–49			41–45							
50–54			46–50							
55–59			52–56							
60–64			57–61	40						
65–69			62–67	41						
70–74			68–72	42–44						
75–79			73–77	45–48						
80–84	40	40	40	78–83	49–52	40	40	40	40	
85–89	40	40	40	84–88	53–55	40	40	40	40	
90–94	40	40	40	89–94	56–59	40	40	40	40	
95–99	40	40	41–42	95–99	60–63	40–41	41–43	40	40	
100–104	41–42	40	43–45	100–104	64–66	42–44	44–46	40–41	41–44	40
105–109	43–45	41–44	46–48	105–110	67–70	45–47	47–49	42–44	45–47	41–43
110–114	46–48	45–47	49–51	111–115	71–74	48–50	50–51	45–48	48–50	44–46
115–119	49–51	48–50	52–54	116–121	75–77	51–53	52–55	49–51	51–52	47–49
120–124	52–54	51–53	55–56	122–126	78–81	54–56	56–57	52–54	53–55	50–52
125–129	55–57	54–56	57–59	127–131	82–85	57–59	58–60	55–57	56–58	53–55
130–134	58–60	57–59	60–62	132–137	86–88	60–61	61–63	58–60	59–61	56–59
135–139	61–63	60–62	63–65	138–142	89–92	62–64	64–66	61–63	62–64	60–62
140–144	64–66	63–65	66–68	143–148	93–96	65–67	67–68	64–66	65–67	63–65
145–149	67–69	66–68	69–71	149–153	96–99	68–70	69–71	67–69	68–70	66–68
150–154	70–72	69–71	72–74	154–158	100–103	71–73	72–74	70–72	71–73	69–71
155–159	73–75	72–75	75–77	159–160	104–107	74–76	75–77	73–75	74–76	72–74
160–164	76–78	76–78	78–79	160	107–110	77–79	78–80	76–78	77–79	75–77
165–169	79–81	79–81	80–82		111–114	80–82	81–83	79–81	80–82	78–81
170–174	82–84	82–84	83–85		115–118	83–85	84–85	82–84	83–85	82–84

SSS TO COMPOSITE SCORE CONVERSION (continued)										
SSS	FA	OF	ST	GT	CL	GM	EL	MM	SC	CO
175–179	85–87	85–87	86–88		119–121	86–88	86–88	85–87	86–88	85–87
180–184	88–90	88–90	89–91		122–125	89–91	89–91	88–90	89–91	88–90
185–189	91–93	91–93	92–94		126–129	92–94	92–94	91–93	92–94	91–93
190–194	94–96	94–96	95–97		130–132	95–97	95–97	94–96	95–97	94–96
195–199	97–99	97–99	98–99		133–136	98–100	98–100	97–99	98–99	97–99
200–204	100–102	100–102	100–102		137–140	101–102	101–102	100–102	100–102	100–103
205–209	103–105	103–106	103–105		141–143	103–105	103–105	103–106	103–105	104–106
210–214	106–108	107–109	106–108		144–147	106–108	106–108	107–109	106–108	107–109
215–219	109–111	110–112	109–111		148–151	109–111	109–111	110–112	109–111	110–112
220–224	112–115	113–115	112–114		152–154	112–114	112–114	113–115	112–114	113–115
225–229	116–118	116–118	115–117		155–158	115–117	115–116	116–118	115–117	116–118
230–234	119–121	119–121	118–120		159–160	118–120	117–119	119–121	118–120	119–121
235–239	122–124	122–124	121–122		160	121–123	120–122	122–124	121–123	122–125
240–244	125–127	125–127	123–125			124–126	123–125	125–127	124–126	126–128
245–249	128–130	128–130	126–128			127–129	126–128	128–130	127–129	129–131
250–254	131–133	131–134	129–131			130–132	129–131	131–133	130–132	132–134
255–259	134–136	135–137	132–134			133–135	132–133	134–136	133–135	135–137
260–264	137–139	138–140	135–137			136–138	134–136	137–139	136–138	138–140
265–269	140–142	141–143	138–140			139–140	137–139	140–142	139–141	141–143
270–274	143–145	144–146	141–143			141–143	140–142	143–145	142–144	144–147
275–279	146–148	147–149	144–145			144–146	143–145	146–148	145–146	148–150
280–284	149–151	150–152	146–148			147–149	146–148	149–151	147–149	151–153
285–289	152–154	153–155	149–151			150–152	149–150	152–154	150–152	154–156
290–294	155–157	156–158	152–154			153–155	151–153	155–157	153–155	157–159
295–299	158–160	159–160	155–157			156–158	154–156	158–160	156–158	160
300–304	160	160	158–160			159–160	157–159	160	159–160	
305–309			160			160	159–160		160	

THE LEARNINGEXPRESS TEST PREPARATION SYSTEM

CHAPTER SUMMARY

Taking the ASVAB can be tough. It demands a lot of preparation if you want to achieve a top score. Whether you get into the military depends on how well you do on the AFQT portion of the exam. The LearningExpress Test Preparation System, developed exclusively for Learning-Express by leading test experts, gives you the discipline and attitude you need to be a winner.

Fact: Taking the ASVAB isn't easy, and neither is getting ready for it. By purchasing this book, you have taken your first step to getting into the military. However, there are all sorts of pitfalls that can prevent you from doing your best on this all-important exam. Here are some obstacles that can stand in the way of your success:

- being unfamiliar with the format of the exam
- being paralyzed by test anxiety
- leaving your preparation until the last minute
- not preparing at all!
- not knowing vital test-taking skills: how to pace yourself through the exam, how to use the process of elimination, and when to guess
- not being in tip-top mental and physical shape
- messing up on test day by arriving late at the test site, having to work on an empty stomach, or shivering through the exam because the room is cold

What is the common denominator in all these test-taking pitfalls? One word: *control*. Who is in control, you or the exam?

Here is some good news: The LearningExpress Test Preparation System puts you in control. In just nine easy-to-follow steps, you will learn everything you need to know to make sure that you are in charge of your preparation and your performance on the exam. Other test takers may let the test get the better of them; other test takers may be unprepared or out of shape, but not you. You will have taken all the steps you need to take to get a high score on the ASVAB.

Here's how the LearningExpress Test Preparation System works: Nine easy steps lead you through everything you need to know and do to get ready to master your exam. Each of the steps listed here includes both reading about the step and one or more activities. It's important that you do the activities along with the reading, or you won't be getting the full benefit of the system. Each step tells you approximately how much time that step will take you to complete.

Step 1. Get Information	30 minutes
Step 2. Conquer Test Anxiety	20 minutes
Step 3. Make a Plan	50 minutes
Step 4. Learn to Manage Your Time	10 minutes
Step 5. Learn to Use the Process of Elimination	20 minutes
Step 6. Know When to Guess	20 minutes
Step 7. Reach Your Peak Performance Zone	10 minutes
Step 8. Get Your Act Together	10 minutes
Step 9. Do It!	10 minutes
Total	**3 hours**

We estimate that working through the entire system will take you approximately three hours, though it's perfectly fine if you work faster or slower than the time estimates assume. If you can take a whole afternoon or evening, you can work through the whole LearningExpress Test Preparation System in one sitting. Otherwise, you can break it up, and do just one or two steps a day for the next several days. It's up to you—remember, you are in control.

Step 1: Get Information

Time to complete: 30 minutes
Activity: Read Chapter l, "About the ASVAB"
Knowledge is power. The first step in the LearningExpress Test Preparation System is finding out everything you can about the ASVAB. Once you have your information, the next steps in the LearningExpress Test Preparation System will show you what to do about it.

Part A: Straight Talk about the ASVAB

Basically, the United States military invented the whole idea of standardized testing, starting around the time of World War I. The Department of Defense wanted to make sure that its recruits were trainable—not that they already knew the skills they needed to serve in the armed forces, but that they could learn them.

The ASVAB started as an intelligence test, but now it is a test of specific aptitudes and abilities. While some of these aptitudes, such as reading and math problem-solving skills, are important in almost any job, others, such as electronics or automotive principles, are quite specialized. These more specialized subtests don't count toward your Armed Forces Qualifying Test (AFQT) score, which determines your eligibility to enlist in the military. Only the four subtests covered in this book count toward the AFQT score.

It's important for you to realize that your score on the ASVAB does not determine what kind of person you are. There are all kinds of things a written exam like this can't test: whether you can follow orders, whether you can become part of a unit that works together to accomplish a task, and so on. Those kinds of things are hard to evaluate, while a test is easy to evaluate.

This is not to say that the exam is not important! Your chances of getting into the military still depend on your getting a good score on the subtests of the ASVAB core. And that's why you're here—using the LearningExpress Test Preparation System to achieve control over the exam.

Part B: What Is on the Test

If you haven't already done so, stop here and read Chapter 1 of this book, which gives you an overview of the ASVAB.

Step 2: Conquer Test Anxiety

Time to complete: 20 minutes
Activity: Take the Test Stress Test

Having complete information about the exam is the first step in getting control of the exam. Next, you have to overcome one of the biggest obstacles to test success: test anxiety. Test anxiety not only impairs your performance on the exam itself; but also keeps you from preparing! In Step 2, you will learn stress management techniques that will help you succeed on your exam. Learn these strategies now, and practice them as you work through the exams in this book, so they will be second nature to you by exam day.

Combating Test Anxiety

The first thing you need to know is that a little test anxiety is a good thing. Everyone gets nervous before a big exam—and if that nervousness motivates you to prepare thoroughly, so much the better. It's said that Sir Laurence Olivier, one of the foremost British actors of the twentieth century, felt ill before every performance. His stage fright didn't impair his performance; in fact, it probably gave him a little extra edge—just the kind of edge you need to do well, whether on a stage or in an examination room.

On page 29 is the Test Stress Test. Stop and answer the questions, to find out whether your level of test anxiety is something you should worry about.

Stress Management before the Test

If you feel your level of anxiety getting the best of you in the weeks before the test, here is what you need to do to bring the level down again:

- **Get prepared.** There is nothing like knowing what to expect and being prepared for it to put you in control of test anxiety. That's why you're reading this book. Use it faithfully, and remind yourself that you are better prepared than most of the people taking the test.

- **Practice self-confidence.** A positive attitude is a great way to combat test anxiety. This is no time to be humble or shy. Stand in front of the mirror and say to your reflection, "I'm prepared. I'm full of self-confidence. I'm going to ace this test. I know I can do it." Say it into a tape recorder and play it back once a day. If you hear it often enough, you will believe it.
- **Fight negative messages.** Every time someone starts telling you how hard the exam is or how it's almost impossible to get a high score, start telling them your self-confidence messages. Don't listen to the negative messages. Turn on your tape recorder and listen to your self-confidence messages.
- **Visualize.** Imagine yourself reporting for duty on your first day as a military trainee. Think of yourself wearing your uniform and learning skills you will use for the rest of your life. Visualizing success can help make it happen—and it reminds you of why you are doing all this work in preparing for the exam.
- **Exercise.** Physical activity helps calm your body down and focus your mind. Besides, being in good physical shape can actually help you do well on the exam. Go for a run, lift weights, go swimming—and do it regularly.

Stress Management on Test Day

There are several ways you can bring down your level of test anxiety on test day. They will work best if you practice them in the weeks before the test, so you know which ones work best for you.

- **Deep breathing.** Take a deep breath while you count to five. Hold it for a count of one, then let it out on a count of five. Repeat several times.
- **Move your body.** Try rolling your head in a circle. Rotate your shoulders. Shake your hands from the wrist. Many people find these movements very relaxing.

- **Visualize again.** Think of the place where you are most relaxed: lying on a beach in the sun, walking through the park, or whatever. Now close your eyes and imagine you are actually there. If you practice in advance, you will find that you only need a few seconds of this exercise to experience a significant increase in your sense of well-being.

When anxiety threatens to overwhelm you right there during the exam, there are still things you can do to manage the stress level:

- **Repeat your self-confidence messages.** You should have them memorized by now. Say them silently to yourself, and believe them!
- **Visualize one more time.** This time, visualize yourself moving smoothly and quickly through the test answering every question right and finishing just before time is up. Like most visualization techniques, this one works best if you have practiced it ahead of time.
- **Find an easy question.** Skim over the test until you find an easy question, and answer it. Getting even one question finished gets you into the test-taking groove.
- **Take a mental break.** Everyone loses concentration once in a while during a long test. It's normal, so you shouldn't worry about it. Instead, accept what has happened. Say to yourself, "Hey, I lost it there for a minute. My brain is taking a break." Put down your pencil, close your eyes, and do some deep breathing for a few seconds. Then you're ready to go back to work.

Try these techniques ahead of time, and see if they work for you!

TEST STRESS TEST

You only need to worry about test anxiety if it is extreme enough to impair your performance. The following questionnaire will provide a diagnosis of your level of test anxiety. In the blank before each statement, write the number that most accurately describes your experience.

0 = Never   1 = Once or twice   2 = Sometimes   3 = Often

_____ I have gotten so nervous before an exam that I simply put down the books and didn't study for it.

_____ I have experienced disabling physical symptoms such as vomiting and severe headaches because I was nervous about an exam.

_____ I have simply not showed up for an exam because I was afraid to take it.

_____ I have experienced dizziness and disorientation while taking an exam.

_____ I have had trouble filling in the little circles because my hands were shaking too hard.

_____ I have failed an exam because I was too nervous to complete it.

_____ **Total: Add up the numbers in the blanks above.**

Your Test Stress Score

Here are the steps you should take, depending on your score:

- **Below 3:** Your level of test anxiety is nothing to worry about; it's probably just enough to give you that little extra edge.

- **Between 3 and 6:** Your test anxiety may be enough to impair your performance, and you should practice the stress management techniques listed in this section to try to bring your test anxiety down to manageable levels.

- **Above 6:** Your level of test anxiety is a serious concern. In addition to practicing the stress management techniques listed in this section, you may want to seek additional, personal help. Call your community college and ask for the academic counselor. Tell the counselor that you have a level of test anxiety that sometimes keeps you from being able to take an exam. The counselor may be willing to help you or may suggest someone else you should talk to.

Step 3: Make a Plan

Time to complete: 50 minutes
Activity: Construct a study plan

Maybe the most important thing you can do to get control of yourself and your exam is to make a study plan. Too many people fail to prepare simply because they fail to plan. Spending hours on the day before the exam poring over sample test questions not only raises your level of test anxiety, it also is simply no substitute for careful preparation and practice over time.

Even more important than making a plan is making a commitment. You can't improve your skills in the areas tested on the ASVAB overnight. You have to set aside some time every day for study and practice. Try for at least 30 minutes a day. Thirty minutes daily will do you much more good than two hours on Saturday.

Don't put off your study until the day before the exam. Start now. Twenty minutes a day, with an hour or more on weekends, can make a big difference in your score.

Step 4: Learn to Manage Your Time

Time to complete: 10 minutes to read, many hours of practice!
Activities: Practice these strategies as you take the sample tests in this book

Each of the subtests of the ASVAB is timed separately. Most allow you enough time to complete the section, though none allows a lot of extra time. You should use your time wisely to avoid making errors. Here are some general tips for the whole exam.

- **Listen carefully to directions.** By the time you get to the exam, you should know how all the subtests work, but listen just in case something has changed.
- **Pace yourself.** Glance at your watch every few minutes, and compare the time to how far you have gotten in the subtest. When one-quarter of the time has elapsed, you should be a quarter of the way through the subtest, and so on. If you're falling behind, pick up the pace a bit.
- **Keep moving.** Don't waste time on one question. If you don't know the answer, skip the question and move on. Circle the number of the question in your test booklet in case you have time to come back to it later.
- **Keep track of your place on the answer sheet.** If you skip a question, make sure you skip on the answer sheet, too. Check yourself every 5–10 questions to make sure the question number and the answer sheet number are still the same.
- **Don't rush.** Though you should keep moving, rushing won't help. Try to keep calm and work methodically and quickly.

Step 5: Learn to Use the Process of Elimination

Time to complete: 20 minutes
Activity: Complete worksheet on Using the Process of Elimination

After time management, your next most important tool for taking control of your exam is using the process of elimination wisely. It's standard test-taking wisdom that you should always read all the answer choices before choosing your answer. This helps you find the right answer by eliminating wrong answer choices. And, sure enough, that standard wisdom applies to your exam, too.

You should always use the process of elimination on tough questions, even if the right answer jumps out at you. Sometimes the answer that jumps out isn't right after all. You should always proceed through the answer choices in order. You can start with answer choice **a** and eliminate any choices that are clearly incorrect.

Let's say you're facing a vocabulary question like this:

"Biology uses a *binomial* system of classification." In this sentence, the word *binomial* most nearly means
   a. understanding the law.
   b. having two names.
   c. scientifically sound.
   d. having a double meaning.

If you happen to know what *binomial* means, of course, you don't need to use the process of elimination, but let's assume you don't. So, you look at the answer choices. "Understanding the law" sure doesn't sound very likely for something having to do with biology. So you eliminate choice **a**—and now you only have three answer choices to deal with. Mark an **X** next to choice **a** so you never have to read it again.

Now, move on to the other answer choices. If you know that the prefix *bi-* means *two,* as in *bicycle,* you will flag answer **b** as a possible answer. Put a check mark beside it, meaning "good answer, I might use this one."

Choice **c**, "scientifically sound," is a possibility. At least it's about science, not law. It could work here, though when you think about it, having a "scientifically sound" classification system in a scientific field is kind of redundant. You remember the *bi-* in *binomial,* and probably continue to like answer **b** better. But you're not sure, so you put a question mark next to **c**, meaning "well, maybe."

Now, choice **d**, "having a double meaning." You're still keeping in mind that *bi-* means *two,* so this one looks possible at first. But then you look again at the sentence the word belongs in, and you think, "Why would biology want a system of classification that has two meanings? That wouldn't work very well!" If you're really taken with the idea that *bi-* means *two,* you might put a question mark here. But if you're feeling a little more confident, you'll put an **X**. You have already got a better answer picked out.

Now your question looks like this:

"Biology uses a *binomial* system of classification." In this sentence, the word *binomial* most nearly means
X **a.** understanding the law.
✓ **b.** having two names.
? **c.** scientifically sound.
? **d.** having a double meaning.

You've got just one checkmark for a good answer. If you're pressed for time, you should simply mark answer **b** on your answer sheet. If you have the time to be extra careful, you could compare your checkmark answer to your question-mark answers to make sure that it's better. (It is: the *binomial* system in biology is the one that gives a two-part genus and species name like *homo sapiens.*)

It's good to have a system for marking good, bad, and maybe answers. Here's one recommendation:

X = bad
✓ = good
? = maybe

If you don't like these marks, devise your own system. Just make sure you do it long before test day—while you're working through the practice exams in this book—so you won't have to worry about it during the test.

Even when you think you are absolutely clueless about a question, you can often use the process of elimination to get rid of one answer choice. If so, you are better prepared to make an educated guess, as you will see in Step 6. More often, the process of elimination allows you to get down to only *two* possibly right answers. Then, you're in a strong position to guess. And sometimes, even though you don't know the right answer, you find it simply by getting rid of the wrong ones, as you did in the preceding example.

Try using your powers of elimination on the questions in the worksheet Using the Process of Elimination beginning on page 32. The answer explanations show one possible way you might use the process to arrive at the right answer.

The process of elimination is your tool for the next step, which is knowing when to guess.

Use the process of elimination to answer the following questions.

1. Ilsa is as old as Meghan will be in five years. The difference between Ed's age and Meghan's age is twice the difference between Ilsa's age and Meghan's age. Ed is 29. How old is Ilsa?

  a. 4
  b. 10
  c. 19
  d. 24

2. "All drivers of commercial vehicles must carry a valid commercial driver's license whenever operating a commercial vehicle." According to this sentence, which of the following people need NOT carry a commercial driver's license?

  a. a truck driver idling his engine while waiting to be directed to a loading dock
  b. a bus operator backing her bus out of the way of another bus in the bus lot
  c. a taxi driver driving his personal car to the grocery store
  d. a limousine driver taking the limousine to her home after dropping off her last passenger of the evening

3. Smoking tobacco has been linked to

  a. increased risk of stroke and heart attack.
  b. all forms of respiratory disease.
  c. increasing mortality rates over the past ten years.
  d. juvenile delinquency.

4. Which of the following words is spelled correctly?

  a. incorrigible
  b. outragous
  c. domestickated
  d. understandible

Answers

Here are the answers, as well as some suggestions as to how you might have used the process of elimination to find them.

1. d. You should have eliminated answer **a** off the bat. Ilsa can't be four years old if Meghan is going to be Ilsa's age in five years. The best way to eliminate other answer choices is to try plugging them in to the information given in the problem. For instance, for answer **b**, if Ilsa is 10, then Meghan must be 5. The difference in their ages is 5. The difference between Ed's age, 29, and Meghan's age, 5, is 24. Is 24 two times 5? No. Then answer **b** is wrong. You could eliminate answer **c** in the same way and be left with answer **d**.

2. c. Note the word *not* in the question, and go through the answers one by one. Is the truck driver in choice **a** "operating a commercial vehicle"? Yes, idling counts as "operating," so he needs to have a commercial driver's license. Likewise, the bus operator in answer **b** is operating a commercial vehicle; the question doesn't say the operator has to be on the street. The limo driver in **d** is operating a commercial vehicle, even if it doesn't have passenger in it. However, the cabbie in answer **c** is *not* operating a commercial vehicle, but his own private car.

3. a. You could eliminate answer **b** simply because of the presence of the word *all*. Such absolutes hardly ever appear in correct answer choices. Choice **c** looks attractive until you think a little about what you know—aren't fewer people smoking these days, rather than more? So how could smoking be responsible for a higher mortality rate? (If you didn't know that *mortality rate* means the rate at which people die, you might keep this choice as a possibility, but you'd still be able to eliminate two answers and have only two to choose from.) Choice **d** is plain silly, so you could eliminate that one, too. You're left with the correct choice, **a**.

4. a. How you used the process of elimination here depends on which words you recognized as being spelled incorrectly. If you knew that the correct spellings were *outrageous*, *domesticated*, and *understandable*, then you were home free. You probably knew that at least one of those words was wrong.

Step 6: Know When to Guess

Time to complete: 20 minutes
**Activity: Complete worksheet on Your
     Guessing Ability**

Armed with the process of elimination, you are ready to take control of one of the big questions in test taking: Should I guess? The first and main answer is Yes. Some exams have what is called a "guessing penalty," in which a fraction of your wrong answers is subtracted from your right answers—but the ASVAB isn't one of them. The number of questions you answer correctly yields your raw score. So you have nothing to lose and everything to gain by guessing.

The more complicated answer to the question "Should I guess?" depends on you—your personality and your "guessing intuition." There are two things you need to know about yourself before you go into the exam:

- Are you a risk taker?
- Are you a good guesser?

You will have to decide about your risk-taking quotient on your own. To find out if you're a good guesser, complete the worksheet "Your Guessing Ability" that begins on this page. Frankly, even if you're a play-it-safe person with lousy intuition, you are still safe in guessing every time. The best thing would be to overcome your anxieties and go ahead and mark an answer. But you may want to have a sense of how good your intuition is before you go into the exam.

YOUR GUESSING ABILITY

The following are ten really hard questions. You are not supposed to know the answers. Rather, this is an assessment of your ability to guess when you don't have a clue. Read each question carefully, just as if you did expect to answer it. If you have any knowledge at all about the subject of the question, use that knowledge to help you eliminate wrong answer choices.

ANSWER GRID

	a	b	c	d			a	b	c	d			a	b	c	d
1.	ⓐ	ⓑ	ⓒ	ⓓ		**5.**	ⓐ	ⓑ	ⓒ	ⓓ		**9.**	ⓐ	ⓑ	ⓒ	ⓓ
2.	ⓐ	ⓑ	ⓒ	ⓓ		**6.**	ⓐ	ⓑ	ⓒ	ⓓ		**10.**	ⓐ	ⓑ	ⓒ	ⓓ
3.	ⓐ	ⓑ	ⓒ	ⓓ		**7.**	ⓐ	ⓑ	ⓒ	ⓓ						
4.	ⓐ	ⓑ	ⓒ	ⓓ		**8.**	ⓐ	ⓑ	ⓒ	ⓓ						

1. September 7 is Independence Day in
   a. India.
   b. Costa Rica.
   c. Brazil.
   d. Australia.

2. Which of the following is the formula for determining the momentum of an object?
   a. $p = mv$
   b. $F = ma$
   c. $P = IV$
   d. $E = mc^2$

3. Because of the expansion of the universe, the stars and other celestial bodies are all moving away from each other. This phenomenon is known as
   a. Newton's first law.
   b. the big bang.
   c. gravitational collapse.
   d. Hubble flow.

4. American author Gertrude Stein was born in
   a. 1713.
   b. 1830.
   c. 1874.
   d. 1901.

5. Which of the following is NOT one of the Five Classics attributed to Confucius?
   a. *I Ching*
   b. *Book of Holiness*
   c. *Spring and Autumn Annals*
   d. *Book of History*

6. The religious and philosophical doctrine that holds that the universe is constantly in a struggle between good and evil is known as
   a. Pelagianism.
   b. Manichaeanism.
   c. neo-Hegelianism.
   d. Epicureanism.

7. The third Chief Justice of the U.S. Supreme Court was
   a. John Blair.
   b. William Cushing.
   c. James Wilson.
   d. John Jay.

8. Which of the following is the poisonous portion of a daffodil?
   a. the bulb
   b. the leaves
   c. the stem
   d. the flowers

9. The winner of the Masters golf tournament in 1953 was
   a. Sam Snead.
   b. Cary Middlecoff.
   c. Arnold Palmer.
   d. Ben Hogan.

10. The state with the highest per capita personal income in 1980 was
    a. Alaska.
    b. Connecticut.
    c. New York.
    d. Texas.

Answers

Check your answers against the correct answers below.

1. c.
2. a.
3. d.
4. c.
5. b.
6. b.
7. b.
8. a.
9. d.
10. a.

How Did You Do?

You may have simply gotten lucky and actually known the answer to one or two questions. In addition, your guessing was more successful if you were able to use the process of elimination on any of the questions. Maybe you didn't know who the third Chief Justice was (question 7), but you knew that John Jay was the first. In that case, you would have eliminated choice **d** and therefore improved your odds of guessing correctly from one in four to one in three.

According to probability, you should get $2\frac{1}{2}$ answers correct, so getting either two or three right would be average. If you got four or more right, you may be a really terrific guesser. If you got one or none right, you may need to work on your guessing skills.

Keep in mind, though, that this is only a small sample. You should continue to keep track of your guessing ability as you work through the sample questions in this book. Circle the numbers of questions you guess on as you make your guess; or, if you don't have time while you take the practice exams, go back afterward and try to remember which questions you guessed at. Remember, on an exam with four answer choices, your chances of getting a right answer is one in four. So keep a separate "guessing" score for each exam. How many questions did you guess on? How many did you get right? If the number you got right is at least one-fourth of the number of questions you guessed on, you are at least an average guesser, maybe better—and you should always go ahead and guess on a real exam. If the number you got right is significantly lower than one-fourth of the number you guessed on, you would, frankly, be safe in guessing anyway, but maybe you would feel more comfortable if you guessed only selectively, when you can eliminate a wrong answer or at least have a good feeling about one of the answer choices.

Step 7: Reach Your Peak Performance Zone

Time to complete: 10 minutes to read; weeks to complete
Activity: Complete the Physical Preparation Checklist

To get ready for a challenge like a big exam, you have to take control of your physical, as well as your mental, state. Exercise, proper diet, and rest will ensure that your body works with, rather than against, your mind on test day, as well as during your preparation.

Exercise

If you don't already have a regular exercise program going, the time during which you are preparing for an exam is actually an excellent time to start one. You will have to be pretty fit to make it through the first weeks of basic training anyway. And if you're already keeping fit—or trying to get that way—don't let the pressure of preparing for an exam fool you into quitting now. Exercise helps reduce stress by pumping wonderful good-feeling hormones called endorphins into your system. It also increases the oxygen supply throughout your body, including your brain, so you will be at peak performance on test day.

A half hour of vigorous activity—enough to raise a sweat—every day should be your aim. If you are really pressed for time, every other day is OK. Choose an activity you like and get out there and do it. Jogging with a friend always makes the time go faster, or take a radio.

But don't overdo it. You don't want to exhaust yourself. Moderation is the key.

Diet

First of all, cut out the junk. Go easy on caffeine and nicotine, and eliminate alcohol and any other drugs from your system at least two weeks before the exam. Promise yourself a treat the night after the exam, if need be.

What your body needs for peak performance is simply a balanced diet. Eat plenty of fruits and vegetables, along with protein and carbohydrates. Foods that are high in lecithin (an amino acid), such as fish and beans, are especially good brain foods.

The night before the exam, you might carboload the way athletes do before a contest. Eat a big plate of spaghetti, rice and beans, or whatever your favorite carbohydrate is.

Rest

You probably know how much sleep you need every night to be at your best, even if you don't always get it. Make sure you do get that much sleep, though, for at least a week before the exam. Moderation is important here, too. Extra sleep will just make you groggy.

If you are not a morning person and your exam will be given in the morning, you should reset your internal clock so that your body doesn't think you're taking an exam at 3:00 A.M. You have to start this process well before the exam. The way it works is to get up half an hour earlier each morning, and then go to bed half an hour earlier that night. Don't try it the other way around: You will just toss and turn if you go to bed early without having gotten up early. The next morning, get up another half an hour earlier, and so on. How long you will have to do this depends on how late you're used to getting up. Use the Physical Preparation Checklist on page 37 to make sure you are in tip-top form.

Step 8: Get Your Act Together

Time to complete: 10 minutes to read; time to complete will vary
Activity: Complete Final Preparations worksheet

You are in control of your mind and body; you are in charge of test anxiety, your preparation, and your test-taking strategies. Now it's time to take charge of external factors, like the testing site and the materials you need to take the exam.

Getting to the MEPS

You will be the guest of the Department of Defense on your trip to the Military Entrance Processing Station (MEPS). Expect to spend up to two days at the MEPS. Most MEPS centers schedule one day for travel and testing and one day for medical/physical tests and administration requirements. Your recruiter will tell you when and where you will be picked up for your trip to the MEPS. Make sure you know how to get to that location, if it's not your recruiting station, and how long it will take to get there. Figure out how early you will have to get up that morning, and get up that early every day for a week before your MEPS day.

PHYSICAL PREPARATION CHECKLIST

For the week before the test, write down (1) what physical exercise you engaged in and for how long and (2) what you ate for each meal. Remember, you're trying for at least half an hour of exercise every other day (preferably every day) and a balanced diet that's light on junk food.

Exam minus 7 days

Exercise: _____ for _____ minutes

Breakfast: _____

Lunch: _____

Dinner: _____

Snacks: _____

Exam minus 6 days

Exercise: _____ for _____ minutes

Breakfast: _____

Lunch: _____

Dinner: _____

Snacks: _____

Exam minus 5 days

Exercise: _____ for _____ minutes

Breakfast: _____

Lunch: _____

Dinner: _____

Snacks: _____

Exam minus 4 days

Exercise: _____ for _____ minutes

Breakfast: _____

Lunch: _____

Dinner: _____

Snacks: _____

Exam minus 3 days

Exercise: _____ for _____ minutes

Breakfast: _____

Lunch: _____

Dinner: _____

Snacks: _____

Exam minus 2 days

Exercise: _____ for _____ minutes

Breakfast: _____

Lunch: _____

Dinner: _____

Snacks: _____

Exam minus 1 day

Exercise: _____ for _____ minutes

Breakfast: _____

Lunch: _____

Dinner: _____

Snacks: _____

Gather Your Materials

The night before the exam, lay out the clothes you will wear and the materials you have to bring with you to the MEPS. Plan on dressing in layers; you won't have any control over the temperature of the examination room. Have a sweater or jacket you can take off if it's warm. Use the checklist on the Final Preparations worksheet on this page to help you pull together what you will need.

Don't Skip Breakfast

Even if you don't usually eat breakfast, do so on exam morning. A cup of coffee doesn't count. Don't do doughnuts or other sweet foods, either. A sugar high will leave you with a sugar low in the middle of the exam. A mix of protein and carbohydrates is best: cereal with milk and just a little sugar, or eggs with toast, will do your body a world of good.

Step 9: Do It!

Time to complete: 10 minutes, plus test-taking time
Activity: Ace the ASVAB!

Fast forward to exam day. You are ready. You made a study plan and followed through. You practiced your test-taking strategies while working through this book. You are in control of your physical, mental, and emotional state. You know when and where to show up and what to bring with you. In other words, you are better prepared than most of the other people taking the ASVAB with you. You are psyched.

Just one more thing. When you're finished at the MEPS, you will have earned a reward. Plan a celebration. Call your friends and plan a party, or have a nice dinner for two—whatever your heart desires. Give yourself something to look forward to.

And then do it. Take the ASVAB, full of confidence, armed with the test-taking strategies you have practiced until they are second nature. You are in control of yourself, your environment, and your performance on the exam. You are ready to succeed. So do it. Go in there and ace the exam. And look forward to your future military career!

FINAL PREPARATIONS

Getting to the MEPS Pickup Site

Location of pickup site: _____

Date:_____

Departure time: _____

Do I know how to get to the pickup site?   Yes ___   No ___

If no, make a trial run.

Time it will take to get to the pickup site: _____

Things to Lay Out the Night Before

Clothes I will wear   ___   Photo ID   ___

Sweater/jacket   ___   4 #2 pencils   ___

Watch   ___

4 ▶ ASVAB DIAGNOSTIC TEST

CHAPTER SUMMARY

This is the first of six practice test batteries in this book. This diagnostic is based on the actual ASVAB—use it to see how you would do if you took the exam today and to determine your strengths and weaknesses as you plan your study schedule.

The ASVAB consists of the following timed subtests: General Science, Arithmetic Reasoning, Word Knowledge, Paragraph Comprehension, Mathematics Knowledge, Electronics Information, Auto and Shop Information, Mechanical Comprehension, and Assembling Objects. The amount of time allowed for completing each subtest will be found at the beginning of that subtest. All the subtests here have the same number of questions found in the paper-and-pencil version of the ASVAB.

It is recommended that you take the tests in as relaxed a manner as you can, using the answer sheet on pages 41–43. After you take the test, use the detailed answer explanations that follow to review each question.

Part 1: General Science (GS)

1. (a) (b) (c) (d)
2. (a) (b) (c) (d)
3. (a) (b) (c) (d)
4. (a) (b) (c) (d)
5. (a) (b) (c) (d)
6. (a) (b) (c) (d)
7. (a) (b) (c) (d)
8. (a) (b) (c) (d)
9. (a) (b) (c) (d)

10. (a) (b) (c) (d)
11. (a) (b) (c) (d)
12. (a) (b) (c) (d)
13. (a) (b) (c) (d)
14. (a) (b) (c) (d)
15. (a) (b) (c) (d)
16. (a) (b) (c) (d)
17. (a) (b) (c) (d)

18. (a) (b) (c) (d)
19. (a) (b) (c) (d)
20. (a) (b) (c) (d)
21. (a) (b) (c) (d)
22. (a) (b) (c) (d)
23. (a) (b) (c) (d)
24. (a) (b) (c) (d)
25. (a) (b) (c) (d)

Part 2: Arithmetic Reasoning (AR)

1. (a) (b) (c) (d)
2. (a) (b) (c) (d)
3. (a) (b) (c) (d)
4. (a) (b) (c) (d)
5. (a) (b) (c) (d)
6. (a) (b) (c) (d)
7. (a) (b) (c) (d)
8. (a) (b) (c) (d)
9. (a) (b) (c) (d)
10. (a) (b) (c) (d)

11. (a) (b) (c) (d)
12. (a) (b) (c) (d)
13. (a) (b) (c) (d)
14. (a) (b) (c) (d)
15. (a) (b) (c) (d)
16. (a) (b) (c) (d)
17. (a) (b) (c) (d)
18. (a) (b) (c) (d)
19. (a) (b) (c) (d)
20. (a) (b) (c) (d)

21. (a) (b) (c) (d)
22. (a) (b) (c) (d)
23. (a) (b) (c) (d)
24. (a) (b) (c) (d)
25. (a) (b) (c) (d)
26. (a) (b) (c) (d)
27. (a) (b) (c) (d)
28. (a) (b) (c) (d)
29. (a) (b) (c) (d)
30. (a) (b) (c) (d)

Part 3: Word Knowledge (WK)

1. (a) (b) (c) (d)
2. (a) (b) (c) (d)
3. (a) (b) (c) (d)
4. (a) (b) (c) (d)
5. (a) (b) (c) (d)
6. (a) (b) (c) (d)
7. (a) (b) (c) (d)
8. (a) (b) (c) (d)
9. (a) (b) (c) (d)
10. (a) (b) (c) (d)
11. (a) (b) (c) (d)
12. (a) (b) (c) (d)

13. (a) (b) (c) (d)
14. (a) (b) (c) (d)
15. (a) (b) (c) (d)
16. (a) (b) (c) (d)
17. (a) (b) (c) (d)
18. (a) (b) (c) (d)
19. (a) (b) (c) (d)
20. (a) (b) (c) (d)
21. (a) (b) (c) (d)
22. (a) (b) (c) (d)
23. (a) (b) (c) (d)
24. (a) (b) (c) (d)

25. (a) (b) (c) (d)
26. (a) (b) (c) (d)
27. (a) (b) (c) (d)
28. (a) (b) (c) (d)
29. (a) (b) (c) (d)
30. (a) (b) (c) (d)
31. (a) (b) (c) (d)
32. (a) (b) (c) (d)
33. (a) (b) (c) (d)
34. (a) (b) (c) (d)
35. (a) (b) (c) (d)

Part 4: Paragraph Comprehension (PC)

1. ⓐ ⓑ ⓒ ⓓ
2. ⓐ ⓑ ⓒ ⓓ
3. ⓐ ⓑ ⓒ ⓓ
4. ⓐ ⓑ ⓒ ⓓ
5. ⓐ ⓑ ⓒ ⓓ

6. ⓐ ⓑ ⓒ ⓓ
7. ⓐ ⓑ ⓒ ⓓ
8. ⓐ ⓑ ⓒ ⓓ
9. ⓐ ⓑ ⓒ ⓓ
10. ⓐ ⓑ ⓒ ⓓ

11. ⓐ ⓑ ⓒ ⓓ
12. ⓐ ⓑ ⓒ ⓓ
13. ⓐ ⓑ ⓒ ⓓ
14. ⓐ ⓑ ⓒ ⓓ
15. ⓐ ⓑ ⓒ ⓓ

Part 5: Mathematics Knowledge (MK)

1. ⓐ ⓑ ⓒ ⓓ
2. ⓐ ⓑ ⓒ ⓓ
3. ⓐ ⓑ ⓒ ⓓ
4. ⓐ ⓑ ⓒ ⓓ
5. ⓐ ⓑ ⓒ ⓓ
6. ⓐ ⓑ ⓒ ⓓ
7. ⓐ ⓑ ⓒ ⓓ
8. ⓐ ⓑ ⓒ ⓓ
9. ⓐ ⓑ ⓒ ⓓ

10. ⓐ ⓑ ⓒ ⓓ
11. ⓐ ⓑ ⓒ ⓓ
12. ⓐ ⓑ ⓒ ⓓ
13. ⓐ ⓑ ⓒ ⓓ
14. ⓐ ⓑ ⓒ ⓓ
15. ⓐ ⓑ ⓒ ⓓ
16. ⓐ ⓑ ⓒ ⓓ
17. ⓐ ⓑ ⓒ ⓓ

18. ⓐ ⓑ ⓒ ⓓ
19. ⓐ ⓑ ⓒ ⓓ
20. ⓐ ⓑ ⓒ ⓓ
21. ⓐ ⓑ ⓒ ⓓ
22. ⓐ ⓑ ⓒ ⓓ
23. ⓐ ⓑ ⓒ ⓓ
24. ⓐ ⓑ ⓒ ⓓ
25. ⓐ ⓑ ⓒ ⓓ

Part 6: Electronics Information (EI)

1. ⓐ ⓑ ⓒ ⓓ
2. ⓐ ⓑ ⓒ ⓓ
3. ⓐ ⓑ ⓒ ⓓ
4. ⓐ ⓑ ⓒ ⓓ
5. ⓐ ⓑ ⓒ ⓓ
6. ⓐ ⓑ ⓒ ⓓ
7. ⓐ ⓑ ⓒ ⓓ

8. ⓐ ⓑ ⓒ ⓓ
9. ⓐ ⓑ ⓒ ⓓ
10. ⓐ ⓑ ⓒ ⓓ
11. ⓐ ⓑ ⓒ ⓓ
12. ⓐ ⓑ ⓒ ⓓ
13. ⓐ ⓑ ⓒ ⓓ
14. ⓐ ⓑ ⓒ ⓓ

15. ⓐ ⓑ ⓒ ⓓ
16. ⓐ ⓑ ⓒ ⓓ
17. ⓐ ⓑ ⓒ ⓓ
18. ⓐ ⓑ ⓒ ⓓ
19. ⓐ ⓑ ⓒ ⓓ
20. ⓐ ⓑ ⓒ ⓓ

Part 7: Auto and Shop Information (AS)

1. ⓐ ⓑ ⓒ ⓓ
2. ⓐ ⓑ ⓒ ⓓ
3. ⓐ ⓑ ⓒ ⓓ
4. ⓐ ⓑ ⓒ ⓓ
5. ⓐ ⓑ ⓒ ⓓ
6. ⓐ ⓑ ⓒ ⓓ
7. ⓐ ⓑ ⓒ ⓓ
8. ⓐ ⓑ ⓒ ⓓ
9. ⓐ ⓑ ⓒ ⓓ

10. ⓐ ⓑ ⓒ ⓓ
11. ⓐ ⓑ ⓒ ⓓ
12. ⓐ ⓑ ⓒ ⓓ
13. ⓐ ⓑ ⓒ ⓓ
14. ⓐ ⓑ ⓒ ⓓ
15. ⓐ ⓑ ⓒ ⓓ
16. ⓐ ⓑ ⓒ ⓓ
17. ⓐ ⓑ ⓒ ⓓ

18. ⓐ ⓑ ⓒ ⓓ
19. ⓐ ⓑ ⓒ ⓓ
20. ⓐ ⓑ ⓒ ⓓ
21. ⓐ ⓑ ⓒ ⓓ
22. ⓐ ⓑ ⓒ ⓓ
23. ⓐ ⓑ ⓒ ⓓ
24. ⓐ ⓑ ⓒ ⓓ
25. ⓐ ⓑ ⓒ ⓓ

Part 8: Mechanical Comprehension (MC)

1.	ⓐ	ⓑ	ⓒ	ⓓ
2.	ⓐ	ⓑ	ⓒ	ⓓ
3.	ⓐ	ⓑ	ⓒ	ⓓ
4.	ⓐ	ⓑ	ⓒ	ⓓ
5.	ⓐ	ⓑ	ⓒ	ⓓ
6.	ⓐ	ⓑ	ⓒ	ⓓ
7.	ⓐ	ⓑ	ⓒ	ⓓ
8.	ⓐ	ⓑ	ⓒ	ⓓ
9.	ⓐ	ⓑ	ⓒ	ⓓ

10.	ⓐ	ⓑ	ⓒ	ⓓ
11.	ⓐ	ⓑ	ⓒ	ⓓ
12.	ⓐ	ⓑ	ⓒ	ⓓ
13.	ⓐ	ⓑ	ⓒ	ⓓ
14.	ⓐ	ⓑ	ⓒ	ⓓ
15.	ⓐ	ⓑ	ⓒ	ⓓ
16.	ⓐ	ⓑ	ⓒ	ⓓ
17.	ⓐ	ⓑ	ⓒ	ⓓ

18.	ⓐ	ⓑ	ⓒ	ⓓ
19.	ⓐ	ⓑ	ⓒ	ⓓ
20.	ⓐ	ⓑ	ⓒ	ⓓ
21.	ⓐ	ⓑ	ⓒ	ⓓ
22.	ⓐ	ⓑ	ⓒ	ⓓ
23.	ⓐ	ⓑ	ⓒ	ⓓ
24.	ⓐ	ⓑ	ⓒ	ⓓ
25.	ⓐ	ⓑ	ⓒ	ⓓ

Part 9: Assembling Objects (AO)

1.	ⓐ	ⓑ	ⓒ	ⓓ
2.	ⓐ	ⓑ	ⓒ	ⓓ
3.	ⓐ	ⓑ	ⓒ	ⓓ
4.	ⓐ	ⓑ	ⓒ	ⓓ
5.	ⓐ	ⓑ	ⓒ	ⓓ
6.	ⓐ	ⓑ	ⓒ	ⓓ
7.	ⓐ	ⓑ	ⓒ	ⓓ
8.	ⓐ	ⓑ	ⓒ	ⓓ
9.	ⓐ	ⓑ	ⓒ	ⓓ

10.	ⓐ	ⓑ	ⓒ	ⓓ
11.	ⓐ	ⓑ	ⓒ	ⓓ
12.	ⓐ	ⓑ	ⓒ	ⓓ
13.	ⓐ	ⓑ	ⓒ	ⓓ
14.	ⓐ	ⓑ	ⓒ	ⓓ
15.	ⓐ	ⓑ	ⓒ	ⓓ
16.	ⓐ	ⓑ	ⓒ	ⓓ
17.	ⓐ	ⓑ	ⓒ	ⓓ

18.	ⓐ	ⓑ	ⓒ	ⓓ
19.	ⓐ	ⓑ	ⓒ	ⓓ
20.	ⓐ	ⓑ	ⓒ	ⓓ
21.	ⓐ	ⓑ	ⓒ	ⓓ
22.	ⓐ	ⓑ	ⓒ	ⓓ
23.	ⓐ	ⓑ	ⓒ	ⓓ
24.	ⓐ	ⓑ	ⓒ	ⓓ
25.	ⓐ	ⓑ	ⓒ	ⓓ

Part 1: General Science

Time: 11 minutes

1. What do humans and mosquitoes share in common?
   a. kingdom
   b. phylum
   c. genus
   d. species

2. Carbon-14 has a half-life of 5,730 years. How much of an 80-gram sample will remain after 17,190 years?
   a. 40 grams
   b. 20 grams
   c. 10 grams
   d. 0 grams

3. How are prokaryote cells different from eukaryote cells?
   a. the lack of ribosomes
   b. the lack of nucleus
   c. the lack of cell membrane
   d. the lack of DNA

4. What is the oxidation number for nitrate in HNO_3?
   a. −1
   b. −3
   c. +1
   d. +3

5. A trait that is only present in men and appears to be passed on only through fathers (mothers are not carriers of the trait)—what type of trait is this?
   a. X-linked trait
   b. recessive trait
   c. Y-linked trait
   d. dominant trait

6. How many electrons do the following have in their outer levels: S_2, Na, Cl, Ar, Mg_2, Al_3?
   a. three
   b. five
   c. seven
   d. eight

7. The resulting single cell from an egg fertilized by sperm is called a(n)
   a. monomer.
   b. embryo.
   c. fetus.
   d. zygote.

8. Which of the following is considered neutral on the pH scale?
   a. pure water
   b. pure saliva
   c. pure blood
   d. pure urine

9. Which organ system is responsible for producing white blood cells in humans?
   a. immune system
   b. skeletal system
   c. circulatory system
   d. integumentary system

10. A substance has the formula $MgSO_4 \cdot 7H_2O$. How many moles of water are in 3.00 moles of this substance?
    a. 3.00
    b. 7.00
    c. 21.0
    d. 30.0

11. Sodium chloride (NaCl) is formed with ionic bonds. This bond is
    a. a very weak bond.
    b. found in compounds of nonmetals.
    c. requires the sharing of electrons.
    d. the attraction of anions and cations.

12. Which adaptation differentiates mammals from other animals?
   a. body temperature regulation
   b. terrestrial mobility
   c. specialized communication
   d. giving birth to live young

13. An experiment you are conducting is difficult to start. Which of the following is NOT a probable reason for this?
   a. high activation energy
   b. low concentration of reactants
   c. it is exothermic
   d. it is endothermic

14. The bonds between amino acids in a polypeptide are
   a. glycosidic bonds.
   b. ester bonds.
   c. peptide bonds.
   d. hydrogen bonds.

15. Which of the following would be best to use in a solution in order to add sulfuric acid without changing the pH?
   a. electrolytes
   b. buffer
   c. water
   d. Bronsted-Lowery acid

16. Which is NOT an example of an endothermic change?
   a. sublimation
   b. evaporation
   c. melting
   d. condensation

17. The Earth's magnetic north pole is located closest to
   a. 0° north latitude.
   b. 90° north latitude.
   c. 90° south latitude.
   d. 0° south latitude.

18. Mammalian mothers provide nutrients to the developing embryo through the
   a. placenta.
   b. uterus.
   c. ovaries.
   d. amnion.

19. Compared to the age of the Earth, the age of the Sun is about
   a. a billion years younger.
   b. the same.
   c. a billion years older.
   d. ten billion years older.

20. The bond between oxygen and hydrogen atoms in a water molecule is a(n)
   a. ionic bond.
   b. polar covalent bond.
   c. hydrogen bond.
   d. nonpolar covalent bond.

21. The most abundant element in Earth's crust is
   a. calcium.
   b. oxygen.
   c. iron.
   d. silicon.

22. Complete the following equation:
   $NaHCO_3 + HCl \rightarrow NaCl +$
   a. CO_2
   b. H_2O
   c. HCO_3
   d. H_2CO_3

23. When calcium (Ca) gives up two electrons it becomes a(n)
   a. cation.
   b. isotope.
   c. electron donor.
   d. anion.

24. What modern organism most resembles prehistoric life from a billion years ago?
- **a.** algae
- **b.** amoeba
- **c.** bacteria
- **d.** protozoa

25. The shallow region of the ocean that is around the shorelines of continents is
- **a.** the oceanic plain.
- **b.** the oceanic sediment floor.
- **c.** the continental slope.
- **d.** the continental shelf.

Part 2: Arithmetic Reasoning

Time: 36 minutes

1. A floppy disk shows 827,036 bytes free and 629,352 bytes used. If you delete a file of size 542,159 bytes and create a new file of size 489,986 bytes, how many free bytes will the floppy disk have?
- **a.** 577,179
- **b.** 681,525
- **c.** 774,863
- **d.** 879,209

2. A train must travel to a certain town in six days. The town is 3,300 miles away. How many miles must the train average each day to reach its destination?
- **a.** 500 miles
- **b.** 525 miles
- **c.** 550 miles
- **d.** 575 miles

3. A trash container, when empty, weighs 27 pounds. If this container is filled with a load of trash that weighs 108 pounds, what is the total weight of the container and its contents?
- **a.** 81 pounds
- **b.** 135 pounds
- **c.** 145 pounds
- **d.** 185 pounds

4. Roberta takes $58 with her on a shopping trip to the mall. She spends $18 on new shoes and another $6 on lunch. How much money does she have left after these purchases?
- **a.** $34
- **b.** $40
- **c.** $52
- **d.** $24

5. A car uses 16 gallons of gas to travel 384 miles. How many miles per gallon does the car get?
- **a.** 22 miles per gallon
- **b.** 24 miles per gallon
- **c.** 26 miles per gallon
- **d.** 28 miles per gallon

6. Sofia bought a pound of vegetables and used $\frac{3}{8}$ of it to make a salad. How many ounces of vegetables are left after she makes the salad?
- **a.** 4 ounces
- **b.** 6 ounces
- **c.** 8 ounces
- **d.** 10 ounces

7. The drivers at G & G trucking must report the mileage on their trucks each week. The mileage reading of Ed's vehicle was 20,907 at the beginning of one week, and 21,053 at the end of the same week. What was the total number of miles driven by Ed that week?
- **a.** 46 miles
- **b.** 145 miles
- **c.** 146 miles
- **d.** 1,046 miles

8. A snack machine accepts only quarters. Candy bars cost 25¢, packages of peanuts cost 75¢, and cans of cola cost 50¢. How many quarters are needed to buy two candy bars, one package of peanuts, and one can of cola?

   a. 8 quarters

   b. 7 quarters

   c. 6 quarters

   d. 5 quarters

9. Dave is 46 years old, twice as old as Rajeeve. How old is Rajeeve?

   a. 30 years old

   b. 28 years old

   c. 23 years old

   d. 18 years old

10. Cheryl lives $5\frac{1}{3}$ miles from where she works. When traveling to work, she walks to a bus stop $\frac{1}{4}$ of the way to catch a bus. How many miles away from her house is the bus stop?

   a. $5\frac{1}{3}$ miles

   b. $4\frac{1}{3}$ miles

   c. $2\frac{1}{3}$ miles

   d. $1\frac{1}{3}$ miles

11. While preparing a dessert, Sue started by using 12 ounces of chocolate in her recipe. Later, she added 10 more ounces for flavor. What was the total amount of chocolate that Sue ended up using?

   a. 1 pound

   b. 1 pound 2 ounces

   c. 1 pound 4 ounces

   d. 1 pound 6 ounces

12. Write ten million, forty-three thousand, seven hundred three in numerals.

   a. 143,703

   b. 1,043,703

   c. 10,043,703

   d. 10,430,703

Use the following table to answer question 13.

STEVE'S BIRD-WATCHING PROJECT	
DAY	NUMBER OF RAPTORS SEEN
Monday	?
Tuesday	7
Wednesday	12
Thursday	11
Friday	4
MEAN	8

13. This table shows the data Steve collected while watching birds for one week. How many raptors did Steve see on Monday?

   a. 6

   b. 7

   c. 8

   d. 10

14. If a vehicle is driven 22 miles on Monday, 25 miles on Tuesday, and 19 miles on Wednesday, what is the average number of miles driven each day?

   a. 19 miles

   b. 21 miles

   c. 22 miles

   d. 23 miles

15. Of the 1,200 videos available for rent at a certain video store, 420 are comedies. What percent of the videos are comedies?

   a. $28\frac{1}{2}\%$

   b. 30%

   c. 32%

   d. 35%

16. Darlene was hired to teach three identical math courses, which entailed being present in the classroom 48 hours altogether. At $35 per class hour, how much did Darlene earn for teaching one course?
- **a.** $105
- **b.** $560
- **c.** $840
- **d.** $1,680

17. Each sprinkler head on an athletic field sprays water at an average of 16 gallons per minute. If five sprinkler heads are flowing at the same time, how many gallons of water will be released in 10 minutes?
- **a.** 80 gallons
- **b.** 160 gallons
- **c.** 800 gallons
- **d.** 1,650 gallons

18. During the last week of track training, Shoshanna achieves the following times in seconds: 66, 57, 54, 54, 64, 59, and 59. Her three best times this week are averaged for her final score on the course. What is her final score?
- **a.** 57 seconds
- **b.** 55 seconds
- **c.** 59 seconds
- **d.** 61 seconds

19. Lefty keeps track of the length of each fish that he catches. Following are the lengths in inches of the fish that he caught one day:
12, 13, 8, 10, 8, 9, 17
What is the median fish length that Lefty caught that day?
- **a.** 8 inches
- **b.** 10 inches
- **c.** 11 inches
- **d.** 12 inches

20. During a fund-raiser, each of the 35 members of a group sold candy bars. If each member sold an average of six candy bars, how many total bars did the group sell?
- **a.** 6
- **b.** 41
- **c.** 180
- **d.** 210

21. If it takes two workers, working separately but at the same speed, 2 hours 40 minutes to complete a particular task, about how long will it take one worker, working at the same speed, to complete the same task alone?
- **a.** 1 hour 20 minutes
- **b.** 4 hours 40 minutes
- **c.** 5 hours
- **d.** 5 hours 20 minutes

22. A piece of gauze 3 feet 4 inches long was divided in five equal parts. How long was each part?
- **a.** 1 foot 2 inches
- **b.** 10 inches
- **c.** 8 inches
- **d.** 6 inches

23. Mr. James Rossen is just beginning a computer consulting firm and has purchased the following equipment:
- three telephone sets, each costing $125
- two computers, each costing $1,300
- two computer monitors, each costing $950
- one printer costing $600
- one answering machine costing $50

Mr. Rossen is reviewing his finances. What should he write as the total value of the equipment he has purchased so far?
- **a.** $3,025
- **b.** $5,400
- **c.** $5,525
- **d.** $6,525

24. An auditorium that holds 350 people currently has 150 seated in it. What part of the auditorium is full?

a. $\frac{1}{4}$

b. $\frac{1}{3}$

c. $\frac{3}{7}$

d. $\frac{3}{5}$

25. Mr. Richard Tupper is purchasing gifts for his family. So far he has purchased the following:

- three sweaters, each valued at $68
- one computer game valued at $75
- two bracelets, each valued at $43

Later, he returned one of the bracelets for a full refund and received a $10 rebate on the computer game. What is the total cost of the gifts after the refund and rebate?

a. $244

b. $312

c. $355

d. $365

26. While bowling in a tournament, Jake and his friends had the following scores:

- Jake, 189
- Charles and Max each scored 120
- Terry, 95

What was the total score for Jake and his friends at the tournament?

a. 404

b. 504

c. 524

d. 526

27. Alex bought 400 hot dogs for the school picnic. If they were contained in packages of eight hot dogs, how many total packages did he buy?

a. 5

b. 50

c. 500

d. 3,200

28. The city's bus system carries 1,200,000 people each day. How many people does the bus system carry each year? (one year = 365 days)

a. 3,288 people

b. 32,880 people

c. 43,800,000 people

d. 438,000,000 people

29. Department regulations require trash collection trucks to have transmission maintenance every 13,000 miles. Truck #B-17 last had maintenance on its transmission at 12,398 miles. The mileage gauge now reads 22,003. How many more miles can the truck be driven before it must be brought in for transmission maintenance?

a. 3,395 miles

b. 4,395 miles

c. 9,003 miles

d. 9,605 miles

30. Roger has completed 78% of his 200-page thesis. How many pages has he written?

a. 150

b. 156

c. 165

d. 160

Part 3: Word Knowledge

Time: 11 minutes

1. *Peripheral* most nearly means
   a. central.
   b. opinion.
   c. secondary.
   d. secret.

2. *Copious* most nearly means
   a. erratic.
   b. abundant.
   c. scarce.
   d. lax.

3. *Impartial* most nearly means
   a. hostile.
   b. prejudiced.
   c. incomplete.
   d. unbiased.

4. *Pensive* most nearly means
   a. oppressed.
   b. caged.
   c. thoughtful.
   d. worried.

5. *Predict* most nearly means
   a. foretell.
   b. decide.
   c. prevent.
   d. forget.

6. *Banish* most nearly means
   a. hate.
   b. welcome.
   c. exile.
   d. fade.

7. *Wary* most nearly means
   a. calm.
   b. curved.
   c. confused.
   d. cautious.

8. *Generic* most nearly means
   a. general.
   b. cheap.
   c. fresh.
   d. elderly.

9. *Distort* most nearly means
   a. wrong.
   b. evil.
   c. deform.
   d. harm.

10. *Solemn* most nearly means
    a. amusing.
    b. harmful.
    c. speech.
    d. serious.

11. *Negligent* most nearly means
    a. pajamas.
    b. morbid.
    c. careless.
    d. dark.

12. *Beneficial* most nearly means
    a. helpful.
    b. wise.
    c. harmful.
    d. generous.

13. *Aloof* most nearly means
    a. above.
    b. tidy.
    c. clever.
    d. reserved.

14. *Reside* most nearly means
   a. remain.
   b. home.
   c. dwell.
   d. sediment.

15. *Placid* most nearly means
   a. lazy.
   b. calm.
   c. solemn.
   d. devious.

16. *Deplete* most nearly means
   a. exhaust.
   b. erase.
   c. hurry.
   d. beg.

17. *Wretched* most nearly means
   a. twisted.
   b. forced.
   c. miserable.
   d. increased.

18. *Refute* most nearly means
   a. garbage.
   b. deny.
   c. offer.
   d. difficult.

19. *Voluntary* most nearly means
   a. willing.
   b. charity.
   c. prisoner.
   d. careless.

20. *Hinder* most nearly means
   a. lose.
   b. loose.
   c. despair.
   d. check.

21. George developed an _____ plan to earn the extra money he needed to start his own business.
   a. elitist
   b. irrational
   c. aloof
   d. ingenious

22. After an hour of heavy rain, the thunderstorm _____, and we were able to continue our golf game.
   a. abated
   b. constricted
   c. evoked
   d. germinated

23. We knew everything about the newest member of our group; she was very _____.
   a. expressive
   b. secretive
   c. reserved
   d. artistic

24. Because Mark needed to pass the exam, he made studying a _____ over watching his favorite television show.
   a. priority
   b. conformity
   c. concept
   d. necessity

25. The narrator's description was an accurate _____ of a true southern family.
   a. council
   b. portrayal
   c. disguise
   d. reunion

26. I don't trust Carl. He always acts in such a _____ manner that I believe he is hiding something.
   a. angry
   b. amicable
   c. secretive
   d. fervent

27. Raheeb was _____ enough to remain silent during Angelica's tirade.
   a. lax
   b. prudent
   c. furtive
   d. happy

28. The participants in the road rally agreed to _____ near the village commons at 5:00.
   a. rendezvous
   b. scatter
   c. filibuster
   d. disperse

29 Meeting my old friend_____ long-forgotten memories of elementary school.
   a. resigned
   b. instituted
   c. divulged
   d. evoked

30. Muhammad fell asleep during the movie because it had a very _____ plot.
   a. monotonous
   b. exciting
   c. ample
   d. detailed

31. *Ecstatic* most nearly means
   a. inconsistent.
   b. positive.
   c. electrified.
   d. thrilled.

32. *Prompt* most nearly means
   a. slack.
   b. question.
   c. late.
   d. punctual.

33. *Corroborate* most nearly means
   a. negate.
   b. confirm.
   c. challenge.
   d. assist.

34. *Erratic* most nearly means
   a. constant.
   b. simple.
   c. irregular.
   d. harmless.

35. *Moderate* most nearly means
   a. original.
   b. average.
   c. final.
   d. excessive.

Part 4: Paragraph Comprehension

Time: 13 minutes

Many lives are lost every year due to drowning, and the majority of drowning victims could have been saved if they or someone nearby had only known the simple rules of water safety. The first and most important rule is to remain calm. Panic is the swimmer's worst enemy! When swimmers allow fear to overwhelm them, they stop making rational decisions and begin to *flounder*. That is the first step in drowning. When fear strikes, the swimmer must choose to remain calm and focused, thinking deliberately about how to escape the situation.

1. According to this passage, what is the first step in drowning?
   a. going underwater
   b. giving in to fear
   c. not wearing a life preserver
   d. not knowing how to swim

2. The word *flounder*, as used in this passage, most nearly means
   a. a fish.
   b. building foundation.
   c. splash about helplessly.
   d. float.

3. According to the passage, the best prevention against drowning is
   a. staying out of the water.
   b. learning how to swim.
   c. having a buddy nearby.
   d. remaining calm.

Braille is a special *tactile* form of printing used to enable blind people to read. It consists of a series of raised dots that a person can feel with the fingertips, and each letter of the alphabet is represented by one to six dots. The six dots form a rectangle if all are present, but most letters use only some of the dots. The letter *A*, for example, is one dot in the upper left corner of the rectangle.

The Braille system was actually a by-product of the Napoleonic wars of the 19th century. Napoleon wanted to devise a code that could be read at night, and a soldier invented a system of raised dots. Napoleon rejected it as too complicated, but Louis Braille simplified it for use by the blind. It is still used today.

4. Napoleon was interested in Braille because
   a. he was blind.
   b. he wanted to help the blind.
   c. he couldn't read.
   d. he wanted a code that could be read at night.

5. The word *tactile*, as used in this passage, most nearly means
   a. a sharp object.
   b. words on a printed page.
   c. something that is sticky.
   d. something that can be felt with the fingers.

6. How many raised dots are used to form each letter of the alphabet in Braille?
   a. three
   b. six
   c. from one to six
   d. none

7. What was Louis Braille's contribution to the invention of this reading system?
   a. He taught blind people how to read.
   b. He urged Napoleon to have it developed.
   c. He named it.
   d. He simplified someone else's complicated idea.

One New York publisher has estimated that 50,000 to 60,000 people in the United States want an *anthology* that includes the complete plays of William Shakespeare. What accounts for this renewed interest in Shakespeare? As scholars point out, the psychological insights that he portrays in both male and female characters are amazing even today.

8. This paragraph best supports the statement that
   a. Shakespeare's characters are more interesting than fictional characters today.
   b. people today are interested in Shakespeare's work because of the characters.
   c. academic scholars are putting together an anthology of Shakespeare's work.
   d. New Yorkers have a renewed interested in the work of Shakespeare.

9. As used in the passage, *anthology* most nearly means
   a. a collection of literature.
   b. a phrase that compares two things.
   c. the history of the human race.
   d. a television program.

People have used mechanical devices to keep track of time throughout history. The hourglass, for example, uses sand falling through a glass tube to count minutes and hours. During the 1500s, however, clock makers created a revolutionary new idea in timekeeping when they invented the pendulum clock. A pendulum is basically a long stick with a weight at the end of it that swings back and forth in a regular rhythm, powered by a spring. The pendulum moves gears inside the clock which count the seconds and minutes and hours, since the pendulum's movement is very stable and consistent. For example, a pendulum that is 10 inches long will swing back and forth once per second, making it easy for the gears to track the passage of seconds and convert them into minutes and hours.

Another major breakthrough occurred in the late 20th century with the invention of the quartz timekeeping mechanism. When electricity is passed through a small piece of quartz, the crystal *oscillates* at a very predictable rate, vibrating back and forth exactly 32,768 times per second. Modern quartz watches have a *rudimentary* computer inside, which simply counts the number of vibrations, converting the quartz crystal's movement into the passage of time. And best of all, quartz is a very common mineral and very inexpensive to work with, far less complicated than man-made mechanical pendulums.

10. Which of the following would be the best title for this passage?
   a. The Development of the Pendulum
   b. What Time Is It?
   c. Timekeeping through History
   d. The Many Uses of Quartz

11. As used in the passage, *oscillates* most nearly means
   a. opens like a clamshell.
   b. vibrates back and forth.
   c. makes a ticking noise.
   d. sits very still.

12. You can infer from this passage that
   a. quartz clocks are less expensive to make than pendulum clocks.
   b. pendulum clocks look nicer than quartz clocks.
   c. timekeeping today is more accurate than ever before.
   d. quartz clocks are waterproof.

13. As used in the passage, *rudimentary* most nearly means
   a. chewing the cud.
   b. written in runes.
   c. alien.
   d. basic.

The Fourth Amendment to the Constitution protects citizens against unreasonable searches and seizures. No search of a person's home or personal effects may be conducted without a written search warrant issued on probable cause. This means that a neutral judge must approve the factual basis justifying a search before it can be conducted.

14. This paragraph best supports the statement that the police cannot search a person's home or private papers unless they have
  a. legal authorization.
  b. direct evidence of a crime.
  c. read the person his or her constitutional rights.
  d. a reasonable belief that a crime has occurred.

15. Which of the following would be considered "probable cause" for a search warrant, according to this passage?
  a. a reasonable belief that a crime has occurred
  b. sworn testimony of the police
  c. direct evidence of a crime
  d. a judge's decision

Part 5: Mathematics Knowledge

Time: 24 minutes

1. What is the reciprocal of $3\frac{7}{8}$?
  a. $\frac{31}{8}$
  b. $\frac{8}{31}$
  c. $\frac{8}{21}$
  d. $\frac{-31}{8}$

2. How many 12-inch square tiles are needed to tile the floor in a room that is 10 feet by 15 feet?
  a. 150
  b. 300
  c. 144
  d. 1,800

3. Express the fraction $\frac{54}{108}$ in lowest terms.
  a. $\frac{27}{54}$
  b. $\frac{9}{18}$
  c. $\frac{3}{6}$
  d. $\frac{1}{2}$

4. What is the value of the expression $\frac{xy + yz}{xy}$ when $x = 1$, $y = 3$, and $z = 6$?
  a. 3
  b. 7
  c. 12
  d. 21

5. In the equation $4p - 10 - 2p = 16$, what is p equal to?
  a. 2
  b. 6
  c. 13
  d. 26

6. If two sides of a triangle measure five and seven, between what two numbers must the length of the third side be?
  a. 2 and 5
  b. 2 and 12
  c. 5 and 7
  d. The third side can be any length.

7. What percentage of 700 is 1,225?
  a. 57%
  b. 60%
  c. 125%
  d. 175%

8. Which of the following is between $\frac{1}{3}$ and $\frac{1}{4}$?

  a. $\frac{1}{5}$

  b. $\frac{2}{3}$

  c. $\frac{2}{5}$

  d. $\frac{2}{7}$

9. Simplify: $3(6x^4)^2$.

  a. $18x^6$

  b. $18x^8$

  c. $108x^6$

  d. $108x^8$

10. To solve for an unknown in an equation, you must always

  a. add it in.

  b. subtract it.

  c. isolate it on one side.

  d. eliminate the inequality.

11. What is the area of the rectangle?

  a. 6 square units

  b. 8 square units

  c. 12 square units

  d. 16 square units

12. If reams of copy paper cost $11.39 for five cases, how much would 100 cases cost?

  a. $56.95

  b. $227.80

  c. $1,139.00

  d. $68.34

13. Which of the following is the word form of the decimal 0.08?

  a. eight hundredths

  b. eight tenths

  c. eight thousandths

  d. eight ten-thousandths

14. The product of a number and its square is 729. What is the number?

  a. 9

  b. 364.5

  c. 18

  d. 182.25

15. Which of the following is equivalent to the product of the expressions $(3x^2y)$ and $(2xy^2)$?

  a. $5x^2y^2$

  b. $5x^3y^3$

  c. $6x^2y^2$

  d. $6x^3y^3$

16. If $x - 1$ represents an odd integer, which of the following represents the next larger odd integer?

  a. $x - 3$

  b. x

  c. $x + 1$

  d. $x + 2$

17. A square television has an area of 676 square inches. How long is each side?

  a. 26 inches

  b. 25 inches

  c. 24 inches

  d. 23 inches

18. What is 42% of 6?

  a. 0.00252

  b. 0.025

  c. 2.52

  d. 0.252

19. Two ships leave from a port. Ship *A* sails west for 300 miles, and Ship *B* sails north for 400 miles. How far apart are the ships after their trips?

  a. 300 miles

  b. 400 miles

  c. 500 miles

  d. 900 miles

20. 625% converted to a mixed number equals

    a. $62\frac{1}{4}$

    b. $6\frac{1}{4}$

    c. $0.6\frac{1}{4}$

    d. 0.625

21. What is the sum of the first four prime numbers?

    a. 17

    b. 18

    c. 19

    d. 20

22. Which value of x will make this number sentence true: $x + 25 \leq 13$?

    a. −13

    b. −11

    c. 12

    d. 38

23. Which of the following numbers is NOT between −0.06 and 1.06?

    a. 0

    b. 0.06

    c. −0.16

    d. −0.016

24. What is another way to write $4.32 \times 1,000$?

    a. 432

    b. 4,320

    c. 43,200

    d. 432,000

25. Solve for x in terms of r and s: $s = 2x - r$.

    a. $x = s + r - 2$

    b. $x = 2s - r$

    c. $x = \frac{s+r}{2}$

    d. $x = \frac{2}{s+r}$

Part 6: Electronics Information

Time: 9 minutes

1. LED stands for which of the following?

    a. light emissions diagram

    b. light emitting diode

    c. lighting electrical diagram

    d. light equivalence delivery

2. Ohm's law defines which of the following?

    a. the relationship between electrons and conductors in a circuit

    b. the relationship between amperes and circuits

    c. the relationship between voltage, current, and resistance in an electrical circuit

    d. the relationship between voltage and capacitors

3. The science of electronics is

    a. the capability to link multiple electrical devices together.

    b. the process of creating electricity.

    c. the practice of using electricity in an electronic device.

    d. the use of the controlled motion of electrons through different media and vacuum.

4. A semiconductor

    a. partially blocks a battery from providing power.

    b. controls the current flowing through a circuit.

    c. controls the speed of electricity.

    d. allows electrical conductivity between a conductor and an insulator.

5. Which is NOT true of a series circuit?
   a. the current through each of the components is the same
   b. the voltage across the components is the sum of the voltages across each component
   c. a series circuit has only one resistor
   d. there is no alternative route for the charge

6. A radio receiver has which of the following electronic components?
   a. antenna, tuner, speakers, detector, amplifier
   b. antenna, detector, tuner, speakers
   c. antenna, tuner, speaker
   d. antenna, speakers, detector

7. Which of the following equations represents Ohm's Law?
   a. $\Omega = A \times C$
   b. $V = I \times R$
   c. $V = A \times C$
   d. $\Omega = V \times R$

8. What is the role of resistance in the flow of electricity?
   a. to direct the flow of electricity
   b. to stop the flow of electricity
   c. to restrict the flow of electricity
   d. to speed up the flow of electricity

9. Increasing resistance will cause
   a. the current to decrease.
   b. the voltage to increase.
   c. the current to increase.
   d. the voltage to decrease.

10. When designing a circuit, Joule's Law can be used to help
   a. determine what type of resistor to use.
   b. determine the level of voltage.
   c. ensure that the components in the circuit can handle the level of current being used.
   d. minimize the current needed.

11. Ten lightbulbs are connected in a series circuit. If one bulb breaks, what will happen?
   a. The other bulbs will still light.
   b. It depends on which bulb breaks.
   c. The other bulbs will break.
   d. The other bulbs will not light.

12. What is another name for *transistor*?
   a. semiconductor
   b. resistor
   c. circuit
   d. attenuator

13. What is the role of a capacitor?
   a. It stores electricity.
   b. It generates electricity.
   c. It burns electricity.
   d. It controls electricity.

14. When the switch is closed in this diagram, what will happen to the current?

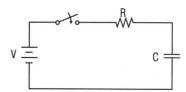

   a. The current will remain steady.
   b. The current will decrease over time as the capacitor charges.
   c. The current will increase over time as the capacitor charges.
   d. There will be no current when the switch is closed.

15. The piezoelectric effect occurs when
   a. electricity is applied to a transformer, which generates a surplus of energy.
   b. certain types of crystals are vibrated or altered, causing them to generate a voltage.
   c. static electricity builds up to a point where it discharges into the nearest object.
   d. none of the above occurs.

16. What is an RC circuit?

    a. a response-conductor circuit

    b. a resistance-current circuit

    c. a response-charge circuit

    d. a resistor-capacitor circuit

17. Which of the following schematic symbols represents an LED?

    a.

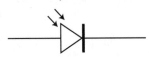

    b.

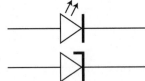

    c.

    d.

18. Transistors may come in many shapes, but all have three leads or legs, which are called the

    a. base, activator, and collector.

    b. base, emitter, and collector.

    c. base, emitter, and activator.

    d. base, collector, and tab.

19. An AA battery produces a potential difference of 1.5 V. Four AA batteries are placed in series to power a portable FM radio. What is the total voltage of the radio?

    a. 0.75 V

    b. 1.5 V

    c. 3.0 V

    d. 6.0 V

20. What is a transmitter used for?

    a. to speed up the current in a circuit

    b. to aid in charging the capacitor

    c. as a resistor

    d. as a switch or an amplifier

Part 7:
Auto and Shop Information

Time: 11 minutes

1. A typical car battery uses how many volts?

    a. 24

    b. 110

    c. 12

    d. 220

2. The following are *all* components of an automobile's engine cooling system EXCEPT the

    a. distributor.

    b. water pump.

    c. thermostat.

    d. pressure cap.

3. In the tire rating "P195/70R14," the "R" stands for

    a. round.

    b. radial.

    c. rim.

    d. rear.

4. What would happen if an automobile thermostat were stuck in the closed position?

    a. The vehicle would run out of gas.

    b. The engine could overheat.

    c. The vehicle heating system would not work.

    d. The RPM limiter would not engage.

5. Why is the sheet metal used to make fuel tanks covered with a lead-tin alloy?

    a. to prevent excessive sloshing of fuel

    b. to prevent static electricity buildup

    c. to prevent rusting

    d. to lessen vibration

6. The two general classes of lubricant are called
  a. flammable and inflammable.
  b. liquids and solids.
  c. oils and greases.
  d. natural and artificial.

7. A class c fire should be extinguished using
  a. water.
  b. carbon dioxide.
  c. all of the above.
  d. none of the above.

8. The automobile engine exhaust gas most lethal if breathed in is
  a. nitrous oxide.
  b. thermocarbons.
  c. dihydrogen monoxide.
  d. carbon monoxide.

9. When referring to an automobile, the term *camber* refers to
  a. the deflection of the headlights between high and low beam usage.
  b. the compression stroke of the cylinders.
  c. the drift of the vehicle when driving at speeds above 25 mile per hour.
  d. the outward or inward tilt of a wheel from its centerline.

10. What piece of equipment would you use to determine engine cylinder compression pressure?
  a.
  b.
  c.
  d.

11. The term *stoichiometric* refers to
  a. the ideal oil viscosity for an internal combustion engine.
  b. the ideal air-fuel mixture for an internal combustion engine.
  c. a method of measurement used by European car manufacturers.
  d. the ideal internal engine temperature for optimal operation.

12. Which of the following is a device used to reduce the toxicity of engine emissions?
a. turbocharger
b. fuel injector
c. carburetor chamber
d. catalytic converter

13. Oxyacetylene is a mixture of gases that is used in
a. lighter-than-air craft.
b. deep sea diving.
c. welding.
d. natural gas powered vehicles.

14. A saw blade that makes wide, grooved cuts so one piece of wood can fit into the groove of another is a
a. rabbet.
b. kerf.
c. rip blade.
d. dado blade.

15. Which power saw has a blade consisting of a continuous band of metal with teeth along one edge, and is used primarily for woodworking and metalworking?
a. the jigsaw
b. the circular saw
c. the band saw
d. the handsaw

16. The best tool to use if you want to make a baseball bat would be a
a. mallet and chisel.
b. hand saw.
c. coping saw.
d. lathe.

17. A plumb line is used
a. as a vertical reference line.
b. to fully charge an electric engine.
c. to align horizontal pieces of wood.
d. to transfer fuel from one tank to another.

18. Pitch, with regard to roofing, pertains to a roof's
a. length.
b. height.
c. slope.
d. width.

19. Cement, sand, gravel, and water are the primary ingredients that make up
a. caulking.
b. mortar.
c. concrete.
d. cement.

20. To remove thin strips of wood from a larger piece of wood, one would use a
a. coping saw.
b. plane.
c. palm sander.
d. mallet and chisel.

21. The following selections are *all* screw drive heads EXCEPT the
a. plow bolt.
b. Phillips.
c. triple square.
d. Robertson.

22. Which of the following would be the best tool to make a curved cut in a sheet of plywood?

a.

b.

c.

d.

23. A length of rope 4 feet 4 inches long was divided into four equal parts. How long was each part?
 a. 8 inches
 b. 13 inches
 c. 16 inches
 d. 22 inches

24. To cut threads in metal, plastics, or similar hard material, you would use
 a. a threaded chamfer.
 b. an auger bit.
 c. tube cutters.
 d. a tap and die.

25. A builder has 27 cubic feet of concrete to pave a sidewalk whose length is 6 times its width. The concrete must be poured 6 inches deep. How long is the sidewalk?
 a. 9 feet
 b. 12 feet
 c. 15 feet
 d. 18 feet

Part 8:
Mechanical Comprehension

Time: 19 minutes

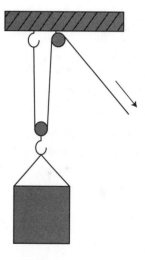

1. Using the pulley system shown here, how much force is required to lift a 276-pound load?
 a. 49 pounds
 b. 92 pounds
 c. 138 pounds
 d. 276 pounds

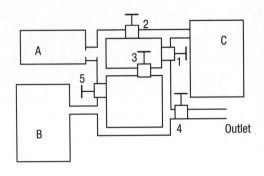

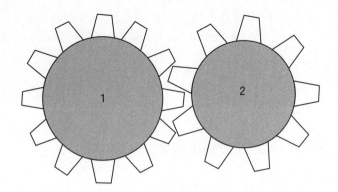

2. The water system in tank A has been contaminated. In what order can the valves be opened to empty tank A through the outlet and then refill it from tank C?
- **a.** open 4, then open 2
- **b.** open 5 and 4, then open 3
- **c.** open 5 and 3, then open 2
- **d.** open 3 and 4, then open 2

5. Gear 1 has 12 teeth and gear 2 has 9. If gear 2 turns at 60 rpm, how fast will gear 1 turn?
- **a.** 15 rpm
- **b.** 30 rpm
- **c.** 45 rpm
- **d.** 60 rpm

3. Ice cubes float on top of water because
- **a.** ice is a solid.
- **b.** ice is hollow.
- **c.** ice is denser than water.
- **d.** ice is less dense than water.

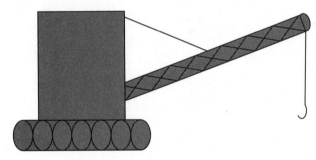

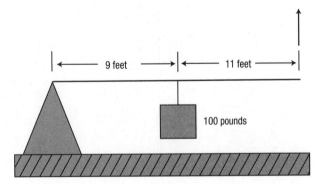

6. The arm of a crane is 16 feet long, and the cable used to lift the arm is attached 10 feet from the crane body. For the crane to lift an object weighing 600 pounds, how much force must be applied by the cable?
- **a.** 160 pounds
- **b.** 600 pounds
- **c.** 960 pounds
- **d.** 1,600 pounds

4. In the diagram shown here, Shannon wants to lift a 100-pound block using a lever. If the block is 9 feet from the pivot point and Shannon is 11 feet beyond that, how much force must she apply to lift the block?
- **a.** 45 pounds
- **b.** 99 pounds
- **c.** 100 pounds
- **d.** 109 pounds

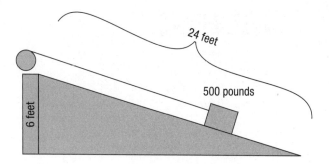

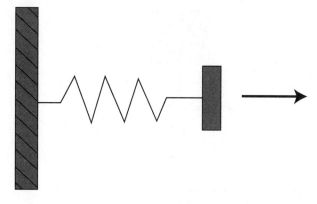

7. A 500-pound block is being pulled up an incline by a pulley. The incline is 24 feet long and rises 6 feet. Neglecting friction, how much force is necessary to move the block up the incline?
   a. 125 pounds
   b. 500 pounds
   c. 144 pounds
   d. 476 pounds

8. Jill leaves her house in a car and travels north at 40 mph. Alex leaves from the same place one hour later and follows the same route at 60 mph. How long will Alex have to drive before he overtakes Jill?
   a. 40 minutes
   b. 1 hour
   c. 2 hours
   d. 3 hours

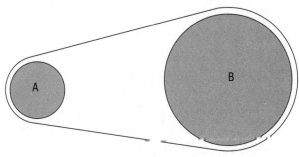

9. Pulley B has twice the circumference of pulley A. If pulley A rotates at 20 revolutions per minute (rpm), how fast must pulley B rotate?
   a. 10 rpm
   b. 20 rpm
   c. 40 rpm
   d. 200 rpm

10. A spring has a force constant of 2.5 pounds per inch. How much force is required to move the spring 10 inches?
   a. 4 pounds
   b. 12.5 pounds
   c. 25 pounds
   d. 50 pounds

11. Styrofoam cups do well at keeping coffee warm because they
   a. are good insulators.
   b. are poor insulators.
   c. absorb light and convert it to heat.
   d. transfer heat from your hand to the coffee.

12. A screw has 20 threads per inch. How many full turns of the nut are required for the nut to travel 1.5 inches?
   a. 15 turns
   b. 20 turns
   c. 25 turns
   d. 30 turns

13. When oil and water are mixed together, the oil forms a layer at the top, and the water sinks to the bottom because
   a. oil is less dense than water.
   b. oil is denser than water.
   c. oil is more acidic than water.
   d. oil is less acidic than water.

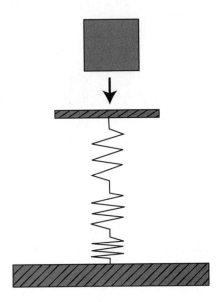

14. A series of springs with force constants of 2, 3, and 6 pounds per inch support a platform. When a 6-pound block is lowered onto it, how many inches does the platform compress?

    a. 4 inches

    b. 5 inches

    c. 6 inches

    d. 7 inches

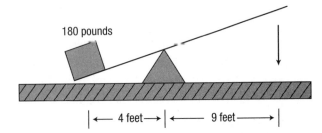

15. In the diagram shown here, Dave wants to lift a 180-pound block using a lever. If the block is 4 feet from the pivot point and Dave is 9 feet from the pivot point, how much force must he apply to lift the block?

    a. 36 pounds

    b. 80 pounds

    c. 120 pounds

    d. 180 pounds

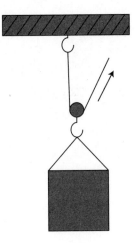

16. Using the pulley system shown here, how much force is required to lift a 200-pound weight?

    a. 50 pounds

    b. 100 pounds

    c. 150 pounds

    d. 200 pounds

17. An ax is a form of what simple machine?

    a. a lever

    b. a pulley

    c. an inclined plane

    d. a gear

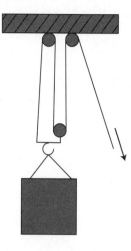

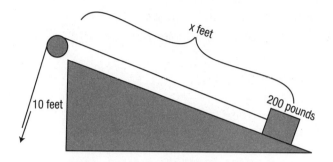

18. What is the mechanical advantage of the pulley system shown here?
- **a.** 1
- **b.** 2
- **c.** 3
- **d.** 4

20. A 200-pound block is being pulled up an incline by a pulley. The incline rises 10 feet. Neglecting friction, if 50 pounds of force is necessary to move the block up the incline, how long is the incline?
- **a.** 30 feet
- **b.** 20 feet
- **c.** 40 feet
- **d.** 100 feet

21. A single-speed bicycle has a front chain ring with 48 teeth. The back gear has 16 teeth. If the bicycle is pedaled for 3 revolutions, how many complete revolutions will the rear wheel make?
- **a.** 3
- **b.** 9
- **c.** 16
- **d.** 48

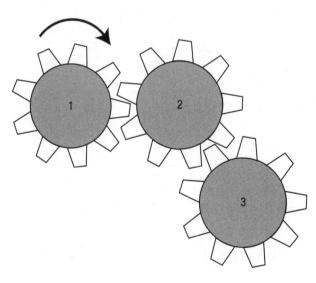

19. If gear 1 turns clockwise, which other gear(s), if any, will also turn clockwise?
- **a.** 2 only
- **b.** 3 only
- **c.** 2 and 3
- **d.** none

22. What causes the pistons in an engine to move when the fuel-air mixture is ignited in the combustion chamber?
- **a.** The heat from the explosion gives the pistons energy.
- **b.** The high pressure created from the ignition forces the piston down.
- **c.** Electrical energy moves the piston.
- **d.** Momentum from the other pistons.

23. Which material would be optimal for constructing a boat anchor?

    a. wood

    b. metal

    c. glass

    d. plastic

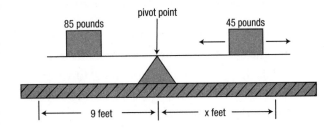

24. In the diagram, Nadine wants to balance two blocks on either side of a lever. One block weighs 85 pounds, and the other weighs 45 pounds. If the 85-pound block is 9 feet to the left of the pivot point, how far to the right of the pivot point should the 45-pound block be placed?

    a. 15 feet

    b. 9 feet

    c. 18 feet

    d. 17 feet

25. A bicycle has one front chain ring with 48 teeth and two possible gears on the back wheel: one with 16 teeth and one with 12 teeth. If the bike with the 16-tooth cog is pedaled at 80 rpm, how fast would the bike with the 12-tooth cog have to be pedaled to go the same speed?

    a. 60 rpm

    b. 80 rpm

    c. 100 rpm

    d. 120 rpm

Part 9: Assembling Objects

Time: 15 minutes

Each question is composed of five separate drawings. The problem is presented in the first drawing, and the remaining four drawings are possible solutions. Determine which of the four choices contains all of the pieces assembled properly that are shown in the first picture. Note: images are not drawn to scale.

1.

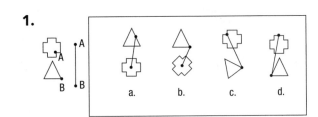

2.

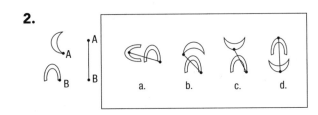

3.

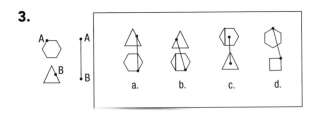

4.

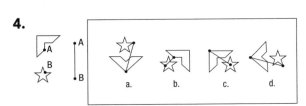

5.

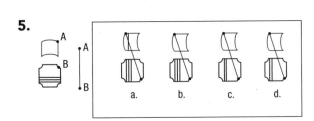

6.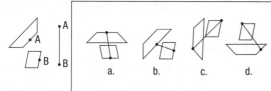

7.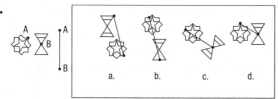

8.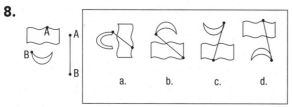

9.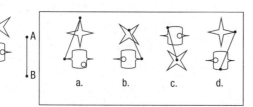

10.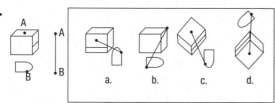

11.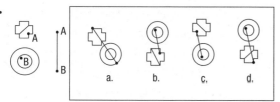

12.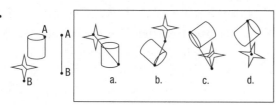

13.

14.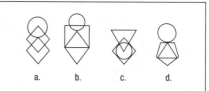

15.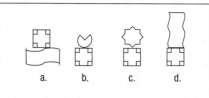

16.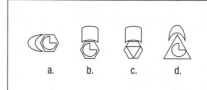

17.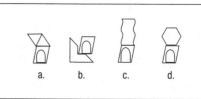

18.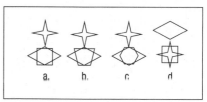

19.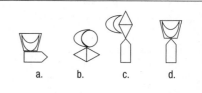

20.

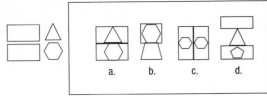

21.

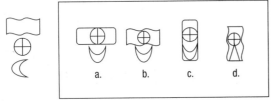

22.

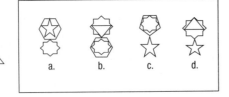

23.

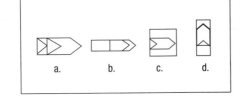

24.

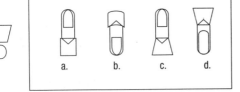

25.

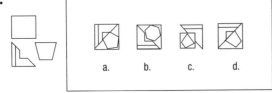

ANSWERS

Part 1: General Science

1. **a.** Humans and mosquitoes are both part of the animal kingdom. The other categories are more specific for each species.
2. **c.** The half-life is the time for 50% of the mass of sample to decay. In this situation three half-lives have passed so 10 grams remain.
3. **b.** Prokaryotes are simple, single-celled microorganisms, but contain ribosomes for protein synthesis, cell membrane, and DNA. However, they do not have a nucleus.
4. **a.** The hydrogen atom (H) has a +1 charge so nitrate molecule (NO_3) has a –1 charge.
5. **c.** Men have to have a Y chromosome, and they can only get this from their fathers. Therefore, because mothers are not carriers of the trait (they do not have the trait linked to their X chromosome) the trait must be passed on through the Y chromosome.
6. **d.** The atoms have complete valences because none of them has a charge. The atoms all have *p* orbitals that have a complete valence number of eight.
7. **d.** When fertilization takes place, the first stage of development is a single-cell zygote. Choices **b** and **c** are later stages in development; the zygote becomes an embryo, which becomes a fetus.
8. **a.** From the choices given, only pure water would be neutral. The other choices would be slightly basic or acidic.
9. **b.** Marrow produces red and white blood cells, and platelets. Marrow is located in the bones of the skeletal system.
10. **c.** The substance $MgSO_4 \cdot 7H_2O$ has seven molecules of water for every mole of the substance. Therefore, three moles will have 21 moles of water.

11. d. Cations of sodium are attracted to anions of chloride, which form a strong bond to make the compound NaCl.

12. a. Mammals and birds are the only animals that can regulate body temperature ("warm-blooded"). Although nearly all mammals give birth to live young, the duck-billed platypus lays eggs.

13. c. An exothermic reaction releases heat energy and is typically associated with low activation energy. Therefore, it is not expected that an exothermic reaction would be difficult to start. If the reaction has a high activation energy, low concentration of reactants, or is an endothermic reaction, it is most likely to be difficult or slow to start.

14. c. Amino acids are peptides, which form peptide bonds between them.

15. b. Sulfuric acid is a strong acid. Buffers are solutions that resist changes in pH with the addition of strong acids or bases.

16. d. Condensation is the phase change from vapor to liquid, which requires the release of energy also known as an endothermic change. The other phase changes require energy, so they are considered endothermic changes.

17. b. Latitude positions start at the equator (the midsection of the planet) and increase in magnitude until they reach 90° at the poles. The north pole is in the northern hemisphere represented by 90° north latitude.

18. a. The placenta is specialized tissue that provides nutrients to the embryo developing in the mother's uterus.

19. b. The Sun and the Earth began to form at the same time, about 4.5 billion years ago.

20. b. The bond formed between oxygen and hydrogen is a polar covalent bond, which is a relatively strong bond.

21. b. Oxygen is the most abundant element found in the Earth's crust, typically in the form of mineral oxides.

22. d. To determine the missing product figure out what elements were not used from the reactants. $NaHCO_3 + HCl \rightarrow NaCl$ shows that CO_3 and two H atoms were not used, so the missing molecule is H_2CO_3.

23. a. Cations are positively charged. With two less electrons, calcium has an excess of two protons, giving it a positive charge.

24. c. Early cells were prokaryotic and resembled bacteria found today. The other options are simple life forms, but bacteria, evolved from single cell prokaryotes, are relatively more complex.

25. d. The continental shelf starts from the continent's shore and extends out to the continental slope.

Part 2: Arithmetic Reasoning

1. d. 827,036 bytes free + 542,159 bytes freed when the document was deleted = 1,369,195 bytes; 1,369,195 bytes – 489,986 bytes put into the new file = 879,209 bytes left free.

2. c. To find the average, divide the total number of miles, 3,300, by 6 days: 3,300 miles ÷ 6 days = 550 miles per day.

3. b. This is a basic addition problem: 108 pounds + 27 pounds = 135 pounds.

4. a. To answer this question, subtract each amount of purchase from the $58 she started with; $58 – $18 = $40 and then $40 – $6 = $34. She has $34 left.

5. b. Take the total number of miles and find the average by dividing: 384 miles ÷ 16 gallons = 24 miles per gallon.

6. d. If she uses $\frac{3}{8}$ of a pound, then $\frac{5}{8}$ of a pound is left. The question asks for the number of ounces left, so convert one pound to 16 ounces. Then find $\frac{5}{8}$ of 16 ounces by multiplying: $\frac{5}{8} \times 16 = 10$ ounces.

7. c. You must subtract the reading at the beginning of the week from the reading at the end of the week: 21,053 − 20,907 = 146.

8. b. Two candy bars require two quarters; one package of peanuts requires three quarters; one can of cola requires two quarters—for a total of seven quarters.

9. c. This is a division problem: 46 ÷ 2 = 23. Rajeeve is 23 years old.

10. d. To determine $\frac{1}{4}$ of $5\frac{1}{3}$, multiply $\frac{1}{4}$ times $5\frac{1}{3}$. Change the mixed number to an improper fraction: $\frac{1}{4} \times \frac{16}{3} = \frac{16}{12} = \frac{4}{3} = 1\frac{1}{3}$.

11. d. Begin by adding: 12 ounces + 10 ounces = 22 ounces. Since this unit of measurement is not an answer choice, convert to pounds. There are 16 ounces in 1 pound, so 22 ounces is equal to 1 pound 6 ounces.

12. c. The correct answer is 10,043,703. The millions place is the third group of numbers from the right. If any group of digits *except the first* has fewer than three digits, you must add a zero at the beginning of that group.

13. a. The mean is equal to the sum of values divided by the number of values. Therefore, 8 raptors per day × 5 days = 40 raptors. The sum of the other six days is 34 raptors; 40 raptors − 34 raptors = 6 raptors.

14. c. This is a two-step problem. First, add the three numbers: 22 + 25 + 19 = 66. Now divide the sum by 3 to find the average: 66 ÷ 3 = 22.

15. d. To find what percent one number is of another, first write out an equation. Since $x\% = \frac{x}{100}$, the equation is $\frac{x}{100} = \frac{420}{1,200}$. Cross multiply: $1,200x = (420)(100)$. Simplify: $x = \frac{42,000}{1,200}$. Thus $x = 35$, which means 35% of the videos are comedies.

16. b. Take the number of classroom hours and divide by the number of courses: 48 ÷ 3 = 16 hours per course. Now multiply the number of hours taught for one course by the pay per hour: 16 × $35 = $560.

17. c. Multiply 16 by 5 to find out how many gallons all five sprinklers will release in one minute. Then multiply the result (80 gallons per minute) by the number of minutes (10) to get the entire amount released: 80 × 10 = 800 gallons.

18. b. Shoshanna's three best (that is, lowest) times are 54, 54, and 57, which add up to 165. Now divide to find the average of these times: 165 ÷ 3 = 55. If you got the wrong answer, you may have added all of Shoshanna's times, rather than just her best three. Even when the problem seems simple and you're in a hurry, be sure to read carefully.

19. b. The median value is the middle value in the list when the numbers are arranged in ascending or descending order. In ascending order this list becomes 8, 8, 9, 10, 12, 13, 17. The middle number is 10.

20. d. Multiply the number of members (35) by the average number of bars per person (6): 35 × 6 = 210.

21. d. It will take one worker about twice as long to complete the task, so you must multiply the original hours and minutes times two: 2 hours 40 minutes × 2 = 4 hours 80 minutes, which is equal to 5 hours 20 minutes.

22. c. First, convert feet to inches: 3 feet = 3 × 12 inches = 36 inches. Now add 4 inches: 36 inches + 4 inches = 40 inches. Then do the final operation: 40 inches ÷ 5 = 8 inches.

23. c. The total value is $5,525. It is important to remember to include all three telephone sets ($375 total), both computers ($2,600 total), and both monitors ($1,900 total) in the total value.

24. c. If 150 of the 350 seats are filled, then $\frac{150}{350}$ represents the part of the auditorium that is full. Divide each by the greatest common factor of 50 to reduce to $\frac{3}{7}$.

25. b. Add the value of the three sweaters ($3 \times 68 = 204$), the computer game after the rebate ($75 - 10 = 65$) and one bracelet (43); $204 + 65 + 43 = \$312$.

26. c. To find their total score, add their individual scores together: $189 + 120 + 120 + 95 = 524$. Don't forget to add 120 twice for both Charles *and* Max.

27. b. Divide the total number of hot dogs (400) by the amount in each package (8), to get the number of packages: $400 \div 8 = 50$.

28. d. This is a problem involving multiplication. The easiest way to solve this problem is to temporarily take away the five zeros, then multiply: $365 \times 12 = 4,380$. Now add back the five zeros for a total of 438,000,000. (If you selected choice **a**, you mistakenly divided when you should have multiplied.)

29. a. This is a two-step subtraction problem. First you must find out how many miles the truck has traveled since its last maintenance. To do this, subtract: $22,003 - 12,398 = 9,605$. Now subtract 9,605 from 13,000 to find out how many more miles the truck can travel before it must have another maintenance: $13,000 - 9,605 = 3,395$.

30. b. $200 \times 78 = 100x$; $x = 156$.

Part 3: Word Knowledge

1. c. *Peripheral* means of or relating to the edge, on the outer boundary; not of central importance or relevance.

2. b. *Copious* means large in number or quantity; abundant, plentiful.

3. d. *Impartial* means to be without prejudice or bias.

4. c. *Pensive* means moodily or dreamily thoughtful.

5. a. To *predict* means to declare in advance or to foretell.

6. c. To *banish* means to drive out from home or country, or to exile.

7. d. To be *wary* means to be attentive especially to danger, or to be cautious.

8. a. *Generic* means having the characteristic of a whole group, or general.

9. c. To *distort* means to twist out of the normal state, or to deform.

10. d. *Solemn* means marked by grave sobriety, or serious.

11. c. *Negligent* means neglectful, or careless.

12. a. *Beneficial* means to confer a benefit, to be advantageous or helpful.

13. d. *Aloof* means distant in feeling, or reserved.

14. c. To *reside* means to occupy a place as one's home, or to dwell.

15. b. *Placid* means free of disturbance, or calm.

16. a. *Deplete* means to reduce or deprive; exhaust means to empty completely.

17. c. *Wretched* means extremely distressed, or miserable.

18. b. To *refute* means to prove wrong, or to deny the truth of a statement.

19. a. *Voluntary* means done by one's own will, or willing.

20. d. To *hinder* means to hold back; one meaning of to *check* means to slow or bring to a stop.

21. d. *Ingenious* means marked by originality, resourcefulness, and cleverness in conception.

22. a. *Abated* means decreased in force or intensity.

23. a. An *expressive* person would be one who is open or emphatic when revealing opinions or feelings.

24. a. *Priority* means having the right to receive attention before others.

25. b. *Portrayal* means a representation or portrait.

26. c. *Secretive* means being disposed to secrecy, or to hiding things from others.

27. b. *Prudent* means careful or wise in practical affairs.

28. a. To *rendezvous* is to meet or assemble by appointment or arrangement.

29. d. *Evoked* means called up, summoned, or produced.

30. a. *Monotonous* means having a tedious sameness.

31. d. A person who is *ecstatic* is in a state of ecstasy, or thrilled.

32. d. *Prompt* means on time, or punctual.

33. b. To *corroborate* is to make certain, support, or confirm.

34. c. *Erratic* means unpredictable, uncertain, or irregular.

35. b. Something that is *moderate* is not subject to extremes, or average.

Part 4: Paragraph Comprehension

1. b. The passage states that fear leads a swimmer to stop making rational decisions, the first step in drowning.

2. c. To *flounder* in the water is to splash around helplessly.

3. d. The author does not discourage the reader from going in the water, nor does the author urge the reader to learn to swim. Having someone nearby is mentioned, but the focus of the passage is on the importance of remaining calm when trouble strikes.

4. d. Napoleon wanted to devise a code that could be read at night, and one of his soldiers invented a system of raised dots that later became Braille.

5. d. The word *tactile* refers to something that can be felt with one's hands.

6. c. The passage states that each letter of the alphabet is represented in Braille by raised dots, each letter using from one to six dots. Some letters may indeed use one dot or six, or even none—but the question asks about the alphabet as a whole, not about any individual letters.

7. d. Napoleon rejected a soldier's idea for a code that could be read at night because it was too complicated. Louis Braille took that idea and simplified it so that blind people could read.

8. b. The last sentence in the paragraph clearly supports the idea that the renewed interest in Shakespeare is due to the development of his characters. Choice **a** is incorrect because the writer never makes this type of comparison. Choice **c** is wrong, because even though scholars are mentioned in the paragraph, there is no indication that the scholars are compiling the anthology. Choice **d** is wrong because there is no support to show that most New Yorkers are interested in this work.

9. a. An *anthology* is a collection of many different pieces of literature, often spanning a historical period. An *anthology* of British poetry, for example, is a book containing a selection of poems written by British writers.

10. c. The passage discusses several mechanical timekeeping devices, including the hourglass, the pendulum clock, and the quartz watch. The information is arranged chronologically, so a title describing the history of timekeeping is most appropriate.

11. b. The word *oscillate* means to vibrate back and forth. The word is also defined in the same sentence of the passage.

12. a. The passage concludes by stating that quartz is "very inexpensive to work with" and "far less complicated" than other types of timekeeping. You might safely infer, then, that quartz clocks cost less to manufacture than traditional pendulum styles. Any of the other choices might be true, but they are not addressed in the passage.

13. d. Something that is *rudimentary* is very basic and simple.

14. a. The second and third sentence combine to give support to choice **a**. The statement stresses that there must be a judge's approval (i.e., legal authorization) before a search can be conducted. Choices **b** and **d** are wrong because it is not enough for the police to have direct evidence or a reasonable belief—a judge must authorize the search for it to be legal. Choice **c** is not mentioned in the passage.

15. c. This question refers to what the judge needs before issuing a search warrant: direct factual evidence of a crime. Neither a reasonable suspicion nor the sworn testimony of the police is enough, according to the passage. The judge's decision must be based on factual evidence.

Part 5: Mathematics Knowledge

1. b. Convert the mixed number $3\frac{7}{8}$ to the improper fraction $\frac{31}{8}$ and then invert to $\frac{8}{31}$.

2. a. Since the area of one tile is 12 inches × 12 inches = 144 square inches, which is one square foot, one tile is needed for each square foot of the floor. The square footage of the room is $10 \times 15 = 150$ square feet, so 150 tiles are needed.

3. d. Although there are other factors that 54 and 108 share, dividing both by the greatest common factor, 54, will result in the lowest terms in one step. The correct answer is $\frac{1}{2}$.

4. b. Substitute the values of each letter and simplify. The expression becomes $\frac{(1)(3) + (3)(6)}{(1)(3)}$, which simplifies to $\frac{3 + 18}{3}$ after performing multiplication. Add $3 + 18$ in the numerator to get $2\frac{1}{3}$, which simplifies to 7.

5. c. First, combine like terms on the left side of the equation to get $2p - 10 = 16$. Add 10 to both sides of the equation: $2p = 26$. Divide both sides of the equation by 2: $p = 13$.

6. b. The third side must measure between the difference and the sum of the two known sides. Since $7 - 5 = 2$ and $7 + 5 = 12$, the third side must measure between 2 and 12 units.

7. d. The correct answer is 175%.

8. d. Find the answer by changing the fractions to decimals: $\frac{1}{3} = 0.333$; $\frac{1}{4} = 0.25$; $\frac{2}{7} = 0.286$. The decimal 0.286, or $\frac{2}{7}$, is between the other two.

9. d. The order of operations dictates addressing the exponents first. Then perform the operations within the parentheses. Finally, perform the operation outside the parentheses: Raising exponents by exponents is done by multiplying: $4 \times 2 = 8$; $3(36x^8)$; the correct answer is $108x^8$.

10. c. One of the most vital steps in solving for an unknown in any algebra problem is to isolate the unknown on one side of the equation.

11. b. Area is equal to base times height: $2 \times 4 = 8$ square units.

12. b. One hundred cases is five times twenty cases, so the cost is 20 times $11.39, or $227.80.

13. a. The 8 is two places to the right of the decimal point, so the correct answer is eight hundredths.

14. a. The square of a number is the number times itself. When you are looking at the answer choices, the only ones that would be possible are either choice **a** or **c**. Trial and error shows that $9 \times 9 = 81$. Then, multiply 81 by 9. The product is 729, so the correct answer is 9.

15. d. The key word *product* tells you to multiply. Therefore, multiply the coefficients of 2 and 3, and multiply the variables by adding the exponents of like bases. Keep in mind that $x = x^1$; $(3x^2y) \times (2xy^2)$ becomes $3 \times 2 \times x^2 \times x \times y \times y^2$. This simplifies to $6x^3y^3$.

16. c. Since odd integers, such as 3, 5 and 7, are two numbers apart, add 2 to the expression: $x - 1 + 2$ simplifies to $x + 1$.

17. a. Take the square root of 676 to find the length of each side; therefore, each side measures 26 inches.

18. c. The correct answer is 2.52.

19. c. Since the ships are going west and north, their paths make a 90° angle. This makes a right triangle where the legs are the distances the ships travel, and the distance between them is the hypotenuse. Using the Pythagorean theorem, $400^2 + 300^2 = distance^2$. The distance is 500 miles.

20. b. First, change the percentage to a fraction: $\frac{625}{100}$. Then, change it to a mixed number and reduce to lowest terms: $6\frac{1}{4}$.

21. a. A prime number is a number that has exactly two factors: one and itself. The first four prime numbers are 2, 3, 5, and 7. The sum of these numbers is 17.

22. a. Since the solution to the problem $x + 25 = 13$ is -12, choices **b**, **c**, and **d** are all too large to be correct.

23. c. The decimal -0.16 is less than -0.06, the smallest number in the range.

24. c. Move the decimal point four places to the right in 4.32 to get the correct answer of 43,200.

25. c. In order to solve for x, get x alone on one side of the equation. First, add r to both sides of the equation: $s + r = 2x - r + r$. The equation becomes $s + r = 2x$. Then divide each side of the equation by 2: $\frac{s+r}{2} = \frac{2x}{2}$. Cancel the 2s on the right side of the equation to get a result of $\frac{s+r}{2} = x$, which is equivalent to answer choice **c**.

Part 6: Electronics Information

1. b. LED stands for light emitting diode.

2. c. Ohm's law deals with the relationship among voltage, current, and resistance in an electrical circuit.

3. d. The science of electronics is the use of the controlled motion of electrons through different media such as a vacuum, in gaseous media, or in semiconductors.

4. d. Two important elements of an electrical device are the conductor and the insulator. A semiconductor allows electrical conductivity between these two items.

5. c. By definition, a series circuit must have more than one resistor.

6. a. The antenna captures the radio waves and transforms them, the tuner selects one of the captured signals, the detector separates the audio signal from the radio signal, the amplifier makes the audio signal loud enough to hear, and the speakers transform the audio signal to sound.

7. b. The equation for Ohm's Law is $V = I \times R$. V represents voltage, I represents current, and R represents resistance.

8. c. Resistance restricts the flow of electricity. The type of circuit (AC or DC) determines in part the direction of the flow of electricity (choice **a**). A switch (when open) will stop the flow of electricity (choice **b**).

9. b. Increasing the resistance in a circuit will cause the voltage to increase.

10. c. Joule's Law allows you to calculate the level of power in watts that is generated in a component based on the voltage in volts and the current in amps ($P = V \times I$).

11. d. In a series circuit, when one bulb no longer works, it acts as an open switch and stops all the other bulbs from working.

12. d. A transistor is a semiconductor device that amplifies a signal.

13. a. A capacitor is a passive device that stores electrical energy from a voltage source.

14. b. The resistor voltage will decrease as the capacitor voltage increases, which in turn decreases the current.

15. b. Certain types of crystals, such as quartz and Rochelle salts, are mechanically vibrated or altered, causing them to generate a voltage. Piezoelectric devices are used in a wide spectrum of consumer devices such as quartz time pieces, the autofocus mechanism in cameras, and inkjet printers where the piezoelectric effect is used to control the flow of ink from the inkjet head to the paper.

16. d. An RC circuit, or resistor-capacitor circuit, is composed of resistors and capacitors driven by a voltage or current source and can be used to filter a signal by blocking certain frequencies while allowing others.

17. c. This schematic symbol represents an LED. The other symbols represent: (**a**) a diode, (**b**) a light sensitive diode, and (**d**) a zener diode.

18. b. All transistors have a base, emitter, and collector.

19. d. Voltages in series are added to determine the total voltage. 1.5 V + 1.5 V + 1.5 V + 1.5 V = 6.0 V.

20. d. A transistor is used to switch or amplify electronic signals.

Part 7: Auto and Shop Information

1. c. A typical car battery uses 12 volts.

2. a. The distributor applies electric current in a proper sequence to spark plugs of an engine.

3. b. In tire ratings, *R* stands for radial. The *P* stands for passenger car tire.

4. b. If a thermostat were stuck in the closed position, no coolant could enter the engine cooling system, resulting in an overheating situation.

5. c. The use of the lead-tin alloy in gas tanks is to prevent rusting from water condensation inside the tank.

6. c. The two general classes of lubricant are oils and greases.

7. b. Class **c** fires are electrical fires, therefore water or other conductive agents should not be used due to the possibility of conducting electricity through the firefighting fluids. CO_2 extinguishers do not leave harmful residues and will not damage electrical equipment.

8. d. Carbon monoxide is one of a number of gaseous byproducts from an automobile engine exhaust and is the most dangerous.

9. d. Camber is the outward or inward tilt of a wheel from its centerline. It is used in the design of automobile steering and suspension.

10. c. The compressor gauge is inserted into a spark plug hole to measure cylinder pressure. The other tools in this question are all measurement tools, but cannot be used to measure engine cylinder pressure.

11. b. The ideal air-fuel mixture for an internal combustion engine is 14.7:1, known as the stoichiometric ratio.

12. d. The catalytic converter creates an environment, using precious metals and chemical reactions, where the toxic byproducts of an internal combustion engine are converted to less toxic substances.

13. c. Oxyacetylene is a combination of the gases oxygen and acetylene.

14. d. A dado blade is a set of saw blades that create a wide cutting edge for use in cutting grooves into pieces of wood.

15. c. A band saw has a blade consisting of a continuous band of metal with teeth along one edge. It used primarily for woodworking and metalworking.

16. d. You would use a lathe if you want to make your own baseball bat from a piece of wood.

17. a. A plumb line is used in conjunction with a plumb bob to determine the verticality of a specific object or point.

18. c. A roof's pitch is its degree of slope or inclination.

19. c. Cement, sand, gravel, and water are the primary ingredients in concrete.

20. b. One would use a plane to remove thin strips of wood from a larger piece of wood.

21. a. A plow bolt is an externally threaded fastener designed to pass through holes in assembled parts. It does not have a screw drive head.

22. a. A jigsaw would provide the variable movement and flexibility necessary to make a curved cut in a piece of wood.

23. b. Convert the 4 feet 4 inches into all inches (52 inches) and divide the total inches by the number of rope lengths; $\frac{52}{4} = 13$.

24. d. Taps are used to cut internal threads, similar to a nut's threads, and dies are used to cut external threads, similar to a bolt's threads.

25. d. The volume of the concrete is 27 cubic feet. Volume is length times width times depth, or (L)(W)(D), so (L)(W)(D) = 27. We're told that the length L is 6 times the width W, so L equals 6W. We're also told that the depth is 6 inches, or 0.5 feet. Substituting what we know about the length and depth into the original equation and solving for W, we get (L)(W)(D) = (6W)(W)(0.5) = 27. $3W^2 = 27$. $W^2 = 9$, so W = 3. To get the length, we remember that L equals 6W, so L equals (6)(3), or 18 feet.

Part 8: Mechanical Comprehension

1. c. The mechanical advantage of this pulley system is 2. The force required to lift the 276 pound load is 276 pounds ÷ 2 = 138 pounds.

2. d. Valves 3 and 4 allow liquid from tank A to flow to the outlet, while opening 2 provides a direct route for liquid to travel from C to A.

3. d. When water freezes into ice, it expands, meaning that it becomes less dense than water. Objects that are less dense than the fluid they are in will float.

4. a. $w_1 \times d_1 = w_2 \times d_2$. Shannon is 20 feet away from the pivot point. 100 pounds × 9 feet = 20 feet × w_2. Solving for w_2 gives 45 pounds.

5. c. For every 1 rotation of gear 2, gear 1 turns 9 teeth ÷ 12 teeth = $\frac{3}{4}$ times. If gear 2 turns at 60 rpm, then gear 1 will turn at 60 rpm × $\frac{3}{4}$ = 45 rpm.

6. c. $w_1 \times d_1 = w_2 \times d_2$. The crane shown is a special type of lever. The weight is 16 feet away from the pivot point, and the lifting cable is 10 feet from the pivot point. 600 pounds × 16 feet = 10 feet × w_2. Solving for w_2 gives 960 pounds.

7. a. The mechanical advantage (MA) of a ramp is determined by the length of the ramp, *l*, divided by the height gained, *h*. In this case, MA = $\frac{l}{h}$ = 24 feet ÷ 6 feet = 4. The force required to pull a 500-pound block up a ramp is 500 pounds ÷ 4 = 125 pounds.

8. c. When Alex departs, Jill is 40 miles ahead. After 1 hour, Alex has traveled 60 miles and Jill 80 miles. After 2 hours, both Alex and Jill will have traveled 120 miles.

9. a. Since the circumference of B is twice that of A, A will have to complete 2 revolutions per 1 revolution of B. Therefore, B must rotate at 10 rpm.

10. c. The force required to stretch a spring is equal to its force constant multiplied by the distance stretch ($F = kx$). The force required to move a spring with a force constant of 2.5 pounds per inch a distance of 10 inches is 2.5 × 10 = 25 pounds.

11. a. Styrofoam is an excellent insulator, meaning that it prevents heat from flowing from the coffee to the surrounding environment. It also keeps one's hands from being burned by hot coffee.

12. d. The nut will move 1 inch down the screw every 20 turns. To travel 1.5 inches, the nut must be turned 1.5 inches × 20 turns per inch = 30 turns.

13. a. Oil is less dense than water. When two immiscible liquids of different density combine, the one that is less dense will always float to the top.

14. c. The 6-pound weight will compress the first spring: 6 pounds ÷ 2 pounds per inch = 3 inches. The second spring compresses 6 pounds ÷ 3 pounds per inch = 2 inches. The third spring compresses 6 pounds ÷ 6 pounds per inch = 1 inch. The total amount the platform compresses is therefore 3 + 2 + 1 = 6 inches.

15. b. $w_1 \times d_1 = w_2 \times d_2$. 180 pounds × 4 feet = w_2 × 9 feet. Solving for w_2 gives 80 pounds.

16. b. A pulley system of this type has a mechanical advantage of 2. So, lifting a 200-pound weight will require 200 pounds ÷ 2 = 100 pounds.

17. c. An ax head is a wedge used to split a piece of wood. It can be thought of as two ramps pressed together.

18. c. In this pulley system, the weight of the box is shared by 3 cables. So, it will have a mechanical advantage of 3.

19. b. If gear 1 turns clockwise, it will cause gear 2 to turn counterclockwise, and gear 3 will turn clockwise.

20. c. Mechanical advantage (MA) is the factor by which a simple machine multiplies for the force put into it. In this case, 50 pounds of force is used to move a 200-pound block, so MA = 200 ÷ 50 = 4. The MA of a ramp is determined by the length of the ramp, l, divided by the height gained, h. In this case, MA = $4 = \frac{l}{h} = \frac{l}{10}$ feet. Solving for l tells us the ramp is 40 feet long.

21. b. Each full turn of the pedals will turn the rear wheel 48 ÷ 16 = 3 revolutions. 3 turns of the pedals will turn the rear wheel 3 × 3 = 9 revolutions.

22. b. Combustion creates a dense, high-pressure gas that rapidly expands and pushes the piston downward.

23. b. Metal boat anchors offer the advantages of being dense and strong.

24. d. $w_1 \times d_1 = w_2 \times d_2$. 85 pounds × 9 feet = 45 pounds × d_2. Solving for d_2 gives 17 feet.

25. a. For the 16-tooth cog, the bike travels 48 ÷ 12 = 4 revolutions per pedal stroke, and 48 ÷ 16 = 3 revolutions per pedal stroke for the 12-tooth cog. At 80 turns of the pedal per minute, the bike wheel completes 80 × 3 = 240 rpm. In order to match that speed using the 12-tooth cog, one must pedal 240 rpm ÷ 4 = 60 rpm.

Part 9: Assembling Objects

1. c.
2. b.
3. a.
4. b.
5. b.
6. a.
7. d.
8. d.
9. b.
10. c.
11. c.
12. b.
13. b.
14. c.
15. a.
16. d.
17. b.
18. b.
19. c.
20. a.
21. b.
22. d.
23. c.
24. d.
25. d.

Scoring

Write your raw score (the number you got right) for each test in the blanks below. Then turn to Chapter 2 to find out how to convert these raw scores into the scores the armed services use.

1. General Science: _____ right out of 25
2. Arithmetic Reasoning: _____ right out of 30
3. Word Knowledge: _____ right out of 35

4. Paragraph Comprehension: _____ right out of 15
5. Mathematics Knowledge: _____ right out of 25
6. Electronics Information: _____ right out of 20
7. Auto and Shop Information: _____ right out of 25
8. Mechanical Comprehension: _____ right out of 25
9. Assembling Objects: _____ right out of 25

5 ▶ ASVAB PRACTICE TEST 1

CHAPTER SUMMARY

Here's another sample ASVAB for you to practice with. Take this test to see how much your score has improved over the diagnostic test.

For this first practice test, simulate the actual test-taking experience as closely as you can. Find a quiet place to work where you won't be disturbed. If you own this book, tear out the answer sheet on the following pages and find some #2 pencils to fill in the circles with. Use a timer or stopwatch to time each section. The times are marked at the beginning of each section. After you take the test, use the detailed answer explanations that follow to review any questions you missed.

Part 1: General Science (GS)

1. (a) (b) (c) (d)
2. (a) (b) (c) (d)
3. (a) (b) (c) (d)
4. (a) (b) (c) (d)
5. (a) (b) (c) (d)
6. (a) (b) (c) (d)
7. (a) (b) (c) (d)
8. (a) (b) (c) (d)
9. (a) (b) (c) (d)

10. (a) (b) (c) (d)
11. (a) (b) (c) (d)
12. (a) (b) (c) (d)
13. (a) (b) (c) (d)
14. (a) (b) (c) (d)
15. (a) (b) (c) (d)
16. (a) (b) (c) (d)
17. (a) (b) (c) (d)

18. (a) (b) (c) (d)
19. (a) (b) (c) (d)
20. (a) (b) (c) (d)
21. (a) (b) (c) (d)
22. (a) (b) (c) (d)
23. (a) (b) (c) (d)
24. (a) (b) (c) (d)
25. (a) (b) (c) (d)

Part 2: Arithmetic Reasoning (AR)

1. (a) (b) (c) (d)
2. (a) (b) (c) (d)
3. (a) (b) (c) (d)
4. (a) (b) (c) (d)
5. (a) (b) (c) (d)
6. (a) (b) (c) (d)
7. (a) (b) (c) (d)
8. (a) (b) (c) (d)
9. (a) (b) (c) (d)
10. (a) (b) (c) (d)

11. (a) (b) (c) (d)
12. (a) (b) (c) (d)
13. (a) (b) (c) (d)
14. (a) (b) (c) (d)
15. (a) (b) (c) (d)
16. (a) (b) (c) (d)
17. (a) (b) (c) (d)
18. (a) (b) (c) (d)
19. (a) (b) (c) (d)
20. (a) (b) (c) (d)

21. (a) (b) (c) (d)
22. (a) (b) (c) (d)
23. (a) (b) (c) (d)
24. (a) (b) (c) (d)
25. (a) (b) (c) (d)
26. (a) (b) (c) (d)
27. (a) (b) (c) (d)
28. (a) (b) (c) (d)
29. (a) (b) (c) (d)
30. (a) (b) (c) (d)

Part 3: Word Knowledge (WK)

1. (a) (b) (c) (d)
2. (a) (b) (c) (d)
3. (a) (b) (c) (d)
4. (a) (b) (c) (d)
5. (a) (b) (c) (d)
6. (a) (b) (c) (d)
7. (a) (b) (c) (d)
8. (a) (b) (c) (d)
0. (a) (b) (c) (d)
10. (a) (b) (c) (d)
11. (a) (b) (c) (d)
12. (a) (b) (c) (d)

13. (a) (b) (c) (d)
14. (a) (b) (c) (d)
15. (a) (b) (c) (d)
16. (a) (b) (c) (d)
17. (a) (b) (c) (d)
18. (a) (b) (c) (d)
19. (a) (b) (c) (d)
20. (a) (b) (c) (d)
21. (a) (b) (c) (d)
22. (a) (b) (c) (d)
23. (a) (b) (c) (d)
24. (a) (b) (c) (d)

25. (a) (b) (c) (d)
26. (a) (b) (c) (d)
27. (a) (b) (c) (d)
28. (a) (b) (c) (d)
29. (a) (b) (c) (d)
30. (a) (b) (c) (d)
31. (a) (b) (c) (d)
32. (a) (b) (c) (d)
33. (a) (b) (c) (d)
34. (a) (b) (c) (d)
35. (a) (b) (c) (d)

Part 4: Paragraph Comprehension (PC)

1.	(a)	(b)	(c)	(d)
2.	(a)	(b)	(c)	(d)
3.	(a)	(b)	(c)	(d)
4.	(a)	(b)	(c)	(d)
5.	(a)	(b)	(c)	(d)

6.	(a)	(b)	(c)	(d)
7.	(a)	(b)	(c)	(d)
8.	(a)	(b)	(c)	(d)
9.	(a)	(b)	(c)	(d)
10.	(a)	(b)	(c)	(d)

11.	(a)	(b)	(c)	(d)
12.	(a)	(b)	(c)	(d)
13.	(a)	(b)	(c)	(d)
14.	(a)	(b)	(c)	(d)
15.	(a)	(b)	(c)	(d)

Part 5: Mathematics Knowledge (MK)

1.	(a)	(b)	(c)	(d)
2.	(a)	(b)	(c)	(d)
3.	(a)	(b)	(c)	(d)
4.	(a)	(b)	(c)	(d)
5.	(a)	(b)	(c)	(d)
6.	(a)	(b)	(c)	(d)
7.	(a)	(b)	(c)	(d)
8.	(a)	(b)	(c)	(d)
9.	(a)	(b)	(c)	(d)

10.	(a)	(b)	(c)	(d)
11.	(a)	(b)	(c)	(d)
12.	(a)	(b)	(c)	(d)
13.	(a)	(b)	(c)	(d)
14.	(a)	(b)	(c)	(d)
15.	(a)	(b)	(c)	(d)
16.	(a)	(b)	(c)	(d)
17.	(a)	(b)	(c)	(d)

18.	(a)	(b)	(c)	(d)
19.	(a)	(b)	(c)	(d)
20.	(a)	(b)	(c)	(d)
21.	(a)	(b)	(c)	(d)
22.	(a)	(b)	(c)	(d)
23.	(a)	(b)	(c)	(d)
24.	(a)	(b)	(c)	(d)
25.	(a)	(b)	(c)	(d)

Part 6: Electronics Information (EI)

1.	(a)	(b)	(c)	(d)
2.	(a)	(b)	(c)	(d)
3.	(a)	(b)	(c)	(d)
4.	(a)	(b)	(c)	(d)
5.	(a)	(b)	(c)	(d)
6.	(a)	(b)	(c)	(d)
7.	(a)	(b)	(c)	(d)

8.	(a)	(b)	(c)	(d)
9.	(a)	(b)	(c)	(d)
10.	(a)	(b)	(c)	(d)
11.	(a)	(b)	(c)	(d)
12.	(a)	(b)	(c)	(d)
13.	(a)	(b)	(c)	(d)
14.	(a)	(b)	(c)	(d)

15.	(a)	(b)	(c)	(d)
16.	(a)	(b)	(c)	(d)
17.	(a)	(b)	(c)	(d)
18.	(a)	(b)	(c)	(d)
19.	(a)	(b)	(c)	(d)
20.	(a)	(b)	(c)	(d)

Part 7: Auto and Shop Information (AS)

1. ⓐ ⓑ ⓒ ⓓ   10. ⓐ ⓑ ⓒ ⓓ   18. ⓐ ⓑ ⓒ ⓓ
2. ⓐ ⓑ ⓒ ⓓ   11. ⓐ ⓑ ⓒ ⓓ   19. ⓐ ⓑ ⓒ ⓓ
3. ⓐ ⓑ ⓒ ⓓ   12. ⓐ ⓑ ⓒ ⓓ   20. ⓐ ⓑ ⓒ ⓓ
4. ⓐ ⓑ ⓒ ⓓ   13. ⓐ ⓑ ⓒ ⓓ   21. ⓐ ⓑ ⓒ ⓓ
5. ⓐ ⓑ ⓒ ⓓ   14. ⓐ ⓑ ⓒ ⓓ   22. ⓐ ⓑ ⓒ ⓓ
6. ⓐ ⓑ ⓒ ⓓ   15. ⓐ ⓑ ⓒ ⓓ   23. ⓐ ⓑ ⓒ ⓓ
7. ⓐ ⓑ ⓒ ⓓ   16. ⓐ ⓑ ⓒ ⓓ   24. ⓐ ⓑ ⓒ ⓓ
8. ⓐ ⓑ ⓒ ⓓ   17. ⓐ ⓑ ⓒ ⓓ   25. ⓐ ⓑ ⓒ ⓓ
9. ⓐ ⓑ ⓒ ⓓ

Part 8: Mechanical Comprehension (MC)

1. ⓐ ⓑ ⓒ ⓓ   10. ⓐ ⓑ ⓒ ⓓ   18. ⓐ ⓑ ⓒ ⓓ
2. ⓐ ⓑ ⓒ ⓓ   11. ⓐ ⓑ ⓒ ⓓ   19. ⓐ ⓑ ⓒ ⓓ
3. ⓐ ⓑ ⓒ ⓓ   12. ⓐ ⓑ ⓒ ⓓ   20. ⓐ ⓑ ⓒ ⓓ
4. ⓐ ⓑ ⓒ ⓓ   13. ⓐ ⓑ ⓒ ⓓ   21. ⓐ ⓑ ⓒ ⓓ
5. ⓐ ⓑ ⓒ ⓓ   14. ⓐ ⓑ ⓒ ⓓ   22. ⓐ ⓑ ⓒ ⓓ
6. ⓐ ⓑ ⓒ ⓓ   15. ⓐ ⓑ ⓒ ⓓ   23. ⓐ ⓑ ⓒ ⓓ
7. ⓐ ⓑ ⓒ ⓓ   16. ⓐ ⓑ ⓒ ⓓ   24. ⓐ ⓑ ⓒ ⓓ
8. ⓐ ⓑ ⓒ ⓓ   17. ⓐ ⓑ ⓒ ⓓ   25. ⓐ ⓑ ⓒ ⓓ
9. ⓐ ⓑ ⓒ ⓓ

Part 9: Assembling Objects (AO)

1. ⓐ ⓑ ⓒ ⓓ   10. ⓐ ⓑ ⓒ ⓓ   18. ⓐ ⓑ ⓒ ⓓ
2. ⓐ ⓑ ⓒ ⓓ   11. ⓐ ⓑ ⓒ ⓓ   19. ⓐ ⓑ ⓒ ⓓ
3. ⓐ ⓑ ⓒ ⓓ   12. ⓐ ⓑ ⓒ ⓓ   20. ⓐ ⓑ ⓒ ⓓ
4. ⓐ ⓑ ⓒ ⓓ   13. ⓐ ⓑ ⓒ ⓓ   21. ⓐ ⓑ ⓒ ⓓ
5. ⓐ ⓑ ⓒ ⓓ   14. ⓐ ⓑ ⓒ ⓓ   22. ⓐ ⓑ ⓒ ⓓ
6. ⓐ ⓑ ⓒ ⓓ   15. ⓐ ⓑ ⓒ ⓓ   23. ⓐ ⓑ ⓒ ⓓ
7. ⓐ ⓑ ⓒ ⓓ   16. ⓐ ⓑ ⓒ ⓓ   24. ⓐ ⓑ ⓒ ⓓ
8. ⓐ ⓑ ⓒ ⓓ   17. ⓐ ⓑ ⓒ ⓓ   25. ⓐ ⓑ ⓒ ⓓ
9. ⓐ ⓑ ⓒ ⓓ

Part 1: General Science

Time: 11 minutes

1. Which planet is next farthest away from the sun after Earth?
   a. Venus
   b. Mercury
   c. Jupiter
   d. Mars

2. Which trait would prevent a new unidentified species from being categorized in the kingdom Animalae?
   a. asexual reproduction
   b. cell walls
   c. no backbone
   d. hard exoskeleton

3. Which of the following represents a possible human nucleotide base pairing?
   a. A–U
   b. G–U
   c. C–T
   d. A–G

4. In order to force the energy from a heat source to fill a space, which process would be best to use?
   a. conduction
   b. convection
   c. radiation
   d. thermal expansion

5. To determine an airplane's velocity, what measurements are needed?
   a. acceleration and time
   b. distance and force
   c. distance and time
   d. airspeed and mass

6. Which law predicts that if the temperature (in Kelvin) doubles, the volume will also double?
   a. Avogadro's Law
   b. Boyle's Law
   c. Gay-Lussac's Law
   d. Charles's Law

7. A cell that is unable to deliver genetic instructions to the ribosome may have problems with
   a. mRNA.
   b. codons.
   c. tRNA.
   d. rRNA.

8. The ribosome structures in all types of cells are responsible for
   a. digesting food.
   b. producing energy.
   c. storing RNA.
   d. producing protein.

9. Solid CO_2 is formed at high pressure and low temperature. Once it is brought to room temperature and atmospheric pressure, it is expected to sublimate. What do you expect to happen?
   a. It will change state from solid to liquid to gas.
   b. It will remain frozen.
   c. It will become a gas.
   d. Its temperature and pressure will increase.

10. Organisms with greater diversity and more adaptations typically utilize
    a. asexual reproduction.
    b. meiosis.
    c. mitosis.
    d. mutualism.

11. The cellular component or organelle where photosynthesis takes place is the
    a. chloroplast.
    b. mitochondrion.
    c. Golgi body.
    d. nucleus.

12. A force is applied to a 30-kg object, resulting in an acceleration of 15 m/s. What is the force being applied to the object?
    a. 15 N
    b. 30 N
    c. 45 N
    d. 450 N

13. How many grams of NaOH would be needed to make 250 mL of 0.200 M solution? (molecular weight of NaOH 40.0)
    a. 8.00 g
    b. 4.00 g
    c. 2.00 g
    d. 2.50 g

14. Cells of various organ systems
    a. have completely different DNA.
    b. have the same DNA.
    c. only have DNA for the specific organ system.
    d. have different organelles.

15. At a fault line where one tectonic plate moves underneath another, what process is occurring?
    a. subduction
    b. transversing
    c. submerging
    d. trenching

16. When sound travels from air into a vacuum, its speed
    a. decreases.
    b. increases.
    c. remains constant.
    d. becomes zero.

17. Blood from the lungs travels to the left atrium of the heart through the
    a. aorta.
    b. vena cava.
    c. pulmonary artery.
    d. pulmonary vein.

18. Which accessory organ detoxifies substances in the blood absorbed through the intestines?
    a. the liver
    b. the kidney
    c. the pancreas
    d. the spleen

19. To measure the flow of electricity through a circuit you need a device reading which unit?
    a. the ohm
    b. the volt
    c. the ampere
    d. the joule

20. Which one of the following elements will resist forming an anion most?
    a. F
    b. N
    c. P
    d. Cl

21. Which does NOT encourage natural selection?
    a. traits learned by parents
    b. some traits that are helpful to survival
    c. harsh climates
    d. competition for limited resources

22. To observe the interactions of different species in a local habitat and the effects of environmental factors, which of the following should be studied?
    a. a food web
    b. a biome
    c. a community
    d. an ecosystem

23. Water and nutrients move through transport tubes, such as xylem and phloem, in which of the following plant groups?
  a. nonvascular plants
  b. tracheophytes
  c. mosses
  d. liverworts

24. What are the products of the following equation?
  sodium chloride(*aq*) + lead(II) nitrate(*aq*) →
  a. sodium nitrate + lead(II) chloride
  b. sodium + chloride
  c. sodium + chloride + lead(II) + nitrate
  d. sodium(II) nitrate + lead chloride

25. What is the maximum number of electrons that the second energy level can hold?
  a. 8
  b. 6
  c. 2
  d. 16

Part 2: Arithmetic Reasoning

Time: 36 minutes

1. Linda needs to read 14 pages for her history class, 26 pages for English, 12 pages for civics, and 28 pages for biology. She has read $\frac{1}{6}$ of the entire number of pages. How many pages has she read?
  a. 80
  b. $13\frac{1}{3}$
  c. $48\frac{1}{2}$
  d. 17

2. George has made a vow to jog for an average of one hour daily five days a week. He cut his workout short on Wednesday by 40 minutes, but was able to make up 20 minutes on Thursday and 13 minutes on Friday. How many minutes of jogging did George lose for the week?
  a. 20 minutes
  b. 13 minutes
  c. 7 minutes
  d. 3 minutes

3. A train travels 300 miles in six hours. If it was traveling at a constant speed the entire time, what was the speed of the train?
  a. 50 miles per hour
  b. 60 miles per hour
  c. 180 miles per hour
  d. 1,800 miles per hour

4. Of 150 people polled, 105 said they rode the city bus at least three times per week. How many people out of 100,000 could be expected to ride the city bus at least three times each week?
  a. 55,000
  b. 70,000
  c. 72,500
  d. 75,000

5. The cost of a certain type of fruit is displayed in the following table.

WEIGHT (IN LBS.)	COST (IN DOLLARS)
4 lbs.	$1.10
5 lbs.	$1.74

Based on the table, estimate the cost for 4 pounds 8 ounces of the same type of fruit.
   a. $1.24
   b. $1.32
   c. $1.35
   d. $1.42

6. Larry buys three puppies at the Furry Friends Kennel for a total cost of $70. Two of the puppies are on sale for $15 apiece. How much does the third puppy cost?
   a. $55
   b. $40
   c. $30
   d. $25

7. If Rita can run around the block five times in 20 minutes, how many times can she run around the block in one hour?
   a. 10
   b. 15
   c. 50
   d. 100

8. Meda arrived at work at 8:14 A.M., and Kirstin arrived at 9:12 A.M. How long had Meda been at work when Kirstin got there?
   a. 1 hour 8 minutes
   b. 1 hour 2 minutes
   c. 58 minutes
   d. 30 minutes

9. How many pounds of chocolates costing $5.95 per pound must be mixed with three pounds of caramels costing $2.95 per pound to obtain a mixture that costs $3.95 per pound?
   a. 1.5 pounds
   b. 3 pounds
   c. 4.5 pounds
   d. 8 pounds

10. Marcia is 10 years older than Fred, who is 16. How old is Marcia?
   a. 6 years old
   b. 20 years old
   c. 26 years old
   d. 30 years old

11. Ralph's newborn triplets weigh $4\frac{3}{8}$ pounds, $3\frac{5}{6}$ pounds, and $4\frac{7}{8}$ pounds. Harvey's newborn twins weigh $7\frac{2}{6}$ pounds and $9\frac{3}{10}$ pounds. Whose babies weigh the most and by how much?
   a. Ralph's triplets by $3\frac{1}{2}$ pounds
   b. Ralph's triplets by $2\frac{1}{4}$ pounds
   c. Harvey's twins by $1\frac{2}{3}$ pounds
   d. Harvey's twins by $3\frac{11}{20}$ pounds

12. How many quarters are there in $12?
   a. 12
   b. 120
   c. 24
   d. 48

13. Marty left his workplace at 5:16 P.M. on Thursday and returned at 7:58 A.M. on Friday. How much time elapsed between the time Marty left work on Thursday and the time he returned on Friday?
   a. 2 hours 42 minutes
   b. 13 hours 42 minutes
   c. 14 hours 42 minutes
   d. 14 hours 52 minutes

14. Carmella and Mariah got summer jobs at the ice cream shop and were supposed to work 15 hours per week each for eight weeks. During that time, Mariah was ill for one week and Carmella took her shifts. How many hours did Carmella work during the eight weeks?
   a. 120 hours
   b. 135 hours
   c. 150 hours
   d. 185 hours

15. Which of the following is a translation of the statement "Twice the sum of six and four"?
   a. $2 + 6 + 4$
   b. $2 \times 6 + 4$
   c. $2(6 + 4)$
   d. $(2 \times 6) \times 4$

16. Jerry's Fish Market was shipped 400 pounds of cod packed into 20-pound crates. How many crates were needed for the shipment?
   a. 80 crates
   b. 40 crates
   c. 20 crates
   d. 10 crates

Use the following table to answer question 17.

DISTANCE TRAVELED FROM CHICAGO WITH RESPECT TO TIME	
TIME (HOURS)	**DISTANCE FROM CHICAGO (MILES)**
1	60
2	120
3	180
4	240

17. A train moving at a constant speed leaves Chicago for Los Angeles (at time $t = 0$). If Los Angeles is 2,000 miles from Chicago, which of the following equations describes the distance (D) from Los Angeles at any time t?
   a. $D(t) = 60t - 2{,}000$
   b. $D(t) = 60t$
   c. $D(t) = 2{,}000 - 60t$
   d. $D(t) = 2{,}000 + 60t$

18. Each week Jaime saves $25. How long will it take her to save $350?
   a. 12 weeks
   b. 14 weeks
   c. 16 weeks
   d. 18 weeks

19. If one pint is $\frac{1}{8}$ of a gallon, how many pints are there in $3\frac{1}{3}$ gallons of ice cream?
   a. $\frac{7}{16}$ pint
   b. $24\frac{1}{2}$ pints
   c. $26\frac{1}{16}$ pints
   d. 28 pints

20. In the music department at a school, a music teacher counted the musical instruments and supplies in storage. There were:
   - one violin valued at $1,200
   - two violin bows, each valued at $350
   - three music stands, each valued at $55
   - one trumpet valued at $235

In addition, there were a number of supplies totaling $125 and some sheet music worth $75. What was the total value of the musical supplies and instruments in storage?
   a. $2,040
   b. $2,500
   c. $3,040
   d. $3,500

21. Which of the following is a translation of the following sentence? Salwa (S) is ten years older than Roland (R).
a. $10 + S = R$
b. $S + R = 10$
c. $R - 10 = S$
d. $S = R + 10$

Use the following table to answer question 22.

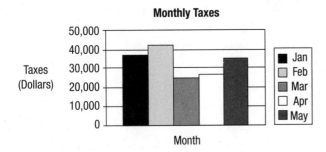

22. Approximately what were the total taxes collected for January, February, and April?
a. $78,000
b. $98,000
c. $105,000
d. $115,000

23. The temperature at 6:00 P.M. was 31°F. By midnight, it had dropped 40°F. What was the temperature at midnight?
a. 9°F
b. −9°F
c. −11°F
d. 0°F

24. Which of the following best represents the following sentence? Rachel (R) had three apples and ate one.
a. $R = 3 - 1$
b. $3 - 2 = R$
c. $R = 3 \times 2$
d. $3R - 2$

25. Find the next number is the following pattern: 320, 160, 80, 40
a. 35
b. 30
c. 10
d. 20

26. A sprinkler system installed in a home that is under construction will cost about 1.5% of the total building cost. The same system, installed after the home is built, costs about 4% of the total building cost. How much would a homeowner save by installing a sprinkler system in a $150,000 home while the home is still under construction?
a. $600
b. $2,250
c. $3,750
d. $6,000

27. Fifth graders Kara and Rani both have lemonade stands. Kara sells her lemonade at five cents a glass, and Rani sells hers at seven cents a glass. Kara sold 17 glasses of lemonade today, and Rani sold 14 glasses. Who made the most money and by what amount?
a. Kara by 13 cents
b. Rani by 13 cents
c. Kara by 85 cents
d. Rani by 98 cents

28. If Linda purchases an item that costs $30 or less, she will pay with cash. If Linda purchases an item that costs between $30 and $70, she will pay with a check. If Linda purchases an item that costs $70 or greater, she will use a credit card. If Linda recently paid for a certain item using a check, which of the following statements could be true?

    a. The item cost $80.
    b. If the item had cost $20 more, she would have paid with cash.
    c. The item cost at least $70.
    d. The item cost more than $25.

29. Joni is 5 feet 11 inches tall, and Pierre is 6 feet 5 inches tall. How much taller is Pierre than Joni?

    a. 1 foot 7 inches
    b. 1 foot
    c. 7 inches
    d. 6 inches

30. Dani spent $6,300 on a used car. She paid $630 as a down payment. What fraction of the original cost was the down payment?

    a. $\frac{1}{10}$
    b. $\frac{1}{18}$
    c. $\frac{1}{20}$
    d. $\frac{1}{40}$

Part 3: Word Knowledge

Time: 11 minutes

1. *Lure* most nearly means
    a. fish.
    b. attract.
    c. resist.
    d. suspect.

2. *Delirious* most nearly means
    a. manic.
    b. calm.
    c. tasty.
    d. suspicious.

3. *Infirm* most nearly means
    a. agree.
    b. strong.
    c. weak.
    d. validate.

4. *Perilous* most nearly means
    a. disciplined.
    b. dangerous.
    c. safe.
    d. honest.

5. *Isolation* most nearly means
    a. fear.
    b. plentitude.
    c. solitude.
    d. disease.

6. *Lull* most nearly means
    a. pause.
    b. hole.
    c. noise.
    d. boring.

7. *Outfit* most nearly means
    a. indoors.
    b. strong.
    c. special.
    d. furnish.

8. *Omit* most nearly means
    a. recluse.
    b. neglect.
    c. mistake.
    d. destroy.

9. *Mutiny* most nearly means
   a. rebellion.
   b. currency.
   c. sailor.
   d. hassle.

10. *Naïve* most nearly means
   a. rural.
   b. secular.
   c. unsophisticated.
   d. church.

11. *Rudimentary* most nearly means
   a. crass.
   b. gracious.
   c. deliberate.
   d. primitive.

12. *Pompous* most nearly means
   a. arrogant.
   b. supportive.
   c. busy.
   d. gaudy.

13. *Prevalent* most nearly means
   a. widespread.
   b. rare.
   c. wind.
   d. servile.

14. *Abundance* most nearly means
   a. trouble.
   b. foolish.
   c. wealth.
   d. love.

15. *Calamity* most nearly means
   a. potion.
   b. silence.
   c. shellfish.
   d. disaster.

16. *Superficial* most nearly means
   a. gorgeous.
   b. shallow.
   c. intelligent.
   d. rich.

17. *Reform* most nearly means
   a. punish.
   b. destroy.
   c. display.
   d. correct.

18. *Methodical* most nearly means
   a. rhythmic.
   b. poetic.
   c. systematic.
   d. disrespectful.

19. *Spite* most nearly means
   a. joy.
   b. beverage.
   c. wonder.
   d. malice.

20. *Scale* most nearly means
   a. climb.
   b. sail.
   c. swim.
   d. skate.

21. *Smudge* most nearly means
   a. gloat.
   b. residue.
   c. blur.
   d. celebrate.

22. *Drizzle* most nearly means
   a. curly.
   b. sprinkle.
   c. sear.
   d. drench.

23. *Mundane* most nearly means
   a. dirty.
   b. commonplace.
   c. confused.
   d. extraordinary.

24. *Mirth* most nearly means
   a. anger.
   b. glee.
   c. sarcasm.
   d. mistrust.

25. *Drudgery* most nearly means
   a. silliness.
   b. evil.
   c. labor.
   d. investigation.

26. *Prerequisite* most nearly means
   a. necessary.
   b. course.
   c. difficult.
   d. tar.

27. Gerard has such a *caustic* sense of humor that most people find his jokes upsetting rather than humorous.
   a. sarcastic
   b. funny
   c. honest
   d. original

28. Sandra is truly an *enigma*; although she's lived here for years and everyone knows her, no one seems to know anything about her.
   a. stranger
   b. enemy
   c. newcomer
   d. mystery

29. Everyone loved Ilona's idea, and she quickly *garnered* enough support for her proposal to present it to the committee.
   a. created
   b. proposed
   c. needed
   d. gathered

30. Hattie's attempt to finally complete the marathon was *thwarted* when she twisted her ankle in the 23rd mile.
   a. injured
   b. prevented
   c. supported
   d. completed

31. Although the plot of the film is admittedly *trite*, the characters are so endearing that the movie is highly entertaining despite the old storyline.
   a. original
   b. exciting
   c. complex
   d. overused

32. Anthony, a meticulous young man, *diligently* watered his neighbors' plants once a week while they were on vacation.
   a. reluctantly
   b. dutifully
   c. haphazardly
   d. predictably

33. Although Hunter was *reticent* about revealing information to us when we first met him, he soon began to talk more than anyone.
   a. quick
   b. voluntary
   c. reluctant
   d. talkative

34. Being a direct relative of the deceased, her claim to the estate was *legitimate*.
   a. lawful
   b. spurious
   c. dubious
   d. honest

35. The Earth Day committee leader placed large garbage bins in the park to *facilitate* Saturday's cleanup.
   a. hinder
   b. assist
   c. plan
   d. begin

Part 4:
Paragraph Comprehension

Time: 13 minutes

Monday, Tuesday, Wednesday, Thursday. . . . We all know the days of the week, but have you ever wondered where their names came from? The answer dates back to the ancient Greeks, who decided to name the weekdays after their *pantheon* of gods. Two of their primary gods were the Sun and the Moon, so they named the first two days of the week after them; these names survive in modern English as Sun-day and Moon-day (Sunday and Monday).

Other day names are not quite so obvious to the modern person, however. This is because English is a Germanic language, influenced by the ancient German peoples, who translated the Greek and Norse gods into their own language. The Greeks, for example, named the third day after Mars, their god of war; the ancient Germanic peoples named it after Tiw (also known as Tyr), their god of war—giving us Tuesday (Tiw's Day). Wednesday is named after Woden, the ancient Germanic god of musical inspiration. Thursday is named for Thor, the Germanic thunder god, while Friday is named for Frigga, Germanic goddess of love (like the Roman god Venus). Finally, Saturday is named after Saturn, ancient god of the harvest.

1. What is the main idea of this passage?
   a. The days of the week are named after the sun, the moon, and ancient gods.
   b. English is a Germanic language.
   c. The ancient Germans had gods that were like the Greeks' gods.
   d. Thursday is named after Thor.

2. According to the passage, Wednesday is named after
   a. the god of speed.
   b. the god of war.
   c. the god of inspiration.
   d. the god of love.

3. As used in the passage, *pantheon* most nearly means
   a. a sports coliseum.
   b. a wild animal.
   c. the days of the week.
   d. a list of ancient gods.

4. From this passage, you can infer that
   a. ancient mythology played a role in the development of modern English.
   b. the Greeks worshiped different gods from the Romans.
   c. ancient Germans spoke English.
   d. Mercury is similar to Thor.

Linoleum was invented in 1860 by a British man named Frederick Walton. It is actually a natural compound made from linseed oil, pine rosin, and pine flour. To that mixture is added wood pulp or other fibers to give it a stiff consistency. Walton named his invention linoleum from the Latin word *linum*, meaning flax (from which linseed oil is made) and *oleum*, meaning oil. Linoleum is still widely used around the world today for floorings and countertops.

5. Linoleum got its name from
   a. Latin words meaning "flax oil."
   b. Greek words meaning "floor covering."
   c. the inventor's imagination.
   d. the British patent office.

6. The main idea of this passage is
   a. that Latin is used in naming inventions.
   b. the many uses of linoleum.
   c. why linoleum is used around the world.
   d. the history of linoleum.

Today's postal service is more efficient than ever. Mail that once took months to move by horse and foot now moves around the country in days or hours by truck, train, and plane. If your letter or package is urgent, the U.S. Postal Service offers Priority Mail and Express Mail services. Priority Mail is guaranteed to go anywhere in the United States in two days or less, while Express Mail will get your package there overnight.

7. This paragraph best supports the statement that
   a. more people use the post office for urgent deliveries than any other delivery service.
   b. Express Mail is a good way to send urgent mail.
   c. Priority Mail usually takes two days or less.
   d. mail service today is more effective and dependable.

8. According to the passage, Priority Mail will get a package delivered
   a. overnight.
   b. in two days or less.
   c. within a week.
   d. in three hours.

Paper clips are such an everyday item that most of us don't even notice them. We use them to get stuck disks out of computers, to clean dirt from tiny *crevices*, to fix our eyeglasses, and a million other things—and sometimes we even use them to clip papers together! But if you think about it, you'll realize that somebody had to invent the paper clip; it didn't suddenly drop out of the sky one day.

That inventor was a Norwegian named Johan Vaaler who registered his idea with the German patent office in 1899 for a "rectangular, triangular, or otherwise shaped hoop" that could be used to fasten papers together. Previously, people had used ribbons, pins, and even string to bind paper, but Vaaler's simple idea changed that forever.

9. The author of this passage thinks that paper clips
   a. are funny.
   b. are a useful invention.
   c. fell from the sky.
   d. should be used for other things besides clipping paper.

10. As used in the passage, *crevices* most nearly means
   a. small cracks.
   b. ceiling paint.
   c. fast-moving water.
   d. tiny bumps.

11. According to the passage, which of the following was once used to bind papers together?
   a. tape
   b. hairpins
   c. string
   d. glue

12. Where was the first paper clip patented, according to the passage?
  a. Norway
  b. Germany
  c. United States
  d. not stated

Daffodil bulbs require well-drained soil and a sunny planting location. They should be planted in holes that are 3 to 6 inches deep, and there should be 2 to 4 inches between bulbs. The bulb should be placed in the hole, pointed side up, root side down. Once the bulb is planted, water the area thoroughly.

13. According to the preceding directions, when planting daffodil bulbs, which of the following conditions is not necessary?
  a. a sunny location
  b. well-drained soil
  c. proper placement of bulbs in soil
  d. proper fertilization

14. According to the directions, which of the following is true?
  a. Daffodils do best in sandy soil.
  b. Daffodil bulbs should be planted in autumn for spring blooming.
  c. It is possible to plant daffodil bulbs upside down.
  d. Daffodil bulbs require daily watering.

Please use the green garbage bags to dispose of all medical waste. White garbage bags are for clean trash only, and red garbage bags are to be used for sensitive paper waste. Adherence to these regulations is vitally important for the safety of all personnel.

15. Why is it important to dispose of medical waste in green garbage bags, according to this passage?
  a. Medical waste can be dangerous if not properly treated.
  b. Green is the universal color for medical waste.
  c. The green bags are stronger than the red and white bags.
  d. The reason is not stated.

Part 5: Mathematics Knowledge

Time: 24 minutes

1. Five more than 20% of a number is 52. Find the number.
  a. 50
  b. 60
  c. 70
  d. 100

2. What is the perimeter of the following polygon?

  a. 12
  b. 16
  c. 24
  d. 32

3. Which of the following phrases means *percent*?
  a. per part
  b. per 100 parts
  c. per fraction
  d. per decimal

4. What is the square root of 64?
   a. 8
   b. 32
   c. 128
   d. 4,096

5. Which of the following numbers can be divided evenly by 19?
   a. 54
   b. 63
   c. 76
   d. 82

6. If pentagon *ABCDE* is similar to pentagon *FGHIJ*, and *AB* = 10, *CD* = 5, and *FG* = 30, what is *HI*?
   a. $\frac{5}{3}$
   b. 5
   c. 15
   d. 30

7. Each of the following figures has exactly two pairs of parallel sides EXCEPT a
   a. parallelogram.
   b. rhombus.
   c. trapezoid.
   d. square.

8. What is the greatest common factor of the following monomials: $3x^2$, $12x$, $6x^3$?
   a. 12
   b. $3x$
   c. $6x$
   d. $3x^2$

9. Which of the following lists three consecutive even integers whose sum is 30?
   a. 9, 10, 11
   b. 8, 10, 12
   c. 9, 11, 13
   d. 10, 12, 14

10. 0.06 =
   a. 0.60%
   b. 6.0%
   c. 60.0%
   d. 600%

11. Forty cents is what percent of $1.30?
   a. 40%
   b. 31%
   c. 20%
   d. 11%

12. A right angle is
   a. 180°.
   b. greater than 90°.
   c. exactly 90°.
   d. less than 90°.

13. Which of the following lengths could form the sides of a triangle?
   a. 1, 2, 3
   b. 2, 2, 5
   c. 2, 3, 6
   d. 2, 3, 2

14. How many faces does a cube have?
   a. 4
   b. 6
   c. 8
   d. 12

15. Which of the following is a prime number?
   a. 6
   b. 9
   c. 11
   d. 27

16. 32% converted to a fraction =
   a. $\frac{1}{32}$
   b. $\frac{8}{32}$
   c. $\frac{8}{25}$
   d. $\frac{1}{25}$

17. $16\sqrt{2} - 4\sqrt{2} =$
a. 12
b. $12\sqrt{2}$
c. $12 - \sqrt{2}$
d. 20

18. If $\frac{2}{5} = \frac{x}{45}$, what is x?
a. 9
b. 12
c. 18
d. 90

19. A triangle has angles of 71° and 62°. Which of the following best describes the triangle?
a. acute scalene
b. obtuse scalene
c. acute isosceles
d. obtuse isosceles

20. $0.75 + 0.518 =$
a. 12.68
b. 0.01268
c. 0.1268
d. 1.268

21. What is the greatest area possible enclosed by a quadrilateral with a perimeter of 24 feet?
a. 6 square feet
b. 24 square feet
c. 36 square feet
d. 48 square feet

22. Solve for p in the following equation:
$$2.5p + 6 = 18.5$$
a. 5
b. 10
c. 15
d. 20

23. Evaluate the expression: $|-14| + -5$
a. −19
b. 19
c. 9
d. −9

24. What is another way to write 7.25×10^3?
a. 72.5
b. 725
c. 7,250
d. 72,500

25. How many inches are there in four feet?
a. 12 inches
b. 36 inches
c. 48 inches
d. 52 inches

Part 6: Electronics Information

Time: 9 minutes

1. Data stored on magnetic tape can be lost by which of the following?
a. exposure to light
b. freezing temperatures
c. exposure to heat
d. low air pressure

2. Fill in the blank to make the following sentence true: "Current is the _____ an electrical charge passes a specific point in a circuit."
a. direction in which
b. rate at which
c. mass with which
d. acceleration with which

3. In a series circuit there are 7 resistors, each with a resistance of 67Ω. What is the total resistance?

   a. 37.5Ω

   b. 67Ω

   c. 234.5Ω

   d. 469Ω

4. In a parallel circuit there are 7 resistors, each with a resistance of 67Ω. What is the total resistance?

   a. 37.5Ω

   b. 67Ω

   c. 234.5Ω

   d. 469Ω

5. This schematic symbol represents what type of switch?

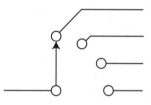

   a. multi-way switch

   b. multi-pole switch

   c. slide switch

   d. rocker switch

6. The pressure of current is called?

   a. voltage

   b. ohms

   c. amperes

   d. none of the above

7. AC refers to what?

   a. ampere current

   b. ampere component

   c. alternating current

   d. alternating component

8. DC refers to what?

   a. diode charge

   b. direct current

   c. direct charge

   d. diode current

9. The process used in electroplating is known as

   a. electrochemistry.

   b. electrocoating.

   c. electrolysis.

   d. electrodeposition.

10. What does this schematic symbol represent?

   a. a bell

   b. a motor

   c. a lamp

   d. a buzzer

11. What does RMS mean?

   a. resistant motor system

   b. real matrix standard

   c. range motion symbol

   d. root mean square

12. What does this schematic symbol represent?

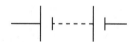

   a. a fuse

   b. a battery

   c. a transformer

   d. a cell

13. What is the speed of radio waves radiated into free space?

   a. 300,000,000 meters per second

   b. 300,000,000 meters per minute

   c. 343 meters per second

   d. 343 meters per minute

14. To cause a current of 10 amps to flow through 20 ohms resistance, the voltage needs to be?
   a. 10
   b. 20
   c. 2
   d. 200

15. Which is NOT an insulator of electricity?
   a. plastic
   b. water
   c. paper
   d. glass

16. Microwave ovens operate by
   a. thermal expansion.
   b. convection heating.
   c. dielectric heating.
   d. trielectric heating.

17. Which of the following is a diode that is used to regulate voltage?
   a. zener diode
   b. photodiode
   c. capacitor
   d. light emitting diode

18. What does this schematic symbol represent?

   a. a cell
   b. an antenna
   c. a wire
   d. a ground

19. The ground wire is always what color in 120-volt wiring in the United States?
   a. white
   b. black
   c. green
   d. orange

20. A 120-volt current is protected by a 30-amp circuit breaker. What is the largest watt appliance that can be used safely?
   a. 36
   b. 3,600
   c. 360
   d. 4

Part 7:
Auto and Shop Information

Time: 11 minutes

1. The gauge shown here is calibrated to read in what measurement?

   a. pounds per linear foot
   b. pounds per square inch
   c. meters per foot
   d. oil temperature

2. An automobile radiator cools the engine coolant by
   a. rapid circulation through a cooling coil.
   b. freon in the air conditioning system.
   c. the flow of air across the radiator grills.
   d. high pressure energy.

3. Which of the following would indicate an overinflated tire?
   a. excessive wear in the middle of the tire tread
   b. excessive wear on the edges of the tire thread
   c. excessive wear on the outer edge of the front right tire tread
   d. none of the above

4. An automobile that bounces a lot on roads would most likely have a problem with
   a. front end alignment.
   b. shock absorbers.
   c. rear end alignment.
   d. engine mounts.

5. What is the primary function of the water pump in a car?
   a. to circulate coolant
   b. to evacuate waste water
   c. to remove exhaust
   d. to filter water

6. The purpose of the crankshaft is
   a. to start the engine.
   b. to convert the up-and-down motion of the pistons and tie rods into rotational movement.
   c. to ensure the universal joint correctly powers the rear axle.
   d. none of the above

7. An automobile differential is located in the
   a. gear box.
   b. distributor.
   c. universal joint.
   d. drive axle.

8. The purpose of a camshaft in an internal combustion engine is to
   a. provide ignition of the fuel.
   b. provide cooling of the fuel.
   c. provide lubrication of the engine.
   d. transfer energy to the drivetrain.

9. Vernier calipers are used to perform which of the following functions?
   a. tightening
   b. measuring
   c. cutting
   d. drilling

10. Which of the following automotive systems uses lubrication fluid?
   a. the transmission system
   b. the exhaust system
   c. the suspension system
   d. the electrical system

11. To which automotive system does the alternator belong?
   a. the steering system
   b. the cooling system
   c. the electrical system
   d. the engine

12. What is the function of the spark plugs in the internal combustion engine in a car?
   a. to transfer electricity to the alternator
   b. to increase the cylinder size
   c. to cool the engine
   d. to ignite the fuel

13. Which fluid is contained in a car radiator?
   a. transmission fluid
   b. cooling fluid
   c. brake fluid
   d. steering fluid

14. A plumber, looking to turn soft iron pipes or fittings with a rounded surface, would most likely use which tool?

a.

b.

c.

d.

15. A floor plan is drawn to scale so that $\frac{1}{4}$ inch represents 2 feet. If a hall on the plan is 4 inches long, how long will the actual hall be when it is built?
   a. 2 feet
   b. 8 feet
   c. 16 feet
   d. 32 feet

16. All the rooms in a building are rectangular, with 8-foot ceilings. One room is 9 feet wide by 11 feet long. What is the combined area of the four walls, including doors and windows?
   a. 99 square feet
   b. 160 square feet
   c. 320 square feet
   d. 72 square feet

17. What tool is used to hold a piece of material in a fixed position?
   a. a biscuit joiner
   b. a router
   c. a vise
   d. a caliper

18. Which of the following is NOT a carpenter's hand tool?
   a. a winch
   b. a level
   c. a compass
   d. a chisel

19. To a welder, what do ammonium chloride, rosin, hydrochloric acid, zinc chloride, and borax have in common?
   a. They are all common types of metal polishing materials.
   b. They are all common types of flux.
   c. They can all be used as solder.
   d. They are all types of metal that can be welded together.

20. Which of the following tools would be best to drill precisely placed holes to a specific depth?
   a. an awl
   b. a chisel
   c. a hand drill
   d. a drill press

21. What type of gauge uses units of rpm?

    a. a pressure gauge

    b. a tachometer

    c. a speedometer

    d. a thermometer

22. What type of outside energy source could be used to operate a pump?

    a. a battery

    b. an internal combustion engine

    c. an electric motor

    d. all of the above

23. Which of the following wrenches is adjustable?

    a. a crescent wrench

    b. a pipe wrench

    c. channel locks

    d. all the above

24. A ball-peen hammer is characterized by

    a. an elongated claw.

    b. a rounded hemispherical head.

    c. a stainless steel construction.

    d. all the above

25. A wood chisel is used for

    a. carving, cutting, or chipping.

    b. slicing, dicing, or paring.

    c. grinding or polishing.

    d. prying.

Part 8:
Mechanical Comprehension

Time: 19 minutes

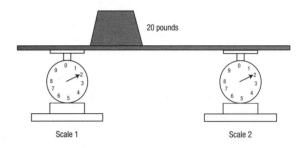

1. According to the figure, assuming the board connecting scales 1 and 2 has no weight, how many pounds will scale 1 register?

    a. less than 10 pounds

    b. 10 pounds

    c. more than 10 pounds

    d. impossible to determine

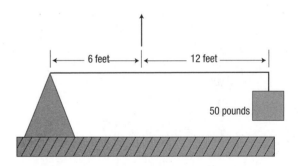

2. In the diagram, Todd wants to lift a 50-pound block using a lever. If the block is 18 feet from the pivot point and Todd is 6 feet from the pivot point, how much force must he apply to lift the block?

    a. 100 pounds

    b. 72 pounds

    c. 150 pounds

    d. 50 pounds

3. A hot air balloon is able to float because
   a. the hot air acts as a jet.
   b. hot air is less dense than the outside air.
   c. hot air is more dense than the outside air.
   d. it is filled with helium.

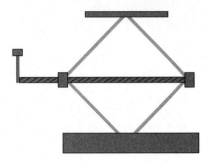

4. To change a tire, a person is able to take advantage of the mechanical advantage of a jack to lift a car. Each complete turn of the screw raises the car $\frac{1}{4}$ inch. If the handle travels 3 feet per revolution, what is the mechanical advantage of the jack?
   a. 12
   b. 36
   c. 14
   d. 144

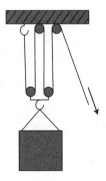

5. Bryan is strong enough to pull a rope with 150 pounds of force. Using the pulley system shown here, what is the maximum weight he can lift?
   a. 50 pounds
   b. 300 pounds
   c. 450 pounds
   d. 600 pounds

6. A wheelbarrow is loaded with 80 pounds of dirt. However, it can be lifted with only 20 pounds of force. What is the mechanical advantage of the wheelbarrow?
   a. 1
   b. 2
   c. 3
   d. 4

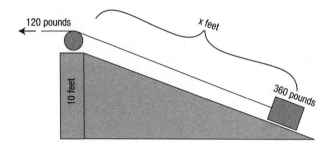

7. A 360-pound block is being pulled up an incline by a pulley. The incline rises 10 feet. Neglecting friction, if 120 pounds of force is necessary to move the block up the incline, how long is the incline?
   a. 30 feet
   b. 360 feet
   c. 20 feet
   d. 60 feet

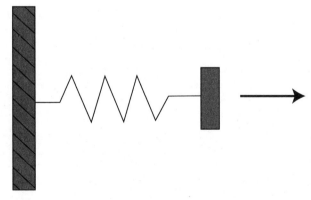

8. A spring has a force constant of 3 pounds per inch. How much force is required to move the spring 1 foot?
   a. 3 pounds
   b. 12 pounds
   c. 24 pounds
   d. 36 pounds

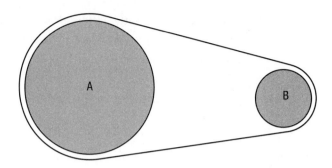

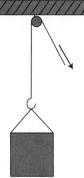

9. Pulley A is three times the diameter pulley B. If pulley A rotates at 45 revolutions per minute (rpm), how fast must pulley B rotate?
  a. 15 rpm
  b. 45 rpm
  c. 90 rpm
  d. 135 rpm

10. A block of wood rests on a level surface. What mechanical principle makes it more difficult to push this block sideways if the surface is made of sandpaper than if it is made of glass?
  a. centrifugal force
  b. gravity
  c. wind resistance
  d. friction

11. A screw has 6 threads per inch. How many full turns are necessary for the nut to travel 2 inches?
  a. 6 turns
  b. 12 turns
  c. 18 turns
  d. 24 turns

12. When you add water to a tank, the water pressure at the top will
  a. change with the water depth.
  b. decrease.
  c. stay the same.
  d. increase.

13. What is the mechanical advantage of the pulley system shown here?
  a. 1
  b. 2
  c. 3
  d. 4

14. A block made of what material will float on water?
  a. metal
  b. glass
  c. styrofoam
  d. rock

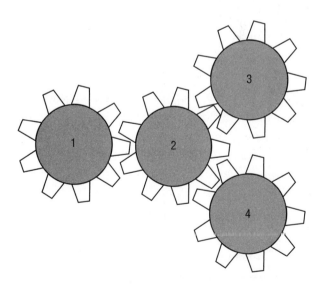

15. If gear 1 turns clockwise, which other gear(s), if any, will also turn clockwise?
  a. 2 only
  b. 3 only
  c. 3 and 4 only
  d. 2, 3, and 4

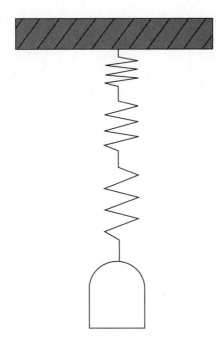

16. A handle is connected to the ceiling by a series of springs with force constants of 400, 200, and 100 pounds per inch. When a 200-pound soldier hangs from the handle, how many inches does the platform stretch?
  a. 2 inches
  b. 2.5 inches
  c. 3 inches
  d. 3.5 inches

17. Matt leaves his barracks and travels east at 45 mph. At the same time, Phil leaves the same barracks and travels west at 35 mph. After 2 hours, how far away from each other will they be?
  a. 20 miles
  b. 80 miles
  c. 135 miles
  d. 160 miles

18. Two men are racing on bicycles. Both have 52-tooth front chain rings. One has a 12-tooth rear cog and the other has a 14-tooth rear cog. If the first bike is being pedaled at 60 rpm, how fast must the other bicycle be pedaled to keep up?
  a. 60 rpm
  b. 70 rpm
  c. 80 rpm
  d. 90 rpm

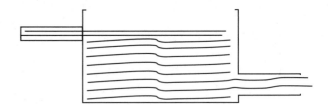

19. Water is flowing into a 20-gallon container through an inlet pipe at a rate of 18 gallons per minute. Water is being evacuated through an outlet at 14 gallons per minute. How much time will it take for the container to overflow?
  a. 1 minute
  b. 5 minutes
  c. 8 minutes
  d. 10 minutes

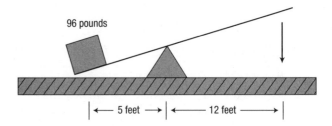

20. In the diagram, James wants to lift a 96-pound block using a lever. If the block is 5 feet from the pivot point and James is 12 feet from the pivot point, how much force must he apply to lift the block?
  a. 40 pounds
  b. 17 pounds
  c. 96 pounds
  d. 60 pounds

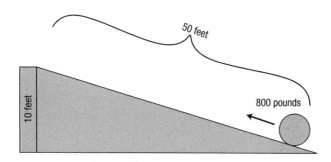

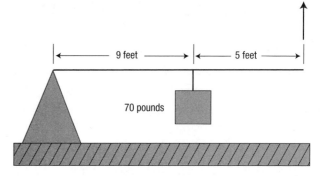

21. An 800-pound block is being pulled up an incline by a pulley. The incline is 50 feet long and rises 10 feet. Neglecting friction, how much force is necessary to move the block up the incline?

a. 50 pounds

b. 160 pounds

c. 800 pounds

d. 60 pounds

24. In the diagram, Stevi wants to lift a 70-pound block using a lever. If the block is 9 feet from the pivot point and Stevi is 5 feet beyond that, how much force must she apply to lift the block?

a. 45 pounds

b. 14 pounds

c. 126 pounds

d. 70 pounds

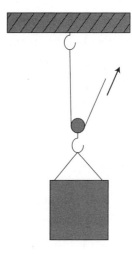

22. Two gears have 12 teeth and 18 teeth. If the larger gear completes two full turns, how many rotations will the smaller gear complete?

a. 1 rotation

b. 1.5 rotations

c. 2 rotations

d. 3 rotations

23. Using the tip of a screwdriver to pry the lid off a paint can is an example of what simple machine?

a. lever

b. pulley

c. inclined plane

d. gear

25. Using the pulley system shown here, how much force is required to lift a 150-pound weight?

a. 25 pounds

b. 50 pounds

c. 75 pounds

d. 100 pounds

Part 9: Assembling Objects

Time: 15 minutes

Each question is composed of five separate drawings. The problem is presented in the first drawing, and the remaining four drawings are possible soutions. Determine which of the four choices contains all of the pieces assembled properly that are shown in the first picture. Note: images are not drawn to scale.

1.
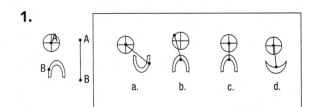

2.
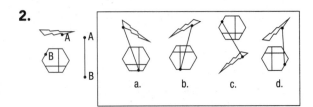

3.
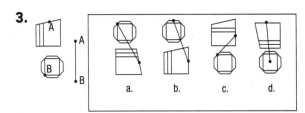

4.
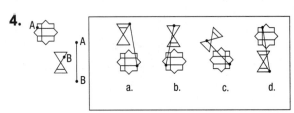

5.
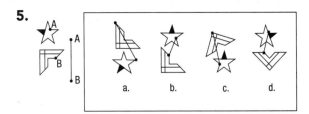

6.
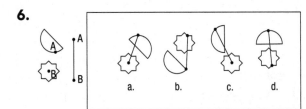

7.
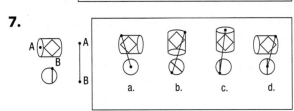

8.
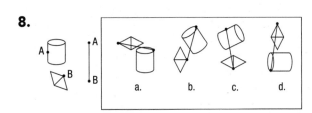

9.
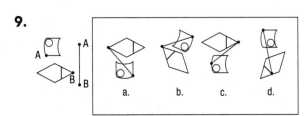

10.
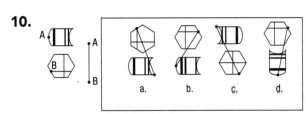

11.
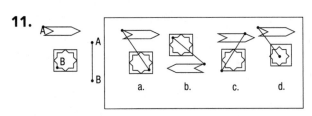

12.
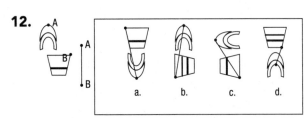

13.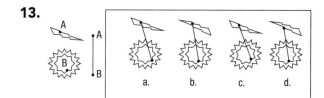

20.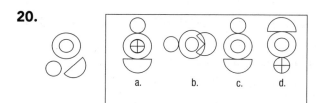

14.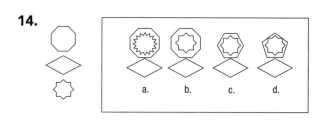

21.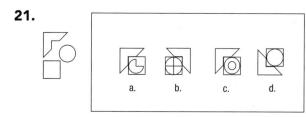

15.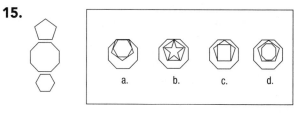

22.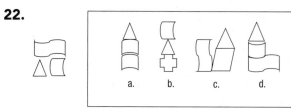

16.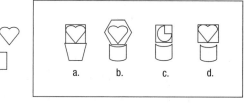

23.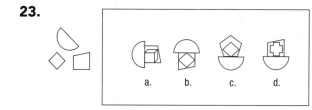

17.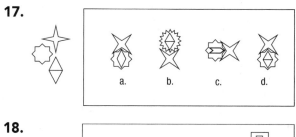

24.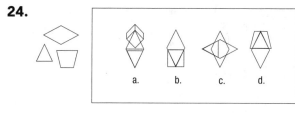

18.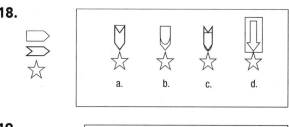

25.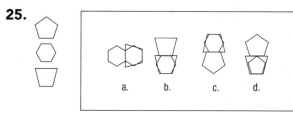

19.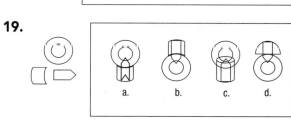

Answers

Part 1: General Science

1. d. Earth is the third planet from the Sun and Mars is the fourth planet and next farthest from the Sun.

2. b. Animal cells do not have cell walls; plant cells do. Animals do exist with the remaining traits.

3. a. Only A-U is a possible human nucleotide pairing, which represents the pairing in RNA between adenosine (A) and uracil (U).

4. b. Convection is the process of transferring heat by moving a fluid in a space, much like a convection oven uses a fan to distribute heat within the oven.

5. c. Velocity is the change in distance over time $(v = \frac{d}{t})$.

6. d. Charles's Law states that a volume of gas maintained at constant pressure is directly proportional to its temperature. Therefore, when the temperature increases so does the volume by the same factor.

7. a. mRNA is responsible for taking the genetic code from DNA out of the nucleus into the cytoplasm of the cell.

8. d. Ribosomes are structures that are present in all cells and are responsible for producing proteins.

9. c. When a substance sublimates, it changes state from a solid to a gas without changing into a liquid first.

10. b. Meiosis results in daughter cells that are genetically different from their parent cell. This leads to greater diversity when compared to reproduction through mitosis or asexual reproduction.

11. a. Chloroplasts contain chlorophyll, which gives plants their green color in leaves and makes photosynthesis possible.

12. d. The force applied to an object is determined by the product of its mass and acceleration ($F = ma$). Therefore, the force on an object weighing 30 kg accelerating at $15\frac{m}{s^2}$ is 450 N ($30 \times 15 = 450$).

13. c. A 0.200 M solution of NaOH contains 0.05 mol NaOH. This is calculated by:

$$\frac{0.200 \text{ mol NaOH}}{1 \text{ L}} \times 250 \text{ mL} \times \frac{1 \text{ L}}{1000 \text{ mL}} =$$

$$0.050 \text{ mol NaOH} \times \frac{40 \text{ g NaOH}}{1 \text{ mol}} = 2.00 \text{ g NaOH}$$

14. b. All cells undergo mitosis to reproduce into identical cells with the same DNA. Cells specialize into different tissue by expressing different parts of their DNA. Only gametes may have different DNA from their parent cells due to meiosis.

15. a. Subduction is when one plate slides underneath another and is the location of earthquakes, fault lines, and deep ocean trenches.

16. d. Sound waves are created by the vibration of matter and make changes in the pressure of the medium in which sound travels. In a vacuum there is no pressure, so sound cannot exist in a vacuum and its speed would be zero.

17. d. Veins carry blood to the heart and arteries carry blood away from the heart. Pulmonary refers to the lungs.

18. a. One of the primary functions of the liver is to process toxins absorbed in the digestive system.

19. c. Electrical current is measured by the unit ampere, which is electrical charge per second.

20. c. To form an anion an element needs to reduce or accept an electron. Electronegativity describes an element's ability to accept electrons and in general electronegativity increases moving from left to right and decreases from top to bottom in the periodic table. Therefore, from this list the element with the least electronegativity would be P.

21. a. Natural selection occurs through genetic traits passed on to offspring that are beneficial to survival, like adapting to harsh climates or living with limited resources. Traits learned by parents are not passed on to generations of offspring.

22. d. An ecosystem is the community of species in a habitat and the environmental factors interacting with the community. Biosphere and biome are too large scale for this question.

23. b. Transport systems in plants is a unique characteristic of vascular plants, otherwise known as tracheophytes.

24. a. This is a double replacement reaction where the cations and anions switch to form new molecules.

25. a. The second energy level can hold up to 8 electrons.

Part 2: Arithmetic Reasoning

1. b. The total number of pages assigned is 80; $\frac{1}{6} \times 80 = \frac{8}{6}$ or $13\frac{1}{3}$.

2. c. This is a three-step problem involving multiplication, subtraction, and addition. First, find out how many fewer minutes George jogged this week than usual. 5 hours $\times$ 60 minutes = 300 minutes – 40 minutes missed = 260 minutes jogged. Now add back the number of minutes George was able to make up: 260 minutes + 20 + 13 minutes = 293 minutes. Now subtract again: 300 minutes – 293 = 7 minutes jogging time lost.

3. a. The train's speed can be found using the formula *Distance = rate × time*. From this we get the formula $rate = \frac{distance}{time}$, since we are looking for the speed. By substituting, $rate = \frac{300}{6}$, which simplifies to 50. The speed is 50 miles per hour.

4. b. To find the percentage of people who said they rode at least three times a week, divide 105 by 150: $105 \div 150 = 0.7$, which is 70%. $0.7 \times 100,000 = 70,000$.

5. d. According to the table, a pound in weight makes a difference of $0.64, or $0.04 per ounce over 4 pounds. Fruit that weighs 4 pounds 8 ounces will cost 8×0.04 or $0.32 more than fruit that costs 4 pounds. Therefore, the cost is $1.10 + 0.32 = $1.42.

6. b. To find the answer, begin by adding the cost of the two sale puppies: $15 + $15 = $30. Now subtract this amount from the total cost: $70 – $30 = $40 paid for the third puppy.

7. b. First, divide to determine the number of 20-minute segments there are in 1 hour: $60 \div 20 = 3$. Now multiply that number by the number of times Rita can circle the block: $3 \times 5 = 15$.

8. c. Between 8:14 and 9:00, 46 minutes elapse, and between 9:00 and 9:12, 12 minutes elapse, so this becomes a simple addition problem: 46 + 12 = 58.

9. a. Let x equal the number of pounds of chocolate to be mixed. You know the mixture's total cost is the cost of the chocolates plus the cost of the caramels, or M = A + B. In terms of x, M = 3.95(x + 3), A = 5.95x, while B = 2.95(3). Combine terms: $3.95(x + 3) = 5.95x + 2.95(3)$. Simplify: $3.95x + 11.85 = 5.95x + 8.85$, or $11.85 – 8.85 = (5.95 – 3.95)x$, which becomes $2x = 3$. Thus, $x = 1.5$ pounds.

10. c. This is a problem of addition. You may simplify the terms: M = F + 10; then substitute: M = 16 + 10, or 26.

11. d. First, add the weight of Ralph's triplets: $4\frac{3}{8} + 3\frac{5}{6} + 4\frac{7}{8}$, or (after finding the least common denominator) $4\frac{9}{24} + 3\frac{20}{24} + 4\frac{21}{24} + 11\frac{50}{24}$, or $13\frac{2}{24}$, or $13\frac{1}{12}$. Now find the weight of Harvey's twins: $7\frac{10}{30} + 9\frac{9}{30} = 16\frac{19}{30}$. Now subtract: $16\frac{19}{30} - 13\frac{1}{12} = 16\frac{38}{60} - 13\frac{5}{60} = 3\frac{33}{60} = 3\frac{11}{20}$. So Harvey's twins outweigh Ralph's triplets by $3\frac{11}{20}$ pounds. (No further reduction of the fraction is possible.)

12. d. There are four quarters for every dollar; $\$12 \times 4$ quarters per dollar = 48 quarters.

13. c. From 5:16 P.M. to 7:16 A.M. the next day is 14 hours. An additional 42 minutes occurs between 7:16 A.M. and 7:58 A.M: $(58 - 16 = 42)$.

14. b. Carmella worked 15 hours per week for 8 weeks: $15 \times 8 = 120$. In addition, she worked 15 hours for Mariah for one week, so $120 + 15 = 135$.

15. c. Take apart the statement and translate each part. The word *twice* tells you to multiply the quantity by two. In the second part of the statement, the word *sum* is a key word for addition. So *the sum of six and four* is translated as $6 + 4$. The whole statement becomes $2(6 + 4)$.

16. c. Divide the amount of cod by the number of crates: $400 \div 20 = 20$.

17. c. The speed of the train, obtained from the table, is 60 miles per hour. Therefore, the distance from Chicago would be equal to $60t$. However, as the train moves on, the distance decreases from Los Angeles, so there must be a function of $-60t$ in the equation. At time $t = 0$, the distance is 2,000 miles, so the function is $2,000 - 60t$.

18. b. Divide $350 by $25; $350 \div 25 = 14$ weeks.

19. d. This is a division problem. First, change the mixed number to a fraction: $3\frac{1}{2} = \frac{7}{2}$. Next, invert $\frac{1}{8}$ and multiply: $\frac{7}{2} \times \frac{8}{1} = 28$.

20. b. The total value of the supplies and instruments is found by adding the cost of each item: $1,200 + (2 \times 350) + (3 \times 55) + 235 + 125 + 75 = 1,200 + 700 + 165 + 235 + 125 + 75$. The total is $2,500.

21. d. If Salwa (S) is 10 years older than Roland (R), then S is equal to R + 10. Therefore, the equation is S = R + 10.

22. c. January is approximately $38,000; February is approximately $41,000; and April is approximately $26,000. These added together give a total of $105,000.

23. b. Visualize a number line. The drop from 31° to 0° is 31°. The are still nine more degrees to drop. They will be below zero, so −9°F is the temperature at midnight.

24. a. This answer is in the correct order and is "translated" correctly: Rachel had (=) 3 apples and ate (−) 1.

25. d. Each number is divided by 2 to find the next number: $40 \div 2 = 20$, so 20 is the next number.

26. c. First you must subtract the percentage of the installation cost during construction (1.5%) from the percentage of the installation cost after construction (4%). To do this, begin by converting the percentages into decimals: 4% = 0.04; 1.5% = 0.015. Now subtract: $0.04 - 0.015 = 0.025$. This is the percentage of the total cost that the homeowner will save. Multiply this by the total cost of the home to find the dollar amount: $0.025 \times \$150,000 = \$3,750$.

27. b. First, simplify the problem: $K = 5 \times 17 = 85$, so Kara made 85 cents; $R = 7 \times 14 = 98$, so Rani made 98 cents, the higher amount of money; $R - K = 98 - 85 = 13$. Therefore, Rani made 13 cents more than Kara.

28. d. Because Linda pays with a check only if an item costs more than $30, the item Linda purchased with a check in this problem must have cost more than $30. If an item costs more than $30, then it must cost more than $25 (choice **d**), as well.

29. d. First, write the problem in columns:

6 feet   5 inches
−5 feet 11 inches

Now subtract, beginning with the rightmost column. Since you cannot subtract 11 inches from 5 inches, you must borrow 1 foot from the 6 in the top left column, then convert it to inches and add: 1 foot = 12 inches; 12 inches + 5 inches = 17 inches. The problem then becomes:

5 feet 17 inches
−5 feet 11 inches
              6 inches

So the answer is choice **d**, 6 inches.

30. a. To find the fraction, compare the down payment with the total cost of the car; 630/6,300 reduces to $\frac{1}{10}$.

Part 3: Word Knowledge

1. b. *Lure* means to entice, tempt, or attract.

2. a. *Delirious* means marked by frenzied excitement, or manic.

3. c. *Infirm* means feeble, unsound, or weak.

4. b. Something *perilous* involved great risk or danger.

5. c. *Isolation* means the state of being alone or withdrawn, or solitude.

6. a. A *lull* is a temporary pause.

7. d. To *outfit* means to supply or to furnish.

8. b. To *omit* means to leave out, fail to perform, or neglect.

9. a. *Mutiny* means resistance to lawful authority, or rebellion.

10. c. *Naïve* means unaffectedly simple, or unsophisticated.

11. d. *Rudimentary* means crude or primitive.

12. a. *Pompous* means self-important, or arrogant.

13. a. *Prevalent* means generally accepted, or widespread.

14. c. *Abundance* means an ample quantity, or wealth.

15. d. A *calamity* is an extraordinarily grave event, or disaster.

16. b. *Superficial* means to be concerned only with the surface or appearance, or shallow.

17. d. To *reform* means to change for the better, or to correct.

18. c. *Methodical* means proceeding according to an order or system, or systematic.

19. d. *Spite* means petty ill will or hatred, or malice.

20. a. When used as a verb, *scale* means to climb.

21. c. A *smudge* is a blurry spot or streak.

22. b. One meaning of to *drizzle* is to rain in very small drops, or to sprinkle.

23. b. *Mundane* means ordinary, or commonplace.

24. b. *Mirth* means gladness expressed with laughter, or glee.

25. c. *Drudgery* means uninspiring or menial behavior.

26. a. *Prerequisite* means necessary for carrying out a function.

27. a. *Caustic* means bitingly sarcastic or cutting; able to burn or dissolve by chemical action. The main context clue is that people find Gerard's jokes upsetting rather than humorous.

28. d. *Enigma* means something that is puzzling or difficult to understand; a baffling problem or riddle. The context tells you that people know who Sandra is, but no one knows anything about her; thus, she remains a mystery.

29. d. To *garner* means to acquire, amass, or gather. The sentence tells you that Ilona quickly found the support she needed to present her idea to the committee; also, because the sentence states that people loved Ilona's idea, it is logical to conclude that she would gather their support.

30. b. To *thwart* means to stop, or prevent the accomplishment or realization of something. Hattie's twisted ankle kept her from realizing her attempt to complete the marathon.

31. d. *Trite* means repeated too often, overly familiar through overuse. The key context clue is the phrase "the old storyline," which indicates that the plot of the movie is overused.

32. b. *Diligently* means attentively, painstakingly, or dutifully. Anthony is described as meticulous, which means careful and attentive.

33. c. *Reticent* means restrained, uncommunicative, or reluctant. The key word here is *although*, because it tells you that first Hunter was quiet, but then later became very talkative.

34. a. *Legitimate* means genuine, in accordance with law, or lawful. Because the deceased is a relative the claim to her estate is justified.

35. b. To *facilitate* something is to help it along, encourage, or assist. By placing garbage bins around the park, the committee leader is helping the cleanup process.

Part 4: Paragraph Comprehension

1. a. Each of the choices is mentioned in the passage, but only **a** states the overall theme or central idea of the passage. The other choices are details of that central idea.

2. c. The passage states that Wednesday is named after Woden, a god associated with musical inspiration. The other choices are not supported in the passage.

3. d. The word *pantheon* comes from the Greek words *pan*, meaning all, and *theos*, meaning gods. Thus, *pantheon* means "all gods," and refers to a list of ancient deities.

4. a. The passage addresses the names of weekdays, demonstrating that they are drawn from ancient gods. Therefore, one can safely conclude that mythology played a role in the development of the English language. The other choices may or may not be true, but they are not sufficiently addressed in the passage to draw an accurate inference.

5. a. The passage states that the word *linoleum* comes from the Latin words *linum* and *oleum*.

6. d. The passage does mention that linoleum is used around the world and that it is named from Latin words, but the main idea is to discuss the floor covering's history.

7. d. Choices **a** and **c** are not supported by the paragraph. Choice **b** only tells us about particular parts of the paragraph and is too specific to be the main idea. Choice **d**, however, is general enough to encompass all the sentences and the paragraph as a whole. Every sentence supports the idea asserted in choice **d**.

8. b. The last sentence states that Priority Mail will deliver a package in two days or less. Express Mail gets a package delivered overnight, while the other options are not addressed in the passage.

9. b. The author does not specifically state that paper clips are a useful invention, but the enthusiastic tone of the passage suggests it. The author's list of uses for paper clips reinforces this tone.

10. a. The word *crevice* refers to a crack or fracture, such as crevices in rocks.

11. c. The last sentence of the passage lists several things that people once used to bind papers together, which included string. The other items are not listed.

12. b. The second paragraph does state that Vaaler was a Norwegian, but he patented his idea with the German patent office, so choice **b** is the correct answer.

13. d. The directions mention nothing about fertilization.

14. c. The third sentence specifically mentions that the pointed side goes up and the root side faces down. This means that there is an up side and a down side and that it is possible for the bulb to be put into the soil upside down if someone didn't know better. The other choices may be true, but are not mentioned in the passage.

15. a. The passage states that the color-coding of garbage is important for the safety of all personnel, so choice **d** is not correct. The other choices are not addressed in the passage.

Part 5: Mathematics Knowledge

1. d. Subtract 5 from 25 to get 20. Then, multiply 20 by 5 to find the correct answer of 100.

2. d. There are four sides measuring 4, and two sides measuring 8. Therefore, the perimeter is $(4 \times 4) + (2 \times 8) = 32$.

3. b. The root *cent* means 100 (think of the word *century*), so the word *percent* literally means "per 100 parts." Thus 25% means 25 out of 100, which can also be expressed as a ratio: 25:100.

4. a. To find the square root of a number, ask the question, "What number times itself equals 64?" The answer is 8.

5. c. $76 \div 19 = 4$; the other division operations will not end in whole numbers.

6. c. If the pentagons are similar, then the sides are in proportion. Because AB is similar to FG, and $AB = 10$ and $FG = 30$, the second pentagon is three times as large as the first pentagon. Therefore, HI is three times as large as CD, which gives a length of 15.

7. c. A trapezoid by definition is a quadrilateral with exactly one pair of parallel sides.

8. b. To find the greatest common factor of $3x^2$, $12x$, and $6x^3$ first start with the coefficients, or numbers in front of the variables. The largest number that divides into 3, 6, and 12 without a remainder is 3. With the variables, the smallest exponent on x is 1, so x^1, or x, is the largest variable factor. Therefore, the greatest common factor of all three terms is $3x$.

9. b. Because the integers must be even, the equation $n + (n + 2) + (n + 4) = 30$ is used. This gives $3n + 6 = 30$; $3n = 24$; $n = 8$. Therefore, 8 is the first number in the series. Choice **a**, (9, 10, 11) would work, but the numbers aren't even integers.

10. b. To convert a decimal to a percent, multiply the decimal by 100, or move the decimal point two places to the right. Therefore, 6.0% is the correct answer.

11. b. Simply set up the equation in the manner in which the problem is written. Since $x\% = \frac{x}{100}$, the equation is $\frac{x}{100} = \frac{0.40}{1.30}$. Cross multply: $1.30x = (0.40)(100)$. Simplify: $x = \frac{40}{1.30}$. Thus, $x = 30.7$, which means that $0.40 is about 31% of $1.30.

12. c. A right angle is exactly 90°.

13. d. In order to form a triangle, the sum of the two shortest sides must be greater than the longest side. In choice **d**, the two shortest sides are 2 and 2; $2 + 2 = 4$, which is greater than the largest side of 3.

14. b. A cube has four sides, a top, and a bottom, which means that it has six faces.

15. c. A prime number is a number that has exactly two factors, 1 and itself. Each of the number choices has more than two factors except 11, whose only factors are 1 and 11.

16. c. The fraction $\frac{32}{100}$ reduced to lowest terms is $\frac{8}{25}$.

17. b. When you are performing addition or subtraction with roots, the terms can be combined only if the radicands (numbers under the square root symbols) are the same. In this case, the radicands are both 2. Subtract the whole numbers in front of the square roots and keep the $\sqrt{2}$. Then, $16 - 4 = \sqrt{12}$, so the final answer is $12\sqrt{2}$.

18. c. Since 45 is nine times larger than five in the denominators, convert to an equivalent fraction by multiplying 2 by 9 to get the resulting numerator: $2 \times 9 = 18$, so $x = 18$. Another way to solve this problem is to cross multiply to get $5x = 90$. Divide both sides of the equation by 5 to get $x = 18$.

19. a. All of the angles are acute, and all are different. Therefore, the triangle is acute scalene.

20. d. The correct answer to this simple addition problem is 1.268.

21. c. The greatest area from a quadrilateral will always be a square. Therefore, a side will be $24 \div 4 = 6$ feet. The area is $6^2 = 36$ square feet.

22. a. The correct answer is 5.

23. c. The bars on either side of −14 indicate the absolute value of −14. The absolute value of a number is its distance away from zero on a number line and, in this case, is 14. Therefore, $14 + -5 = 9$. Since the signs are different, subtract and keep the sign of the larger number.

24. c. Ten times 10 times 10 is 1,000. One thousand times 7.25 is 7,250.

25. c. First ask how many inches are in one foot; the answer is 12 inches. Now multiply: $12 \times 4 = 48$ inches.

Part 6: Electronics Information

1. c. Data stored on magnetic tape can be lost by exposure to heat; damage can also be done by stretching the tape or by exposure to other magnetic fields.

2. b. Current is the *rate at which* an electrical charge passes a specific point in a circuit.

3. d. In a series circuit, the total resistance is the sum of each resistor value. 7 resistors $\times 67\Omega = 469\Omega$.

4. b. In a parallel circuit, the total resistance is the value of a single resistor.

5. a. The symbol actually shows a single-pole 4-way switch.

6. a. Ohms is the resistance of the current and amperes is the strength of the current.

7. c. AC stands for alternating current.

8. b. DC stands for direct current.

9. d. The coating process used in electroplating is known as *electrodeposition*.

10. c. This is the schematic symbol for a lamp.

11. d. RMS stands for root mean square, which is the peak value of voltage multiplied by 0.707.

12. b. This is the schematic symbol for a battery.

13. a. The velocity of radio waves radiated into free space is 300,000,000 meters per second, which is the speed of light. Choice **c**, 343 meters per second, is the speed of sound.

14. d. Volts = ohms × amps. $V = 10 \times 20$. $V = 200$.

15. b. Water is not an insulator. Rubber is another insulator not listed in the choices.

16. c. Dielectric heating is the process by which a dielectric material is subjected to a rapidly altering electrical field. Heat is generated as the radio wave or microwave electromagnetic radiation heats the material.

17. a. A zener diode is used to regulate voltage. A photodiode (**b**) converts light to electricity, a capacitor (**c**) stores electricity, and a light emitting diode (**d**) converts electricity to light.

18. d. This is the schematic symbol for a ground.

19. c. The neutral wire is white or silver in 120-volt wiring in the United States. The hot or live wire can be black, red, blue, or brass. Orange or yellow wire is often used for input signals.

20. b. Watts = amps × volts. W = 30 × 120. W = 3,600.

Part 7: Auto and Shop Information

1. b. The gauge abbreviation "PSI" stands for "pounds per square inch."

2. c. The circulation of coolant through the engine block picks up waste heat generated by the operation of the engine. This hot coolant is routed back to the radiator where the passage of ambient air over the radiator grill cause the coolant to exchange heat.

3. a. Overinflated tires would result in the center part of the tread contacting the road more often than the outer, side surfaces. Underinflated tires would show excessive tread wear on the outer edges because the weight of the automobile makes more of the tire surface contact the road.

4. b. Poor or malfunctioning shock absorbers could result in an extremely bouncy ride, as the suspension springs absorb the bumps in the road but the shock absorbers do not dampen out this spring movement.

5. a. The job of the water pump is to circulate coolant throughout the engine's cooling system.

6. b. The job of the crankshaft is to convert the up-and-down motion of the pistons and tie rods into the rotational movement of the driveshaft.

7. d. The differential is located in the drive axle. This allows the wheels to turn at different speeds as a car rounds corners.

8. d. The purpose of a camshaft in an internal combustion engine is to transfer energy to the drivetrain.

9. b. A caliper is a tool with which one can obtain precise measurements between two opposing objects. Vernier calipers use the highly precise Vernier measurement scale to gain an even more precise measurement.

10. a. The transmission system uses specialized transmission fluid to ensure the elements involved in the automobile transmission are lubricated.

11. c. An automobile's electrical system uses the alternator to recharge the battery.

12. d. Spark plugs provide the spark to ignite the air/fuel mixture during the power cycle of the internal combustion engine operation.

13. b. The cooling fluid used is typically a mixture of water and ethylene glycol ($C_2H_6O_2$), the former for its ability to retain heat and the latter for improving the boiling and freezing points as necessary.

14. d. A plumber looking to turn soft iron pipes or fittings with a rounded surface would most likely use a pipe wrench.

15. d. Four inches is equal to 16 quarter inches. Each quarter inch is 2 feet, so 16 quarter inches is 32 feet.

16. c. Each 9-foot wall has an area of 9(8), or 72 square feet. There are two such walls, so those two walls combined have an area of 144 square feet. Each 11-foot wall has an area of 11(8) or 88 square feet, and again there are two such walls: 88(2) = 176. Finally, add 144 and 176 to get 320 square feet.

17. c. A vise has an adjustable grip that can be used to securely hold a piece of wood or other material, allowing the carpenter more freedom to perform work that could require both hands and a steady, secure material.

18. a. A winch is a mechanical device used to hoist, haul, or pull an item. A level, a compass, and a chisel are all tools that are used by a carpenter's hand in his work.

19. b. Ammonium chloride, rosin, hydrochloric acid, zinc chloride and borax are all common types of flux, necessary to remove oxidation from the metals to be welded together.

20. d. A drill press can be set to drill to a specific depth and is mounted to a rig allowing for precise placement of the drill bit.

21. b. A tachometer would typically use units of revolutions per minute (rpm) as a measurement. A pressure gauge would typically use pounds per square inch (psi), a speedometer would typically use miles per hour (mph) or kilometers per hour (kph), and a thermometer would typically use degrees Fahrenheit or Celsius.

22. d. All the selections are used to power various pumps. A battery is used to power a portable sump pump, an internal combustion engine is used to power a number of pumps in an automobile (e.g., oil pump, fuel pump) and an electric motor powers pumps used in places like water wells or pools.

23. d. A crescent wrench, a pipe wrench, and channel locks are all adjustable wrenches.

24. b. The ball-peen hammer, typically used in metalworking, has a rounded hemispherical head as one of its usable ends.

25. a. A wood chisel is used for carving, cutting, or chipping wood.

Part 8: Mechanical Comprehension

1. c. The 20-pound block is located closer to scale 1 than scale 2. Scale 1 will support more than half the weight of the block.

2. c. $w_1 \times d_1 = w_2 \times d_2$. Todd is 6 feet away from the pivot point, and the block is 18 feet away. 50×18 feet $= 6$ feet $\times w_2$. Solving for w_2 gives 150 pounds.

3. b. When air is heated it expands and becomes less dense than cold air, making the entire balloon buoyant and allowing it to float.

4. d. Mechanical advantage describes the factor that force is multiplied by a simple machine. Here, by moving the screw handle 3 feet (3 feet × 12 inches per foot = 36 inches), the jack is raised $\frac{1}{4}$ inch. Thus the mechanical advantage of the jack is $36 \div \frac{1}{4} = 144$.

5. d. A pulley system of this type has a mechanical advantage of 4. So, if Bryan can pull a rope with 150 pounds of force, he will be able to lift a weight of 150 pounds × 4 = 600 pounds.

6. d. Mechanical advantage = output force ÷ input force. Here, 20 pounds of force is input to lift 80 pounds of dirt. The mechanical advantage is $80 \div 20 = 4$.

7. a. Mechanical advantage (MA) is the factor by which a simple machine multiplies for the force put into it. In this case, 120 pounds of force is used to move a 360-pound block, so MA = $360 \div 120 = 3$. The MA of a ramp is determined by the length of the ramp, l, divided by the height gained, h. In this case, MA $= 3 = \frac{l}{h} = \frac{l}{10}$ feet. Solving for l tells us the ramp is 30 feet long.

8. d. The force required to stretch a spring is equal to its force constant multiplied by the distance stretch ($F = kx$). The force required to move a spring with a force constant of 3 pounds per inch a distance of 12 inches is $3 \times 12 = 36$ pounds.

9. d. Since pulley A is three times greater in diameter than pulley A, each revolution of A will lead to 3 revolutions of B. If A rotates at 45 rpm, then B will rotate at 45 rpm × 3 = 135 rpm.

10. d. Friction is the force that must be overcome in order to slide on object across another.

11. b. There are 6 threads per inch. To move the nut 2 inches will require $6 \times 2 = 12$ turns.

12. c. Water pressure at the bottom of a tank increases as the weight of water above it increases, but pressure at the top remains the same, since it has a finite amount of water above it.

13. a. The entire weight is supported by a single cable and no mechanical advantage is achieved using this pulley system. So the mechanical advantage is 1.

14. c. All other materials are denser than water and will sink. Styrofoam is not very dense and will float on water.

15. c. Gear 1 turning clockwise will cause gear 2 to turn counterclockwise. In turn, this counterclockwise movement will cause gears 3 and 4 to turn clockwise.

16. d. The 200-pound weight will stretch the first spring 200 pounds ÷ 400 pounds per inch = 0.5 inches. The second spring stretches 200 pounds ÷ 200 pounds per inch = 1 inch. The third spring stretches 200 pounds ÷ 100 pounds per inch = 2 inches. The total amount the platform compresses is therefore 0.5 + 1 + 2 = 3.5 inches.

17. d. Since the two are traveling in opposite directions, the rate at which they move farther apart is equal to the sum of their two speeds (35 mph + 45 mph = 80 mph). After 2 hours, the two will be 80 mph × 2 hours = 160 miles.

18. b. The first bike has 12 teeth on its rear cog and 52 teeth on front chain ring. At 60 rpm, the bike will travel 60 rpm × 52 front teeth ÷ 12 rear teeth = 260 revolutions. For the bicycle with 14 teeth on its rear cog to travel 260 revolutions, it must be pedaled at 260 revolutions × 14 rear teeth ÷ 52 front teeth = 70 rpm.

19. b. If the container is being filled at 18 gallons per minute (gpm) and evacuated at 14 gpm, then it is filling at an overall rate of (18 − 14 = 4 gpm). Since the tank can hold 20 gallons, it will fill in 20 gallons ÷ 4 gallons per minute = 5 minutes.

20. a. $w_1 \times d_1 = w_2 \times d_2$. 96 pounds × 5 feet = w_2 × 12 feet. Solving for w_2 gives 40 pounds.

21. b. The mechanical advantage (MA) of a ramp is determined by the length of the ramp, l, divided by the height gained, h. In this case, MA = $\frac{l}{h}$ = 50 feet ÷ 10 feet = 5. The force required to pull a 800-pound block up a ramp is 800 pounds ÷ 5 = 160 pounds.

22. d. Every full turn of the larger gear will result in 18 teeth ÷ 12 teeth = 1.5 rotations. In two turns of the larger gear, the smaller will complete 3 rotations.

23. a. The lip of the paint can acts as a fulcrum of a lever when trying to pry off a lid. The long arm of a screwdriver provides a sizeable mechanical advantage.

24. a. $w_1 \times d_1 = w_2 \times d_2$. Stevi is 14 feet away from the pivot point. 70 pounds × 9 feet = 14 feet × w_2. Solving for w_2 gives 45 pounds.

25. c. A pulley system of this type has a mechanical advantage of 2. So, to lift a 150-pound weight will require 150 pounds ÷ 2 = 75 pounds.

Part 9: Assembling Objects

1. a.
2. d.
3. a.
4. c.
5. b.
6. a.
7. c.

8. c.
9. b.
10. d.
11. a.
12. c.
13. c.
14. b.
15. a.
16. d.
17. d.
18. a.
19. b.
20. c.
21. d.
22. d.
23. b.
24. d.
25. c.

Scoring

Write your raw score (the number you got right) for each test in the blanks below. Then turn to Chapter 2 to find out how to convert these raw scores into the scores the armed services use.

1. General Science: _____ right out of 25
2. Arithmetic Reasoning: _____ right out of 30
3. Word Knowledge: _____ right out of 35
4. Paragraph Comprehension: _____ right out of 15
5. Mathematics Knowledge: _____ right out of 25
6. Electronics Information: _____ right out of 20
7. Auto and Shop Information: _____ right out of 25
8. Mechanical Comprehension: _____ right out of 25
9. Assembling Objects: _____ right out of 25

6 ▶ ASVAB PRACTICE TEST 2

CHAPTER SUMMARY

Here's another sample ASVAB for you to practice with.

For this practice exam, again simulate the actual test-taking experience as closely as you can. Work in a quiet place where you won't be interrupted. If you own this book, tear out the answer sheet and use your #2 pencils to fill in the circles. As you did for the practice exam in Chapter 5, set a timer or stopwatch, and give yourself the appropriate amount of time marked at the beginning of each section. After you take the test, use the detailed answer explanations that follow to review any questions you missed.

Part 1: General Science (GS)

1.	ⓐ	ⓑ	ⓒ	ⓓ	10.	ⓐ	ⓑ	ⓒ	ⓓ	18.	ⓐ	ⓑ	ⓒ	ⓓ
2.	ⓐ	ⓑ	ⓒ	ⓓ	11.	ⓐ	ⓑ	ⓒ	ⓓ	19.	ⓐ	ⓑ	ⓒ	ⓓ
3.	ⓐ	ⓑ	ⓒ	ⓓ	12.	ⓐ	ⓑ	ⓒ	ⓓ	20.	ⓐ	ⓑ	ⓒ	ⓓ
4.	ⓐ	ⓑ	ⓒ	ⓓ	13.	ⓐ	ⓑ	ⓒ	ⓓ	21.	ⓐ	ⓑ	ⓒ	ⓓ
5.	ⓐ	ⓑ	ⓒ	ⓓ	14.	ⓐ	ⓑ	ⓒ	ⓓ	22.	ⓐ	ⓑ	ⓒ	ⓓ
6.	ⓐ	ⓑ	ⓒ	ⓓ	15.	ⓐ	ⓑ	ⓒ	ⓓ	23.	ⓐ	ⓑ	ⓒ	ⓓ
7.	ⓐ	ⓑ	ⓒ	ⓓ	16.	ⓐ	ⓑ	ⓒ	ⓓ	24.	ⓐ	ⓑ	ⓒ	ⓓ
8.	ⓐ	ⓑ	ⓒ	ⓓ	17.	ⓐ	ⓑ	ⓒ	ⓓ	25.	ⓐ	ⓑ	ⓒ	ⓓ
9.	ⓐ	ⓑ	ⓒ	ⓓ										

Part 2: Arithmetic Reasoning (AR)

1.	ⓐ	ⓑ	ⓒ	ⓓ	11.	ⓐ	ⓑ	ⓒ	ⓓ	21.	ⓐ	ⓑ	ⓒ	ⓓ
2.	ⓐ	ⓑ	ⓒ	ⓓ	12.	ⓐ	ⓑ	ⓒ	ⓓ	22.	ⓐ	ⓑ	ⓒ	ⓓ
3.	ⓐ	ⓑ	ⓒ	ⓓ	13.	ⓐ	ⓑ	ⓒ	ⓓ	23.	ⓐ	ⓑ	ⓒ	ⓓ
4.	ⓐ	ⓑ	ⓒ	ⓓ	14.	ⓐ	ⓑ	ⓒ	ⓓ	24.	ⓐ	ⓑ	ⓒ	ⓓ
5.	ⓐ	ⓑ	ⓒ	ⓓ	15.	ⓐ	ⓑ	ⓒ	ⓓ	25.	ⓐ	ⓑ	ⓒ	ⓓ
6.	ⓐ	ⓑ	ⓒ	ⓓ	16.	ⓐ	ⓑ	ⓒ	ⓓ	26.	ⓐ	ⓑ	ⓒ	ⓓ
7.	ⓐ	ⓑ	ⓒ	ⓓ	17.	ⓐ	ⓑ	ⓒ	ⓓ	27.	ⓐ	ⓑ	ⓒ	ⓓ
8.	ⓐ	ⓑ	ⓒ	ⓓ	18.	ⓐ	ⓑ	ⓒ	ⓓ	28.	ⓐ	ⓑ	ⓒ	ⓓ
9.	ⓐ	ⓑ	ⓒ	ⓓ	19.	ⓐ	ⓑ	ⓒ	ⓓ	29.	ⓐ	ⓑ	ⓒ	ⓓ
10.	ⓐ	ⓑ	ⓒ	ⓓ	20.	ⓐ	ⓑ	ⓒ	ⓓ	30.	ⓐ	ⓑ	ⓒ	ⓓ

Part 3: Word Knowledge (WK)

1.	ⓐ	ⓑ	ⓒ	ⓓ	13.	ⓐ	ⓑ	ⓒ	ⓓ	25.	ⓐ	ⓑ	ⓒ	ⓓ
2.	ⓐ	ⓑ	ⓒ	ⓓ	14.	ⓐ	ⓑ	ⓒ	ⓓ	26.	ⓐ	ⓑ	ⓒ	ⓓ
3.	ⓐ	ⓑ	ⓒ	ⓓ	15.	ⓐ	ⓑ	ⓒ	ⓓ	27.	ⓐ	ⓑ	ⓒ	ⓓ
4.	ⓐ	ⓑ	ⓒ	ⓓ	16.	ⓐ	ⓑ	ⓒ	ⓓ	28.	ⓐ	ⓑ	ⓒ	ⓓ
5.	ⓐ	ⓑ	ⓒ	ⓓ	17.	ⓐ	ⓑ	ⓒ	ⓓ	29.	ⓐ	ⓑ	ⓒ	ⓓ
6.	ⓐ	ⓑ	ⓒ	ⓓ	18.	ⓐ	ⓑ	ⓒ	ⓓ	30.	ⓐ	ⓑ	ⓒ	ⓓ
7.	ⓐ	ⓑ	ⓒ	ⓓ	19.	ⓐ	ⓑ	ⓒ	ⓓ	31.	ⓐ	ⓑ	ⓒ	ⓓ
8.	ⓐ	ⓑ	ⓒ	ⓓ	20.	ⓐ	ⓑ	ⓒ	ⓓ	32.	ⓐ	ⓑ	ⓒ	ⓓ
9.	ⓐ	ⓑ	ⓒ	ⓓ	21.	ⓐ	ⓑ	ⓒ	ⓓ	33.	ⓐ	ⓑ	ⓒ	ⓓ
10.	ⓐ	ⓑ	ⓒ	ⓓ	22.	ⓐ	ⓑ	ⓒ	ⓓ	34.	ⓐ	ⓑ	ⓒ	ⓓ
11.	ⓐ	ⓑ	ⓒ	ⓓ	23.	ⓐ	ⓑ	ⓒ	ⓓ	35.	ⓐ	ⓑ	ⓒ	ⓓ
12.	ⓐ	ⓑ	ⓒ	ⓓ	24.	ⓐ	ⓑ	ⓒ	ⓓ					

Part 4: Paragraph Comprehension (PC)

1. (a) (b) (c) (d)
2. (a) (b) (c) (d)
3. (a) (b) (c) (d)
4. (a) (b) (c) (d)
5. (a) (b) (c) (d)

6. (a) (b) (c) (d)
7. (a) (b) (c) (d)
8. (a) (b) (c) (d)
9. (a) (b) (c) (d)
10. (a) (b) (c) (d)

11. (a) (b) (c) (d)
12. (a) (b) (c) (d)
13. (a) (b) (c) (d)
14. (a) (b) (c) (d)
15. (a) (b) (c) (d)

Part 5: Mathematics Knowledge (MK)

1. (a) (b) (c) (d)
2. (a) (b) (c) (d)
3. (a) (b) (c) (d)
4. (a) (b) (c) (d)
5. (a) (b) (c) (d)
6. (a) (b) (c) (d)
7. (a) (b) (c) (d)
8. (a) (b) (c) (d)
9. (a) (b) (c) (d)

10. (a) (b) (c) (d)
11. (a) (b) (c) (d)
12. (a) (b) (c) (d)
13. (a) (b) (c) (d)
14. (a) (b) (c) (d)
15. (a) (b) (c) (d)
16. (a) (b) (c) (d)
17. (a) (b) (c) (d)

18. (a) (b) (c) (d)
19. (a) (b) (c) (d)
20. (a) (b) (c) (d)
21. (a) (b) (c) (d)
22. (a) (b) (c) (d)
23. (a) (b) (c) (d)
24. (a) (b) (c) (d)
25. (a) (b) (c) (d)

Part 6: Electronics Information (EI)

1. (a) (b) (c) (d)
2. (a) (b) (c) (d)
3. (a) (b) (c) (d)
4. (a) (b) (c) (d)
5. (a) (b) (c) (d)
6. (a) (b) (c) (d)
7. (a) (b) (c) (d)

8. (a) (b) (c) (d)
9. (a) (b) (c) (d)
10. (a) (b) (c) (d)
11. (a) (b) (c) (d)
12. (a) (b) (c) (d)
13. (a) (b) (c) (d)
14. (a) (b) (c) (d)

15. (a) (b) (c) (d)
16. (a) (b) (c) (d)
17. (a) (b) (c) (d)
18. (a) (b) (c) (d)
19. (a) (b) (c) (d)
20. (a) (b) (c) (d)

Part 7: Auto and Shop Information (AS)

1.	ⓐ	ⓑ	ⓒ	ⓓ	10.	ⓐ	ⓑ	ⓒ	ⓓ	18.	ⓐ	ⓑ	ⓒ	ⓓ
2.	ⓐ	ⓑ	ⓒ	ⓓ	11.	ⓐ	ⓑ	ⓒ	ⓓ	19.	ⓐ	ⓑ	ⓒ	ⓓ
3.	ⓐ	ⓑ	ⓒ	ⓓ	12.	ⓐ	ⓑ	ⓒ	ⓓ	20.	ⓐ	ⓑ	ⓒ	ⓓ
4.	ⓐ	ⓑ	ⓒ	ⓓ	13.	ⓐ	ⓑ	ⓒ	ⓓ	21.	ⓐ	ⓑ	ⓒ	ⓓ
5.	ⓐ	ⓑ	ⓒ	ⓓ	14.	ⓐ	ⓑ	ⓒ	ⓓ	22.	ⓐ	ⓑ	ⓒ	ⓓ
6.	ⓐ	ⓑ	ⓒ	ⓓ	15.	ⓐ	ⓑ	ⓒ	ⓓ	23.	ⓐ	ⓑ	ⓒ	ⓓ
7.	ⓐ	ⓑ	ⓒ	ⓓ	16.	ⓐ	ⓑ	ⓒ	ⓓ	24.	ⓐ	ⓑ	ⓒ	ⓓ
8.	ⓐ	ⓑ	ⓒ	ⓓ	17.	ⓐ	ⓑ	ⓒ	ⓓ	25.	ⓐ	ⓑ	ⓒ	ⓓ
9.	ⓐ	ⓑ	ⓒ	ⓓ										

Part 8: Mechanical Comprehension (MC)

1.	ⓐ	ⓑ	ⓒ	ⓓ	10.	ⓐ	ⓑ	ⓒ	ⓓ	18.	ⓐ	ⓑ	ⓒ	ⓓ
2.	ⓐ	ⓑ	ⓒ	ⓓ	11.	ⓐ	ⓑ	ⓒ	ⓓ	19.	ⓐ	ⓑ	ⓒ	ⓓ
3.	ⓐ	ⓑ	ⓒ	ⓓ	12.	ⓐ	ⓑ	ⓒ	ⓓ	20.	ⓐ	ⓑ	ⓒ	ⓓ
4.	ⓐ	ⓑ	ⓒ	ⓓ	13.	ⓐ	ⓑ	ⓒ	ⓓ	21.	ⓐ	ⓑ	ⓒ	ⓓ
5.	ⓐ	ⓑ	ⓒ	ⓓ	14.	ⓐ	ⓑ	ⓒ	ⓓ	22.	ⓐ	ⓑ	ⓒ	ⓓ
6.	ⓐ	ⓑ	ⓒ	ⓓ	15.	ⓐ	ⓑ	ⓒ	ⓓ	23.	ⓐ	ⓑ	ⓒ	ⓓ
7.	ⓐ	ⓑ	ⓒ	ⓓ	16.	ⓐ	ⓑ	ⓒ	ⓓ	24.	ⓐ	ⓑ	ⓒ	ⓓ
8.	ⓐ	ⓑ	ⓒ	ⓓ	17.	ⓐ	ⓑ	ⓒ	ⓓ	25.	ⓐ	ⓑ	ⓒ	ⓓ
9.	ⓐ	ⓑ	ⓒ	ⓓ										

Part 9: Assembling Objects (AO)

1.	ⓐ	ⓑ	ⓒ	ⓓ	10.	ⓐ	ⓑ	ⓒ	ⓓ	18.	ⓐ	ⓑ	ⓒ	ⓓ
2.	ⓐ	ⓑ	ⓒ	ⓓ	11.	ⓐ	ⓑ	ⓒ	ⓓ	19.	ⓐ	ⓑ	ⓒ	ⓓ
3.	ⓐ	ⓑ	ⓒ	ⓓ	12.	ⓐ	ⓑ	ⓒ	ⓓ	20.	ⓐ	ⓑ	ⓒ	ⓓ
4.	ⓐ	ⓑ	ⓒ	ⓓ	13.	ⓐ	ⓑ	ⓒ	ⓓ	21.	ⓐ	ⓑ	ⓒ	ⓓ
5.	ⓐ	ⓑ	ⓒ	ⓓ	14.	ⓐ	ⓑ	ⓒ	ⓓ	22.	ⓐ	ⓑ	ⓒ	ⓓ
6.	ⓐ	ⓑ	ⓒ	ⓓ	15.	ⓐ	ⓑ	ⓒ	ⓓ	23.	ⓐ	ⓑ	ⓒ	ⓓ
7.	ⓐ	ⓑ	ⓒ	ⓓ	16.	ⓐ	ⓑ	ⓒ	ⓓ	24.	ⓐ	ⓑ	ⓒ	ⓓ
8.	ⓐ	ⓑ	ⓒ	ⓓ	17.	ⓐ	ⓑ	ⓒ	ⓓ	25.	ⓐ	ⓑ	ⓒ	ⓓ
9.	ⓐ	ⓑ	ⓒ	ⓓ										

Part 1: General Science

Time: 11 minutes

1. Which of the following elements is expected to be least reactive?
   a. Kr
   b. F
   c. Ca
   d. K

2. When the Moon is new, which is true?
   a. A solar eclipse could occur.
   b. A lunar eclipse could occur.
   c. An Earth eclipse could occur.
   d. A corona eclipse could occur.

3. What is the mass number of an atom with 60 protons, 60 electrons, and 75 neutrons?
   a. 60
   b. 120
   c. 135
   d. 195

4. Which of the following is the main function of the urinary bladder?
   a. to convert urea to urine
   b. to absorb water
   c. to store bile salts
   d. to store urine for excretion

5. Which of the following is known as the "powerhouse of the cell"?
   a. chloroplast
   b. vacuole
   c. endoplasmic reticulum
   d. mitochondrion

6. Which of the following represents the ground state of an ion in the alkaline earth family?
   a. $1s^2 2s^2$
   b. $1s^2 2s^2 2p^1$
   c. $1s^2 2s^2 2p^2$
   d. $1s^2 2s^2 2p^3$

7. Which process requires the most energy for a cell to transport material through its cell membrane?
   a. facilitated diffusion
   b. osmosis
   c. active transport
   d. filtration

8. In the reaction $2Cu_2S + 3O_2 \rightarrow 3Cu_2O + 2SO_2$, if 24 moles of Cu_2O are to be prepared, then how many moles of O_2 are needed?
   a. 24
   b. 36
   c. 16
   d. 27

9. In a food chain, which of the following are the producers?
   a. dead organic matter
   b. plant-eating animals
   c. meat-eating animals
   d. green plants

10. A mixture consisting of 8.0 g of oxygen (MW = 16) and 14 g of nitrogen (MW = 14) is prepared in a container such that the total pressure is 750 mm Hg. The partial pressure of oxygen in the mixture is
    a. 125 mm Hg.
    b. 500 mm Hg.
    c. 135 mm Hg.
    d. 250 mm Hg.

11. Membranes in cells are used for all of the following EXCEPT
   a. providing rigid support.
   b. regulating transport of substances.
   c. containing DNA.
   d. creating cellular organelles.

12. The energy of the Sun is created through which chemical reaction?
   a. single combination of molecules
   b. splitting larger elements into smaller elements
   c. combustion of fuel and oxygen
   d. combining of smaller elements to larger elements

13. The Himalayas are the result of
   a. a continental collision zone.
   b. a plate subduction zone.
   c. a volcanic zone.
   d. a ridge spreading zone.

14. The time required for half the atoms in a sample of a radioactive element to disintegrate is known as the element's
   a. decay period.
   b. lifetime.
   c. radioactive period.
   d. half-life.

15. Bacteria are part of which of the following kingdoms?
   a. protist
   b. monera
   c. animal
   d. plant

16. A 10 g sample of hydrogen sulfide gas is in a closed vessel at 127°C and 6 atm. What would the pressure be in the vessel when the temperature of the sample is changed to 27°C and the volume remains the same?
   a. 2 atm
   b. 4 atm
   c. 6 atm
   d. 8 atm

17. If a cell is in an environment that lacks oxygen, how will it get its energy?
   a. photosynthesis
   b. transpiration
   c. fermentation
   d. cellular respiration

18. A pressure of 740 mm Hg is the same as
   a. 1 atm.
   b. 0.974 atm.
   c. 1.03 atm.
   d. 0.740 atm.

19. Which adaptation do protists and plants share that separate them from fungi?
   a. chloroplasts
   b. nucleus
   c. cell wall
   d. specialized tissue

20. When aluminum (Al) and oxygen (O) form an ionic compound, it is represented as
   a. AlO
   b. Al_3O_2
   c. Al_2O_3
   d. $Al_{13}O_8$

21. In a cell with 16 chromosomes, how many gametes with how many chromosomes would be present after meiosis?
  a. 2 with 8 chromosomes
  b. 2 with 16 chromosomes
  c. 4 with 4 chromosomes
  d. 4 with 8 chromosomes

22. To get the most accurate data, where would be the best placement of a weather balloon?
  a. the mesosphere
  b. the troposphere
  c. the stratosphere
  d. the thermosphere

23. What is the proper nomenclature for the covalent molecule CCl_4?
  a. carbon chloride
  b. carbon chlorine
  c. carbon tetrachloride
  d. carbon quadrachloride

24. If the half-life for a radioactive element is 6 minutes, what was the initial mass of a sample with 40 g left after 18 minutes?
  a. 320 g
  b. 160 g
  c. 80 g
  d. 40 g

25. Viruses appear to be living organisms for the following characteristics EXCEPT
  a. nucleic acids.
  b. enzymes.
  c. adaptation.
  d. cellular reproduction.

Part 2: Arithmetic Reasoning

Time: 36 minutes

1. Michael scores 260 points during his junior year on the school basketball team. He scored 25% more points during his senior year. How many points did he score during his senior year?
  a. 195
  b. 65
  c. 325
  d. 345

2. The dwarf planet Pluto is estimated at a mean distance of 3,666 million miles from the Sun. The planet Mars is estimated at a mean distance of 36 million miles from the Sun. How much closer to the Sun is Mars than Pluto?
  a. 36,300,000 million miles
  b. 36,300 million miles
  c. 3,630 million miles
  d. 363 million miles

3. How many acres are contained in a parcel 121 feet wide and 240 yards deep? (one acre = 43,560 square feet)
  a. 1 acre
  b. $1\frac{1}{2}$ acres
  c. 2 acres
  d. $2\frac{1}{2}$ acres

4. On a certain day, the nurses at a hospital worked the following number of hours: Nurse Howard worked 8 hours; Nurse Pease worked 10 hours; Nurse Campbell worked 9 hours; Nurse Grace worked 8 hours; Nurse McCarthy worked 7 hours; and Nurse Murphy worked 12 hours. What is the average number of hours worked per nurse on this day?

  a. 7
  b. 8
  c. 9
  d. 10

Use the following table to answer question 5.

PRODUCTION OF FARM-IT TRACTORS FOR THE MONTH OF APRIL	
FACTORY	APRIL OUTPUT
Dallas	450
Houston	425
Lubbock	?
Amarillo	345
TOTAL:	1,780

  5. What was Lubbock's production in the month of April?

    a. 345
    b. 415
    c. 540
    d. 560

6. At the movies, Lucinda bought food for herself and her friend Rae, including: one box of popcorn to share at $5, one box of Junior Mints for each of them at $2 a box, and one soft drink for each at $3 apiece. Rae bought a ticket for each at $7 apiece. Who spent the most money and by how much?

  a. Rae by $3
  b. Rae by $7
  c. Lucinda by $1
  d. Lucinda by $2

7. John has started an egg farm. His chickens produce 480 eggs per day, and his eggs sell for $2 a dozen. How much does John make on eggs per week? (one week = seven days)

  a. $480
  b. $500
  c. $560
  d. $600

8. Maria made $331.01 last week. She worked $39\frac{1}{2}$ hours. What is her hourly wage?

  a. $8.28
  b. $8.33
  c. $8.38
  d. $8.43

9. For health reasons, Amir wants to drink eight glasses of water a day. He's already had six glasses. What fraction does Amir have left to drink?

  a. $\frac{1}{8}$
  b. $\frac{1}{6}$
  c. $\frac{1}{4}$
  d. $\frac{1}{3}$

10. Rita is eight decades old. How many years old is Rita?
- **a.** 40 years old
- **b.** 16 years old
- **c.** 64 years old
- **d.** 80 years old

11. A street sign reads "Loading Zone 15 Minutes." If a truck pulls into this zone at 11:46 A.M., by what time must it leave?
- **a.** 11:59 A.M.
- **b.** 12:01 P.M.
- **c.** 12:03 P.M.
- **d.** 12:06 P.M.

12. It takes three firefighters $1\frac{2}{5}$ hours to clean their truck. At that same rate, how many hours would it take one firefighter to clean the same truck?
- **a.** $2\frac{4}{7}$ hours
- **b.** $3\frac{4}{5}$ hours
- **c.** $4\frac{1}{5}$ hours
- **d.** $4\frac{2}{5}$ hours

13. One colony of bats consumes 36 tons of mosquitoes per year. At that rate, how many pounds of mosquitoes does the same colony consume in a month?
- **a.** 36,000 pounds
- **b.** 12,000 pounds
- **c.** 6,000 pounds
- **d.** 3,000 pounds

14. At birth, Winston weighed $6\frac{1}{2}$ pounds. At one year of age, he weighed $23\frac{1}{8}$ pounds. How much weight, in pounds, did he gain?
- **a.** $16\frac{5}{8}$ pounds
- **b.** $16\frac{7}{8}$ pounds
- **c.** $17\frac{1}{6}$ pounds
- **d.** $17\frac{3}{4}$ pounds

15. A recipe calls for $\frac{1}{4}$ teaspoon of red pepper. How much red pepper would you need for half a recipe?
- **a.** $\frac{1}{10}$ teaspoon
- **b.** $\frac{1}{8}$ teaspoon
- **c.** $\frac{1}{6}$ teaspoon
- **d.** $\frac{1}{2}$ teaspoon

16. Fifty-four students are to be separated into six groups of equal size. How many students are in each group?
- **a.** 8
- **b.** 9
- **c.** 10
- **d.** 12

17. Yetta just got a raise of $3\frac{1}{4}$%. Her original salary was $30,600. How much does she make now?
- **a.** $30,594.50
- **b.** $31,594.50
- **c.** $32,094.50
- **d.** $32,940.50

18. Ashley's car insurance costs her $115 per month. How much does it cost her per year?
- **a.** $1,150
- **b.** $980
- **c.** $1,380
- **d.** $1,055

19. It is 19.85 miles from Jacqueline's home to her job. If she works five days a week and drives to work, how many miles does Jacqueline drive each week?
- **a.** 99.25 miles
- **b.** 188.5 miles
- **c.** 190.85 miles
- **d.** 198.5 miles

20. On a four-day trip, Carrie drove 135 miles the first day, 213 miles the second day, 159 miles the third day, and 189 miles the fourth day. Which of the following choices is the best approximation of the total miles Carrie drove during the trip?

    a. 600

    b. 700

    c. 400

    d. 800

21. How many inches are there in four feet?

    a. 12 inches

    b. 36 inches

    c. 48 inches

    d. 52 inches

22. On a particular morning the temperature went up 1° every two hours. If the temperature was 53° at 5 A.M., at what time was it 57°?

    a. 7 A.M.

    b. 8 A.M.

    c. 12 P.M.

    d. 1 P.M.

23. Of 360 students polled, 150 participate in extracurricular activities. Approximately what percent of the students do NOT participate in extracurricular activities?

    a. 32%

    b. 42%

    c. 52%

    d. 58%

24. How many ways can four students line up in a line, if the order matters?

    a. 4

    b. 8

    c. 16

    d. 24

25. Ted has to write a $5\frac{1}{2}$-page paper. He's finished $3\frac{1}{3}$ pages. How many pages does he have left to write?

    a. $1\frac{3}{5}$

    b. $1\frac{7}{8}$

    c. $2\frac{2}{3}$

    d. $2\frac{1}{6}$

26. Larry purchased three pairs of pants for $18 each and five shirts for $24 each. How much did Larry spend?

    a. $42

    b. $54

    c. $174

    d. $186

27. The light on a lighthouse blinks 45 times a minute. How long will it take the light to blink 405 times?

    a. 11 minutes

    b. 4 minutes

    c. 9 minutes

    d. 6 minutes

28. Brian's 100-yard dash time was 2.68 seconds more than the school record. His time was 13.4 seconds. What is the school record?

    a. 10.72 seconds

    b. 11.28 seconds

    c. 10.78 seconds

    d. 16.08 seconds

29. Jason's hair salon charges $63 for a haircut and color, which is $\frac{3}{4}$ of what Lisa's hair salon charges. How much does Lisa's hair salon charge?

    a. $65

    b. $21

    c. $42

    d. $84

30. Two quarters are equivalent to how many dimes?
 a. 2
 b. 4
 c. 5
 d. 10

Part 3: Word Knowledge

Time: 11 minutes

1. *Glare* most nearly means
 a. scowl.
 b. hide.
 c. display.
 d. summon.

2. *Civil* most nearly means
 a. unkind.
 b. trite.
 c. public.
 d. questionable.

3. *Peer* most nearly means
 a. apple.
 b. connote.
 c. fellow.
 d. dock.

4. *Fiasco* most nearly means
 a. festival.
 b. disaster.
 c. happenstance.
 d. ceremony.

5. *Chasm* most nearly means
 a. gorge.
 b. charm.
 c. bridle.
 d. criticize.

6. *Expertise* most nearly means
 a. activity.
 b. courage.
 c. mastery.
 d. effort.

7. *Outlandish* most nearly means
 a. distant.
 b. absurd.
 c. pastoral.
 d. belligerent.

8. *Pine* most nearly means
 a. clean.
 b. hate.
 c. resolve.
 d. crave.

9. *Exploit* most nearly means
 a. answer.
 b. abuse.
 c. enquire.
 d. persuade.

10. *Culmination* most nearly means
 a. realization.
 b. disaster.
 c. serendipity.
 d. persuasion.

11. *Feign* most nearly means
 a. jab.
 b. swoon.
 c. pretend.
 d. dread.

12. *Heed* most nearly means
 a. trek.
 b. consider.
 c. consolidate.
 d. bound.

13. *Edge* most nearly means
  a. diffuse.
  b. point.
  c. force.
  d. dissuade.

14. *Elevate* most nearly means
  a. lessen.
  b. mention.
  c. affix.
  d. hoist.

15. *Appoint* most nearly means
  a. score.
  b. discuss.
  c. nominate.
  d. ensure.

16. *Hoard* most nearly means
  a. stockpile.
  b. burrow.
  c. mine.
  d. dessert.

17. *Hub* most nearly means
  a. counsel.
  b. elder.
  c. center.
  d. extension.

18. *Tame* most nearly means
  a. lost.
  b. wild.
  c. pushy.
  d. submissive.

19. *Irk* most nearly means
  a. shrug.
  b. irritate.
  c. devour.
  d. avoid.

20. *Loom* most nearly means
  a. disappear.
  b. sew.
  c. surface.
  d. teach.

21. *Fitful* most nearly means
  a. erratic.
  b. angry.
  c. tired.
  d. strong.

22. *Gaudy* most nearly means
  a. massive.
  b. mindful.
  c. tasteful.
  d. flashy.

23. *Flaunt* most nearly means
  a. conceal.
  b. parade.
  c. trust.
  d. fray.

24. *Flex* most nearly means
  a. bend.
  b. binge.
  c. rid.
  d. consume.

25. *Tantalize* most nearly means
  a. pronounce.
  b. reign.
  c. bother.
  d. tease.

26. Even though she's almost 80, my grandmother seems _____; she still plays golf three times a week and has an active social life.
a. indefatigable
b. persistent
c. feeble
d. senile

27. The treasure hunter's interest was _____ by a small glimmer of gold at the bottom of the pit.
a. piqued
b. enhanced
c. lessened
d. questioned

28. Although the novice doctor had just started his internship, he was already _____ by the amount of work required.
a. perplexed
b. overwhelmed
c. energized
d. negated

29. Desert dwellers tend to be _____, moving from place to place as water sources dry up.
a. listless
b. nomadic
c. spontaneous
d. conscientious

30. Mr. Crane did not say anything about being fired from his last job because he did not want to _____ his chances of being hired by the new company.
a. jeopardize
b. stigmatize
c. evade
d. divulge

31. Carlos found the movie so _____ that he continued to feel immersed in the film's world for hours afterward.
a. engrossing
b. enlightening
c. enchanting
d. inventive

32. The king furiously declared that the philosopher should be _____ by society for his anti-authoritarian views.
a. embraced
b. lauded
c. reprimanded
d. ostracized

33. Climbing Mount Everest may be a daunting prospect, but successful climbing expeditions in the past have proved that the peak is not _____.
a. formidable
b. frigid
c. insurmountable
d. mundane

34. As a pacifist, I _____ all forms of violence.
a. deride
b. entreat
c. endorse
d. deplore

30. General Wilkenson ordered his troops to charge at the invading forces and _____ them from the vulnerable town.
a. sequester
b. incense
c. condense
d. repel

Part 4:
Paragraph Comprehension

Time: 13 minutes

Our daily lives are filled with machines. We drive cars, operate computers, ride bicycles, talk on telephones, and use a *myriad* number of machines without even thinking about it. But did you know that all machines are based on six simple machines? What's more, all simple machines fall into one of two categories: the lever or the wedge. The lever is a simple machine that allows a person to lift a heavy weight using less energy than would be required to lift it directly. A wedge is a simple machine that separates two or more objects.

There are six basic machines, each of which uses either lever action or wedge action. The screw, for example, uses wedge action to separate the wood that it's being screwed into. A pulley uses lever action to enable a person to use less force to lift heavy objects. An inclined plane uses wedge action to separate an object from the ground; you can even see the wedge shape of an inclined plane if you look at it from the side. And the sixth simple machine, the wheel and axle, uses lever action to force the wheel to turn using less energy than would be required by manually spinning it.

1. What is the main idea of this passage?
   a. Wheels and pulleys are simple machines.
   b. All machines are based on six simple machines.
   c. Screws use lever action.
   d. Machines are complicated.

2. Which of the following statements is best supported by this passage?
   a. Screwdrivers are complex machines.
   b. Computers are simple machines.
   c. A car uses many simple machines to run.
   d. Gravity was discovered by Isaac Newton.

3. Which of the following is *not* a simple machine?
   a. a screw
   b. a pushbutton
   c. a wedge
   d. a pulley

4. As used in the passage, *myriad* most nearly means
   a. mythical.
   b. confusing.
   c. mirror image.
   d. many.

The town council met Wednesday night to discuss the recent vandalism at the park. Police have stated that the vandalism is caused by several youths in town who are angry because the park closes at sunset. Several parents spoke out, however, to say that the problems are being caused by *transient* workers who have no place to sleep. The mayor disagreed and suggested that the vandalism is the work of students from the rival high school in the next town.

Since the council can't take any action before the next meeting on the 3rd of next month, police have been instructed to increase security at the park at night. Town council members also asked the school board to *implement* stronger methods of policing at high school athletic events to ensure that students do not bring cans of spray paint or other tools of vandalism.

5. According to the passage, who believes that the vandalism is being caused by rivalry between two local schools?
   a. the police
   b. parents
   c. the mayor
   d. not stated

6. As used in this passage, *transient* most nearly means
  a. passing through.
  b. a window above a doorway.
  c. athletic.
  d. angry.

7. The town council will next meet on
  a. June 4.
  b. the 3rd of next month.
  c. the first Wednesday of the month.
  d. the 3rd of this month.

8. As used in the passage, *implement* most nearly means
  a. an eating utensil.
  b. a tool.
  c. put into practice.
  d. a small unit of measurement.

Critical reading is a demanding process. To read critically, you must slow down your reading and, with pencil in hand, perform specific operations on the text. Mark up the text with your reactions, conclusions, and questions. When you read, become an active participant.

9. This paragraph best supports the statement that
  a. critical reading is a slow, dull, but essential process.
  b. the best critical reading happens at critical times in a person's life.
  c. readers should get into the habit of questioning the truth of what they read.
  d. critical reading requires thoughtful and careful attention.

10. What does being "an active participant" in reading mean?
  a. A good reader will be writing books.
  b. A good reader takes notes, asks questions, and draws conclusions.
  c. A good book will get an emotional reaction from the reader.
  d. Reading out loud is better than reading silently.

It has recently come to the attention of management that employees are using their sick days for purposes of vacation time. Effective June 1, all sick days not used prior to May 31 will be canceled, and all employees will begin to *accrue* new sick time effective June 1. The purpose of this new policy is to *curtail* abuse of employee sick days.

11. The author of this passage most likely believes that employees are
  a. underpaid and overworked.
  b. highly skilled in their jobs.
  c. abusing their job benefits.
  d. showing up late for work too often.

12. As used in the passage, *accrue* most nearly means
  a. gather together.
  b. turn sideways.
  c. take time off.
  d. report to work.

13. Why is the company restarting sick time beginning June 1?
  a. It is the beginning of the company's fiscal year.
  b. The company has improved its sick-time benefits.
  c. Congress has passed a new law.
  d. Employees have been using sick time inappropriately.

14. As used in the passage, *curtail* most nearly means
  a. an appendage.
  b. increase.
  c. cut back.
  d. leave alone.

If you're a fitness walker, there is no need for a commute to a health club. Your neighborhood can be your health club. You don't need a lot of fancy equipment to get a good workout, either. All you need is a well-designed pair of athletic shoes.

15. This paragraph best supports the statement that
  a. fitness walking is a better form of exercise than weight lifting.
  b. a membership in a health club is a poor investment.
  c. walking outdoors provides a better workout than walking indoors.
  d. fitness walking is a convenient and valuable form of exercise.

Part 5: Mathematics Knowledge

Time: 24 minutes

1. What is the area of the following isosceles triangle?

  a. 12 square units
  b. 15 square units
  c. 6 square units
  d. 24 square units

2. Which of the following expressions best represents the sum of two numbers, *a* and *b*, divided by a third number, *c*?
  a. $a + b \div c$
  b. $(a + b) \div c$
  c. $a \div (b + c)$
  d. $a \div b + c$

3. A line is drawn within a right angle. One angle that is formed by the line and the vertex of the right angle measures 32°. What does the other angle measure?
  a. 148°
  b. 58°
  c. 328°
  d. 45°

4. Change $\frac{160}{40}$ to a whole number.
  a. 16
  b. 10
  c. 8
  d. 4

5. Which number sentence is true?
  a. $0.43 < 0.043$
  b. $0.0043 > 0.43$
  c. $0.00043 > 0.043$
  d. $0.043 > 0.0043$

6. What is the mean of the following numbers: 76, 34, 78, and 56?
  a. 244
  b. 61
  c. 49
  d. 56

7. Which of the following terms is best described as *a comparison of two numbers*?
  a. variable
  b. coefficient
  c. ratio
  d. radical

8. An equation of the form $\frac{a}{b} = \frac{d}{c}$ is
  a. an inequality.
  b. a variable.
  c. a proportion.
  d. a monomial.

9. 184 is evenly divisible by
  a. 46
  b. 43
  c. 41
  d. 40

10. The base of a triangle is twice the height of the triangle. If the area is 16 square inches, what is the height?
  a. 4 inches
  b. 8 inches
  c. 12 inches
  d. 16 inches

11. When both six and nine are added to a number, the sum is 49. What is the number?
  a. 15
  b. 34
  c. 43
  d. 21

12. Find the sum of $4x - 7y$ and $7x + 7y$.
  a. $11x$
  b. $14y$
  c. $11x + 14y$
  d. $11x - 14y$

13. What is the sum of the measures of the exterior angles of a regular pentagon?
  a. 72°
  b. 108°
  c. 360°
  d. 540°

14. How many inches are there in $3\frac{1}{3}$ yards?
  a. 126 inches
  b. 120 inches
  c. 160 inches
  d. 168 inches

15. 1 hour 20 minutes + 3 hours 30 minutes =
  a. 4 hours
  b. 4 hours 20 minutes
  c. 4 hours 50 minutes
  d. 5 hours

16. Which of the following is equivalent to $x^3 + 6x$?
  a. $x(x^2 + 6)$
  b. $x(x + 6)$
  c. $x(x^2 + 6x)$
  d. $x^2(x + 6)$

17. What is five and four hundredths written as a decimal?
  a. 0.54
  b. 0.054
  c. 5.4
  d. 5.04

18. The square root of a number is three times four. What is the number?
  a. 100
  b. 121
  c. 144
  d. 169

19. The circumference of a circle is 131.88. Assuming π is 3.14, what is the diameter of the circle?
  a. 42 inches
  b. 44 inches
  c. 46 inches
  d. 48 inches

20. Which of the following is 16% of 789?
  a. 126.24
  b. 12.624
  c. 662.76
  d. 66.276

21. What is the value of x when $y = 8$ and $x = 4 + 6y$?
  a. 48
  b. 52
  c. 24
  d. 36

22. Thirty-five cents is what percent of $1.40?
  a. 25%
  b. 40%
  c. 45%
  d. 105%

23. Find the perimeter of a regular octagon that has sides measuring 13 centimeters each.
  a. 78 centimeters
  b. 91 centimeters
  c. 104 centimeters
  d. 117 centimeters

24. Which of the following decimals has the greatest value?
  a. 8.241
  b. 8.0241
  c. 8.2
  d. 8.2041

25. What is the value of the expression $xy - 6z$, when $x = -3$, $y = 6$, and $z = -5$?
  a. −48
  b. 48
  c. −12
  d. 12

Part 6: Electronics Information

Time: 9 minutes

1. Sources of electromagnetic interference (EMI) can include
  a. an electrical power supply located too close to an audio transmission source.
  b. electrical transmission wires placed too close to digital communications wires.
  c. atmospheric events involving the Earth's magnetic field.
  d. all the above

2. What class of fire would an electrical fire be?
  a. Class A
  b. Class B
  c. Class C
  d. Class D

3. The national standard in the United States for the safe installation of electrical wiring and equipment is the National Electrical Code (NEC). This standard is maintained and modified, as needed, every three years by the
  a. individual state or county governments.
  b. National Fire Protection Association (NFPA).
  c. National Institute for Standards and Technology (NIST).
  d. Environmental Protection Agency (EPA).

4. Which schematic symbol represents a NOR gate?

a.

b.

c.

d.

5. Which of the following is not a sensor?
a. a photocell
b. a light-emitting diode
c. a photodiode
d. a phototransistor

6. Microphones convert sound waves into electrical energy. Which type of microphone uses a magnet to convert sound waves to electrical signals?
a. the crystal microphone
b. the condenser microphone
c. the dynamic microphone
d. the fiber optic microphone

7. Which of the following criteria is NOT used to rate speakers?
a. polarity
b. frequency range
c. impedance
d. power

8. What does a hertz measure?
a. the amperage of a device
b. the voltage of a device
c. the decibels of a sound
d. the frequency of a sound wave

9. According to North American electrical standards, what is the standard configuration for ground wire insulation?
a. green wires
b. bare copper wires
c. both **a** and **b**
d. neither **a** nor **b**

10. What type of pliers is depicted here?

a. wire cutting pliers
b. combination pliers
c. needlenose pliers
d. crimping pliers

11. Which of the following is needed to produce electrical power from fossil fuels?
a. a dam
b. a wind turbine
c. tidal forces
d. heat

12. Compressed air can be used to
a. put out a fire.
b. cool solder joints.
c. provide air to breathe in an emergency.
d. blow dust off electric parts.

13. What would probably be the effect of 6–9mA of 60 Hz of AC current on a body?
a. There will be a slight tingling sensation.
b. Pain will be felt but muscle control is still possible.
c. Pain will be felt and muscle control is lost.
d. There will be difficulty breathing.

14. What does the following schematic symbol represent?

   a. a battery
   b. a chassis ground
   c. an earth ground
   d. a signal ground

15. Which of the following will NOT help to minimize static electricity?
   a. wearing cotton clothing
   b. anti-static wrist straps
   c. wearing polyester clothing
   d. anti-static mats

16. Copper electrical wiring is preferable to aluminum electrical wiring because
   a. aluminum heats up and expands more than copper wire.
   b. aluminum cools down and contracts more than copper wire.
   c. aluminum oxidation creates a resistance to the electrical flow.
   d. all the above

17. Which of the following schematic symbols depicts a single on-off switch?
   a.
   b.
   c.
   d.

18. If in a schematic's parts list you see "R2: 47 kΩ," what does this indicate?
   a. There are at least two relays and the second one relays 47 kΩ.
   b. There are at least two resistors and the second one handles 47 kΩ.
   c. There are at least two relays that handle a total of 47 kΩ.
   d. There are at least two resistors and combined they handle 47 kΩ.

19. What do the following schematic symbols represent?

   a. I is a capacitor and II is a resistor.
   b. I is a battery and II is a resistor.
   c. Both are resistors.
   d. I is a capacitor and II is a resistor.

20. In Europe, how is a brown wire used?
   a. Brown wires are not allowed.
   b. It is a ground.
   c. It is neutral.
   d. It is live.

Part 7:
Auto and Shop Information

Time: 11 minutes

1. Neutral (N) position on an automatic transmission indicator means the transmission
   a. is locked and cannot be moved.
   b. is engaged in a maximum load configuration.
   c. has disengaged all gear trains within the transmission.
   d. none of the above

2. What type of mechanical device is used to aid in the cooling of an internal combustion engine?
   a. a pump
   b. a lever
   c. a hinge
   d. a pulley

3. Of the following mechanical devices on an automobile, which one uses friction to accomplish its purpose?
   a. the distributor
   b. the alternator
   c. the brakes
   d. the radiator

4. A pair of gears that convert rotational motion into linear motion in the steering mechanism of an automobile is called
   a. the rack and pinion.
   b. the tap and die.
   c. the flywheel.
   d. the overhead cam.

5. The clutch on an automobile is used to
   a. lock the rear axle.
   b. disconnect the engine from the transmission so that you can shift gears.
   c. connect the universal joint to the transaxle.
   d. connect the drivetrain to the differential.

6. A universal joint
   a. transforms linear motion into stored energy.
   b. can be attached to any rotational object.
   c. transmits rotary motion between two shafts that aren't in a straight line.
   d. converts kinetic energy to potential energy.

7. With the engine off, battery power can be used to
   a. power the catalytic converter.
   b. power the alternator to recharge the battery.
   c. run the power windows.
   d. power the lights and accessories.

8. Which system on an automobile uses shock absorbers?
   a. electrical
   b. suspension
   c. braking
   d. power steering

9. An automobile burns oil when which of the following parts are worn?
   a. the spark plugs
   b. the piston rings
   c. the rocker arms
   d. the connecting rods

10. It is recommended that engine oil in an automobile be changed at what mileage interval?
   a. 1,500 miles
   b. 3,000 miles
   c. 4,500 miles
   d. none of the above

11. A typical 12-volt automobile battery provides
   a. 3 cells.
   b. 6 cells.
   c. 12 cells.
   d. 24 cells.

12. Which automotive system uses universal joints, a driveshaft, and a clutch?
   a. drivetrain
   b. braking
   c. electrical
   d. fuel

13. To measure the inside diameter of a tube, which tool would be best to use?

a.

b.

c.

d.

14. A metal punch would be used in sheet metal work to
   a. cut along a scored line.
   b. create 45-degree cuts.
   c. create a curved edge.
   d. make holes in the metal.

15. What saw would be used to cut a hole in Sheetrock for an electrical outlet?
   a. a crosscut saw
   b. a keyhole saw
   c. a hacksaw
   d. a coping saw

16. What would the moisture content be in a piece of lumber with the following stamp?

   a. 12% or less
   b. 15% or less
   c. 19% or less
   d. more than 19%

17. A hacksaw is best used for cutting
   a. intricate patterns in soft wood.
   b. long crosscuts.
   c. iron, steel, and other softer metals.
   d. sheets of plywood.

18. What is the standard size of a claw hammer?
   a. 16 oz.
   b. 24 oz.
   c. 32 oz.
   d. none of the above

19. A nail set is used to
   a. start a nail hole.
   b. drive finish nails below the surface of the surrounding wood.
   c. provide a variety of nails for any circumstance.
   d. none of the above

20. A baluster is a
   a. tool used to shape long pieces of wood.
   b. decorative piece of wood on top of a pole.
   c. one of a set of closely spaced supports on a railing.
   d. guide used for cutting.

21. A *cat's paw* is a type of
 a. pry bar.
 b. nail remover.
 c. multi-utility bar.
 d. all the above

22. Which of the following would be the best tool to use to make the most precise angular cuts?
 a. a handsaw
 b. a coping saw
 c. a jigsaw
 d. a miter saw

23. Local building codes generally set the minimum diameter for concrete footings at
 a. 4 inches.
 b. 6 inches.
 c. 8 inches.
 d. 16 inches.

24. A 2 × 4 piece of lumber has dimensions that are actually
 a. $1\frac{1}{2}'' \times 3\frac{1}{2}''$.
 b. $1\frac{3}{4}'' \times 3\frac{3}{4}''$.
 c. $2'' \times 4''$.
 d. none of the above

25. A carpenter's compass is used to
 a. calculate angles.
 b. draw circles.
 c. estimate distance.
 d. determine area.

Part 8:
Mechanical Comprehension

Time: 19 minutes

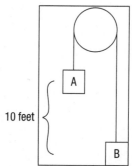

10 feet

1. Two blocks of equal weight are suspended by a pulley. The blocks are 10 vertical feet apart. How far must block A be pulled down to be at equal height with block B?
 a. 5 feet
 b. 10 feet
 c. 15 feet
 d. 20 feet

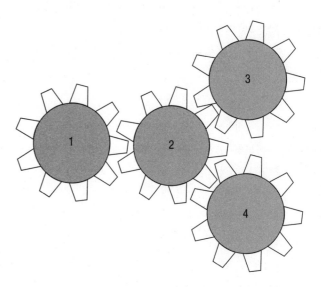

2. If gear 2 turns counterclockwise, which other gear(s), if any, will turn clockwise?
 a. 1 only
 b. 3 only
 c. 3 and 4 only
 d. 1, 3, and 4

3. Lenny leaves camp at 6:00 A.M. and jogs north at 8 mph. George leaves camp half an hour later and follows the same path as Lenny at 10 mph. At what time will George catch Lenny?

    a. 7:00 A.M.

    b. 7:30 A.M.

    c. 8:00 A.M.

    d. 8:30 A.M.

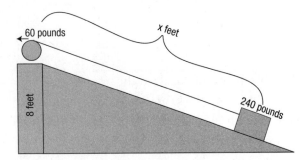

4. A 240-pound block is being pulled up an incline by a pulley. The incline rises 8 feet. Neglecting friction, if 60 pounds of force is necessary to move the block up the incline, how long is the incline?

    a. 60 feet

    b. 32 feet

    c. 16 feet

    d. 30 feet

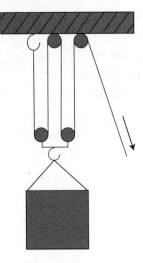

5. What is the mechanical advantage of the pulley system shown here?

    a. 1

    b. 2

    c. 3

    d. 4

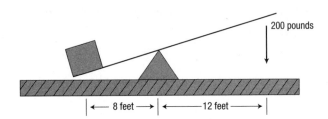

6. In the diagram, Cory wants to lift a block using a lever. The block is 8 feet from the pivot point and Cory is 12 feet from the pivot point. If it takes 200 pounds of force to lift the block, how much does it weigh?

    a. 96 pounds

    b. 400 pounds

    c. 300 pounds

    d. 200 pounds

7. The same type of plastic is used to make blocks of 3 cubes of different sizes. The first has a weight of 0.5 pounds, the second has a weight of 0.75 pounds, and the third has a weight of 1.5 pounds. Which of the following statements is true?

   a. All three cubes will either float or sink.

   b. Cube 1 will float and cubes 2 and 3 will sink.

   c. Cube 3 will float and cubes 1 and 2 will sink.

   d. Cubes 1 and 2 will float and cube 3 will sink.

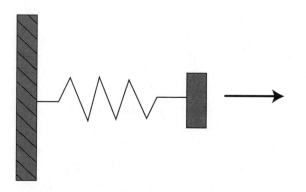

8. A force of 8 pounds is required to move a spring 4 inches. How much force is required to move the spring 1 foot?

   a. 3 pounds

   b. 12 pounds

   c. 24 pounds

   d. 36 pounds

9. A screw has 7 threads per inch. How many full turns are necessary for the nut to travel 3 inches?

   a. 12 turns

   b. 15 turns

   c. 18 turns

   d. 21 turns

10. Why is oil added to an engine?

   a. Engines burn oil.

   b. Oil helps gasoline burn better.

   c. Oil increases friction in the engine.

   d. Oil decreases friction in the engine.

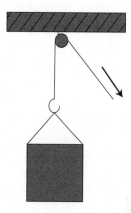

11. Using the pulley system shown, how much force is required to lift an 80-pound weight?

   a. 20 pounds

   b. 40 pounds

   c. 80 pounds

   d. 160 pounds

12. Raising a flag up a flagpole is most commonly accomplished with what simple machine?

   a. a lever

   b. a pulley

   c. an inclined plane

   d. a gear

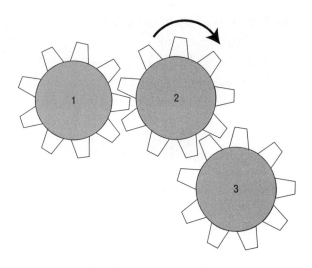

13. If gear 2 turns clockwise, which other gear(s), if any, will turn clockwise?

   a. 1 only

   b. 3 only

   c. 1 and 3

   d. none

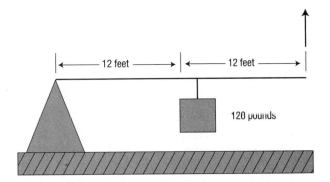

14. In the diagram, Andre wants to lift a 126-pound block using a lever. If the block is 12 feet from the pivot point and Andre is 12 feet beyond that, how much force must he apply to lift the block?

   a. 126 pounds

   b. 63 pounds

   c. 75 pounds

   d. 144 pounds

15. The shock absorber on a car is a very large spring. If a car hits a pothole with 500 pounds of force and the shock absorber compresses 2.5 inches, what is its force constant?

   a. 200 pounds per inch

   b. 300 pounds per inch

   c. 350 pounds per inch

   d. 400 pounds per inch

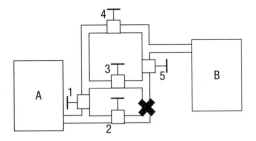

16. A cracked pipe, marked in the figure by an ×, has caused all valves to automatically close. Which valves can be opened to allow water to flow from tank A to tank B while avoiding the broken section?

   a. 1 and 3

   b. 1 and 4

   c. 1, 2, and 5

   d. 1, 3, and 5

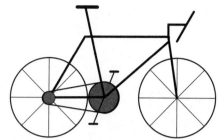

17. A single-speed bicycle has a front gear with 48 teeth and a rear gear with 12 teeth. If the bicycle is pedaled at 90 rpm, how fast will the rear wheel rotate?

a. 90 rpm

b. 180 rpm

c. 270 rpm

d. 360 rpm

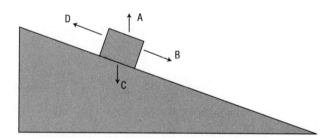

18. A block is held in place on a ramp by friction. Which arrow shows the direction of the frictional force?

a. A

b. B

c. C

d. D

19. If the following items are placed into a hot oven, which will warm most quickly?

a. a metal fork

b. a plastic spoon

c. a ceramic mug

d. a glass bowl

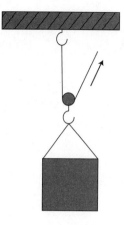

20. Using the pulley system shown in the figure, how much force is required to lift a 300-pound weight?

a. 75 pounds

b. 100 pounds

c. 150 pounds

d. 300 pounds

21. A screw can be thought of as a special type of what simple machine?

a. the lever

b. the inclined plane

c. the pulley

d. the wheel and axle

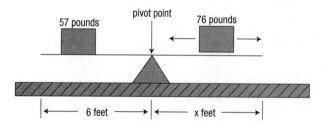

22. In the diagram, Steven wants to balance two blocks on either side of a lever. One block weighs 57 pounds and the other weighs 76 pounds. If the 57-pound block is 6 feet to the left of the pivot point, how far to the right of the pivot point should the 76-pound block be placed?

a. 4.5 feet

b. 6 feet

c. 19 feet

d. 4 feet

23. Two ramps can be used to raise a heavy barrel up to a platform. Neglecting friction, which ramp requires less work to raise the barrel?

a. Ramp A requires less work.
b. Ramp B requires less work.
c. They require the same amount of work.
d. It is impossible to determine.

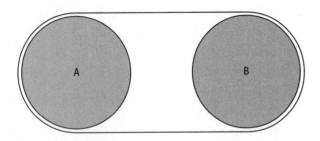

24. Pulleys A and B are identical in size and connected by a belt. If pulley A rotates at 20 rpm clockwise, at what rate and in what direction will pulley B rotate?

a. 20 rpm, clockwise
b. 20 rpm, counterclockwise
c. 40 rpm, clockwise
d. 40 rpm, counterclockwise

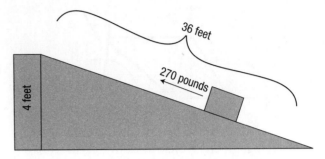

25. A 270-pound block is being pulled up an incline by a pulley. The incline is 36 feet long and rises 4 feet. Neglecting friction, how much force is necessary to move the block up the incline?

a. 30 pounds
b. 270 pounds
c. 40 pounds
d. 144 pounds

Part 9: Assembling Objects

Time: 15 minutes

Each question is composed of five separate drawings. The problem is presented in the first drawing, and the remaining four drawings are possible solutions. Determine which of the four choices contains all of the pieces assembled properly that are shown in the first picture. Note: images are not drawn to scale.

1.

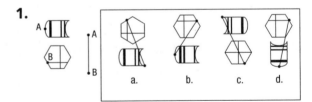

2.

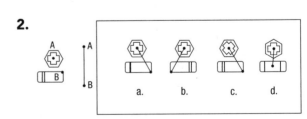

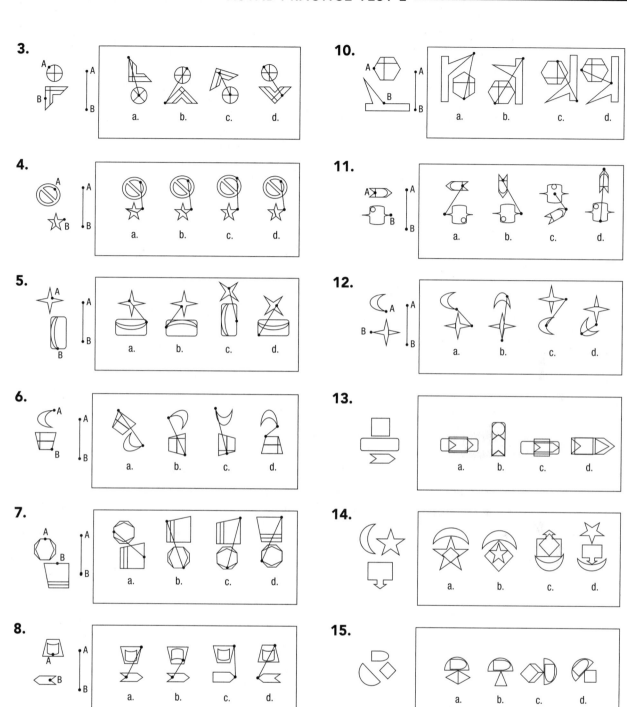

17.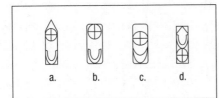

18.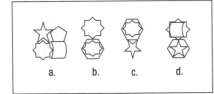

19.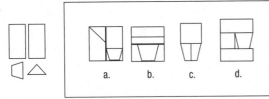

20.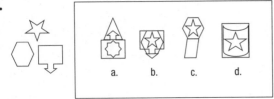

21.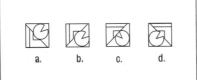

22.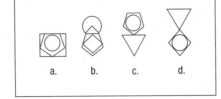

23.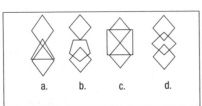

24.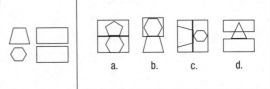

25.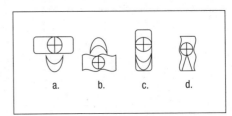

Scoring

Write your raw score (the number you got right) for each test in the blanks below. Then turn to Chapter 2 to find out how to convert these raw scores into the scores the armed services use.

1. General Science: _____ right out of 25
2. Arithmetic Reasoning: _____ right out of 30
3. Word Knowledge: _____ right out of 35
4. Paragraph Comprehension: _____ right out of 15
5. Mathematics Knowledge: _____ right out of 25
6. Electronics Information: _____ right out of 20
7. Auto and Shop Information: _____ right out of 25
8. Mechanical Comprehension: _____ right out of 25
9. Assembling Objects: _____ right out of 25

Answers

Part 1: General Science

1. **a.** Krypton (Kr) is a noble gas found in the last column of the periodic table. These elements have complete outer valence shells, making them very unreactive to other elements.

2. **a.** When a Moon is new it is between the Sun and Earth. A solar eclipse occurs when the Moon crosses the path of the Sun's light rays between the Earth and Sun, which can happen only during the new Moon phase.

3. **c.** The mass number of an atom is the sum of protons and neutrons. In this case, $60 + 75 = 135$.

4. **d.** The urinary bladder stores urine after it is created in the kidneys.

5. **d.** A mitochondrion in a cell produces energy for cellular functions through processing ATP.

6. **a.** The alkaline earth metals are in group 2, which all have a valence electron configuration of s^2.

7. **c.** Active transport requires energy to transport substances through the membrane. Diffusion and osmosis rely on concentration differences, and filtration relies on pressure differences.

8. **a.** According to the balanced reaction, 3 moles of O_2 in the reactants is equivalent to 3 moles of Cu_2O in the products. Therefore, to make 24 moles Cu_2O, 24 moles of O_2 are needed.

9. **d.** In the food chain green plants "produce" energy through photosynthesis, which is transferred to consumers—first plant eaters, then animal eaters.

10. **d.** Partial pressure of each component is proportional to its molar ratio of the mixture. Using the mass and molecular weights given, there are 0.5 mol oxygen ($8 \text{ g} \times \frac{1 \text{ mol}}{16 \text{ g}} = 0.5$ mol) and 1 mol nitrogen ($14 \text{ g} \times \frac{1 \text{ mol}}{14 \text{ g}} = 1.0$ mol). Therefore, the molar ratio of oxygen in this mixture is $\frac{0.5}{0.5 + 1.0} = \frac{0.5}{1.5} = \frac{1}{3}$ and oxygen's partial pressure is $\frac{1}{3} \times 750$ mm Hg $= 250$ mm Hg.

11. **a.** Membranes are not rigid and do not provide support like cell walls do. The cell membrane is responsible for transporting substances and forming structures to contain cytoplasm and DNA.

12. **d.** Nuclear fusion is the combining of smaller nuclei to form a larger one. This reaction releases extremely large amounts of energy and is the reaction occurring at the Sun and other stars.

13. **a.** Mountains that are not volcanic are formed at a continental collision zone.

14. **c.** The time for a radioactive element to lose half its atoms is referred to as its radioactive period. Be careful not to confuse this with half-life, which is the time it takes for the concentration of a sample of nuclei to decompose by one half.

15. **b.** Bacteria are a part of the kingdom *monera*, the classification for the simplest single cell life.

16. **d.** Use Gay-Lussac's law, $P_1 T_1 = P_2 T_2$. Don't forget to convert temperature from Celsius to Kelvin by adding 273. $\frac{(400 \text{ K})(6 \text{ atm})}{300 \text{ K}} = 8$ atm

17. **c.** Fermentation is a process that produces energy without oxygen.

18. **b.** 1 atm is equal to 760 mm Hg. Since 740 mm Hg is just a little bit less than 760 mm Hg, the answer should be just a little less than 1 atm.

19. a. Fungi and plants evolved from protists. Some protists are autotrophs and contain chloroplasts like plants. Fungi are not autotrophic. Protists do not have specialized tissue.

20. c. When two elements form an ionic compound, the charge of the ion needs to be determined. Aluminum (Al) has three valence electrons and will give those up, while oxygen (O) has six valence electrons, so it favors taking two electrons in. This gives the Al ion a +3 charge and the O ion a –2 charge. The number of ions in the ionic compound is determined by balancing the overall charge. In this case, two Al ions will give a charge of +6, which will be balanced by three O ions with a total charge of –6.

21. d. Meiosis results in four haploid gametes with half the number of chromosomes as their parent. This is unlike mitosis that results in two daughter cells with the same number of chromosomes as their parent.

22. b. Weather and almost all clouds are located in the troposphere.

23. c. Covalent molecules are named using prefixes to describe the number of atoms and generally end in the suffix *-ide*. In this case, *tetra-* represents four chlorine atoms.

24. a. After 18 minutes, three half-life cycles have occurred.
$$\left(\frac{1}{2}\right)^3 = \frac{1}{8}$$
unknown mass $\cdot \frac{1}{8} = 40$ g $\Rightarrow$ unknown mass $= 320$ g

25. d. Viruses are unable to reproduce because they lack cells. Viruses rely on host cells to express their genetic material. Viruses contain enzymes and nucleic acid, and have evolved through natural selection similar to other living organisms, but are still considered nonliving because they lack cellular reproduction.

Part 2: Arithmetic Reasoning

1. c. If the number of points is increased by 25%, the number of points in his senior year is 125% of the number of points in his junior year (100% + 25% = 125%). To find 125% of the number of points in his junior year, multiply the junior year points by the decimal equivalent of 125%; $260 \times 1.25 = 325$. If you chose **a**, you calculated what his points would be if he scored 25% *less* than he did in his junior year.

2. c. This is a subtraction problem. First, simplify the problem by dropping the word *million*. The problem then becomes P = 3,666 and M = 36. So P – M = 3,666 – 36 = 3,630. Now add back the word *million*, and the answer becomes 3,630 million.

3. c. This is a three-step problem involving multiplication and division. First, change yards to feet: 240 yards × 3 feet in a yard = 720 feet. Now find the number of square feet in the parcel: 121 feet × 740 feet = 87,120 square feet. Now find the number of acres: 87,120 square feet ÷ 43,560 square feet in an acre = 2 acres.

4. c. First, find the total hours worked by all six nurses: 8 + 10 + 9 + 8 + 7 + 12 = 54. Then find the average by dividing the total hours by the number of nurses: 54 ÷ 6 = 9.

5. d. The production for Lubbock is equal to the total minus the other productions: 1,780 – 450 – 425 – 345 = 560.

6. c. First, simplify the problem: L = $5 + $4 + $6 = $15; R = $14. Lucinda spent the most by $1. Don't forget that only the popcorn was shared; the other items must be multiplied by two.

7. c. This is a multistep problem. First, figure out how many dozen eggs John's chickens produce per day: $480 \div 12 = 40$ dozen eggs per day. Now figure out how much money John makes on eggs per day: $2 \times 40 = \$80$ per day. Finally, figure out how much money John makes per week: $\$80 \times 7 = \$560$ per week. The most common mistake for this problem is to forget to do the last step. It is important to read each problem carefully, so you won't skip a step.

8. c. To find the hourly wage, divide the total salary by the number of hours worked, or 331.01 divided by $39\frac{1}{2}$, or 39.5, which equals 8.38.

9. c. There are two glasses out of eight left to drink, or $\frac{2}{8}$, which reduces to $\frac{1}{4}$.

10. d. Multiply the number of years in a decade by the given number of decades. A decade is ten years. Eight decades is therefore 80 years: 8×10 years $= 80$ years.

11. b. If it is 11:46 A.M., in 14 minutes it will be noon. In 15 minutes, then, it will be 12:01 P.M.

12. c. This is a multiplication problem. To multiply a whole number by a mixed number, first convert the mixed number to a fraction: $1\frac{2}{5} = \frac{7}{5}$. Then, multiply: $\frac{7}{5} \times \frac{3}{1} = \frac{21}{5}$. Now reduce: $\frac{21}{5} = 4\frac{1}{5}$.

13. c. First, convert tons to pounds; 1 ton = 2,000 pounds; 36 tons (per year) = 72,000 pounds (per year); 1 year = 12 months, so the average number of pounds of mosquitoes the colony of bats can consume in a month is $72,000 \div 12$, or 6,000 pounds.

14. a. This is a subtraction of mixed numbers problem. The common denominator is 8. Convert $\frac{1}{2}$ to $\frac{4}{8}$. Because $\frac{4}{8}$ is larger than $\frac{1}{8}$, you must borrow from the whole number 23. Then subtract: $22\frac{9}{8} - 6\frac{4}{8} = 16\frac{5}{8}$.

15. b. $\frac{1}{2}$ of $\frac{1}{4}$ is expressed as $\frac{1}{2} \times \frac{1}{4}$ or $\frac{1}{8}$.

16. b. The number 54 divided by 6 is 9.

17. b. First, change the percent to a decimal: $3\frac{1}{4}\% = 0.0325$. Now multiply: $30,600 \times 0.0325 = 994.5$. Finally, add: $\$30,600 + 994.50 = \$31,594.50$ for Yetta's current salary.

18. c. Multiply $115 by 12 because there are 12 months in a year; $\$115 \times 12 = \$1,380$ per year.

19. d. This is a two-step multiplication problem. First, multiply: $5 \times 2 = 10$, which is the number of trips Jacqueline drives to get to work and back. Then multiply 19.85 by 10 by simply moving the decimal one place to the right.

20. b. Add the amount of miles for each day for a total of 696 miles; 696 rounded to the nearest ten or nearest hundred is 700.

21. c. First ask how many inches are in one foot; the answer is 12 inches. Now multiply: $12 \times 4 = 48$ inches.

22. d. First, find the number of degrees that the temperature will increase; $57° - 53° = 4°$. Since the temperature increases $1°$ every two hours, $4° \times 2$ hours is 8 hours. Add eight hours to 5 A.M. It will be 1:00 P.M.

23. d. First, calculate the number of students that do not participate in extracurricular activities: $360 - 150 = 210$ students. Next, find the percent 210 is of 360 by setting up the proportion $\frac{210}{360} = \frac{x}{100}$. Cross multiply to get $360x = 21,000$. Divide each side of the equation by 360 to get $x = 58.33$, which rounds to 58%.

24. d. If four students are lining up, then there are four choices of students for the first spot in line, three choices for the second, two choices for the third, and one choice for the fourth spot. The counting principle tells you to take the possible choices and multiply them together: $4 \times 3 \times 2 \times 1 = 24$. This type of situation is also called a *permutation*, because the order matters.

25. d. To subtract, convert to improper fractions, find a common denominator, and subtract the numerators: $1\frac{1}{2} - \frac{10}{3} = \frac{33}{6} - \frac{20}{6} = \frac{13}{6}$ or $2\frac{1}{6}$.

26. c. He spent $54 on pants ($3 \times \$18 = \$54$) and $120 on shirts ($5 \times \$24 = \$120$). Altogether he spent $174 ($\$54 + \$120 = \$174$). If you chose **a**, you calculated the cost of *one* pair of pants plus *one* shirt instead of *three* pairs of pants and *five* shirts.

27. c. Divide 405 by 45 to get 9 minutes.

28. a. The school record is less than Brian's time. Therefore, 2.68 must be subtracted from 13.4; $13.4 - 2.68 = 10.72$. To subtract decimals, line up the numbers vertically so that the numbers are aligned. Since 13.4 has one less decimal place than 2.68, you must add a zero after the 4 (13.40) before subtracting. After you have done this, subtract normally. If you chose **d**, you added instead of subtracted.

29. d. If Jason's price is $\frac{3}{4}$ of Lisa's, that would mean that if $63 is divided by 3, the quotient will be $\frac{1}{4}$. Add this to Jason's price, and the sum is Lisa's price: $\$63 \div 3 = \$21$; $\$63 + \$21 = \$84$. Lisa's salon charges $84.

30. c. Each quarter is worth $0.25, so two quarters are equal to $0.50 ($2 \times 0.25 = 0.50$). Each dime is worth $0.10: $\$0.50 \div \$0.10 = 5$ dimes.

Part 3: Word Knowledge

1. a. To *glare* means to stare angrily; to *scowl* means to have an angry expression.

2. c. One meaning of *civil* is involving the general public.

3. c. A *peer* is a person belonging to the same group; a *fellow* is an equal in rank, or a member of the same group.

4. b. A *fiasco* is a complete failure, or a disaster.

5. a. A *chasm* is a deep split in the earth, or a gorge.

6. c. *Expertise* and mastery both mean special skills or knowledge.

7. b. *Outlandish* means extremely out of the ordinary; absurd means ridiculously unreasonable.

8. d. To *pine* means to long for, or to crave.

9. b. To *exploit* means to use selfishly for one's own ends, to misuse or abuse.

10. a. *Culmination* means the act of reaching the highest point, or decisive action; realization means the act of bringing into concrete existence.

11. c. To *feign* means to assert as if true, or to pretend.

12. b. To *heed* means to pay attention to, or to consider.

13. a. To *edge* means to force or move gradually (as in to edge off the road).

14. d. To *elevate* means to lift up, or raise; to hoist means to raise into position.

15. c. To *appoint* means to name officially, often to a position; to nominate means to appoint or propose for office.

16. a. To *hoard* means to gather a hidden supply; to stockpile means accumulate a reserve of something.

17. c. A *hub* is a center of activity.

18. d. *Tame* means deficient in spirit or courage, or submissive.

19. b. To *irk* means to annoy or irritate.

20. c. To *loom* means to come into sight in enlarged or distorted form; to surface means to come to the surface or into view.

21. a. *Fitful* means having intermittent or irregular character; erratic means lacking regularity.

22. d. *Gaudy* means ostentatiously or tastelessly ornamented; flashy means ostentatious or showy.

23. b. To *flaunt* means to display ostentatiously or impudently; to parade means to exhibit ostentatiously.

24. a. To *flex* means to bend.

25. d. To *tantalize* means to tease by presenting something desirable.

26. a. The phrase *even though she's almost 80* indicates that the correct answer will seem contrary to what we would normally think of as being a quality of an elderly person. Therefore, choices **c** and **d** are incorrect. Choice **b**, *persistent*, is a possibility, but there is a better answer choice—choice **a**, *indefatigable*, meaning "untiring."

27. a. A treasure hunter would most likely be interest by a glimmer of gold, so choices **c** and **d** do not make sense. Answer choice **b** is almost correct, but the best word is choice **a**, *piqued*, which means aroused or excited.

28. b. It makes the most sense that a *novice*, or new, doctor would be overwhelmed by the amount of work required.

29. b. Although desert dwellers might be classified as any of these words, the sentence is really looking for a word describing people who are constantly moving—the word that best fits his definition is choice **b**, *nomadic*.

30. a. The implication is that Mr. Crane might harm his chances of being hired if he divulged the previous firing; therefore, the best answer is choice **a**, *jeopardize*, meaning "endanger."

31. a. Although all four choices fit the sentence, the only word that explains why Carlos would continue to feel immersed in the film's world is engrossing.

32. d. An anti-authoritarian philosopher would hold views that were against the king, so choices **a** and **b** are incorrect. Although choice **c** could make sense, it is more likely that a furious king would call for the philosopher to be ostracized.

33. c. The keyword *but* indicates that the second half of the sentence should provide evidence against the first half. If the task of climbing the mountain is daunting, then the second half should say something that suggests otherwise. Therefore the best choice is *insurmountable*, meaning incapable of being overcome or achieved. In this case, *not insurmountable* would mean still possible.

34. d. A pacifist is someone who refuses to engage in violence; therefore the best answer is *deplore*, meaning "hate."

35. d. The correct answer choice would explain what an army would do to an invading force if it were to charge them; of the four choices, *repel* most accurately fits the sentence.

Part 4: Paragraph Comprehension

1. b. The passage states that all machines are based on six simple machines, and it goes into detail to explain the principles of simple machines and give examples of each type. The other choices might refer to details in the passage, but only choice **b** states the overall theme.

2. c. The passage states that most machines use one or more of the six basic simple machines to operate. Cars are listed among the complicated machines that we use daily, so we can infer that it uses simple machines to operate.

3. b. Each of the choices is listed as a simple machine in the passage except for a pushbutton.

4. d. The word *myriad* means "a very large, indefinite number." Therefore, many is the best choice.

5. c. The mayor stated in the last sentence of the first paragraph that the vandalism was being caused by students from a rival high school.

6. a. The word *transient* refers to someone or something that will not remain in one place for very long. Thus, a transient person is just "passing through" town.

7. b. The first sentence of the second paragraph states that the town council will meet again on the 3rd of next month.

8. c. When *implement* is used as a verb, it means "to put something into practice." When it is used as a noun, it can refer to a tool or even an eating utensil, so you need to determine from the context whether it is being used as a noun or a verb. In this passage, it is used as a verb, a word that describes some form of action.

9. d. This answer is implied by the whole paragraph. The author stresses the need to read critically by performing operations on the text in a slow and specific manner. Choice **a** is incorrect because the author never says that reading is dull. Choices **b** and **c** are not supported by the paragraph.

10. b. The passage urges the reader to mark up the text, ask questions, and draw conclusions, which is what is meant by being *an active participant.* The other options may or may not be true, but they are not addressed in the passage.

11. c. In the first sentence, the passage states that employees have been abusing their sick-time benefits in order to increase their vacation time. The writer's tone makes it clear that he or she does not approve of the practice, particularly since he or she refers to it as an "abuse" in the last sentence.

12. a. The word *accrue* means to gather together or to collect.

13. d. The new policy beginning June 1 is designed, according to the passage, to discourage employees from misusing their sick-time benefits.

14. c. The word *curtail* means to cut back on something or to decrease something. To curtail abuse means to cut back on or decrease how much abuse is taking place.

15. d. The author stresses the convenience of fitness walking by stating that it does not require a commute to a health club. The paragraph also implies that fitness walking will result in a good workout. Choice **a** is incorrect because no comparison to weight lifting is made. Choice **b** may seem like a logical answer, but the paragraph only refers to people who are fitness walkers, so for others, a health club might be a good investment. Choice **c** is not in the passage.

Part 5: Mathematics Knowledge

1. a. $Area = \frac{1}{2}(b \times h)$. To get the height of the triangle, use the Pythagorean theorem: $3^2 + height^2 = 5^2$, so height = 4. When this is plugged into the area equation, you'll get an area of 6 square units for half of the triangle. Double this, and the answer is 12 square units.

2. b. Break the statement down into smaller parts. The first part, "the sum of two numbers, *a* and *b*," can be translated $(a + b)$. This part needs to be in parentheses to ensure that the correct order of operations is executed. The second part, "divided by a third number, *c*," takes the first part and divides it by *c*. This now becomes $(a + b) \div c$.

3. b. The line right, or 90°, angle is split into two complementary angles. The given angle is 32°; therefore, $90 - 32 = 58°$.

4. d. Divide the top number by the bottom number: $160 \div 40 = 4$.

5. d. The farther to the right the nonzero digits are, the smaller the number. Forty-three thousandths is greater than 43 ten-thousandths.

6. b. Add the four numbers together for a sum of 244. Then, divide by 4 to get a quotient of 61.

7. c. A ratio is a comparison of two numbers.

8. c. This equation is a proportion, expressing the equivalence of two ratios.

9. a. Forty-six goes into 184 four times. The other choices cannot be divided evenly into 184.

10. a. The area of a triangle is $A = \frac{1}{2}(b \times h)$. Since $b = 2h$, you have $16 = \frac{1}{2}(2h)(h)$ or $h^2 = 16$; $h = 4$ inches.

11. b. Subtract both 6 and 9 from 49. The correct answer is 34.

12. a. Only like terms can be added: $4x - 7y + 7x + 7y$; $4x + 7x$ and $-7y + 7y$. The y terms cancel each other out, leaving $11x$ as the correct answer.

13. c. The sum of the measures of the exterior angles of any convex polygon is 360°.

14. b. To solve this problem, you must first convert yards to inches. There are 36 inches in one yard; $36 \times 3\frac{1}{3} = \frac{36}{1} \times \frac{10}{3} = \frac{360}{3} = 120$.

15. c. Add the hours first, and then the minutes: 1 hour + 3 hours = 4 hours. 20 minutes + 30 minutes = 50 minutes. Combine: 4 hours 50 minutes.

16. a. The correct answer is $x(x^2 + 6)$.

17. d. This is a mixed decimal, which included a whole number placed to the left of the decimal point. The zero is in the tenths place and the 4 is in the hundredths place: 5.04.

18. c. First, find the product of the given values, which is 12. Then, square that number. Twelve squared equals 144. The correct answer is 144.

19. a. Divide the circumference by 3.14 to find the diameter; therefore, the correct answer is 42 inches.

20. a. The correct answer is 126.24.

21. b. Substitute 8 for y in the expression and perform the operations: $x = 4 + 6(8)$; $x = 52$.

22. a. Simply set up the equation in the manner in which the problem is written. Since $x\% = \frac{x}{100}$, the equation is $\frac{x}{100} = \frac{35}{1.40}$. Cross multiply: $1.40x = (0.35)(100)$. Simplify: $x = \frac{35}{1.40}$. Thus, $x = 25$, which means \$0.35 is 25% of \$1.40.

23. c. A regular octagon has eight equal sides; therefore, the perimeter equals 8×13. The correct answer is 104 centimeters.

24. a. The greatest value to the right of the decimal point can be determined by the tenths place. Choices **a**, **c**, and **d** all have a two in the tenths place. Choice **a** is correct because its values in the hundredths and thousandths places are greater than the other two possible answers.

25. d. When the given values are plugged into the expression, it reads: $(-3)(6) - 6(-5)$; $-18 + 30 = 12$.

Part 6: Electronics Information

1. d. Electromagnetic interference (EMI) is electromagnetic energy that adversely affects the performance of electrical/electronic equipment by affecting the performance and operation of the equipment in various degrees to the point of failure.

2. c. Class C fires are those that consist of energized electrical equipment. Class A fires are combustible solid materials and Class B fires are flammable liquids. Class D fires involve combustible metals. If electrical power is shut off in a Class C fire, it then becomes a Class A, B, or D fire depending on what remains aflame.

3. b. The National Fire Protection Association (NFPA), while not a federal agency, first established the National Electrical Code (NEC) in 1897, and its incorporation as a national standard has been mandated and/or adopted by all 50 states.

4. d. This is the component symbol for a NOR gate. Choice **a** is the symbol for an AND gate, choice **b** for an OR gate, and choice **c** represents a NOT gate.

5. b. A light emitting diode (LED) emits light, whereas the others receive or sense light.

6. c. Dynamic microphones use electromagnetic induction to produce sound waves. Crystal microphones (**a**) use piezoelectricity; condenser microphones (**b**) use a capacitor; fiber optic microphones (**d**) use a laser.

7. a. A speaker converts electrical signals to sound waves. Of the choices, only polarity is not a speaker rating.

8. d. Hertz is a term used to measure the frequency of a sound wave. It is also known as cycles per second and abbreviated as Hz.

9. c. Green wires and bare copper wires are used only for grounding. These wires will ensure the appliance is grounded and should be attached from the junction boxes to the appliance receiving power.

10. a. Wire cutters are one of the electrician's most important tools.

11. d. Producing electrical power from fossil fuels such as oil, coal, or natural gas requires heat to release the hydrocarbon energy held within the fuel. A dam uses stored water from a reservoir or tidal movement to generate electricity through the hydroelectric process while a wind turbine generates electricity through the rotational motion of the turbine.

12. d. You should use compressed air for parts that are too delicate to dust with cloth.

13. b. A current of .3 – .4 mA will produce a slight tingling sensation; a current of 10 – 16 mA will cause pain; and will prevent muscles from responding, causing you to not be able to break the connection; and 15 – 23 mA will cause difficulty breathing. A current of 65 – 100 mA will cause heart fibrillation.

14. d. This is the schematic symbol for a signal ground.

15. c. Synthetic materials such as polyester generate a great deal of static electricity due to the triboelectric effect of the fibers rubbing against one another and skin. Cotton (**a**) is predominantly a low-static material. Anti-static devices such as wrist bands (**d**) and mats (**c**) do much to minimize static electricity.

16. d. When aluminum wiring warms up from the passage of electricity, it expands more than copper does; when it cools down, it contracts more than copper does. This expansion and contraction, over time, can cause the loosening of attachment screws, creating a potential fire hazard. Aluminum oxidation (corrosion when exposed to oxygen) develops as a resistor, causing additional heat, creating additional concerns of a fire hazard.

17. c. Choice **a** is a push switch, choice **b** is a push-to-break switch, and choice **d** is a dual on-off switch.

18. b. The R indicates the part is a resistor and the 2 indicates it is the second out of at least 2 resistors in the schematic. The 47 kΩ is the amount of resistance of the individual resistor.

19. c. The symbol with the rectangle is used in the EU for resistors whereas the zigzag symbol is used in the United States.

20. d. In Europe, brown wires are live wires. The neutral (**c**) wire is blue and the ground (**b**) is green and yellow.

Part 7: Auto and Shop Information

1. c. The neutral (N) position setting disengages all gear trains within the transmission, meaning the transmission is disconnected from the drivetrain. The automobile can be towed in this configuration and is one of the two positions, along with park (P) when the automobile can be started.

2. a. The water pump is used to circulate cooling fluid throughout the engine.

3. c. The braking system uses friction in both drum brakes and disc brakes to slow the car down.

4. a. In a rack and pinion steering system, the gear teeth of a pinion gear operate along a rack where the teeth engage, causing the linkage mechanism to turn the car wheels.

5. b. The clutch disconnects the engine from the transmission so that you can shift gears.

6. c. The universal joint is where the main driveshaft connects with the drive axle and transmits the rotary motion between these two shafts that aren't in a straight line.

7. d. In a typical automobile electrical system with the engine off, battery power can power only the lights and certain accessories, such as internal lighting and the horn. The other items listed need the engine or alternator running (such as power windows) or are a system that doesn't require electrical power (catalytic converter).

8. b. Shock absorbers are a part of the suspension system of a car. The car springs absorb any bumps in the road and the shock absorbers dampen out the spring action.

9. b. When the piston rings are worn, the pressure in the engine system will force oil into the compression chamber of the engine (called *blow by*) where it will be burned in the power cycle of the internal combustion engine.

10. b. Most auto manufacturers recommend that engine oil should be changed every 3,000 miles, unless severe conditions are experienced while driving.

11. b. A typical 12-volt car starter battery connects six galvanic cells in a series, each of which provides 2.1 volts, for a total of 12.6 volts at full charge.

12. a. The universal joint, driveshaft, and the clutch are all part of the drive train of an automobile.

13. d. An inside caliper would be the measuring device that could measure the inside diameter of a tube. The other measuring devices could provide you a measurement but it would not be as precise or exact.

14. d. A metal punch is used to make holes in sheet metal.

15. b. A keyhole saw is the type of saw used to cut an outlet or light switch hole in a piece of Sheetrock. The other saws listed could cut the Sheetrock, but not in the manner needed.

16. c. A piece of lumber stamped with S-DRY or KD indicates 19% maximum moisture content. A piece of lumber stamped with MC-15 or KD-15 indicates 15% maximum moisture content (choice **b**); a piece of lumber stamped with S-GRN indicates greater than 19% moisture content (choice **d**) unseasoned.

17. c. The blade tooth pattern and kerf of a hacksaw is designed to cut iron, steel, and other softer metals.

18. a. A standard claw hammer weighs 16 ounces.

19. b. A carpenter would use a nail set to drive the head of a finish nail just below the surface of the wood. The hole would then be treated with wood filler, sanded, and painted to hide the nail hole.

20. c. On stairs or decks, a baluster is one of a set of closely spaced supports.

21. d. A cat's paw is a combination tool that can be used as a nail remover, pry bar, and multi-utility tool.

22. d. A miter saw is designed to make precise, exact angled cuts. All the other saws listed could be used to make angled cuts, however nowhere near as precise or exact.

23. c. Concrete footings that support structures need to be at least 8 inches in diameter to ensure stability and strength.

24. a. Due to the drying process and the planing of lumber, its true size is reduced by one half of an inch to its finished size.

25. b. A carpenter's compass is used to draw circles or arcs.

Part 8: Mechanical Comprehension

1. a. Every foot block A is lowered will raise block B by the same amount. To equalize the 10-foot difference, block A must be lowered 10 feet ÷ 2 = 5 feet.

2. d. Gear 2 turning counterclockwise will lead all gears it touches to turn clockwise.

3. d. When George leaves, Lenny will have already traveled 8 mph × 0.5 hours = 4 miles. George runs 2 mph faster than Lenny. Since Lenny got a 4-mile head start, it will take George 4 miles ÷ 2 mph = 2 hours to catch Lenny. Since George left at 6:30 A.M., he will catch Lenny at 8:30 A.M.

4. b. Mechanical advantage (MA) is the factor by which a simple machine multiplies for the force put into it. In this case, 60 pounds of force is used to move a 240-pound block, so MA = 240 ÷ 60 = 4. The MA of a ramp is determined by the length of the ramp, l, divided by the height gained, h. In this case, MA = $3 = \frac{l}{h} = \frac{l}{8}$ feet . Solving for l tells us the ramp is 32 feet long.

5. d. The weight of the load is spread over 4 cables, so the mechanical advantage is 4.

6. c. $w_1 \times d_1 = w_2 \times d_2$. $w_1 \times 8$ feet = 200 pounds × 12 feet. Solving for w_1 gives 300 pounds.

7. a. Each block will have a different size and weight, but, since each is made from the same material, they will all have the same density. Since an object's density determines whether it will float or sink in water, all three objects will either float or sink.

8. c. If 8 pounds of force will move a spring 4 inches, it has a force constant of 8 pounds ÷ 4 inches = 2 pounds per inch. Moving the spring 12 inches will require 12 inches × 2 pounds per inch = 24 pounds of force.

9. d. There are 7 threads per inch. To move the nut 3 inches will require 7 × 3 = 21 turns.

10. d. Oil is a lubricant used to decrease the amount of friction between the many moving parts in an engine.

11. c. The mechanical advantage of this pulley system is 2. The force required to lift the 80-pound load is 80 pounds ÷ 1 = 80 pounds.

12. b. A single fixed pulley has the advantage of being able to change the direction of force. Thus, a flag can be raised up a flagpole without having to climb and lift it.

13. d. Gear 2 turning clockwise will cause the neighboring gears to turn counterclockwise, so no other gears will turn clockwise.

14. b. $w_1 \times d_1 = w_2 \times d_2$. Andre is 24 feet away from the pivot point. 126 pounds × 12 feet = 12 feet × w_2. Solving for w_2 gives 63 pounds.

15. a. 500 pounds ÷ 2.5 inches = 200 pounds per inch.

16. b. Valves 2, 3, and 5 are all directly connected to the break and so must remain closed. 1 and 4 may be opened to successfully route the flow from A to B.

17. d. Each full turn of the pedals will turn the rear wheel 48 ÷ 12 = 4 revolutions. If the pedals are turning at 90 rpm, the rear wheel will move at 4 × 90 rpm = 360 rpm.

18. d. Frictional forces point in the opposite direction of motion (arrow B).

19. a. Of the materials listed, metal objects are the best at conducting heat and therefore will warm the fastest. Plastic, glass, and ceramic are all good insulators and thus will take a long time to absorb heat.

20. c. A pulley system of this type has a mechanical advantage of 2. So, to lift a 300-pound weight will require 300 pounds ÷ 2 = 150 pounds.

21. b. A screw is a special type of inclined plane where the ramp is wrapped around a cylindrical object.

22. a. $w_1 \times d_1 = w_2 \times d_2$. 57 pounds × 6 feet = 76 pounds × d_2. Solving for d_2 gives 4.5 feet.

23. c. While ramp B offers a greater mechanical advantage, the amount of work is determined by the overall change in height of the barrel. Since the barrel is raised the same height regardless of which ramp is used, the amount of work done is the same.

24. a. Since A and B are identical in size, they will rotate at the same rate. The belt connects the two, so A and B also rotate in the same direction.

25. a. The mechanical advantage (MA) of a ramp is determined by the length of the ramp, l, divided by the height gained, h. In this case, MA = $\frac{l}{h}$ = 36 feet ÷ 4 feet = 9. The force required to pull a 270-pound block up a ramp is 270 pounds ÷ 9 = 30 pounds.

Part 9: Assembling Objects

1. d.
2. b.
3. d.
4. d.

5. b.
6. d.
7. a.
8. b.
9. c.
10. d.
11. a.
12. a.
13. c.
14. d.
15. d.
16. b.
17. a.
18. d.
19. a.
20. b.
21. a.
22. a.
23. a.
24. c.
25. b.

Scoring

Write your raw score (the number you got right) for each test in the blanks below. Then turn to Chapter 2 to find out how to convert these raw scores into the scores the armed services use.

1. General Science: _____ right out of 25
2. Arithmetic Reasoning: _____ right out of 30
3. Word Knowledge: _____ right out of 35
4. Paragraph Comprehension: _____ right out of 15
5. Mathematics Knowledge: _____ right out of 25
6. Electronics Information: _____ right out of 20
7. Auto and Shop Information: _____ right out of 25
8. Mechanical Comprehension: _____ right out of 25
9. Assembling Objects: _____ right out of 25

ASVAB PRACTICE TEST 3

CHAPTER SUMMARY

Here's another sample ASVAB for you to practice with.

For this test, simulate the actual test-taking experience as closely as you can. Find a quiet place to work where you won't be disturbed. If you own this book, tear out the answer sheet on the following pages and find some #2 pencils to fill in the circles with. Use a timer or stopwatch to time each section. The times are marked at the beginning of each section. After you take the test, use the detailed answer explanations that follow to review any questions you missed.

Part 1: General Science (GS)

1.	ⓐ	ⓑ	ⓒ	ⓓ	10.	ⓐ	ⓑ	ⓒ	ⓓ	18.	ⓐ	ⓑ	ⓒ	ⓓ
2.	ⓐ	ⓑ	ⓒ	ⓓ	11.	ⓐ	ⓑ	ⓒ	ⓓ	19.	ⓐ	ⓑ	ⓒ	ⓓ
3.	ⓐ	ⓑ	ⓒ	ⓓ	12.	ⓐ	ⓑ	ⓒ	ⓓ	20.	ⓐ	ⓑ	ⓒ	ⓓ
4.	ⓐ	ⓑ	ⓒ	ⓓ	13.	ⓐ	ⓑ	ⓒ	ⓓ	21.	ⓐ	ⓑ	ⓒ	ⓓ
5.	ⓐ	ⓑ	ⓒ	ⓓ	14.	ⓐ	ⓑ	ⓒ	ⓓ	22.	ⓐ	ⓑ	ⓒ	ⓓ
6.	ⓐ	ⓑ	ⓒ	ⓓ	15.	ⓐ	ⓑ	ⓒ	ⓓ	23.	ⓐ	ⓑ	ⓒ	ⓓ
7.	ⓐ	ⓑ	ⓒ	ⓓ	16.	ⓐ	ⓑ	ⓒ	ⓓ	24.	ⓐ	ⓑ	ⓒ	ⓓ
8.	ⓐ	ⓑ	ⓒ	ⓓ	17.	ⓐ	ⓑ	ⓒ	ⓓ	25.	ⓐ	ⓑ	ⓒ	ⓓ
9.	ⓐ	ⓑ	ⓒ	ⓓ										

Part 2: Arithmetic Reasoning (AR)

1.	ⓐ	ⓑ	ⓒ	ⓓ	11.	ⓐ	ⓑ	ⓒ	ⓓ	21.	ⓐ	ⓑ	ⓒ	ⓓ
2.	ⓐ	ⓑ	ⓒ	ⓓ	12.	ⓐ	ⓑ	ⓒ	ⓓ	22.	ⓐ	ⓑ	ⓒ	ⓓ
3.	ⓐ	ⓑ	ⓒ	ⓓ	13.	ⓐ	ⓑ	ⓒ	ⓓ	23.	ⓐ	ⓑ	ⓒ	ⓓ
4.	ⓐ	ⓑ	ⓒ	ⓓ	14.	ⓐ	ⓑ	ⓒ	ⓓ	24.	ⓐ	ⓑ	ⓒ	ⓓ
5.	ⓐ	ⓑ	ⓒ	ⓓ	15.	ⓐ	ⓑ	ⓒ	ⓓ	25.	ⓐ	ⓑ	ⓒ	ⓓ
6.	ⓐ	ⓑ	ⓒ	ⓓ	16.	ⓐ	ⓑ	ⓒ	ⓓ	26.	ⓐ	ⓑ	ⓒ	ⓓ
7.	ⓐ	ⓑ	ⓒ	ⓓ	17.	ⓐ	ⓑ	ⓒ	ⓓ	27.	ⓐ	ⓑ	ⓒ	ⓓ
8.	ⓐ	ⓑ	ⓒ	ⓓ	18.	ⓐ	ⓑ	ⓒ	ⓓ	28.	ⓐ	ⓑ	ⓒ	ⓓ
9.	ⓐ	ⓑ	ⓒ	ⓓ	19.	ⓐ	ⓑ	ⓒ	ⓓ	29.	ⓐ	ⓑ	ⓒ	ⓓ
10.	ⓐ	ⓑ	ⓒ	ⓓ	20.	ⓐ	ⓑ	ⓒ	ⓓ	30.	ⓐ	ⓑ	ⓒ	ⓓ

Part 3: Word Knowledge (WK)

1.	ⓐ	ⓑ	ⓒ	ⓓ	13.	ⓐ	ⓑ	ⓒ	ⓓ	25.	ⓐ	ⓑ	ⓒ	ⓓ
2.	ⓐ	ⓑ	ⓒ	ⓓ	14.	ⓐ	ⓑ	ⓒ	ⓓ	26.	ⓐ	ⓑ	ⓒ	ⓓ
3.	ⓐ	ⓑ	ⓒ	ⓓ	15.	ⓐ	ⓑ	ⓒ	ⓓ	27.	ⓐ	ⓑ	ⓒ	ⓓ
4.	ⓐ	ⓑ	ⓒ	ⓓ	16.	ⓐ	ⓑ	ⓒ	ⓓ	28.	ⓐ	ⓑ	ⓒ	ⓓ
5.	ⓐ	ⓑ	ⓒ	ⓓ	17.	ⓐ	ⓑ	ⓒ	ⓓ	29.	ⓐ	ⓑ	ⓒ	ⓓ
6.	ⓐ	ⓑ	ⓒ	ⓓ	18.	ⓐ	ⓑ	ⓒ	ⓓ	30.	ⓐ	ⓑ	ⓒ	ⓓ
7.	ⓐ	ⓑ	ⓒ	ⓓ	19.	ⓐ	ⓑ	ⓒ	ⓓ	31.	ⓐ	ⓑ	ⓒ	ⓓ
8.	ⓐ	ⓑ	ⓒ	ⓓ	20.	ⓐ	ⓑ	ⓒ	ⓓ	32.	ⓐ	ⓑ	ⓒ	ⓓ
9.	ⓐ	ⓑ	ⓒ	ⓓ	21.	ⓐ	ⓑ	ⓒ	ⓓ	33.	ⓐ	ⓑ	ⓒ	ⓓ
10.	ⓐ	ⓑ	ⓒ	ⓓ	22.	ⓐ	ⓑ	ⓒ	ⓓ	34.	ⓐ	ⓑ	ⓒ	ⓓ
11.	ⓐ	ⓑ	ⓒ	ⓓ	23.	ⓐ	ⓑ	ⓒ	ⓓ	35.	ⓐ	ⓑ	ⓒ	ⓓ
12.	ⓐ	ⓑ	ⓒ	ⓓ	24.	ⓐ	ⓑ	ⓒ	ⓓ					

Part 4: Paragraph Comprehension (PC)

1.	ⓐ	ⓑ	ⓒ	ⓓ
2.	ⓐ	ⓑ	ⓒ	ⓓ
3.	ⓐ	ⓑ	ⓒ	ⓓ
4.	ⓐ	ⓑ	ⓒ	ⓓ
5.	ⓐ	ⓑ	ⓒ	ⓓ

6.	ⓐ	ⓑ	ⓒ	ⓓ
7.	ⓐ	ⓑ	ⓒ	ⓓ
8.	ⓐ	ⓑ	ⓒ	ⓓ
9.	ⓐ	ⓑ	ⓒ	ⓓ
10.	ⓐ	ⓑ	ⓒ	ⓓ

11.	ⓐ	ⓑ	ⓒ	ⓓ
12.	ⓐ	ⓑ	ⓒ	ⓓ
13.	ⓐ	ⓑ	ⓒ	ⓓ
14.	ⓐ	ⓑ	ⓒ	ⓓ
15.	ⓐ	ⓑ	ⓒ	ⓓ

Part 5: Mathematics Knowledge (MK)

1.	ⓐ	ⓑ	ⓒ	ⓓ
2.	ⓐ	ⓑ	ⓒ	ⓓ
3.	ⓐ	ⓑ	ⓒ	ⓓ
4.	ⓐ	ⓑ	ⓒ	ⓓ
5.	ⓐ	ⓑ	ⓒ	ⓓ
6.	ⓐ	ⓑ	ⓒ	ⓓ
7.	ⓐ	ⓑ	ⓒ	ⓓ
8.	ⓐ	ⓑ	ⓒ	ⓓ
9.	ⓐ	ⓑ	ⓒ	ⓓ

10.	ⓐ	ⓑ	ⓒ	ⓓ
11.	ⓐ	ⓑ	ⓒ	ⓓ
12.	ⓐ	ⓑ	ⓒ	ⓓ
13.	ⓐ	ⓑ	ⓒ	ⓓ
14.	ⓐ	ⓑ	ⓒ	ⓓ
15.	ⓐ	ⓑ	ⓒ	ⓓ
16.	ⓐ	ⓑ	ⓒ	ⓓ
17.	ⓐ	ⓑ	ⓒ	ⓓ

18.	ⓐ	ⓑ	ⓒ	ⓓ
19.	ⓐ	ⓑ	ⓒ	ⓓ
20.	ⓐ	ⓑ	ⓒ	ⓓ
21.	ⓐ	ⓑ	ⓒ	ⓓ
22.	ⓐ	ⓑ	ⓒ	ⓓ
23.	ⓐ	ⓑ	ⓒ	ⓓ
24.	ⓐ	ⓑ	ⓒ	ⓓ
25.	ⓐ	ⓑ	ⓒ	ⓓ

Part 6: Electronics Information (EI)

1.	ⓐ	ⓑ	ⓒ	ⓓ
2.	ⓐ	ⓑ	ⓒ	ⓓ
3.	ⓐ	ⓑ	ⓒ	ⓓ
4.	ⓐ	ⓑ	ⓒ	ⓓ
5.	ⓐ	ⓑ	ⓒ	ⓓ
6.	ⓐ	ⓑ	ⓒ	ⓓ
7.	ⓐ	ⓑ	ⓒ	ⓓ

8.	ⓐ	ⓑ	ⓒ	ⓓ
9.	ⓐ	ⓑ	ⓒ	ⓓ
10.	ⓐ	ⓑ	ⓒ	ⓓ
11.	ⓐ	ⓑ	ⓒ	ⓓ
12.	ⓐ	ⓑ	ⓒ	ⓓ
13.	ⓐ	ⓑ	ⓒ	ⓓ
14.	ⓐ	ⓑ	ⓒ	ⓓ

15.	ⓐ	ⓑ	ⓒ	ⓓ
16.	ⓐ	ⓑ	ⓒ	ⓓ
17.	ⓐ	ⓑ	ⓒ	ⓓ
18.	ⓐ	ⓑ	ⓒ	ⓓ
19.	ⓐ	ⓑ	ⓒ	ⓓ
20.	ⓐ	ⓑ	ⓒ	ⓓ

Part 7: Auto and Shop Information (AS)

	a	b	c	d
1.	ⓐ	ⓑ	ⓒ	ⓓ
2.	ⓐ	ⓑ	ⓒ	ⓓ
3.	ⓐ	ⓑ	ⓒ	ⓓ
4.	ⓐ	ⓑ	ⓒ	ⓓ
5.	ⓐ	ⓑ	ⓒ	ⓓ
6.	ⓐ	ⓑ	ⓒ	ⓓ
7.	ⓐ	ⓑ	ⓒ	ⓓ
8.	ⓐ	ⓑ	ⓒ	ⓓ
9.	ⓐ	ⓑ	ⓒ	ⓓ

	a	b	c	d
10.	ⓐ	ⓑ	ⓒ	ⓓ
11.	ⓐ	ⓑ	ⓒ	ⓓ
12.	ⓐ	ⓑ	ⓒ	ⓓ
13.	ⓐ	ⓑ	ⓒ	ⓓ
14.	ⓐ	ⓑ	ⓒ	ⓓ
15.	ⓐ	ⓑ	ⓒ	ⓓ
16.	ⓐ	ⓑ	ⓒ	ⓓ
17.	ⓐ	ⓑ	ⓒ	ⓓ

	a	b	c	d
18.	ⓐ	ⓑ	ⓒ	ⓓ
19.	ⓐ	ⓑ	ⓒ	ⓓ
20.	ⓐ	ⓑ	ⓒ	ⓓ
21.	ⓐ	ⓑ	ⓒ	ⓓ
22.	ⓐ	ⓑ	ⓒ	ⓓ
23.	ⓐ	ⓑ	ⓒ	ⓓ
24.	ⓐ	ⓑ	ⓒ	ⓓ
25.	ⓐ	ⓑ	ⓒ	ⓓ

Part 8: Mechanical Comprehension (MC)

	a	b	c	d
1.	ⓐ	ⓑ	ⓒ	ⓓ
2.	ⓐ	ⓑ	ⓒ	ⓓ
3.	ⓐ	ⓑ	ⓒ	ⓓ
4.	ⓐ	ⓑ	ⓒ	ⓓ
5.	ⓐ	ⓑ	ⓒ	ⓓ
6.	ⓐ	ⓑ	ⓒ	ⓓ
7.	ⓐ	ⓑ	ⓒ	ⓓ
8.	ⓐ	ⓑ	ⓒ	ⓓ
9.	ⓐ	ⓑ	ⓒ	ⓓ

	a	b	c	d
10.	ⓐ	ⓑ	ⓒ	ⓓ
11.	ⓐ	ⓑ	ⓒ	ⓓ
12.	ⓐ	ⓑ	ⓒ	ⓓ
13.	ⓐ	ⓑ	ⓒ	ⓓ
14.	ⓐ	ⓑ	ⓒ	ⓓ
15.	ⓐ	ⓑ	ⓒ	ⓓ
16.	ⓐ	ⓑ	ⓒ	ⓓ
17.	ⓐ	ⓑ	ⓒ	ⓓ

	a	b	c	d
18.	ⓐ	ⓑ	ⓒ	ⓓ
19.	ⓐ	ⓑ	ⓒ	ⓓ
20.	ⓐ	ⓑ	ⓒ	ⓓ
21.	ⓐ	ⓑ	ⓒ	ⓓ
22.	ⓐ	ⓑ	ⓒ	ⓓ
23.	ⓐ	ⓑ	ⓒ	ⓓ
24.	ⓐ	ⓑ	ⓒ	ⓓ
25.	ⓐ	ⓑ	ⓒ	ⓓ

Part 9: Assembling Objects (AO)

	a	b	c	d
1.	ⓐ	ⓑ	ⓒ	ⓓ
2.	ⓐ	ⓑ	ⓒ	ⓓ
3.	ⓐ	ⓑ	ⓒ	ⓓ
4.	ⓐ	ⓑ	ⓒ	ⓓ
5.	ⓐ	ⓑ	ⓒ	ⓓ
6.	ⓐ	ⓑ	ⓒ	ⓓ
7.	ⓐ	ⓑ	ⓒ	ⓓ
8.	ⓐ	ⓑ	ⓒ	ⓓ
9.	ⓐ	ⓑ	ⓒ	ⓓ

	a	b	c	d
10.	ⓐ	ⓑ	ⓒ	ⓓ
11.	ⓐ	ⓑ	ⓒ	ⓓ
12.	ⓐ	ⓑ	ⓒ	ⓓ
13.	ⓐ	ⓑ	ⓒ	ⓓ
14.	ⓐ	ⓑ	ⓒ	ⓓ
15.	ⓐ	ⓑ	ⓒ	ⓓ
16.	ⓐ	ⓑ	ⓒ	ⓓ
17.	ⓐ	ⓑ	ⓒ	ⓓ

	a	b	c	d
18.	ⓐ	ⓑ	ⓒ	ⓓ
19.	ⓐ	ⓑ	ⓒ	ⓓ
20.	ⓐ	ⓑ	ⓒ	ⓓ
21.	ⓐ	ⓑ	ⓒ	ⓓ
22.	ⓐ	ⓑ	ⓒ	ⓓ
23.	ⓐ	ⓑ	ⓒ	ⓓ
24.	ⓐ	ⓑ	ⓒ	ⓓ
25.	ⓐ	ⓑ	ⓒ	ⓓ

Part 1: General Science

Time: 11 minutes

1. What is adipose tissue composed of?
   a. lipids
   b. amino acids
   c. white blood cells
   d. nucleotides

2. What is needed to balance the reaction
   $N_2 + ?H_2 \leftrightarrow 2NH_3$?
   a. 1
   b. 2
   c. 3
   d. 4

3. Fungi eating the nutrients of a dead plant is an example of
   a. decomposition.
   b. mutualism.
   c. commensalism.
   d. parasitism.

4. Which of the following equations is balanced?
   a. $Ag + Cl_2 \rightarrow 2AgCl$
   b. $2H_2O_2 \rightarrow 2H_2O + O_2$
   c. $KClO_3 \rightarrow KCl + O_2$
   d. $Na + H_2O \rightarrow NaOH + H_2$

5. An internal fan to blow out the excessive heat produced from operating a computer processor is an example of which process?
   a. convection
   b. conduction
   c. active transport
   d. radiation

6. A new solar system in the universe would form at the location of a
   a. supernova.
   b. nebula.
   c. white dwarf.
   d. neutron star.

7. What is the codon responsible for the third amino acid in the sequence represented in the genetic code UACUUCGCU?
   a. CUU
   b. GCU
   c. UUC
   d. UAC

8. For a certain carnation plant, R is the dominant allele for red flowers over r for white flowers. What explains that some plants have pink flowers?
   a. incomplete dominance
   b. mutation
   c. codominance
   d. heterozygous traits

9. What type of chemical equation is
   $2NH_3 \rightarrow N_2 + 3H_2$?
   a. combination reaction
   b. decomposition reaction
   c. single-displacement reaction
   d. double-displacement reaction

10. Which of the following does a cell use to transport amino acids within the cell to the site of protein synthesis?
    a. DNA
    b. rRNA
    c. mRNA
    d. tRNA

11. If the electron configuration of an element is written as $1s^2 2s^2 2px^2 2py^2 2pz^2 3s^1$, the element's atomic
   a. number is 11.
   b. number is 12.
   c. weight is 11.
   d. weight is 12.

12. The asteroid belt orbits between which two planets?
   a. Mars and Earth
   b. Jupiter and Saturn
   c. Saturn and Neptune
   d. Mars and Jupiter

13. A defect in an organism's alveoli would affect which process organ system?
   a. constant blood pressure by the circulatory system
   b. air exchange by the respiratory system
   c. nutrient absorption by the digestion system
   d. secretion of enzymes by the endocrine system

14. When moving down the first column of the periodic table, what can be expected of the elements' radii?
   a. The atomic radii increase.
   b. The atomic radii decrease.
   c. The atomic radii stay the same.
   d. The atomic radii increase and decrease.

15. The resulting single cell from an egg fertilized by sperm is called a(n)
   a. fetus.
   b. zygote.
   c. embryo.
   d. gamete.

16. If you wanted to change the state of the substance you are observing in an experiment from liquid to solid, what would you do?
   a. agitate the substance
   b. decrease its pressure
   c. increase its temperature
   d. increase its pressure

17. A flowering plant relies on fruit for which of the following?
   a. competition with other plants
   b. energy storage
   c. protection of the embryo
   d. pollination

18. What factor affects weather most?
   a. water content
   b. pressure at the Equator
   c. wind
   d. temperature differences

19. A red-tailed hawk is an example of
   a. a primary producer.
   b. a primary consumer.
   c. a secondary consumer.
   d. a migratory consumer.

20. Which of the following is NOT a form of potential energy?
   a. a ball at the top of a hill
   b. a battery powering a cell phone
   c. an apple in a tree
   d. a runner about to race

21. Which of the following electron configurations represents a halogen?
   a. $1s^2 2s^2 2p^4$
   b. $1s^2 2s^2 2p^5$
   c. $1s^2 2s^2 2p^6$
   d. $1s^2 2s^2 2p^6 3s^1$

22. Which of the following molecules has a double bond?

a. H_2O

b. O_3

c. NH_3

d. O_2

23. In an organism, the allele **X** is dominant over **x**. If one parent is homozygous dominant (**XX**) and the other is homozygous recessive (**xx**), what percentage of their offspring will express the recessive trait?

a. 0%

b. 25%

c. 50%

d. 100%

24. The rocky remains of an object from outer space that has collided with Earth are called

a. meteorites.

b. meteoroids.

c. meteors.

d. asteroids.

25. Which region of the spectrum represents radiation with the highest energy?

a. radio waves

b. gamma rays

c. microwave

d. X-rays

Part 2: Arithmetic Reasoning

Time: 36 minutes

1. For a science project, Stacy and Tina are measuring the length of two caterpillars. Stacy's caterpillar is 2.345 centimeters long. Tina's caterpillar is 0.0005 centimeter longer. How long is Tina's caterpillar?

a. 2.0345 centimeters

b. 2.3455 centimeters

c. 2.0345 centimeters

d. 2.845 centimeters

2. An elevator sign reads "Maximum weight 600 pounds." Which of the following may ride the elevator?

a. three people: one weighing 198 pounds, one weighing 185 pounds, one weighing 200 pounds

b. one person weighing 142 pounds with a load weighing 500 pounds

c. one person weighing 165 pounds with a load weighing 503 pounds

d. three people: one weighing 210 pounds, one weighing 101 pounds, one weighing 298 pounds

3. Laura saves at three times the rate Hazel does. If it takes Laura $1\frac{1}{2}$ years to save \$1,000, how many years will it take Hazel to save this amount?

a. 1

b. 3.5

c. 4.5

d. 6

4. On Wednesday morning, Yoder's Appliance Service had a balance of $2,354.82 in its checking account. If the bookkeeper wrote a total of $867.59 worth of checks that day, how much was left in the checking account?
   a. $1,487.23
   b. $1,487.33
   c. $1,496.23
   d. $1,587.33

5. At the city park, 32% of the trees are oaks. If there are 400 trees in the park, how many trees are NOT oaks?
   a. 128
   b. 272
   c. 278
   d. 312

6. Jake grew 0.6 inch during his senior year in high school. If he was 68.8 inches tall at the beginning of his senior year, how tall was he at the end of the year?
   a. 69.0 inches
   b. 69.2 inches
   c. 69.4 inches
   d. 74.8 inches

7. Phil and Alice went out to dinner and spent a total of $42.09. If they tipped the waiter $6.25 and the tip was included in their total bill, how much did their meal alone cost?
   a. $35.84
   b. $36.84
   c. $36.74
   d. $48.34

Answer question 8 on the basis of the following paragraph.

Basic cable television service, which includes 16 channels, costs $15 a month. The initial labor fee to install the service is $25. A $65 deposit is required but will be refunded within two years if the customer's bills are paid in full. Other cable services may be added to the basic service: The movie channels service is $9.40 a month; the news channels are $7.50 a month; the arts channels are $5.00 a month; and the sports channels are $4.80 a month.

8. A customer's first bill after having cable television installed totaled $110. This customer chose basic cable and one additional cable service. Which additional service was chosen?
   a. the news channels
   b. the movie channels
   c. the arts channels
   d. the sports channels

9. A loaf of bread has 35 slices. Ann eats eight slices, Betty eats six slices, Carl eats five slices, and Derrick eats nine slices. What fraction of the loaf is left?
   a. $\frac{2}{11}$
   b. $\frac{1}{9}$
   c. $\frac{2}{7}$
   d. $\frac{1}{5}$

10. The butcher at Al's Meat Market divided ground beef into eight packages. If each package weighs 0.75 pound and he has 0.04 pound of ground beef left over, how many pounds of ground beef did he start with?
   a. 5.064 pounds
   b. 5.64 pounds
   c. 6.04 pounds
   d. 6.4 pounds

11. While on a three-day vacation, the Wilsons spent the following amounts on motel rooms: $52.50, $47.99, and $49.32. What is the total amount they spent?
   a. $139.81
   b. $148.81
   c. $148.83
   d. $149.81

12. Dan rented two movies to watch last night. The first was 1 hour 40 minutes long, the second 1 hour 50 minutes long. How much time did it take for Dan to watch the two videos?
   a. 4.5 hours
   b. 3.5 hours
   c. 2.5 hours
   d. 1.5 hours

13. The Benton High School girls' relay team ran the mile in 6.32 minutes in April. By May, they were able to run the same race in 6.099 minutes. By how much time had their time improved?
   a. 0.221 minute
   b. 0.339 minute
   c. 0.467 minute
   d. 0.67 minute

14. If one pound of chicken costs $2.79 a pound, how much does 0.89 pound of chicken cost, rounded to the nearest cent?
   a. $2.40
   b. $2.48
   c. $2.68
   d. $4.72

15. In order to pass a certain exam, candidates must answer 70% of the test questions correctly. If there are 70 questions on the exam, how many questions must be answered correctly in order to pass?
   a. 49
   b. 52
   c. 56
   d. 60

16. Rashaard went fishing six days in the month of June. He caught eleven, four, zero, five, four, and six fish respectively. On the days that Rashaard fished, what was his average catch?
   a. 4
   b. 5
   c. 6
   d. 7

17. Ingrid has two pieces of balsa wood. Piece A is 0.724 centimeter thick. Piece B is 0.0076 centimeter thicker than Piece A. How thick is Piece B?
   a. 0.7164 centimeter
   b. 0.7316 centimeter
   c. 0.8 centimeter
   d. 0.08 centimeter

18. How many different meals can be ordered from a restaurant if there are three choices of soup, five choices of entrées, and two choices of dessert if a meal consists of a soup, entrée, and dessert?
   a. 10
   b. 15
   c. 30
   d. 60

19. If Nanette cuts a length of ribbon that is 13.5 inches long into four equal pieces, how long will each piece be?

   a. 3.3075 inches

   b. 3.375 inches

   c. 3.385 inches

   d. 3.3805 inches

20. Marty and Phyllis arrive late for a movie and miss 10% of it. The movie is 90 minutes long. How many minutes did they miss?

   a. 10 minutes

   b. 9 minutes

   c. 8 minutes

   d. 7 minutes

21. During an eight-hour workday, Bob spends two hours on the phone. What fraction of the day does he spend on the phone?

   a. $\frac{1}{5}$

   b. $\frac{1}{3}$

   c. $\frac{1}{4}$

   d. $\frac{1}{8}$

22. To reach his tree house, Raymond has to climb $9\frac{1}{3}$ feet up a rope ladder, then $8\frac{5}{6}$ feet up the tree trunk. How far does Raymond have to climb altogether?

   a. $17\frac{7}{12}$ feet

   b. $17\frac{1}{6}$ feet

   c. $18\frac{1}{6}$ feet

   d. $18\frac{1}{2}$ feet

23. About how many quarts of water will a 3.25-liter container hold? (one liter = 1.06 quarts)

   a. 3.066 quarts

   b. 3.045 quarts

   c. 3.445 quarts

   d. 5.2 quarts

24. How many $5\frac{1}{4}$-ounce glasses can be completely filled from a $33\frac{1}{2}$-ounce container of juice?

   a. 4

   b. 5

   c. 6

   d. 7

25. Lucille spent 12% of her weekly earnings on DVDs and deposited the rest into her savings account. If she spent $42 on DVDs, how much did she deposit into her savings account?

   a. $42

   b. $308

   c. $318

   d. $350

26. Millie is a night security guard at the art museum. Each night, she is required to walk through each gallery once. The museum contains 52 galleries. This night, Millie has walked through 16 galleries. What fraction of the total galleries has she already visited?

   a. $\frac{4}{13}$

   b. $\frac{1}{16}$

   c. $\frac{5}{11}$

   d. $\frac{3}{14}$

27. At age six, Zack weighed 40.6 pounds. By age seven, Zack weighed 46.1 pounds. How much weight did he gain in that one year?

   a. 4.5 pounds

   b. 5.5 pounds

   c. 5.7 pounds

   d. 6.5 pounds

28. Michael has a $20 bill and a $5 bill in his wallet and $1.29 in change in his pocket. If he buys a half gallon of ice cream that costs $4.89, how much money will he have left?

   a. $22.48

   b. $22.30

   c. $21.48

   d. $21.40

29. Land consisting of a quarter section is sold for $1,850 per acre (one quarter section = 160 acres). The total sale price is
a. $296,000.
b. $592,000.
c. $1,184,000.
d. $1,850,000.

30. Emilio is 1 year 7 months old, and Brooke is 2 years 8 months old. How much older is Brooke than Emilio?
a. 1 year 1 month
b. 2 years
c. 1 month
d. 1 year 2 months

Part 3: Word Knowledge

Time: 11 minutes

1. *Incredulous* most nearly means
a. faithful.
b. trustworthy.
c. skeptical.
d. incredible.

2. *Disabuse* most nearly means
a. heal.
b. correct.
c. harm.
d. praise.

3. *Laconic* most nearly means
a. lazy.
b. concise.
c. fleeting.
d. wordy.

4. *Spurious* most nearly means
a. genuine.
b. antique.
c. inauthentic.
d. sharp.

5. *Nadir* most nearly means
a. honor.
b. median.
c. peak.
d. bottom.

6. *Allay* most nearly means
a. soothe.
b. vary.
c. arrange.
d. postpone.

7. *Disingenuous* most nearly means
a. reliable.
b. insincere.
c. smart.
d. honest.

8. *Adversely* most nearly means
a. instantly.
b. mildly.
c. regularly.
d. negatively.

9. *Courtesy* most nearly means
a. civility.
b. congruity.
c. conviviality.
d. rudeness.

10. *Frail* most nearly means
a. vivid.
b. delicate.
c. robust.
d. adaptable.

11. *Recuperate* most nearly means
   a. mend.
   b. endorse.
   c. persist.
   d. worsen.

12. *Meager* most nearly means
   a. majestic.
   b. scarce.
   c. tranquil.
   d. adequate.

13. *Apathetic* most nearly means
   a. pitiable.
   b. indifferent.
   c. suspicious.
   d. evasive.

14. *Surreptitious* most nearly means
   a. expressive.
   b. secretive.
   c. emotional.
   d. gullible.

15. *Droll* most nearly means
   a. boring.
   b. slobbering.
   c. amusing.
   d. gullible.

16. *Commendable* most nearly means
   a. admirable.
   b. accountable.
   c. irresponsible.
   d. noticeable.

17. *Disperse* most nearly means
   a. gather.
   b. agree.
   c. scatter.
   d. vary.

18. *Domain* most nearly means
   a. entrance.
   b. rebellion.
   c. formation.
   d. territory.

19. *Ludicrous* most nearly means
   a. ridiculous.
   b. lecherous.
   c. loud.
   d. reasonable.

20. *Augment* most nearly means
   a. repeal.
   b. evaluate.
   c. increase.
   d. criticize.

21. *Archaic* most nearly means
   a. tangible.
   b. modern.
   c. ancient.
   d. haunted.

22. *Vindictive* most nearly means
   a. outrageous.
   b. insulting.
   c. spiteful.
   d. offensive.

23. *Orient* most nearly means
   a. confuse.
   b. arouse.
   c. deter.
   d. adjust.

24. *Expendable* most nearly means
   a. flexible.
   b. replaceable.
   c. expensive.
   d. extraneous.

25. *Revolutionize* most nearly means
   a. cancel.
   b. preserve.
   c. maintain.
   d. transform.

26. The dry modeling clay was no longer *malleable* after the young boys left it uncovered overnight.
   a. useful
   b. wet
   c. hardened
   d. shapeable

27. The tutoring Sheila received had a *salutary* effect on her grade point average.
   a. negligible
   b. welcoming
   c. beneficial
   d. negative

28. The *florid* ceiling of the palace contained a very colorful and detailed painting that was surrounded by gold leaf moldings.
   a. high
   b. ornate
   c. flat
   d. bare

29. Carl realized he had hit the jackpot when he opened his grandfather's safe deposit box and found a 1921 baseball card in *pristine* condition.
   a. worn
   b. untouched
   c. valuable
   d. fair

30. Running out of gas in the middle of the desert in August was an *abysmal* turn of events.
   a. terrible
   b. fortunate
   c. unexpected
   d. preventable

31. The CIA agent put herself in a very *precarious* situation by sneaking into the embassy.
   a. haphazard
   b. embarrassing
   c. dangerous
   d. comfortable

32. The minor earthquake left everything in my house *askew*.
   a. destroyed
   b. crooked
   c. untouched
   d. dirty

33. Matthew's sneakers were *sodden* after jumping in every puddle on the block.
   a. soaked
   b. dirty
   c. ruined
   d. cleaned

34. As a novice mountain climber, Maria wasn't prepared for the *precipitous* face of El Capitan.
   a. dangerous
   b. slippery
   c. steep
   d. level

35. The museum has a broad array of archeological displays from contemporary society to *primeval* artifacts from the age of the caveman.
   a. cursed
   b. ancient
   c. wrecked
   d. mysterious

Part 4: Paragraph Comprehension

Time: 13 minutes

The card game known as poker is an American tradition and has become immensely popular in recent years around the world. The modern version of the game was largely developed during the 1800s when the United States was expanding into the west, and it was played by pioneers and frontiersmen seeking some entertainment and human fellowship to relieve the hard *toil* of their daily lives.

Poker has also influenced our daily speech in many ways. Elements of the game have found their way into common phrases that form colorful ways of describing things. For example, people frequently speak of "calling a person's bluff," which refers to the act of forcing someone to prove that he's telling the truth—and this comes directly from the art of bluffing that forms the foundation of modern poker. A person will "up the ante" if he increases the amount of risk in an undertaking, similar to increasing the amount of one's bet. Other examples include *ace in the hole, ace up the sleeve, cash in,* and *poker face.* It's just a simple game, but it's had a big influence in American culture.

1. Which of the following would be the best title for this passage?
   a. Poker in Modern Times
   b. A History of Betting
   c. The Dangers of Gambling Addiction
   d. The Rules of Poker

2. The author of this passage most likely would agree that
   a. poker is an evil game.
   b. gambling is dangerous.
   c. poker has influenced modern culture.
   d. bluffing requires a straight face.

3. As used in the passage, *toil* most nearly means
   a. dirt.
   b. hard work.
   c. pioneering.
   d. something shiny.

4. The phrase *poker face* most likely means
   a. to look ugly.
   b. to be weary from playing cards too long.
   c. to up the ante.
   d. to hide one's emotions behind a blank expression.

In criminal cases, the availability of readable fingerprints is often critical in establishing evidence of a major crime. It is necessary, therefore, to follow proper procedures when taking fingerprints. In major cases, prints should be obtained from all persons who may have touched areas associated with a crime scene in order to *diminish* the number of suspects.

5. The main idea of the paragraph is that
   a. because fingerprints are so important in many cases, it is important to follow the correct course in taking them.
   b. all fingerprints found at a crime scene should be taken and thoroughly investigated.
   c. if the incorrect procedure is followed in gathering fingerprints, the ones taken may be useless.
   d. the first step in investigating fingerprints is to eliminate those of non-suspects.

6. The paragraph best supports the statement that
   a. no crimes can be solved without readable fingerprints.
   b. all persons who have touched an area in a crime scene are suspects.
   c. all fingerprints found at a crime scene are used in court as evidence.
   d. all persons who have touched a crime scene area should be fingerprinted.

7. As used in the passage, *diminish* most nearly means
   a. to make larger.
   b. to make smaller.
   c. a guilty person.
   d. an innocent person.

Tobacco is used in a variety of ways, including old-fashioned snuff, chewing tobacco, and tobacco for smoking. It is actually dried and crushed plant leaves that are grown widely throughout the world, but what distinguishes one tobacco from another is the way in which it is *cured*. The curing process determines what the tobacco will taste like, and that largely determines how it will be used.

Tobacco used in cigars, for example, is air cured, hung in odd-looking barns that have wide spaces between the exterior wall boards, which allows air to ventilate through. This process takes four to eight weeks, but it produces a light, sweet-tasting tobacco. Chewing tobacco is cured using *smoldering* fires that fill a barn with smoke. This process takes less time but also removes the natural sugars, making a tobacco that is less sweet. Tobacco used in cigarettes is cured by heat, but the fires are burned outside the barn rather than inside, and the hot air is circulated through the interior of the structure. This process is far more complicated, but it is fast and allows the tobacco to retain its natural sweetness.

8. Which of the following describes the author's attitude toward smoking in this passage?
   a. Smoking is a nasty habit and should be outlawed.
   b. Smoking is a harmless pastime.
   c. The author believes that people should be forbidden from smoking in public areas, but free to smoke at home.
   d. The author does not address the moral implications of smoking.

9. As used in the passage, *cured* most nearly means
   a. made well.
   b. medicated.
   c. mentholated.
   d. dried.

10. According to the passage, which type of tobacco is air cured?
   a. pipe
   b. cigar
   c. chewing
   d. cigarette

11. As used in the passage, *smoldering* most nearly means
   a. angry.
   b. low-burning.
   c. smelly.
   d. moldy.

In the summer, the Northern Hemisphere is slanted toward the Sun, making the days longer and warmer than in winter. The first day of summer, June 21, is called summer solstice and is also the longest day of the year. However, June 21 marks the beginning of winter in the Southern Hemisphere, when that hemisphere is tilted away from the Sun.

12. According to the passage, when it is summer in the Northern Hemisphere, it is _____ in the Southern Hemisphere.
   a. spring
   b. summer
   c. autumn
   d. winter

13. It can be inferred from the passage that, in the Southern Hemisphere, June 21 is the
   a. autumnal equinox.
   b. winter solstice.
   c. vernal equinox.
   d. summer solstice.

The competitive civil service system is designed to give candidates fair and equal treatment and to ensure that federal applicants are hired based on objective criteria. Hiring has to be based solely on a candidate's knowledge, skills, and abilities (which you'll sometimes see abbreviated as *ksa*), and not on external factors such as race, religion, sex, and so on. Whereas employers in the private sector can hire employees for subjective reasons, federal employers must be able to justify their decision with objective evidence that the candidate is qualified.

14. The paragraph best supports the statement that
  a. hiring in the private sector is inherently unfair.
  b. *ksa* is not as important as test scores to federal employers.
  c. federal hiring practices are simpler than those employed by the private sector.
  d. the civil service strives to hire on the basis of a candidate's abilities.

15. The federal government's practice of hiring on the basis of *ksa* frequently results in the hiring of employees
  a. based on race, religion, sex, and so forth.
  b. who are unqualified for the job.
  c. who are qualified for the job.
  d. on the basis of subjective judgment.

Part 5: Mathematics Knowledge

Time: 24 minutes

1. Which of these equations is incorrect?
  a. $\sqrt{16} + \sqrt{3} = \sqrt{16+3}$
  b. $\sqrt{6} + \sqrt{12} = \sqrt{6+12}$
  c. Neither is incorrect.
  d. Both are incorrect.

2. Sixteen less than six times a number is 20. What is the number?
  a. 12
  b. 10
  c. 8
  d. 6

3. The most ergonomically correct angle between the keyboard and the screen of a laptop computer is 100°. This is called
  a. an acute angle.
  b. a complimentary angle.
  c. an obtuse angle.
  d. a right angle.

4. Which of these angle measures form a right triangle?
  a. 40°, 40°, 100°
  b. 20°, 30°, 130°
  c. 40°, 40°, 40°
  d. 40°, 50°, 90°

5. Evaluate the following expression if $a = 3$, $b = 4$, and $c = -2$: $(ab - ac) \div abc$.
  a. $-\frac{7}{8}$
  b. $-\frac{3}{4}$
  c. $-\frac{1}{4}$
  d. $\frac{1}{4}$

6. Which value of a will make this number sentence false? $a \leq 5$
  a. 0
  b. −3
  c. 5
  d. 6

7. Change this mixed number to an improper fraction: $5\frac{1}{2}$.
  a. $\frac{11}{2}$
  b. $\frac{5}{1}$
  c. $\frac{7}{2}$
  d. $\frac{5}{2}$

8. Which of the following choices is equivalent to 2^5?

   a. 7

   b. 10

   c. 16

   d. 32

9. Which of the following is equivalent to $2y^2$?

   a. $2(y + y)$

   b. $2y(y)$

   c. $y^2 + 2$

   d. $y + y + y + y$

10. If $\frac{2}{x} + \frac{x}{6} = 4$, what is x?

   a. $\frac{1}{24}$

   b. $\frac{1}{6}$

   c. 3

   d. 6

11. What is the value of $16^{1/2}$?

   a. 2

   b. 4

   c. 8

   d. 32

12. What is the smallest prime number?

   a. 0

   b. 1

   c. 2

   d. 3

13. If $5a + 50 = 150$, then a is

   a. 10

   b. 20

   c. 30

   d. 40

14. If the following figure is a regular decagon with a center at Q, what is the measure of the indicated angle?

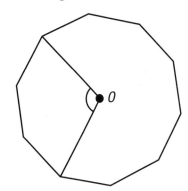

   a. 45°

   b. 80°

   c. 90°

   d. 108°

15. Which of the following choices is divisible by both 7 and 8?

   a. 42

   b. 78

   c. 112

   d. 128

16. Which of the following is a simplification of $(x^2 + 4x + 4) \div (x + 2)$?

   a. $x - 2$

   b. $x + 4$

   c. $x^2 + 3x + 2$

   d. $x + 2$

17. If $\frac{x}{72} = 2$, then x is

   a. 9

   b. 36

   c. 144

   d. 72

18. The area of a rectangular table is 72 square inches. The longer sides are 12 inches long. What is the width?
  a. 5 inches
  b. 6 inches
  c. 7 inches
  d. 8 inches

19. A triangle has sides that are consecutive even integers. The perimeter of the triangle is 24 inches. What is the length of the shortest side?
  a. 10 inches
  b. 8 inches
  c. 6 inches
  d. 4 inches

20. The tens digit is four times the ones digit in a certain number. If the sum of the digits is 10, what is the number?
  a. 93
  b. 82
  c. 41
  d. 28

21. $\frac{x}{4} + \frac{3x}{4} =$
  a. $\frac{1}{2}x$
  b. $\frac{x^3}{4}$
  c. 1
  d. x

22. Two angles are supplementary. One measures 84°. What does its supplement measure?
  a. 90°
  b. 276°
  c. 6°
  d. 96°

23. What lines must be parallel in the following diagram?

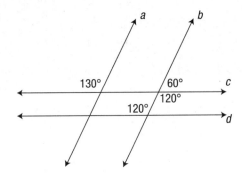

  a. a and b
  b. a and d
  c. b and c
  d. c and d

24. What is the value of 56,515 ÷ 4, rounded to the nearest whole number?
  a. 10,000
  b. 14,000
  c. 14,128
  d. 14,129

25. Five oranges, when removed from a basket containing three more than seven times as many oranges, leaves how many in the basket?
  a. 21
  b. 28
  c. 33
  d. 38

Part 6: Electronics Information

Time: 9 minutes

1. A circuit breadboard is used
  a. to easily build and break down circuits.
  b. to solder parts together.
  c. to prepare all the parts of a circuit.
  d. to build permanent circuits.

2. Why is flux used with electronic soldering?
   a. to prevent the formation of oxides
   b. to facilitate the flow of solder onto an electronic connection
   c. to enhance the fusing of the solder as it cools
   d. none of the above

3. A cold solder joint is
   a. brittle and weaker than a hot solder joint.
   b. not good at conducting electricity.
   c. both **a** and **b**
   d. neither **a** nor **b**

4. "Wire wrapping" is
   a. used only in large electronic arrays.
   b. a means of identifying electronic parts.
   c. a means of assembling electronics.
   d. used as an emergency repair.

5. What does the following schematic symbol represent?

   a. a speaker
   b. a thermostat
   c. a piezoelectric buzzer
   d. a microphone

6. What does a multimeter measure?
   a. voltage
   b. current
   c. resistance
   d. all the above

7. What does the abbreviation "mA" mean in relation to amperes?
   a. microamps
   b. multiamps
   c. milliamps
   d. none of the above

8. What does the following schematic symbol represent?

   a. a waveguide
   b. an open circuit
   c. a multimeter
   d. an oscilloscope

9. What does the following schematic symbol represent?

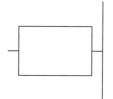

   a. an unspecified output
   b. a shielded jack
   c. a jack and plug
   d. an unspecified component

10. An oscilloscope is a useful tool for
   a. displaying how signal voltage varies over time.
   b. calculating ohms based on voltage detected.
   c. measuring amperage.
   d. testing the current to confirm AC or DC.

11. The two most important features of an oscilloscope are
   a. resolution and digital storage.
   b. delayed sweep and digital storage.
   c. bandwidth and resolution.
   d. bandwidth and delayed sweep.

12. What function does the inductor perform in the circuit diagram?

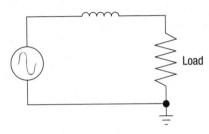

a. band stop filter
b. band pass filter
c. low pass filter
d. high pass filter

13. What is the biggest advantage of fiber optic data lines over coaxial or conventional data transmission lines?
a. Fiber optic lines carry more data.
b. Fiber optic lines are easier to configure and use.
c. Fiber optic lines cost less.
d. Fiber optic lines are more robust than conventional lines.

14. When building a simple series circuit, which of the following should always be connected last?
a. the capacitor
b. the fixed resistor
c. the potentiometer
d. the power

15. A potentiometer is commonly used to
a. control power input to a transformer.
b. provide power to lamps.
c. control volume in audio equipment.
d. provide power to televisions.

16. A difference between high definition television (HDTV) and standard definition television (SDTV) is
a. SDTV is in black and white, whereas HDTV is in color.
b. HDTV raster has more lines than SDTV raster.
c. SDTV is transmitted by cable whereas HDTV is transmitted by satellite.
d. HDTV requires fiber optic cable whereas SDTV does not.

17. In electronics, CRT stands for
a. cathode ray tube.
b. capacitor reduction tool.
c. current refinement tool.
d. coulomb relay trend.

18. What does the following schematic symbol represent?

a. an antenna
b. a semiconductor
c. a chassis ground
d. an earth ground

19. An example of an output transducer would be a(n)
a. lamp.
b. loudspeaker.
c. light-emitting diode (LED).
d. all the above

20. What type of electronic memory can be accessed but not changed?
a. diode memory
b. bipolar memory
c. read only memory (ROM)
d. random access memory (RAM)

Part 7:
Auto and Shop Information

Time: 11 minutes

1. A higher viscosity rating for a given oil signifies that
   a. the oil is thicker.
   b. the oil is thinner.
   c. the oil is better in winter.
   d. the oil will last longer in the engine environment.

2. Which of the following items is part of the braking system in an automobile?
   a. hydraulic fluid
   b. electrolyte
   c. antifreeze
   d. high-viscosity oil

3. Which of the following items is part of the air-conditioning system in an automobile?
   a. the condenser
   b. the compressor
   c. the evaporator
   d. all the above

4. Which of the following items is part of the electrical system in an automobile?
   a. fuses
   b. a distributor cap
   c. an alternator
   d. all the above

5. Which of the following items is part of the engine start system in an automobile?
   a. the ignition coil
   b. the oil pump
   c. the catalytic converter
   d. the thermometer

6. Where does combustion occur in an internal combustion engine?
   a. in the oil pan
   b. in the fuel bladders
   c. in the cylinders
   d. in the carburetor

7. The four cycles of an internal compression engine in proper order are
   a. intake, compression, ignition, exhaust.
   b. compression, intake, power, exhaust.
   c. intake, power, compression, exhaust.
   d. intake, compression, power, exhaust.

8. In which of the internal combustion engine cycles does the spark plug fire?
   a. the intake cycle
   b. the compression cycle
   c. the power cycle
   d. the exhaust cycle

9. What must happen for the exhaust cycle to complete?
   a. The power cycle is initiated.
   b. Both the exhaust valve and the intake valves are closed.
   c. The exhaust valve opens and the intake valve is open.
   d. The exhaust valve opens and the intake valve is closed.

10. In a conventional camshaft engine, the camshaft pushes on which of the following?
    a. the rocker arm
    b. the solenoid
    c. the camshaft lobe
    d. none of the above

11. Blue smoke in an automobile exhaust indicates
    a. the water pump is failing.
    b. wear of the rings and/or cylinders.
    c. the radiator needs attention.
    d. the catalytic converter needs replacing.

12. An internal combustion engine needs what three basic items in order to operate properly?
   a. fuel, oxygen, and oil
   b. fire, fuel, and transmission fluid
   c. fire, fuel, and oxygen
   d. coolant, fuel, and oxygen

13. Approximately what percent of the energy in gasoline is converted to energy to drive the car?
   a. 10%
   b. 15%
   c. 30%
   d. 50%

14. Which of the following tools is an Allen wrench?
   a.

   b.

   c.

   d.

15. Which of the following would you use with a slotted head screw driver?
   a.

   b.

   c.

   d.

16. Which hand tool listed here is used to tighten a nut and bolt?
   a. a crescent wrench
   b. a reamer
   c. calipers
   d. pipe clamps

17. What gauge is used to determine the number of threads per inch on a standard screw?
   a. a depth gauge
   b. a wire gauge
   c. a thickness gauge
   d. a thread gauge

18. Which of the following items is used to measure angles?

    a. a protractor

    b. a level

    c. a tachometer

    d. a gear

19. Which of the following woodworking objects would most likely be created with a lathe?

    a. a bench slat

    b. a baseball bat

    c. a bookshelf

    d. a chair seat

20. The tool shown here should only be used to

    a. cut copper pipe.

    b. put a finished surface on lumber.

    c. cut, grind, or polish metal.

    d. cut rabbet joints.

21. The part of a drill bit that is grabbed and held by the drill chuck is called the

    a. root.

    b. trunk.

    c. stem.

    d. shank.

22. One of the drawbacks in using steel with outdoor construction is

    a. the need to paint and treat the steel.

    b. its inability to flex in cold weather.

    c. its rigidity during warm weather.

    d. the need to use rivets to join pieces together.

23. What is the tool shown here?

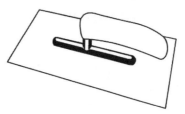

    a. a level

    b. a trowel

    c. a bench plane

    d. a mortar brush

24. What is the tool shown here?

    a. a pipe wrench

    b. a pipe threader

    c. an Allen wrench

    d. a pipe cutter

25. The tool shown here would be used to

    a. apply adhesive by melting glue sticks.

    b. drive small brads or nails into wood.

    c. melt solder to join pieces of material.

    d. attach pop rivets to join pieces of material.

Part 8:
Mechanical Comprehension

Time: 19 minutes

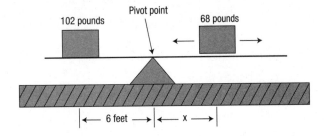

1. In the diagram, Vartan wants to balance two blocks on either side of a lever. One block weighs 102 pounds and the other weighs 68 pounds. If the 102-pound block is 6 feet to the left of the pivot point, how far to the right of the pivot point should the 68-pound block be placed?

   a. 12 feet

   b. 6 feet

   c. 4 feet

   d. 9 feet

2. Two ramps can be used to raise a heavy barrel up to a platform. Neglecting friction, which ramp requires less force to raise the barrel?

   a. ramp A

   b. ramp B

   c. It requires the same amount of work.

   d. It is impossible to determine.

3. If a pulley is attached to the top of a flagpole, what is the mechanical advantage of using the pulley to raise a flag up the pole?

   a. 1

   b. 2

   c. 3

   d. 4

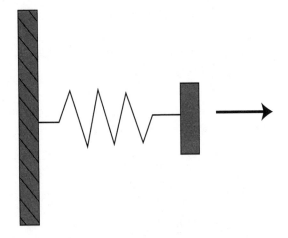

4. A force of 4 pounds is required to move a spring 6 inches. How far will the spring stretch under 6 pounds of force?

   a. 6 inches

   b. 9 inches

   c. 12 inches

   d. 15 inches

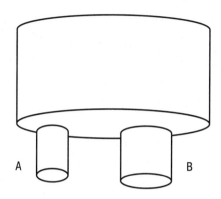

5. Two pipes are used to drain liquid from a 100-gallon barrel. Pipe A is 2 inches in diameter and pipe B is 4 inches in diameter. How much faster does liquid leave the barrel through pipe B compared to pipe A?
   a. Liquid leaves both pipes at the same rate.
   b. Liquid flows out of pipe B twice as fast.
   c. Liquid flows out of pipe B four times as fast.
   d. Liquid flows out of pipe B eight times as fast.

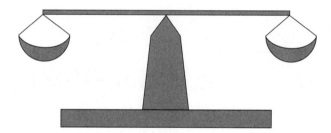

6. The type of scale shown in the diagram is based on what simple machine?
   a. the lever
   b. the pulley
   c. the inclined plane
   d. the screw

7. Steel battleships are able to float because
   a. steel is less dense than water.
   b. steel is denser than water.
   c. the ship displaces its weight in water.
   d. the ship displaces less than its weight in water.

8. If 9 full turns are required to move the nut 0.75 inches, how many threads per inch does the screw have?
   a. 10
   b. 12
   c. 14
   d. 16

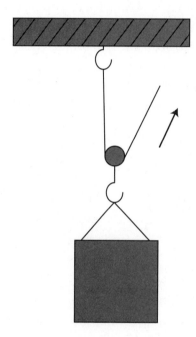

9. What is the mechanical advantage of the pulley system shown here?
   a. 1
   b. 2
   c. 3
   d. 4

10. A cold beverage will stay cold longest in which of the following containers?
   a. a glass bottle
   b. an aluminum can
   c. a plastic bottle
   d. a paper cup

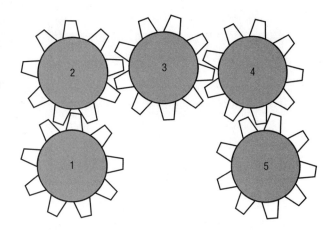

11. If gear 3 turns counterclockwise, which other gear(s), if any, will turn clockwise?
   a. 1 and 5
   b. 2 and 4
   c. All will turn clockwise.
   d. None will turn clockwise.

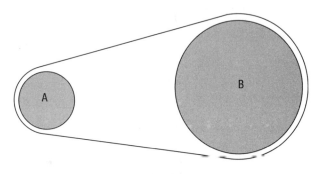

12. Pulley B has four times the circumference of pulley A. If pulley A rotates at 60 revolutions per minute (rpm), how fast must pulley B rotate?
   a. 15 rpm
   b. 30 rpm
   c. 60 rpm
   d. 240 rpm

13. An object is most likely to slide the farthest on which surface?
   a. ice
   b. wood
   c. dirt
   d. rubber

14. A single-speed bicycle has a front chain ring with 54 teeth. The back gear has 12 teeth. If the bicycle is pedaled at 90 rpm, how fast does the rear wheel rotate?
   a. 90 rpm
   b. 180 rpm
   c. 405 rpm
   d. 500 rpm

15. A balloon is filled with helium. It is then taken to a special room where the air pressure is decreased. What will happen to the balloon?
   a. Its size will increase.
   b. Its size will decrease.
   c. Its size will stay the same.
   d. It will begin to sink.

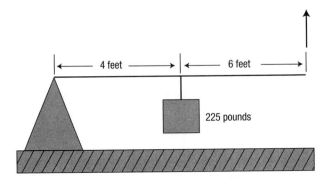

16. In the diagram, Daniel wants to lift a 225-pound block using a lever. If the block is 4 feet from the pivot point and Daniel is 6 feet beyond that, how much force must he apply to lift the block?
   a. 100 pounds
   b. 24 pounds
   c. 90 pounds
   d. 225 pounds

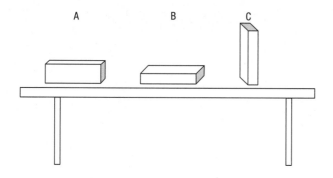

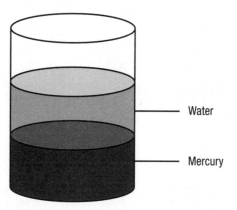

17. Three identical objects are placed on a table in different orientations. Which orientation is most stable?

a. orientation A

b. orientation B

c. orientation C

d. A and C are equally the most stable.

18. A rock is shown to have a density of 10 g/cm³. It is then cut precisely in half. What is the density of the two pieces?

a. 5 g/cm³

b. 8 g/cm³

c. 10 g/cm³

d. 20 g/cm³

20. A lead plug is dropped into a beaker containing mercury and water. Mercury is a liquid with a density of 8 g/cm³ and water has a density of 1 g/cm³. If the plug has a density of 10 g/cm³, where will it settle in the beaker?

a. at the bottom of the beaker

b. in the middle of the mercury layer

c. in between the mercury and water layers

d. on top of the water layer

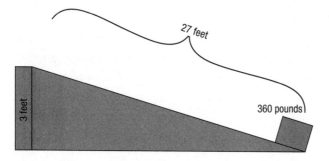

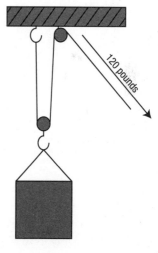

19. A 360-pound block is being pulled up an incline by a pulley. The incline is 27 feet long and rises 3 feet. Neglecting friction, how much force is necessary to move the block up the incline?

a. 81 pounds

b. 360 pounds

c. 387 pounds

d. 40 pounds

21. Keiko is strong enough to pull a rope with 120 pounds of force. Using the pulley system shown here, what is the maximum weight she can lift?

a. 480 pounds

b. 360 pounds

c. 240 pounds

d. 120 pounds

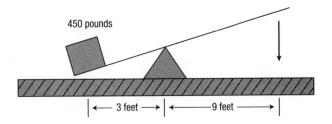

22. In the diagram, Robert wants to lift a 450-pound block using a lever. If the block is 3 feet from the pivot point and Robert is 9 feet from the pivot point, how much force must he apply to lift the block?
   a. 450 pounds
   b. 27 pounds
   c. 150 pounds
   d. 462 pounds

23. Two men are leave checkpoint 1 at the same time in the same direction. One travels at 25 mph and the other at 15 mph. How far apart are they after one hour?
   a. 5 miles
   b. 10 miles
   c. 25 miles
   d. 40 miles

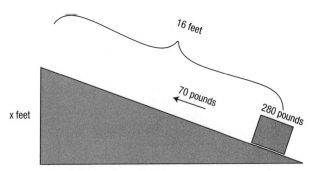

24. A 280-pound block is being pulled up an incline by a pulley. The incline is 16 feet long. Neglecting friction, if 70 pounds of force is necessary to move the block up the incline, how tall is the incline?
   a. 4 feet
   b. 8 feet
   c. 16 feet
   d. 2.5 feet

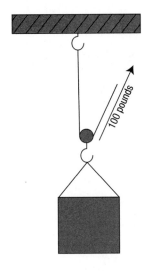

25. Maria is strong enough pull a rope with 100 pounds of force. Using the pulley system shown here, what is the maximum weight she can lift?
   a. 50 pounds
   b. 100 pounds
   c. 150 pounds
   d. 200 pounds

Part 9: Assembling Objects

Time: 15 minutes

Each question is composed of five separate drawings. The problem is presented in the first drawing, and the remaining four drawings are possible solutions. Determine which of the four choices contains all of the pieces assembled properly that are shown in the first picture. Note: images are not drawn to scale.

1.

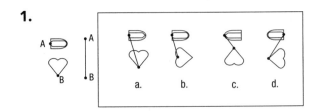

2.
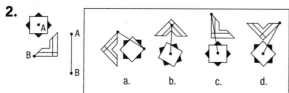
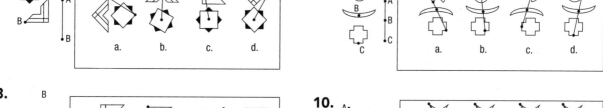

a.   b.   c.   d.

9.

a.   b.   c.   d.

3.
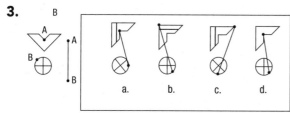

a.   b.   c.   d.

10.
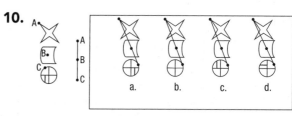

a.   b.   c.   d.

4.
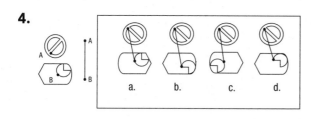

a.   b.   c.   d.

11.
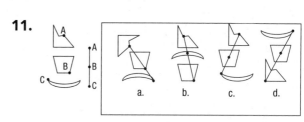

a.   b.   c.   d.

5.
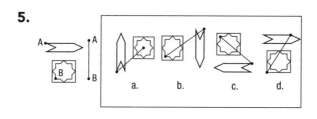

a.   b.   c.   d.

12.
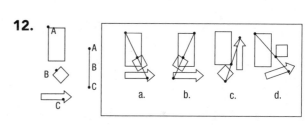

a.   b.   c.   d.

6.
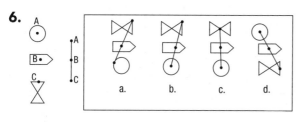

a.   b.   c.   d.

13.
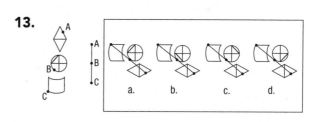

a.   b.   c.   d.

7.
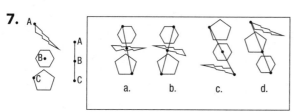

a.   b.   c.   d.

14.
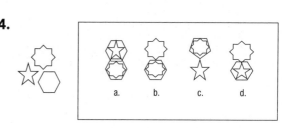

a.   b.   c.   d.

8.
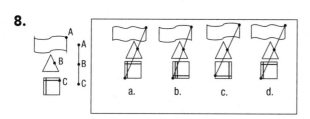

a.   b.   c.   d.

15.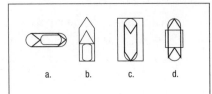

      a.   b.   c.   d.

22.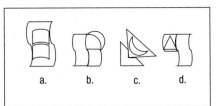

      a.   b.   c.   d.

16.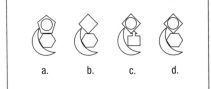

      a.   b.   c.   d.

23.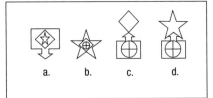

      a.   b.   c.   d.

17.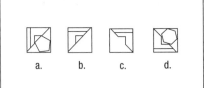

      a.   b.   c.   d.

24.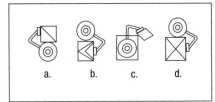

      a.   b.   c.   d.

18.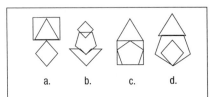

      a.   b.   c.   d.

25.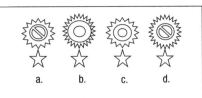

      a.   b.   c.   d.

19.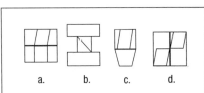

      a.   b.   c.   d.

20.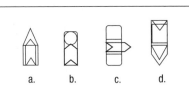

      a.   b.   c.   d.

21.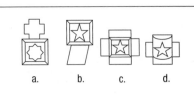

      a.   b.   c.   d.

Answers

Part 1: General Science

1. a. Adipose tissue is the connective tissue otherwise known as fat. Adipose is made up of lipids, also referred to as fatty acids or triglycerides.

2. c. The same number of elements must be on both sides of the equation. For example, there are two nitrogen elements on the reactant and product sides of the reaction in the question. There are six hydrogen elements in the products, so six hydrogens are needed on the reactant side. Because hydrogen is present as H_2, three molecules are needed.

3. a. Fungi are decomposers that return nutrients into soil by breaking down nutrients from decaying organic matter. Fungi rely on dead organisms for nutrients, like the dead plant, but this is not a form of symbiosis, which is considered a relationship between living organisms. Choices **b** through **d** are examples of symbiosis.

4. b. When balancing chemical equations, make sure the number of each element is balanced on each side. For example, choice **b** has 4 hydrogen atoms and 4 oxygen atoms on each side of the equation.

5. a. The transport of heat energy by movement of a fluid, in this case air, is convection.

6. b. The first stage of a star similar to the Sun is in the form of a nebula, a cloud of dust, hydrogen, and plasma.

7. b. Genetic code is broken down into codons of three base-pairs. It is helpful to separate the codons as follows: UAC UUC GCU.

8. a. When two traits appear to blend, one is not completely dominant over the other. This is referred to as incomplete dominance.

9. b. A decomposition reaction is when a molecule is broken down into its component elements.

10. c. tRNA is responsible for delivering amino acids to the ribosome according to the sequence on mRNA.

11. a. The electron configuration given has 11 electrons, which corresponds to 11 protons in the nucleus. Therefore, the atomic number is 11 and the atomic weight would be determined by the sum of the number of protons and neutrons in the nucleus, which is not given.

12. d. The asteroid belt of the solar system orbits between Mars and Jupiter.

13. b. Alveoli are found in the lungs and are the site of oxygen and carbon dioxide exchange.

14. a. Moving down a column of the periodic table the elements have more electrons in their valence shells, hence the atomic radii are expected to increase.

15. b. After sexual reproduction leads to fertilization, the first stage of development is a single cell zygote. Choices **a** and **c** are later stages in development; the zygote becomes an embryo, which becomes a fetus.

16. d. Pressure and temperature affect the state of substances. To move from liquid to solid, the pressure needs to be increased or its temperature decreased.

17. c. The fruit of a tree is formed after pollination and serves to protect the resulting embryo.

18. d. Temperature differences from incoming solar energy and ocean currents largely affect weather. Temperature differences lead to pressure differences, wind, and precipitation.

19. c. Red-tailed hawks typically eat other animals (primary consumers) for energy, making them secondary consumers. Primary consumers get their energy by eating producers, plants that make their own energy.

20. b. Potential energy is the amount of energy to do work, but not the process of doing work. Choice **b** is a form of electrical energy.

21. b. Halogens are the elements in group 7A, the first family to the left of the noble gases. They all share the valence electron configuration of p^5.

22. d. The only molecule in this list that has a double bond is O_2. Choice **a** has two single bonds, choice **b** has a triple bond, and choice **c** has three single bonds.

23. a. The homozygous dominant parent has a genotype of **XX**, and will always give **X** to its offspring. The homozygous recessive parent has a genotype of **xx**, and will always give **x** to its offspring. Therefore, all the offspring will have the genotype **Xx** and the chance of offspring expressing the recessive trait is 0%.

24. a. Meteorites are the remains of meteors that have survived the entry into the Earth's atmosphere.

25. b. Energy of electromagnetic radiation is proportional to the frequency of its waves. Therefore, the radiation with the most energy has the largest frequency. Radio waves and microwaves have the smallest frequency and X-rays and gamma rays have the largest, with gamma rays being the larger of the two.

Part 2: Arithmetic Reasoning

1. b. This is an addition problem. Arrange the numbers in a column so that the decimal points are aligned: $2.345 + 0.0005 = 2.3455$.

2. a. To arrive at the answer quickly, begin by rounding off the numbers, and you will see that choice **a** is less than 600 pounds, whereas choices **b**, **c**, and **d** are all more than 600 pounds.

3. c. The problem is to find H, the number of years Hazel will take to save $1,000. You are told Laura saves three times faster than Hazel, a ratio of 3:1. Therefore, 3L = H. You are given L = 1.5 years. Substitute: 3(1.5) = H, or H = 4.5 years.

4. a. This is a basic subtraction problem. Line up the decimals and subtract: $2,354.82 - 867.59 = 1,487.23$.

5. b. This is a two-step problem. First, determine what percent of the trees are not oaks by subtracting: 100% − 32% = 68%. Change 68% to a decimal and multiply: $0.68 \times 400 = 272$.

6. c. This is a basic addition problem. Be sure to align the decimal points before you add $68.8 + 0.6 = 69.4$.

7. a. This is a simple subtraction problem: $\$42.09 - \$6.25 = \$35.84$.

8. c. The labor fee ($25) plus the deposit ($65) plus the basic service ($15) equals $105. The difference between the total bill, $110, and $105 is $5.00, the cost of the arts channels.

9. d. Since 28 of the 35 slices have been eaten, there are 35 − 28 = 7 slices left. This means $\frac{7}{35}$, or $\frac{1}{5}$ of the loaf is left.

10. c. This is a two-step problem. First, multiply to determine how many pounds of beef were contained in the eight packages: $0.75 \times 8 = 6$. Then add: $6 + 0.04 = 6.04$.

11. d. This is an addition problem. To add these three decimals, line them up in a column so that their decimal points are aligned: $52.50 + 47.99 + 49.32 = 149.81$. Move the decimal point directly down into the answer.

12. b. Change the hours to minutes: 1 hour 40 minutes = 100 minutes; 1 hour 50 minutes = 110 minutes. Now add: 100 minutes + 110 minutes = 210 minutes. Now change back to hours and minutes: 210 minutes ÷ 60 minutes = 3.5 hours.

13. a. This is a subtraction problem. Be sure to align the decimal points: $6.32 - 6.099 = 0.221$.

14. b. This is a multiplication problem. First, multiply 279 by 89. Then, because there are four decimal places, count off four places from the right. Your answer should be 2.4831. Because the 3 in the thousandths place is less than 5, round to 2.48.

15. a. First, change 70% to a decimal, which is 0.7. Then multiply: $70 \times 0.7 = 49$.

16. b. The average is the sum divided by the number of observations: $(11 + 4 + 0 + 5 + 4 + 6) \div 6 = 5$.

17. b. This is an addition problem. Be sure the decimal points are aligned before you add: $0.724 + 0.0076 = 0.7316$.

18. c. The counting principle shows the number of ways an event can occur and tells you to take the total choices for each item and multiply them together: $3 \times 5 \times 2 = 30$.

19. b. This is a division problem: $13.5 \div 4 = 3.375$. Move the decimal straight up into the quotient.

20. b. Set up the problem this way: $\frac{x}{90} = \frac{10}{100}$. If you're getting good at percentages, you may just see the answer, but if you don't, cross multiply: $10 \times 90 = 100x$. Solve: $x = 9$.

21. c. Change the information into a fraction: $\frac{2}{8}$. Now, reduce the fraction: $\frac{1}{4}$.

22. c. First, find the least common denominator of the fractions, which is 6. Then add: $9\frac{2}{6} + 8\frac{5}{6} = 17\frac{7}{6}$, or $18\frac{1}{6}$.

23. c. This is a multiplication problem. Multiply 3.25 times 1.06. Be sure to count four decimal places from the right: $3.25 \times 1.06 = 3.445$.

24. c. This is a division problem with mixed numbers. First, convert the mixed numbers to fractions: $33\frac{1}{2} = \frac{67}{2}$ and $5\frac{1}{4} = \frac{21}{4}$. Next, invert the second fraction and multiply: $\frac{67}{2} \times \frac{4}{21} = \frac{134}{21}$. Reduce to a mixed number: $\frac{134}{21} = 6\frac{8}{21}$. With this result, you know that only six glasses can be completely filled.

25. b. First, ask the question: "$42 is 12% of what number?" Change the percent to a decimal and divide $42 by 0.12. This is equal to $350, which represents the total weekly earnings. Now subtract the amount she spent on DVDs from $350: $350 − $42 = $308. She deposited $308 into her savings account.

26. a. Millie has completed $\frac{16}{52}$, or $\frac{4}{13}$, of the total galleries.

27. b. This is a simple subtraction problem. Line up the decimals and subtract: $46.1 - 40.6 = 5.5$.

28. d. This problem involves two steps: addition and subtraction. Add to determine the amount of money Michael has: $20.00 + $5.00 + $1.29 = $26.29. Then, subtract the amount spent for the ice cream: $26.29 − $4.89 = $21.40.

29. a. This is a multiplication problem. A quarter section contains 160 acres, so you must multiply: $160 \times \$1,850 = \$296,000$.

30. a. Subtract the months first, then the years. Remember that it is best to write the problem in columns and subtract the right-most column (months) first, then the left-most column (years): 8 months – 7 months = 1 month; 2 years – 1 year = 1 year. So, Brook is 1 year 1 month older than Emilio.

Part 3: Word Knowledge

1. c. *Incredulous* means showing disbelief, or skeptical.

2. b. To *disabuse* someone means to free from error or deception.

3. b. *Laconic* means using few words, or concise.

4. c. Something that is *spurious* is not genuine or authentic.

5. d. *Nadir* means lowest point, or bottom.

6. a. *Allay* means to relieve or soothe.

7. b. *Disingenuous* means to lack candor, candidness, or sincerity.

8. d. *Adversely* means unfavorably, harmfully, or negatively.

9. a. A *courtesy* implies being courteous or mannerly; it is civility.

10. b. A *frail* person is weak and delicate.

11. a. *Recuperate* means to heal; to mend.

12. b. *Meager* and scarce both mean lacking.

13. b. To be *apathetic* is to show little emotion or interest; to be indifferent is to have no particular interest or concern.

14. b. *Surreptitious* is acting in a stealthy or secretive manner.

15. c. *Droll* means oddly humorous or amusing.

16. a. Both *commendable* and admirable mean worthy, qualified, or desirable.

17. c. *Disperse* means to spread, disseminate, or scatter.

18. d. A *domain* is an area governed by a ruler; a territory is an area for which someone is responsible.

19. a. Both *ludicrous* and ridiculous mean absurd or outrageous.

20. c. To *augment* means to increase or expand in size or extent.

21. c. Something *archaic* is marked by characteristics from an earlier period.

22. c. To be *vindictive* is to be vengeful; to be spiteful means to be malicious.

23. d. To *orient* something means to direct or set in position.

24. b. Something that is *expendable* is unnecessary, disposable, or replaceable.

25. d. To *revolutionize* means to radically change or improve something; to transform means to change the appearance or form of something.

26. d. *Malleable* means easily molded, controlled, or pressed into shape. If clay were left overnight uncovered, it would harden, and could no longer be molded.

27. c. *Salutary* means having or producing a beneficial effect. Tutoring would have such an effect on one's grades.

28. b. *Florid* means elaborate or ornate. That is essentially how one would describe a painted ceiling with gold leaf molding.

29. b. *Pristine* means in its original and unspoiled condition. A card in perfect condition would explain why it is a "jackpot."

30. a. While choices **c** and **d** might make sense, *abysmal* means extremely bad.

31. c. Something *precarious* is fraught with danger.

32. b. *Askew* means crooked; not straight or level. A minor earthquake would probably not destroy everything in a house, nor would it leave everything unmoved.

33. a. After jumping in so many puddles, Matthew's sneakers would be *sodden*, which means thoroughly saturated; soaked. Choices **b** and **c** might make sense, but they are not definitions of sodden.

34. c. *Precipitous* means extremely steep. Choices **a** and **b** might make sense—a precipitous slope might indeed be dangerous or slippery—but these words do not define precipitous.

35. b. Something *primeval* belongs to or is from the earliest ages.

Part 4: Paragraph Comprehension

1. a. The passage is focused on how poker has influenced modern culture, specifically in the things people say in common speech. It does mention some historical elements of the game, but that is not the focus of the passage overall.

2. c. The author addresses poker's effect on modern culture throughout the passage, but he or she does not address any of the other topics. Specifically, the author does not teach any strategies of poker, nor does he or she make any value assessments on the game itself.

3. b. The word *toil* means hard work or physical labor. The pioneers are pictured as working hard during the day and relaxing with poker in the evenings.

4. d. To have a *poker face* means to hide one's emotions behind a neutral facial expression, thus preventing one's opponents from knowing whether one is bluffing.

5. a. This idea is expressed in two of the three sentences in the passage and sums up the overall meaning of the passage.

6. d. This is stated in the final paragraph. The other choices are not reflected in the passage.

7. b. The word *diminish* means to reduce or make smaller. Getting fingerprints from everyone present at a crime scene would remove some people from suspicion, thereby diminishing the number of potential suspects.

8. d. The author does not address any moral questions concerning smoking in this passage. The focus is on the various methods used to cure tobacco, and the author does not comment on how it should be used.

9. d. *Curing* is the process of drying plants and other products.

10. b. The second paragraph begins by describing how cigar tobacco is cured, using the air-curing method.

11. b. Something that is *smoldering* is burning on low heat. A charcoal fire used in a barbecue grill generally smolders rather than blazes.

12. d. In the Northern Hemisphere, June 21 would be the beginning of summer; however, according to the passage, it is the beginning of winter in the Southern Hemisphere.

13. b. Logically, if June 21 is called the summer solstice in the Northern Hemisphere, then that same day would be the winter solstice in the Southern Hemisphere.

14. d. See the final sentence of the passage.

15. c. See the second sentence, which defines *ksa*. The other choices are refuted in the passage.

Part 5: Mathematics Knowledge

1. a. Square roots can be multiplied and divided, but they cannot be added or subtracted.

2. d. Start by adding 16 to 20. The sum is 36. Then, divide 36 by 6. The correct answer is 6.

3. c. An angle that is more than 90° is an obtuse angle.

4. d. This is the only choice that includes a 90° angle.

5. b. The simplest way to solve this problem is to cancel the *a* term that occurs in both the numerator and denominator. This leaves $\frac{b-c}{bc}$. This is $\frac{4-(-2)}{4(-2)}$, which simplifies to $-\frac{3}{4}$.

6. d. The symbol means that *a* is "less than or equal to" 5. The only choice that makes this statement false is 6.

7. a. Multiply the whole number by the fraction's denominator: $5 \times 2 = 10$. Add the fraction's numerator to the answer: $1 + 10 = 11$. Now place that answer over the fraction's denominator: $\frac{11}{2}$.

8. d. In this problem, 2 is the base and 5 is the exponent. *Two raised to the power of 5* means to use 2 as a factor five times: $2 \times 2 \times 2 \times 2 \times 2 = 32$.

9. b. Since $y \times y = y^2$, then $2y(y)$ is equal to $2y^2$.

10. d. To solve this problem, you must first find the common denominator, which is 6. The equation then becomes $\frac{3x}{6} + \frac{x}{6} = 4$; then, $\frac{4x}{6} = 4$; and then $4x = 24$, so $x = 6$.

11. b. In a fractional exponent, the numerator (number on top) is the power, and the denominator (number on the bottom) is the root. Since 2 is the denominator, take the square root of 16. Since $4 \times 4 = 16$, 4 is the square root of 16. Then the numerator (power) is 1, so $4^1 = 4$.

12. c. A common error is to think that 1 is a prime number. But, it is not, because one has only 1 factor: itself. The correct answer is 2.

13. b. Isolate the variable by subtracting 50 from both sides of the equation. Then divide both sides by 5. The correct answer is 20.

14. d. If the figure is a regular decagon, it can be divided into 10 equal sections by lines passing through the center. Two such lines form the indicated angle, which includes three of the 10 sections; $\frac{3}{10}$ of 360° is equal to 108°.

15. c. The number 112 is divisible by both 7 and 8 because each can divide into 112 without a remainder; $112 \div 7 = 16$ and $112 \div 8 = 14$. Choice **a** is divisible only by 7, choice **b** is not divisible by either, and choice **d** is divisible only by 8.

16. d. $x^2 + 4x + 4$ factors into $(x + 2)(x + 2)$. Therefore, one of the $(x + 2)$ terms can be canceled with the denominator. This leaves $x + 2$.

17. c. Ask the question, *What number divided by 72 equals 2*? The correct answer is 144.

18. b. Find the correct answer by dividing the area by the given side length, because area = length × width: $72 \div 12 = 6$ inches.

19. c. An algebraic equation must be used to solve this problem. The shortest side can be denoted s. Therefore, $s + (s + 2) + (s + 4) = 24$; $3s + 6 = 24$, and $s = 6$.

20. b. Two equations are used: $T = 4O$, and $T + O = 10$. This gives $5O = 10$, and $O = 2$. Therefore, $T = 8$. The number is 82.

21. d. The first step in solving this problem is to add the fractions to get the sum of $\frac{4x}{4}$. This fraction reduces to x.

22. d. Supplementary angles add up to 180°. When given one and asked to find its supplement, subtract the given angle from 180°. The correct answer is 96°.

23. d. The angles labeled 120° are alternate interior angles of the lines c and d. When the alternate interior angles are congruent (the same measure), the lines are parallel. Therefore, lines c and d are parallel.

24. d. $56,515 \div 4 = 14,128.75$, or, rounded to the nearest whole number, 14,129.

25. c. Let x equal the number of oranges left in the basket. Three more than seven times as many oranges as five is $7(5) + 3 = 38$. Removing five leaves $x = 38 - 5 = 33$ oranges.

Part 6: Electronics Information

1. a. A circuit breadboard is also called a solderless breadboard. It is typically used in one-of-a-kind or prototype electronic designs as proof-of-concept. Soldered contacts are not used in a circuit breadboard, making it reusable.

2. d. Flux, or a specific material such as ammonium chloride or hydrochloric acid, is used to prevent the formation of oxides, which can act as an inhibitor to electrical flow. It is also added to a solder to make it easier for the flow of solder onto an electronic connection and assists in the fusing of the solder as it cools.

3. c. A cold solder is the result of not sufficiently heating up the metal surface that will be accepting the solder. A cold solder joint will have an unsmooth, unfinished look to it.

4. c. Wire wrapping is a means of assembling electronics. Wires on a circuit board are attached or wound by hand or soldered in place by machine vise.

5. d. This is the schematic symbol for a microphone.

6. d. A multimeter is an electronic measuring instrument that combines several measurement functions in one unit. Some models can be used to test diodes, capacitors, and transistors in addition to the test functions listed as answers.

7. c. 1A (1 amp) is quite a large current for electronics, so mA (milliamps) are often used; "m" (milli) means "thousandth," so 1mA = 0.001A, or 1000mA = 1A.

8. d. This is the schematic symbol for an oscilloscope.

9. d. This is the schematic symbol for an unspecified component.

10. a. An oscilloscope is an electronic test instrument that displays how signal voltage varies over time. The display is usually as a two-dimensional graph of one or more electrical potential differences.

11. c. Bandwidth is measured in the megahertz and will be the limit of the frequency signal that can be measured. Resolution is the accuracy in microseconds.

12. c. Finding the location of the inductor on the schematic will give its function. The higher frequencies coming from the source will be attenuated more by the inductor than the lower frequencies will. An inductor located downstream from the source will result in attenuating higher frequencies, while passing lower frequencies. This is a function of a low pass filter.

13. a. Fiber optic lines, since the medium used is pulses of light, can carry more data than conventional data transmission lines that use packets of electronic energy. The negatives on fiber optic lines are difficult to configure and use and are expensive. Lastly, the glass center of fiber optic lines makes them less robust than a conventional coaxial or metal-cored line.

14. d. Connecting the power early in the process could result in electrical shock.

15. c. A potentiometer is a three-terminal resistor with a rotating knob usually used to control electrical devices, such as volume controls on audio equipment.

16. b. The raster is the grid of pixels that make up the picture. HDTV has more lines, so the picture is sharper. Color or black and white has no bearing on HDTV or SDTV, nor does the data delivery mode (cable or fiber optic).

17. a. CRT stands for cathode ray tube and was typically used for television screens, computer monitors, and oscilloscopes. The advent of plasma and liquid-crystal displays is causing CRTs to become closer to obsolete.

18. d. This is the schematic symbol for an earth ground.

19. d. An output transducer converts an electrical signal to another quantity. A lamp and an LED convert electrical energy to light, while a loudspeaker converts electrical signals to sound.

20. c. Read only memory (ROM) is characterized by data that is permanently stored and cannot be modified, hence the ability to read the data, but not alter it.

Part 7: Auto and Shop Information

1. a. Oil with a higher viscosity means it is thicker, or will have a higher resistance to flow.

2. a. The fluid located in the braking system of an automobile is hydraulic fluid. Hydraulic fluid cannot be compressed, so when you push on the brake pedal, hydraulic fluid from the master cylinder is ported to the brakes on the wheels, in turn forcing the brake mechanisms on the wheels to close.

3. d. All three selections are part of an automobile air-conditioning system.

4. d. All three selections are parts that make up an automobile electrical system.

5. a. The ignition coil helps transform the battery's 12 volts into the thousands of volts needed to fire the spark plugs.

6. c. The combustion part of the internal combustion engine occurs in the cylinders, where the air/fuel mixture is ignited by the spark plug.

7. d. The proper sequence for an internal combustion engine operation is intake, compression, power, exhaust.

8. c. The spark plug fires during the power cycle.

9. d. To complete the exhaust cycle, the exhaust valve must open and the intake valve must be closed.

10. a. The camshaft rotates and actuates a pushrod connected to the rocker arm, which depresses the valve, which is forced back into place by the valve spring.

11. b. Blue smoke is an indication of worn rings in the cylinders, allowing oil to blow by and be burned in the power cycle of the process.

12. c. As with any fire triangle, to get the internal combustion engine operating properly, you will need fire, fuel, and oxygen.

13. c. Approximately 30% of the energy in gasoline is used to power the engine. The remaining 70% ends up as heat and excess energy, needed to be vented from the vehicle via the engine cooling system.

14. b. The Allen wrench is characterized by a hexagonal cross-sectional shape and is used to drive bolts and screws that have a corresponding hexagonal socket in the head.

15. d. The subject screwdriver is a slotted type, thus it would be used to screw in the slotted-head screw.

16. a. A reamer is used to shape or enlarge holes; calipers are used to measure internal and external dimensions. Pipe clamps are used to clamp boards or framing together so they can be bonded by glue.

17. d. A thread gauge is used to determine the thread pitch and diameter of screws.

18. a. A level measures how vertical or horizontal something is. A tachometer measures the revolutions per minute (rpm) of an engine. A hydrometer measures specific gravity of liquids.

19. b. A lathe is a woodworking tool that turns a piece of wood so that rotational cuts can be made to create items such as a baseball bat, a table leg, or baluster spindles.

20. c. The tool shown is an angle grinder and should be used to cut, grind, or polish metal.

21. d. The chuck of a drill tightens on the shank of a drill bit.

22. a. Steel, when used outdoors, needs to be treated and/or painted to keep rust and other degenerative effects of the environment from affecting its structural integrity.

23. b. A trowel is used to smooth, level, spread, or shape substances such as cement, plaster, or mortar.

24. d. A pipe cutter would be used by plumbers to score and cut pipe.

25. a. A glue gun applies adhesive by melting glue sticks.

Part 8: Mechanical Comprehension

1. d. $w_1 \times d_1 = w_2 \times d_2$. 102 pounds $\times$ 6 feet = 68 pounds $\times d_2$. Solving for d_2 gives 9 feet.

2. b. The mechanical advantage of a ramp is determined by its length divided by the height. Since ramp B is much longer (and the slope is much shallower) it provides a greater mechanical advantage and thus less force is required to raise the barrel.

3. a. A single fixed pulley offers no mechanical advantage. Pulleys are used at the top of flagpoles because they change the direction of force required to raise the flag.

4. b. The force constant of the spring is 4 pounds $\div$ 6 inches = $\frac{2}{3}$ pounds per inch. Using the equation, $F = kx$, we have 6 pounds = $\frac{2}{3}$ pounds per inch $\times x$. Solving for x gives 9 inches.

5. c. The area of opening of a pipe is pi times the square of half the diameter. So, the area of pipe A is $\pi(1)^2 = \pi$ and the opening of pipe B is $\pi(2)^2 = 4\pi$. The rate at which liquid flows out of the pipes is equal to the ratio of the area of their opening. A $\div$ B = $\pi \div 4\pi$ = 0.25. Water flows out of pipe B four times faster than pipe A.

6. a. The scale works by balancing the weight of an object on one side of the pivot point with objects of known weight on the other side.

7. c. For an object to float, its weight must be equal to the weight of water it displaces. Steel is much denser than water; however, the overall density of the ship is decreased due to numerous inner rooms filled with air.

8. b. If 9 full turns move the nut 0.75 inches, there are 9 turns $\div$ 0.75 inches = 12 threads per inch.

9. b. In this pulley system, the weight of the load is shared over 2 cables and so the mechanical advantage is 2.

10. a. A glass bottle is the best insulator of the choices given. Thus, it will keep the beverage colder for a longer period of time. Metals such as aluminum are good conductors and will rapidly transfer heat.

11. b. If gear 3 turns counterclockwise, it will lead its neighboring gears (2 and 4) to turn clockwise.

12. a. Since pulley B is four times greater in circumference than pulley A, pulley A must rotate 4 times for every revolution of B. If A rotates at 60 rpm, then B will rotate at 60 rpm $\div$ 4 = 15 rpm.

13. a. Ice is a slippery surface, meaning that it has a very low coefficient of friction. An object sliding on ice will take longer to slow down than it will on the other surfaces.

14. c. Each turn of the pedals will move the bike 54 $\div$ 12 = 4.5 revolutions. If the bike is pedaled at 90 rpm, the rear wheel will rotate at 90 rpm $\times$ 4.5 revolutions = 405 rpm.

15. a. A decrease in air pressure means that air is hitting the outside of the balloon with less force, meaning that the helium inside the balloon will expand.

16. c. $w_1 \times d_1 = w_2 \times d_2$. Daniel is 10 feet away from the pivot point. 225 pounds $\times$ 4 feet = 10 feet $\times w_2$. Solving for w_2 gives 90 pounds.

17. b. Orientation B has the widest base and lowest center of mass compared to orientations A and C.

18. c. The density of an object is unchanged when it is cut in half. Density = mass ÷ volume. If the object is cut in half, both the mass and volume are decreased by half, so the density will remain unchanged.

19. d. The mechanical advantage (MA) of a ramp is determined by the length of the ramp, l, divided by the height gained, h. In this case, MA = $\frac{l}{h}$ = 27 feet ÷ 3 feet = 9. The force required to pull a 360-pound block up a ramp is 360 pounds ÷ 9 = 40 pounds.

20. a. An object will float on top of a liquid if its density is less than the density of the liquid it is in and sink if its density is greater. In this case, the lead plug is denser than water and mercury, so it will sink to the bottom of the beaker.

21. c. A pulley system of this type has a mechanical advantage of 2. So if Keiko can pull a rope with 120 pounds of force, she will be able to lift a weight of 120 pounds × 2 = 240 pounds.

22. c. $w_1 \times d_1 = w_2 \times d_2$. 450 pounds × 3 feet = w_2 × 9 feet. Solving for w_2 gives 150 pounds.

23. b. After 1 hour, the first man has traveled 25 miles and the second has traveled 15 miles. 25 miles − 15 miles = 10 miles.

24. a. The mechanical advantage (MA) of a ramp is equal to the ratio of ouput force (280 pounds) to input force (70 pounds). It is also equal to the length of the ramp (16 feet) divided by the height gained by the ramp (x feet). The MA is 280 pounds ÷ 70 pounds = 4. So, we know that the length of the ramp (16 feet) divided by the height must equal 4 as well. The height of the ramp must be 4 feet.

25. d. A pulley system of this type has a mechanical advantage of 2. So, if Maria can pull a rope with 100 pounds of force, she will be able to lift a weight of 100 pounds × 2 = 200 pounds.

Part 9: Assembling Objects

1. d.
2. c.
3. d.
4. c.
5. b.
6. d.
7. c.
8. c.
9. d.
10. d.
11. a.
12. a.
13. a.
14. d.
15. d.
16. d.
17. b.
18. c.
19. a.
20. c.
21. c.
22. b.
23. d.
24. a.
25. a.

Scoring

Write your raw score (the number you got right) for each test in the blanks below. Then turn to Chapter 2 to find out how to convert these raw scores into the scores the armed services use.

1. General Science: _____ right out of 25
2. Arithmetic Reasoning: _____ right out of 30
3. Word Knowledge: _____ right out of 35
4. Paragraph Comprehension: _____ right out of 15
5. Mathematics Knowledge: _____ right out of 25
6. Electronics Information: _____ right out of 20
7. Auto and Shop Information: _____ right out of 25
8. Mechanical Comprehension: _____ right out of 25
9. Assembling Objects: _____ right out of 25

CHAPTER

ASVAB PRACTICE TEST 4

CHAPTER SUMMARY

Here's another sample ASVAB test for you to practice with.

For this test, simulate the actual test-taking experience as closely as you can. Find a quiet place to work where you won't be disturbed. If you own this book, tear out the answer sheet on the following pages and find some #2 pencils to fill in the circles with. Use a timer or stopwatch to time each section. The times are marked at the beginning of each section. After you take the test, use the detailed answer explanations that follow to review any questions you missed.

Part 1: General Science (GS)

1. (a) (b) (c) (d)
2. (a) (b) (c) (d)
3. (a) (b) (c) (d)
4. (a) (b) (c) (d)
5. (a) (b) (c) (d)
6. (a) (b) (c) (d)
7. (a) (b) (c) (d)
8. (a) (b) (c) (d)
9. (a) (b) (c) (d)

10. (a) (b) (c) (d)
11. (a) (b) (c) (d)
12. (a) (b) (c) (d)
13. (a) (b) (c) (d)
14. (a) (b) (c) (d)
15. (a) (b) (c) (d)
16. (a) (b) (c) (d)
17. (a) (b) (c) (d)

18. (a) (b) (c) (d)
19. (a) (b) (c) (d)
20. (a) (b) (c) (d)
21. (a) (b) (c) (d)
22. (a) (b) (c) (d)
23. (a) (b) (c) (d)
24. (a) (b) (c) (d)
25. (a) (b) (c) (d)

Part 2: Arithmetic Reasoning (AR)

1. (a) (b) (c) (d)
2. (a) (b) (c) (d)
3. (a) (b) (c) (d)
4. (a) (b) (c) (d)
5. (a) (b) (c) (d)
6. (a) (b) (c) (d)
7. (a) (b) (c) (d)
8. (a) (b) (c) (d)
9. (a) (b) (c) (d)
10. (a) (b) (c) (d)

11. (a) (b) (c) (d)
12. (a) (b) (c) (d)
13. (a) (b) (c) (d)
14. (a) (b) (c) (d)
15. (a) (b) (c) (d)
16. (a) (b) (c) (d)
17. (a) (b) (c) (d)
18. (a) (b) (c) (d)
19. (a) (b) (c) (d)
20. (a) (b) (c) (d)

21. (a) (b) (c) (d)
22. (a) (b) (c) (d)
23. (a) (b) (c) (d)
24. (a) (b) (c) (d)
25. (a) (b) (c) (d)
26. (a) (b) (c) (d)
27. (a) (b) (c) (d)
28. (a) (b) (c) (d)
29. (a) (b) (c) (d)
30. (a) (b) (c) (d)

Part 3: Word Knowledge (WK)

1. (a) (b) (c) (d)
2. (a) (b) (c) (d)
3. (a) (b) (c) (d)
4. (a) (b) (c) (d)
5. (a) (b) (c) (d)
6. (a) (b) (c) (d)
7. (a) (b) (c) (d)
8. (a) (b) (c) (d)
9. (a) (b) (c) (d)
10. (a) (b) (c) (d)
11. (a) (b) (c) (d)
12. (a) (b) (c) (d)

13. (a) (b) (c) (d)
14. (a) (b) (c) (d)
15. (a) (b) (c) (d)
16. (a) (b) (c) (d)
17. (a) (b) (c) (d)
18. (a) (b) (c) (d)
19. (a) (b) (c) (d)
20. (a) (b) (c) (d)
21. (a) (b) (c) (d)
22. (a) (b) (c) (d)
23. (a) (b) (c) (d)
24. (a) (b) (c) (d)

25. (a) (b) (c) (d)
26. (a) (b) (c) (d)
27. (a) (b) (c) (d)
28. (a) (b) (c) (d)
29. (a) (b) (c) (d)
30. (a) (b) (c) (d)
31. (a) (b) (c) (d)
32. (a) (b) (c) (d)
33. (a) (b) (c) (d)
34. (a) (b) (c) (d)
35. (a) (b) (c) (d)

Part 4: Paragraph Comprehension (PC)

1. (a) (b) (c) (d)
2. (a) (b) (c) (d)
3. (a) (b) (c) (d)
4. (a) (b) (c) (d)
5. (a) (b) (c) (d)

6. (a) (b) (c) (d)
7. (a) (b) (c) (d)
8. (a) (b) (c) (d)
9. (a) (b) (c) (d)
10. (a) (b) (c) (d)

11. (a) (b) (c) (d)
12. (a) (b) (c) (d)
13. (a) (b) (c) (d)
14. (a) (b) (c) (d)
15. (a) (b) (c) (d)

Part 5: Mathematics Knowledge (MK)

1. (a) (b) (c) (d)
2. (a) (b) (c) (d)
3. (a) (b) (c) (d)
4. (a) (b) (c) (d)
5. (a) (b) (c) (d)
6. (a) (b) (c) (d)
7. (a) (b) (c) (d)
8. (a) (b) (c) (d)
9. (a) (b) (c) (d)

10. (a) (b) (c) (d)
11. (a) (b) (c) (d)
12. (a) (b) (c) (d)
13. (a) (b) (c) (d)
14. (a) (b) (c) (d)
15. (a) (b) (c) (d)
16. (a) (b) (c) (d)
17. (a) (b) (c) (d)

18. (a) (b) (c) (d)
19. (a) (b) (c) (d)
20. (a) (b) (c) (d)
21. (a) (b) (c) (d)
22. (a) (b) (c) (d)
23. (a) (b) (c) (d)
24. (a) (b) (c) (d)
25. (a) (b) (c) (d)

Part 6: Electronics Information (EI)

1. (a) (b) (c) (d)
2. (a) (b) (c) (d)
3. (a) (b) (c) (d)
4. (a) (b) (c) (d)
5. (a) (b) (c) (d)
6. (a) (b) (c) (d)
7. (a) (b) (c) (d)

8. (a) (b) (c) (d)
9. (a) (b) (c) (d)
10. (a) (b) (c) (d)
11. (a) (b) (c) (d)
12. (a) (b) (c) (d)
13. (a) (b) (c) (d)
14. (a) (b) (c) (d)

15. (a) (b) (c) (d)
16. (a) (b) (c) (d)
17. (a) (b) (c) (d)
18. (a) (b) (c) (d)
19. (a) (b) (c) (d)
20. (a) (b) (c) (d)

Part 7: Auto and Shop Information (AS)

1.	ⓐ	ⓑ	ⓒ	ⓓ	10.	ⓐ	ⓑ	ⓒ	ⓓ	18.	ⓐ	ⓑ	ⓒ	ⓓ
2.	ⓐ	ⓑ	ⓒ	ⓓ	11.	ⓐ	ⓑ	ⓒ	ⓓ	19.	ⓐ	ⓑ	ⓒ	ⓓ
3.	ⓐ	ⓑ	ⓒ	ⓓ	12.	ⓐ	ⓑ	ⓒ	ⓓ	20.	ⓐ	ⓑ	ⓒ	ⓓ
4.	ⓐ	ⓑ	ⓒ	ⓓ	13.	ⓐ	ⓑ	ⓒ	ⓓ	21.	ⓐ	ⓑ	ⓒ	ⓓ
5.	ⓐ	ⓑ	ⓒ	ⓓ	14.	ⓐ	ⓑ	ⓒ	ⓓ	22.	ⓐ	ⓑ	ⓒ	ⓓ
6.	ⓐ	ⓑ	ⓒ	ⓓ	15.	ⓐ	ⓑ	ⓒ	ⓓ	23.	ⓐ	ⓑ	ⓒ	ⓓ
7.	ⓐ	ⓑ	ⓒ	ⓓ	16.	ⓐ	ⓑ	ⓒ	ⓓ	24.	ⓐ	ⓑ	ⓒ	ⓓ
8.	ⓐ	ⓑ	ⓒ	ⓓ	17.	ⓐ	ⓑ	ⓒ	ⓓ	25.	ⓐ	ⓑ	ⓒ	ⓓ
9.	ⓐ	ⓑ	ⓒ	ⓓ										

Part 8: Mechanical Comprehension (MC)

1.	ⓐ	ⓑ	ⓒ	ⓓ	10.	ⓐ	ⓑ	ⓒ	ⓓ	18.	ⓐ	ⓑ	ⓒ	ⓓ
2.	ⓐ	ⓑ	ⓒ	ⓓ	11.	ⓐ	ⓑ	ⓒ	ⓓ	19.	ⓐ	ⓑ	ⓒ	ⓓ
3.	ⓐ	ⓑ	ⓒ	ⓓ	12.	ⓐ	ⓑ	ⓒ	ⓓ	20.	ⓐ	ⓑ	ⓒ	ⓓ
4.	ⓐ	ⓑ	ⓒ	ⓓ	13.	ⓐ	ⓑ	ⓒ	ⓓ	21.	ⓐ	ⓑ	ⓒ	ⓓ
5.	ⓐ	ⓑ	ⓒ	ⓓ	14.	ⓐ	ⓑ	ⓒ	ⓓ	22.	ⓐ	ⓑ	ⓒ	ⓓ
6.	ⓐ	ⓑ	ⓒ	ⓓ	15.	ⓐ	ⓑ	ⓒ	ⓓ	23.	ⓐ	ⓑ	ⓒ	ⓓ
7.	ⓐ	ⓑ	ⓒ	ⓓ	16.	ⓐ	ⓑ	ⓒ	ⓓ	24.	ⓐ	ⓑ	ⓒ	ⓓ
8.	ⓐ	ⓑ	ⓒ	ⓓ	17.	ⓐ	ⓑ	ⓒ	ⓓ	25.	ⓐ	ⓑ	ⓒ	ⓓ
9.	ⓐ	ⓑ	ⓒ	ⓓ										

Part 9: Assembling Objects (AO)

1.	ⓐ	ⓑ	ⓒ	ⓓ	10.	ⓐ	ⓑ	ⓒ	ⓓ	18.	ⓐ	ⓑ	ⓒ	ⓓ
2.	ⓐ	ⓑ	ⓒ	ⓓ	11.	ⓐ	ⓑ	ⓒ	ⓓ	19.	ⓐ	ⓑ	ⓒ	ⓓ
3.	ⓐ	ⓑ	ⓒ	ⓓ	12.	ⓐ	ⓑ	ⓒ	ⓓ	20.	ⓐ	ⓑ	ⓒ	ⓓ
4.	ⓐ	ⓑ	ⓒ	ⓓ	13.	ⓐ	ⓑ	ⓒ	ⓓ	21.	ⓐ	ⓑ	ⓒ	ⓓ
5.	ⓐ	ⓑ	ⓒ	ⓓ	14.	ⓐ	ⓑ	ⓒ	ⓓ	22.	ⓐ	ⓑ	ⓒ	ⓓ
6.	ⓐ	ⓑ	ⓒ	ⓓ	15.	ⓐ	ⓑ	ⓒ	ⓓ	23.	ⓐ	ⓑ	ⓒ	ⓓ
7.	ⓐ	ⓑ	ⓒ	ⓓ	16.	ⓐ	ⓑ	ⓒ	ⓓ	24.	ⓐ	ⓑ	ⓒ	ⓓ
8.	ⓐ	ⓑ	ⓒ	ⓓ	17.	ⓐ	ⓑ	ⓒ	ⓓ	25.	ⓐ	ⓑ	ⓒ	ⓓ
9.	ⓐ	ⓑ	ⓒ	ⓓ										

Part 1: General Science

Time: 11 minutes

1. Some of the world's land is unusable because it's desert, ice, or rock. Another fraction of the world's land is already used for crops and grazing. About how much, after accounting for these two categories, of the world's land could still be developed for exclusively human use?
   a. $\frac{1}{2}$
   b. $\frac{1}{3}$
   c. $\frac{1}{8}$
   d. $\frac{1}{20}$

2. Why might angiosperms recover faster than conifers from a devastating environmental phenomenon?
   a. Conifers requires more sunlight.
   b. Angiosperms reproduce more quickly.
   c. Angiosperms depend on mammals to spread seeds.
   d. Conifers have tougher seeds.

3. Blood moving through the pulmonary vein is
   a. oxygenated.
   b. not oxygenated.
   c. mixed oxygenated and nonoxygenated blood.
   d. full of carbon dioxide.

4. The last column of the periodic table is the family of noble gases. Which of the following characteristics is NOT true?
   a. They have low boiling points.
   b. They are inert.
   c. They have full valence orbitals.
   d. They are highly reactive.

5. What do nuclear power plants do to control nuclear fission reactions to safely produce electricity?
   a. They use only small amounts of radioactive materials.
   b. Radioactive waste is securely contained.
   c. Materials are used to slow down the flow of neutrons.
   d. Fission reactors are located deep underground.

6. Which of the following is a mixture?
   a. sodium chloride
   b. rice and bean
   c. magnesium sulfate
   d. water

7. The specialized organ system that is responsible for filtering out impurities from the blood and excreting them is the
   a. renal system.
   b. respiratory system.
   c. circulatory system.
   d. endocrine system.

8. Mammalian mothers provide nutrients to the developing embryo through the
   a. fallopian tube.
   b. uterus.
   c. placenta.
   d. ovaries.

9. When light travels from a vacuum into air it is expected to undergo
   a. reflection.
   b. a change in wavelength.
   c. a change in frequency.
   d. refraction.

10. Nucleic acids are large molecules made up of smaller molecules called
   a. amino acids.
   b. nucleotides.
   c. lipids.
   d. carbohydrates.

11. The dinosaurs became extinct due to an impact from space
   a. 65 million years ago, which left a chemical imprint of radium.
   b. 65 million years ago, which left a chemical imprint of iridium.
   c. 540 million years ago, which left a chemical imprint of radium.
   d. 540 million years ago, which left a chemical imprint of iridium.

12. Which of the following atoms or ions is largest?
   a. Kr
   b. Br^-
   c. Ca^{2+}
   d. N^{2-}

13. All the following are forms of connective tissue EXCEPT
   a. tendons.
   b. adipose.
   c. blood.
   d. nerves.

14. A sample of 7 g of CO_2 contains
   a. 0.75 g of carbon.
   b. 1.5 g of carbon.
   c. 3.0 g of carbon.
   d. 7.0 g of carbon.

15. What type of rock is expected to be found at a site of extreme pressure and temperature?
   a. igneous
   b. metamorphic
   c. stratified
   d. sedimentary

16. The population of species will continue to increase until it reaches the habitat's carrying capacity, which will limit the population. All the following are limiting factors of population in a habitat EXCEPT
   a. limited water supply.
   b. excessive food supply.
   c. food web relationships.
   d. competition.

17. You find a unique species of ants living in tunnels formed by termites in a specific tree. The tree is lush and appears healthy. When you put your hand on the tree for a closer look, the ants race out of the tree to attack your hand. This is an example of
   a. predator-prey.
   b. parasitism.
   c. mutualism.
   d. commensalism.

18. Which is an example of an endothermic change?
   a. condensation
   b. combustion
   c. freezing
   d. sublimation

19. Sickle cell anemia is a recessive genetic disorder that decreases the amount of oxygen carried by red blood cells. Individuals will have painful attacks and their life expectancy is shortened. Which of the following statements is true?
   a. Both parents must pass the defective allele to offspring with the disease.
   b. The allele should disappear from the gene pool in the future.
   c. One parent must show symptoms of the disorder.
   d. The mutation is not useful at all.

20. The isomers butane and isobutane are expected to have different properties EXCEPT for which of the following?
   a. molecular weight
   b. freezing point
   c. vapor pressure
   d. shape

21. A cell experiences a genetic mutation and is unable to deliver the appropriate amino acids according to the genetic code. Which of the following is affected?
   a. DNA
   b. mRNA
   c. rRNA
   d. tRNA

22. How many grams of sugar are needed to make 500 mL of a 5% (weight/volume) solution of sugar?
   a. 20
   b. 25
   c. 50
   d. 10

23. Masses of ice, dust, and small rock particles orbiting the solar system and seen as patches of light with long tails are
   a. meteors.
   b. asteroids.
   c. meteor showers.
   d. comets.

24. Which of the following groups of organisms produce flowers?
   a. angiosperms
   b. gymnosperms
   c. mosses
   d. fungi

25. A gas that follows the ideal gas law is contained in a sealed piston at 25°C and 1 atm. What would you expect to happen if the temperature were increased to 35°C?
   a. The volume would decrease.
   b. The pressure would decrease.
   c. The volume and pressure would decrease.
   d. The volume would increase.

Part 2: Arithmetic Reasoning

Time: 36 minutes

1. In New York City, two out of every five people surveyed bicycle to work. Out of a population sample of 200,000 people, how many bicycle to work?
   a. 4,000
   b. 8,000
   c. 40,000
   d. 80,000

2. Serena has to choose between two jobs. One is at Books R Us and pays $18,000 with yearly raises of $800. The other, at Readers Galore, pays $16,400 per year with yearly raises of $1,200. In how many years will the two yearly salaries be equal?
   a. 6
   b. 5
   c. 4
   d. 3

Use the following pie chart to answer questions 3 through 5.

Ricardo's Budget
(cents per $1.00)

3. For which item does Ricardo spend half as much as he puts in his savings account?
   a. his car
   b. clothes
   c. housing
   d. food

4. For which two items does Ricardo spend 50% of each budgeted dollar?
   a. savings and housing
   b. clothes and housing
   c. car and medical
   d. medical and food

5. Last year, Ricardo made $46,500. About how much more did he spend on housing during the year than he put away in savings?
   a. $2,000
   b. $2,600
   c. $2,800
   d. $3,000

6. The number of red blood corpuscles in one cubic millimeter is about 5,000,000, and the number of white blood corpuscles in one cubic millimeter is about 8,000. What, then, is the ratio of white blood corpuscles to red blood corpuscles?
   a. 1:625
   b. 1:40
   c. 4:10
   d. 5:1,250

7. The living room in Donna's home is 182 square feet. How many square yards of carpet should she purchase to carpet the room?
   a. 9 square yards
   b. 1,638 square yards
   c. 61 square yards
   d. 21 square yards

8. During a basketball game, Jack has made 20 free-throw shots out of his 50 tries. How many of his next 25 free-throw attempts is Jack most likely to make?
   a. 5
   b. 10
   c. 15
   d. 20

9. Twelve people entered a room. Three more than two-thirds of these people then left. How many people remain in the room?
   a. 0
   b. 1
   c. 2
   d. 7

10. A map of Nevada has the following scale: 0.5 inches = 15 miles. Which expression tells the actual distance, d, between points that are 5.25 inches apart on the map?

a. $\frac{0.5}{15} = \frac{5.25}{d}$

b. $\frac{15}{0.5} = \frac{5.25}{d}$

c. $\frac{0.5}{d} = \frac{15}{5.25}$

d. $\frac{d}{2.5} = \frac{0.5}{15}$

11. The Cougars played three basketball games last week. Monday's game lasted 113.9 minutes; Wednesday's game lasted 106.7 minutes; and Friday's game lasted 122 minutes. What is the average time, in minutes, for the three games?

a. 77.6 minutes

b. 103.2 minutes

c. 114.2 minutes

d. 115.6 minutes

12. A helicopter flies over a river at 6:02 A.M. and arrives at a heliport 20 miles away at 6:17 A.M. How many miles per hour was the helicopter traveling?

a. 120 miles per hour

b. 300 miles per hour

c. 30 miles per hour

d. 80 miles per hour

13. How many minutes are there in 12 hours?

a. 24 minutes

b. 1,440 minutes

c. 720 minutes

d. 1,200 minutes

14. Five people in Sonja's office are planning a party. Sonja will buy a loaf of French bread ($3 per loaf) and a platter of cold cuts ($23). Barbara will buy the soda ($1 per person) and two boxes of crackers ($2 per box). Mario and Rick will split the cost of two packages of Cheese Doodles ($1 per package). Danica will supply a package of five paper plates ($4 per package). How much more will Sonja spend than the rest of the office put together?

a. $14

b. $13

c. $12

d. $11

15. Kathy charges $7.50 per hour to mow a lawn. Sharon charges 1.5 times as much to do the same job. How much does Sharon charge to mow a lawn?

a. $5.00 per hour

b. $11.25 per hour

c. $10.00 per hour

d. $9.00 per hour

16. The height of the Eiffel Tower is 986 feet. A replica of the tower made to scale is 4 inches tall. What is the scale of the replica to the real tower?

a. 1 to 246.5

b. 1 to 3,944

c. 246.5 to 1

d. 1 to 2,958

17. On Sundays, Mike gives half-hour drum lessons from 10:30 A.M. to 5:30 P.M. He takes a half-hour lunch break at noon. If Mike is paid $20 for each lesson, what is the total amount he makes on Sunday?

a. $260

b. $190

c. $170

d. $140

18. Driving 60 miles per hour, it takes one-half hour to drive to work. How much *additional* time will it take to drive to work if the speed is now 40 miles per hour?

   a. 1 hour

   b. 2 hours

   c. 15 minutes

   d. 30 minutes

19. An 8″ × 10″ photograph is blown up to a billboard size that is in proportion to the original photograph. If 8″ is considered the height of the photo, what would be the length of the billboard if its height is 5.6 feet?

   a. 7 feet

   b. 400 feet

   c. 56 feet

   d. 9 feet

20. Membership dues at Arnold's Gym are $53 per month this year, but were $50 per month last year. What was the percentage increase in the gym's prices?

   a. 5.5%

   b. 6.0%

   c. 6.5%

   d. 7.0%

21. Which of the following best represents the following statement? Patricia (P) has four times the number of marbles Sean (S) has.

   a. $P = S + 4$

   b. $S = P - 4$

   c. $P = 4S$

   d. $S = 4P$

22. A piggy bank contains $8.20 in coins. If there are an equal number of quarters, nickels, dimes, and pennies, how many of each denomination are there?

   a. 10

   b. 20

   c. 30

   d. 40

23. Two saline solutions are mixed. Twelve liters of 5% solution are mixed with four liters of 4% solution. What percent saline is the final solution?

   a. 4.25%

   b. 4.5%

   c. 4.75%

   d. 5%

24. A neighbor has three dogs. Fluffy is half the age of Muffy, who is one-third as old as Spot, who is half the neighbor's age, which is 24. How old is Fluffy?

   a. 2

   b. 4

   c. 6

   d. 12

25. Mario has finished 35 out of 45 of his test questions. Which of the following fractions of the test does he have left?

   a. $\frac{2}{9}$

   b. $\frac{7}{9}$

   c. $\frac{4}{5}$

   d. $\frac{3}{5}$

26. D'Andre rides the first half of a bike race in two hours. If his partner, Adam, rides the return trip five miles per hour less, and it takes him three hours, how fast was D'Andre traveling?
- **a.** 10 miles per hour
- **b.** 15 miles per hour
- **c.** 20 miles per hour
- **d.** 25 miles per hour

27. Kate earns $26,000 a year. If she receives a 4.5% salary increase, how much will she earn?
- **a.** $26,450
- **b.** $27,170
- **c.** $27,260
- **d.** $29,200

28. Rudy forgot to replace his gas cap the last time he filled his car with gas. The gas is evaporating out of his 14-gallon tank at a constant rate of $\frac{1}{3}$ gallon per day. How much gas does Rudy lose in one week?
- **a.** 2 gallons
- **b.** $2\frac{1}{3}$ gallons
- **c.** $4\frac{2}{3}$ gallons
- **d.** 6 gallons

29. Veronica took a trip to the lake. If she drove steadily for five hours traveling 220 miles, what was her average speed for the trip?
- **a.** 44 miles per hour
- **b.** 55 miles per hour
- **c.** 60 miles per hour
- **d.** 66 miles per hour

30. A rectangular tract of land measures 860 feet by 560 feet. Approximately how many acres is this? (one acre = 43,560 square feet)
- **a.** 12.8 acres
- **b.** 11.06 acres
- **c.** 10.5 acres
- **d.** 8.06 acres

Part 3: Word Knowledge

Time: 11 minutes

1. *Lucid* most nearly means
- **a.** confusing.
- **b.** quick.
- **c.** understandable.
- **d.** slippery.

2. *Mourning* most nearly means
- **a.** early.
- **b.** sorrowing.
- **c.** celebration.
- **d.** night.

3. *Resolute* most nearly means
- **a.** yielding.
- **b.** agreeable.
- **c.** cowardly.
- **d.** determined.

4. *Ambivalent* most nearly means
- **a.** left-handed.
- **b.** right-handed.
- **c.** uncertain.
- **d.** energetic.

5. *Dissent* most nearly means
- **a.** fall.
- **b.** disagreement.
- **c.** average.
- **d.** stop.

6. *Grave* most nearly means
- **a.** dead.
- **b.** serious.
- **c.** angry.
- **d.** excited.

7. *Hapless* most nearly means
a. unlucky.
b. careless.
c. joyful.
d. fortunate.

8. *Dreary* most nearly means
a. dull.
b. sleepy.
c. interesting.
d. awake.

9. *Arid* most nearly means
a. big.
b. lost.
c. busy.
d. dry.

10. *Deter* most nearly means
a. shortcut.
b. chose.
c. discourage.
d. clean.

11. *Covert* most nearly means
a. altered.
b. secret.
c. obvious.
d. missed.

12. *Allusion* most nearly means
a. reference.
b. mirage.
c. escape.
d. rhyme.

10. *Desist* most nearly means
a. help.
b. stop.
c. want.
d. chose.

14. *Pariah* most nearly means
a. sage.
b. fish.
c. outcast.
d. leader.

15. *Precede* most nearly means
a. lead.
b. follow.
c. continue.
d. profit.

16. *Forgive* most nearly means
a. commute.
b. remember.
c. pardon.
d. skip.

17. *Potent* most nearly means
a. ominous.
b. uniform.
c. secretive.
d. powerful.

18. *Succinct* most nearly means
a. heavy.
b. tasteful.
c. clever.
d. concise.

19. *Console* most nearly means
a. ask.
b. comfort.
c. associate.
d. worry.

20. *Surmise* most nearly means
a. complete.
b. shock.
c. guess.
d. fill.

21. Certain predators *mimic* a harmless species, allowing them to avoid detection by their prey.
   a. intimate
   b. intimidate
   c. imitate
   d. interpret

22. Sleeping during class is *tantamount* to being absent; you might as well not come at all.
   a. equal
   b. encouraged
   c. unlike
   d. preferable

23. Without a goal in mind, Greg wandered *aimlessly* through the woods.
   a. purposefully
   b. nervously
   c. quickly
   d. randomly

24. Surprisingly, the very *meticulous* writer made many typos on her latest manuscript.
   a. careless
   b. fast
   c. intelligent
   d. thorough

25. It is *imperative* that you finish the reports this morning; they are due at the end of the day!
   a. optional
   b. acceptable
   c. crucial
   d. encouraged

26. Because he got no sleep the night before, the boy was so *lethargic* that he did not get up from the couch all day.
   a. exhausted
   b. hurt
   c. awake
   d. frightened

27. The *overbearing* supervisor would not approve anyone's ideas except his own.
   a. friendly
   b. arrogant
   c. busy
   d. judicious

28. Do not *deviate* from the instructions; just one small error will ruin the project!
   a. follow
   b. stray
   c. undervalue
   d. read

29. Burnett was scared and *anxious* about meeting new people on her first day at school.
   a. confident
   b. relaxed
   c. nervous
   d. bored

30. The gopher was a *menace* on the golf course; it kept ruining the carefully mowed grass.
   a. asset
   b. nuisance
   c. pet
   d. rival

31. The speaker was so *riveting* that no one in the audience got up from his or her seat during the presentation.
   a. boring
   b. short
   c. long
   d. fascinating

32. The notes on the document were *incomprehensible*; no one could read them.
   a. illegible
   b. numerous
   c. sparse
   d. tiny

33. The *callow* intern made many mistakes at his first job.
- a. experienced
- b. inexperienced
- c. friendly
- d. intelligent

34. Don't bother me with small, *trivial* details; we have more important things to think about!
- a. essential
- b. specific
- c. petty
- d. general

35. After being pestered for weeks, the boy's parents finally *acceded* to his requests and bought him a puppy.
- a. disagreed
- b. agreed
- c. asked
- d. stopped

Part 4:
Paragraph Comprehension

Time: 13 minutes

The taxpayers' association rose up in protest at the town meeting when it was announced that the school budget would be increased by 50% over the next year. "We will no longer tolerate wasting money on swimming pools and skating rinks," stated Bob Smith. "It is time for this council to be held accountable for proper use of the taxpayers' money."

Other members of the taxpayers' association stated that they intend to run for town council in the coming election in order to remove members of the board who have *persistently* raised taxes over the last three fiscal years.

1. Why was the taxpayers' association upset at the recent town meeting?
- a. They had not been allowed to speak.
- b. Taxes keep going up.
- c. The town council had not fulfilled the school budget.
- d. Students were learning to skate instead of studying.

2. As used in the passage, *persistently* most nearly means
- a. ongoing.
- b. increasingly.
- c. overused.
- d. ended.

3. Bob Smith complained about swimming pools and skating rinks because
- a. he is not athletic.
- b. he was concerned about the environment.
- c. he felt that such things are a waste of taxpayers' money.
- d. he was at the wrong meeting.

4. One of the solutions offered by the taxpayers' association was
- a. to drain the swimming pool.
- b. to close the local schools.
- c. to pass a bill lowering taxes.
- d. to run for town council and replace the existing members.

Recent flooding in the county has caused a shortage of sump pumps, vacuum cleaners, and other cleanup utilities. Recently, one hardware store resorted to handing out numbered tickets to customers, because they had a limited number of pumps on hand and wanted to ensure that each customer purchased only one on a first-come, first-served basis. This led to resentment on the part of those who had stood in the rain, waiting for an hour to get inside, only to discover that they had to take a numbered ticket and come back the next day when another shipment of pumps would arrive.

These hardships, however, were small compared to the suffering of many residents. Hundreds of houses were *deluged* with the rising waters, and residents were forced to flee their homes in boats. The anger of those who were forced to take numbered tickets seemed childish in the eyes of those people whose homes were destroyed.

5. Why did the hardware store hand out numbered tickets to people buying pumps?
   a. They were holding a raffle for free sump pumps.
   b. They didn't have enough pumps to sell more than one to a customer.
   c. The customers were getting angry.
   d. Ownership of sump pumps is regulated by law.

6. As used in the passage, *deluge* most nearly means
   a. strong winds.
   b. a new law.
   c. a flood.
   d. cold weather.

7. What is the main idea of this passage?
   a. There is always someone who is suffering more than you are.
   b. The area should have been declared a national disaster zone.
   c. The hardware store owners were heartless people.
   d. Raffle tickets should be outlawed.

8. Why does the author describe the hardware store customers as "childish"?
   a. They were playing games while waiting to get inside.
   b. The hardware store owners were their parents.
   c. They were angry about a small problem.
   d. They were being irresponsible by not helping their neighbors.

Light pollution is a growing problem worldwide. Like other forms of pollution, light pollution degrades the quality of the environment. Where it was once possible to look up at the night sky and see thousands of twinkling stars in the inky blackness, one now sees little more than the yellow glare of urban sky. When we lose the ability to connect visually with the vastness of the universe by looking up at the night sky, we lose our connection with something profoundly important to the human spirit, our sense of wonder.

9. The passage implies that the most serious damage done by light pollution is to our
   a. artistic appreciation.
   b. sense of physical well-being.
   c. cultural advancement.
   d. spiritual selves.

10. According to the passage, which of the following is important to the human spirit?
   a. a clean environment
   b. our sense of wonder
   c. dark skies
   d. looking at the stars

George walked out of his boss's office in anger after being *reprimanded* for his *slovenly* appearance. "I dress as well as anyone else," he fumed. "I think the boss is just singling me out." Two days later, George resigned from his job and went to work at the competitor's company for a smaller salary.

11. Which of the following was probably the reason that George left his job?
a. He was angry at his boss.
b. The new job was closer to home.
c. He was bored with his old job.
d. The new job paid more than the old job.

12. As used in the passage, *reprimanded* most nearly means
a. fired.
b. demoted.
c. scolded.
d. given an award.

13. George got in trouble at work because
a. he was a careless employee.
b. he didn't dress properly.
c. he wanted more money.
d. the boss didn't like him.

14. As used in the passage, *slovenly* most nearly means
a. lazy.
b. tardy.
c. heavenly.
d. sloppy.

When writing business letters or memos, it's not practical to be personal. The first-person point of view may make the reader feel close to the writer, but it also implies a certain subjectivity. That is, the writer is expressing a personal view from a personal perspective.

15. This paragraph best supports the statement that
a. writing a first-person business correspondence will prevent the writer from getting promoted.
b. effective business writing is one of the most important skills to have in an office environment.
c. using the first-person point of view in business correspondence is not a wise choice.
d. the first-person point of view expresses a personal view and a personal perspective.

Part 5: Mathematics Knowledge

Time: 24 minutes

1. Which of the following has the greatest value?
a. $\frac{7}{8}$
b. $\frac{3}{4}$
c. $\frac{2}{3}$
d. $\frac{5}{6}$

2. Factor the expression completely: $x^2 - 25$.
a. $x(x - 25)$
b. $(x + 5)(x - 5)$
c. $(x + 5)(x + 5)$
d. $(x - 5)(x - 5)$

3. Solve the equation for b: $\sqrt{b-4} = 5$.
a. 1
b. 9
c. 21
d. 29

4. If one angle of a triangle measures 42° and the second measures 59°, what does the third angle measure?
   a. 101°
   b. 89°
   c. 90°
   d. 79°

5. What is the perimeter of the following figure?

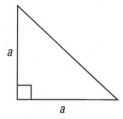

   a. $a^2 \div 2$
   b. $2a + 2a^2$
   c. $2a + \sqrt{2a^2}$
   d. $4a$

6. The area of a right triangle is 60 square centimeters. The height is 15 centimeters. How many centimeters is the base?
   a. 8 centimeters
   b. 4 centimeters
   c. 6 centimeters
   d. 12 centimeters

7. Which of the following number statements is true?
   a. 4 feet > 3 feet
   b. 7 feet < 6 feet
   c. 5 feet > 6 feet
   d. 3 feet < 2 feet

8. Choose the answer to the following problem:
$10^5 \div 10^2 =$
   a. 1^3
   b. 10^3
   c. 10^7
   d. 10^{10}

9. Which of the following is the equivalent of $\frac{18}{45}$?
   a. 0.45
   b. 0.5
   c. 0.42
   d. 0.4

10. One side of a rectangle measures 834 centimeters and another side measures 1,288 centimeters. What is the perimeter of the rectangle?
   a. 2,148,384 square feet
   b. 1,074,192 square feet
   c. 4,244 feet
   d. 2,122 feet

11. How many minutes are in $7\frac{1}{6}$ hours?
   a. 258 minutes
   b. 430 minutes
   c. 2,580 minutes
   d. 4,300 minutes

12. What is the area of a circle that has a diameter of 94 centimeters?
   a. 188π square centimeters
   b. 47π square centimeters
   c. 94π square centimeters
   d. 2,209π square centimeters

13. How does the area of a rectangle change if the base and the height of the original rectangle are tripled?
   a. The area is tripled.
   b. The area is six times larger.
   c. The area is nine times larger.
   d. The area remains the same.

14. Plattville is 80 miles west and 60 miles north of Quincy. How long is a direct route from Plattville to Quincy?
   a. 100 miles
   b. 110 miles
   c. 120 miles
   d. 140 miles

15. Which of the following numbers is divisible by six?
   a. 232
   b. 341
   c. 546
   d. 903

16. A triangle has two congruent sides, and the measure of one angle is 40°. Which of the following types of triangles is it?
   a. isosceles
   b. equilateral
   c. right
   d. scalene

17. Multiply the binomials: $(3x + 4)(x - 6)$.
   a. $3x^2 - 22x - 24$
   b. $3x^2 + 14x - 24$
   c. $3x^2 - 14x - 24$
   d. $3x^2 + 14x + 24$

18. An acute angle is
   a. 180°.
   b. greater than 90°.
   c. 90°.
   d. less than 90°.

19. Choose the answer to the following problem:
   $|4 - 15| =$
   a. −11
   b. 11
   c. −19
   d. 19

20. Which of the following is equivalent to $2\sqrt{6}$?
   a. $\sqrt{24}$
   b. $6\sqrt{2}$
   c. $12\sqrt{2}$
   d. $\sqrt{12}$

21. Which of the following answer choices is equivalent to 10^4?
   a. $10 \times 10 \times 10 \times 10$
   b. 10×4
   c. $(10 + 4) \times 10$
   d. $10 + 4$

22. 56.73647 rounded to the nearest hundredth is equal to
   a. 100
   b. 57
   c. 56.7
   d. 56.74

23. In the following decimal, which digit is in the hundredths place: 0.2153
   a. 2
   b. 1
   c. 5
   d. 3

24. Solve for all values of x in the equation: $x^2 - 25 = 0$.
   a. 5
   b. 0, 5
   c. −5
   d. 5, −5

25. How many $5\frac{1}{4}$-ounce glasses can be completely filled from a $33\frac{1}{2}$-ounce container of juice?
   a. 4
   b. 5
   c. 6
   d. 7

Part 6: Electronics Information

Time: 9 minutes

1. In which of the following is a quartz crystal most likely to be found?
   a. a transformer
   b. a capacitor
   c. a battery
   d. an oscillator

2. What type of voltage is available from a typical domestic wall outlet?
   a. DC
   b. AC
   c. static
   d. dynamic

3. Which of the following has the longest wavelength?
   a. ultraviolet waves
   b. radio waves
   c. X-rays
   d. microwaves

4. What is needed to convert 120 volts to 12 volts?
   a. a step-down transformer
   b. a step-up transformer
   c. a rectifier
   d. a diode reduction device

5. What does the following schematic symbol represent?

   a. a battery
   b. a circuit breaker
   c. a fuse
   d. a headphone

6. One coulomb per second is equal to one
   a. ampere.
   b. volt.
   c. watt.
   d. decibel.

7. Which of the following functions would be performed by a diode?
   a. amplifier
   b. capacitor
   c. filter
   d. rectifier

8. A photovoltaic cell produces
   a. direct current.
   b. alternating current.
   c. square wave current.
   d. all the above

9. Which symbol represents a wattmeter?
   a.
   b.
   c.
   d.

10. *Low potential,* for electricians, most closely means
    a. 600 watts or lower.
    b. circuits that have low chance of overload.
    c. a low risk of fire.
    d. a low cost of wiring.

11. The frequency of a signal is *inversely* proportional to which of the following?
 a. power
 b. phase
 c. amplitude
 d. period

12. What would the expected power level be at the input to the receiver?

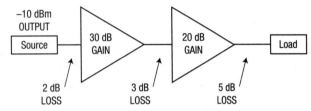

 a. 20 dBm
 b. 30 dBm
 c. 40 dBm
 d. 50 dBm

13. A capacitor's storage potential, or capacitance, is measured in
 a. coulombs.
 b. decibels.
 c. Fahrenheit.
 d. farads.

14. What is true of a random access memory (RAM) electronic chip?
 a. Its contents are erased when power is turned off.
 b. Its contents are saved when power is turned off.
 c. It is no different from a read-only-memory (ROM) chip.
 d. all the above

15. Electrons have a _____ charge while protons have a _____ charge.
 a. neutral, positive
 b. negative, neutral
 c. positive, negative
 d. negative, positive

16. If you have a 10-ohm resistor and a 55-ohm resistor in series, what is the total resistance?
 a. 15 ohms
 b. 35 ohms
 c. 65 ohms
 d. 110 ohms

17. Amplification factor is typically stated in
 a. volts.
 b. watts.
 c. hertz.
 d. decibels.

18. An ammeter reads 287 microamps. Which of the following is equivalent to the meter reading?
 a. 0.00287 A
 b. 0.287 A
 c. 0.0287 A
 d. 0.000287 A

19. What is the minimum gauge of wire that must be used for a piece of equipment that draws 55 amps?
 a. #14
 b. #10
 c. #8
 d. #4

20. What would be the rated amps for the fuse shown here?

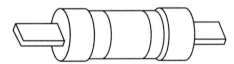

 a. 20
 b. 40
 c. 60
 d. unknown

Part 7:
Auto and Shop Information

Time: 11 minutes

1. Using only water in an automobile's cooling system can result in
   a. engine parts rusting.
   b. the water boiling away.
   c. the water freezing during winter.
   d. all the above

2. Which of the following systems connects directly to the internal combustion engine in an automobile?
   a. the suspension system
   b. the braking system
   c. the oil system
   d. the electrical system

3. Of which automotive system does the driver have the most direct control while driving?
   a. the emissions system
   b. the steering system
   c. the fuel system
   d. the drive train

4. A "knock" or "ping" sound when accelerating typically indicates
   a. the suspension needs adjusting.
   b. the tires need rotating.
   c. the fuel-air mixture is igniting too soon inside the engine cylinders.
   d. the ignition timing sequence needs adjusting.

5. Solving the knock or ping sound heard when accelerating usually entails
   a. using a higher octane gasoline.
   b. changing the spark plugs.
   c. changing the timing sequence.
   d. all the above

6. If you press down on your brake pedal and the reaction feels "spongy," what could be the problem?
   a. misaligned brake pads
   b. an overfilled master cylinder
   c. air in the hydraulic system
   d. water in the hydraulic system

7. Engine oil S.A.E. numbers measure
   a. flash point of the oil.
   b. oil viscosity.
   c. chemical composition.
   d. none of the above

8. Tires on a typical car will generally last how long?
   a. 10,000 to 30,000 miles
   b. 15,000 to 25,000 miles
   c. 30,000 to 80,000 miles
   d. 100,000 miles and up

9. Looking at what on a tire will give you an indication of when it should be replaced?
   a. the valve stem
   b. the sidewalls
   c. the steel-belted radials
   d. the wear bars

10. A squealing noise from your engine as you accelerate usually indicates
    a. problems with the steering gearbox.
    b. worn tires.
    c. a worn or loose fan belt.
    d. all the above

11. A spark plug that is not firing will usually result in
    a. the environmental control system not operating properly.
    b. a higher rate of gasoline consumption.
    c. an engine not starting.
    d. an engine running rough.

12. Before an oil change, the engine should be
   a. off for at least one hour to let the oil settle.
   b. at minimum rpm.
   c. running at idle.
   d. run for at least 10 minutes to warm the oil up, increasing viscosity.

13. When making a circular cut in a piece of metal, the best chisel to use is a
   a. butt chisel.
   b. round chisel.
   c. framing chisel.
   d. socket chisel.

14. If you want to thin paint, which of the following should be used?
   a. varnish
   b. turpentine
   c. mineral spirits
   d. benzene

15. The tool shown here is used to

   a. drive screws.
   b. drill holes.
   c. melt solder.
   d. melt glue.

16. What would be the strongest material to use when building a permanent building foundation?
   a. wood timbers
   b. concrete
   c. cinder blocks
   d. brick and mortar

17. A Forstner bit is characterized by
   a. its quick release mechanism.
   b. its wide circular cutting edge with a spur in the middle of the drill.
   c. its extended length to drill through multiple pieces of lumber.
   d. none of the above

18. Which of the following is the small thin nail with a small head often used in picture frames and light assembly?
   a. the spiral
   b. the tack
   c. the brad
   d. the sinker

19. A torque wrench is used to
   a. maximize the leverage needed to overcome resistance.
   b. tighten bolts to a specific tightness.
   c. apply the maximum amount of torque allowed to a bolt.
   d. none of the above

20. Which of the following is not considered a carpenter's hand tool?
   a. a hammer
   b. a coping saw
   c. a table saw
   d. a wood chisel

21. The best tool to use to dig a small, circular hole a foot or two deep would be a
   a. posthole digger.
   b. shovel.
   c. backhoe.
   d. garden trowel.

22. The word *kerf* describes
   a. the length of a saw cut.
   b. the depth of a saw cut.
   c. the width of the saw cut.
   d. none of the above

23. Which of the following tools are most likely to be used together?

   a. a lathe and a claw hammer

   b. an electric winch and a center punch

   c. a ball-peen hammer and a Phillips-head screwdriver

   d. a table saw and a fence guide

24. What is the tool shown here?

   a. an open-end wrench

   b. a rivet tool.

   c. a pair of pliers

   d. a bolt cutter

25. What is the abrasive material used on most sandpapers?

   a. pumice

   b. aluminum oxide

   c. emery

   d. none of the above

Part 8: Mechanical Comprehension

Time: 19 minutes

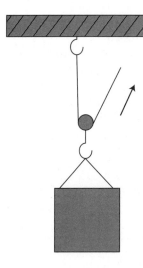

1. A 250-pound weight is being lifted using the pulley system shown here. How much force is necessary to lift the weight?

   a. 50 pounds

   b. 100 pounds

   c. 125 pounds

   d. 250 pounds

2. When a mercury thermometer is placed in hot liquid, mercury will travel up the thermometer to provide an accurate temperature reading. Why does mercury rise in a thermometer when it is exposed to heat?

   a. Heat causes mercury to expand.

   b. Mercury is repelled by heat.

   c. Heat causes mercury to contract.

   d. Air bubbles push mercury up the thermometer.

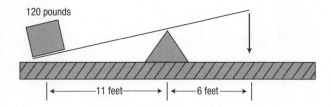

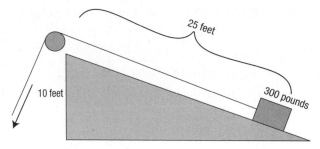

3. In the diagram, Holly wants to lift a 120-pound block using a lever. If the block is 11 feet from the pivot point and Holly is 6 feet from the pivot point, how much force must she apply to lift the block?

a. 220 pounds

b. 66 pounds

c. 120 pounds

d. 720 pounds

6. A 300-pound block is being pulled up an incline by a pulley. The incline is 25 feet long and rises 10 feet. Neglecting friction, how much force is necessary to move the block up the incline?

a. 120 pounds

b. 250 pounds

c. 300 pounds

d. 35 pounds

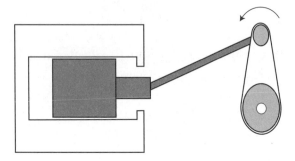

4. The vertical motion of a piston is transferred to rotational motion at the crank. Based on the figure, what description best describes the position and direction of the piston when the crank arm is pointing downward?

a. far left and stationary

b. in the center and moving to the left

c. in the center and moving to the right

d. far right and stationary

5. Ian goes on a trail run and covers 12 miles in 1.5 hours. How fast was Ian running?

a. 6 mph

b. 8 mph

c. 10 mph

d. 18 mph

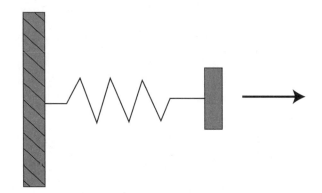

7. A force of 10 pounds is required to move a spring 8 inches. How far will the spring stretch under 15 pounds of force?

a. 12 inches

b. 14 inches

c. 16 inches

d. 18 inches

8. If 18 full turns are required to move a nut 1.2 inches, how many threads per inch does the screw have?

a. 10

b. 12

c. 15

d. 20

9. Using a lever, a man is able to lift a 120-pound load with only 40 pounds of force. What is the mechanical advantage of the lever?
   a. $\frac{1}{3}$
   b. 3
   c. 20
   d. 80

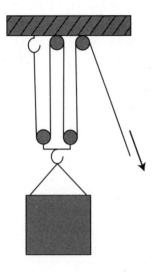

10. How much force is required to lift a 300-pound weight using the pulley system shown above?
   a. 75 pounds
   b. 100 pounds
   c. 150 pounds
   d. 900 pounds

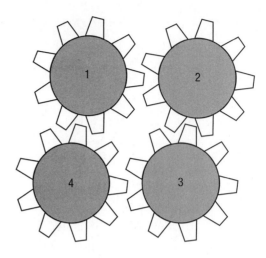

11. If gear 1 turns clockwise, which other gears, if any, will also turn clockwise?
   a. 2 only
   b. 3 only
   c. 2 and 4
   d. None

12. When a submarine dives, it fills its ballast tanks with water, causing all the following EXCEPT
   a. the density of the submarine to increase.
   b. the buoyancy of the submarine to decrease.
   c. the weight of the submarine to increase.
   d. the volume of the submarine to increase.

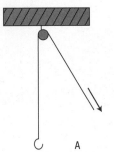

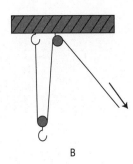

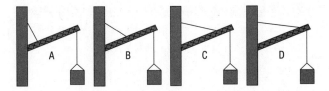

13. Pulley system A offers no mechanical advantage, whereas pulley system B has a mechanical advantage of 2. In pulley system A, if the rope is pulled 10 feet, the hook will rise 10 feet. How many feet of rope must be pulled to raise the hook in pulley system B by 10 feet?

  a. 5 feet
  b. 10 feet
  c. 15 feet
  d. 20 feet

15. The cable supporting the arm of the crane is attached to the arm in four different positions. In which position is the cable strained the most?

  a. cable A
  b. cable B
  c. cable C
  d. cable D

16. A steel block has a density of 0.3 pounds per cubic inch. Its dimensions are $2'' \times 2'' \times 5''$. What is the weight of the block?

  a. 6 pounds
  b. 10 pounds
  c. 20 pounds
  d. 27 pounds

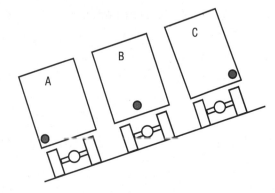

14. Three trucks are parked on an incline. Their centers of gravity are marked by dots. Which truck is most likely to tip over?

  a. truck A
  b. truck B
  c. truck C
  d. All trucks are stable.

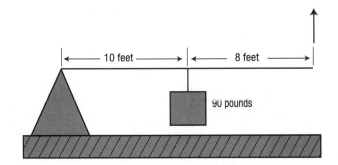

17. In the diagram, Talia wants to lift a 90-pound block using a lever. If the block is 10 feet from the pivot point and Talia is 8 feet beyond that, how much force must she apply to lift the block?

  a. 45 pounds
  b. 80 pounds
  c. 90 pounds
  d. 50 pounds

18. Which material is best suited for building a raft?

    a. metal

    b. wood

    c. glass

    d. concrete

19. A single-speed bicycle has a front chain ring with 48 teeth and a back gear with 12 teeth. If the bicycle is pedaled at 90 rpm, how fast will the rear wheel turn?

    a. 15 rpm

    b. 90 rpm

    c. 180 rpm

    d. 360 rpm

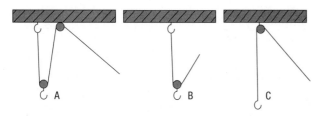

20. Which of the following pulley systems offers the least mechanical advantage?

    a. A

    b. B

    c. C

    d. They all offer the same advantage.

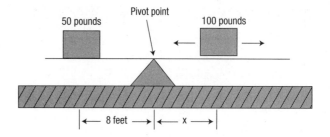

21. In the diagram, two blocks are balanced on either side of a lever. One block weighs 50 pounds and the other weighs 100 pounds. If the 50-pound block is 8 feet to the left of the pivot point, how far to the right of the pivot point is the 100 pound block?

    a. 2 feet

    b. 4 feet

    c. 8 feet

    d. 16 feet

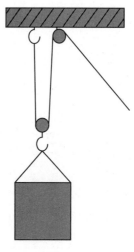

22. What is the mechanical advantage of the pulley system shown here?

    a. 1

    b. 2

    c. 3

    d. 4

23. Which of the following is heaviest?

  a. 1 cubic foot of water

  b. 1 cubic foot of lead

  c. 1 cubic foot of wood

  d. 1 cubic foot of ice

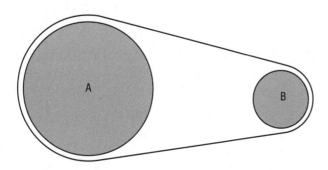

24. Pulley A has 2.5 times the circumference of pulley B. If pulley A rotates at 50 revolutions per minute (rpm), how fast must pulley B rotate?

  a. 20 rpm

  b. 50 rpm

  c. 125 rpm

  d. 250 rpm

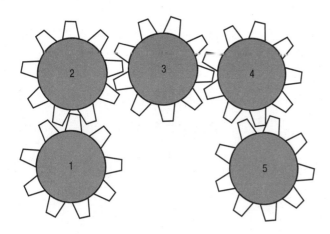

25. If gear 3 turns counterclockwise, which other gear(s), if any, will turn clockwise?

  a. 1 and 5

  b. 2 and 4

  c. All will turn clockwise.

  d. None will turn clockwise.

Part 9: Assembling Objects

Time: 15 minutes

Each question is composed of five separate drawings. The problem is presented in the first drawing, and the remaining four drawings are possible solutions. Determine which of the four choices contains all of the pieces assembled properly that are shown in the first picture. Note: images are not drawn to scale.

1.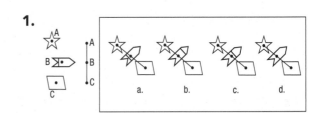

2.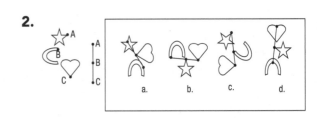

3.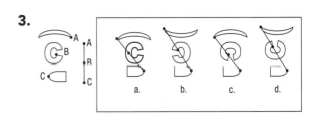

4.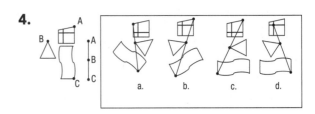

5.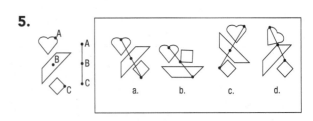

6.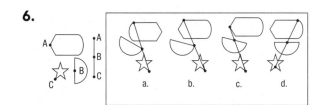

13.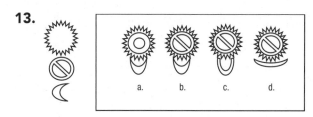

7.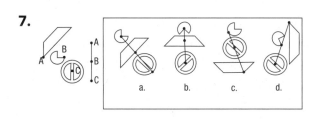

14.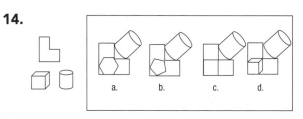

8.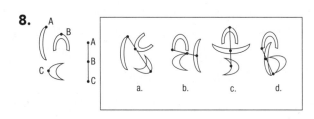

15.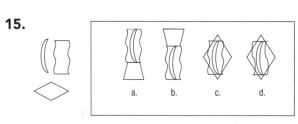

9.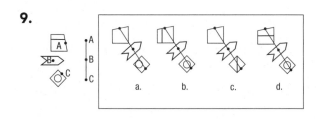

16.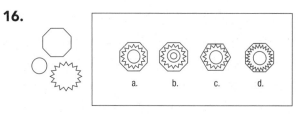

10.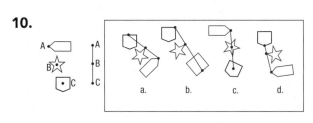

17.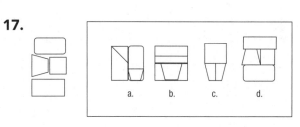

11.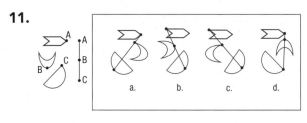

18.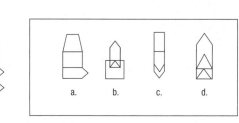

12.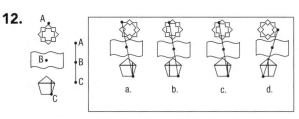

19.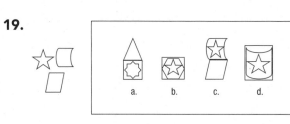

20.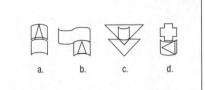

21.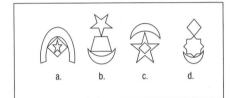

22.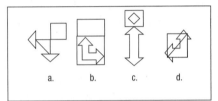

23.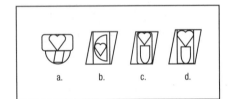

24.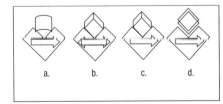

25.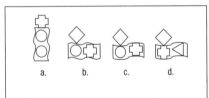

Answers

Part 1: General Science

1. b. About a third of the world's land is unusable and another third is already used for agriculture, leaving about a third remaining for human development.

2. b. Flowering plants (angiosperms) might reproduce faster because their reproduction involves flowers, which attract insects to help pollinate and other animals to spread seeds. Also, the seeds of angiosperms have a tough skin, which may have helped them tolerate harsh conditions.

3. a. Veins transport blood to the heart and pulmonary refers to the lungs. Therefore, the blood coming from the lungs to the heart is full of oxygen.

4. d. Noble gases have eight valence electrons and full orbital shells, making them stable and nonreactive. Noble gases have very low boiling points.

5. c. Materials, such as water, are used to slow the acceleration of neutrons, which prevents the uncontrolled release of energy.

6. b. A mixture is a combination of two or more components that do not change chemically. Choices **a** and **c** are compounds.

7. a. The renal system, also called the excretory system, consists of the kidneys and excretory accessory organs.

8. c. The placenta is specialized tissue that provides nutrients to the developing embryo in the mother's uterus.

9. d. When light moves from one medium to another it undergoes refraction, which is the bending of light.

10. b. Nucleotides are linked together according to genetic code and form nucleic acids.

11. b. Iridium is a rare element and occurs at high concentrations in meteorites. There is evidence of a huge impact on Earth 65 million years ago, which left high concentrations of iridium.

12. b. Generally, atomic radii increase when moving from left to right in the periodic table. Anions are much larger than their corresponding atoms and cations are much smaller than their corresponding atoms. In the case of Br^-, it accepts another electron, but does not change its number of protons. As a result, Br^- has a lesser pull on the electrons than Kr does, which has 8 protons and 8 electrons.

13. d. Nerves are composed of nervous tissue, which would exclude it from connective tissue.

14. c. The molecular mass of carbon (C) is 12 g and the molecular mass of oxygen (O) is 8 g. Therefore, the molecular mass of carbon dioxide (CO_2) is 28 g. With 7 g of CO_2 there is $\frac{1}{4}$ mole, equivalent to 3.0 g carbon.
$\frac{1}{4}$ mole $CO_2 \times \frac{\text{mol C}}{\text{mol CO}_2} \times \frac{12\text{ g}}{\text{mol C}} = 3.0$ g.

15. b. Metamorphic rock is formed from other rock types at extreme temperature and pressure.

16. b. With an excessive food supply, animals would not have to compete with other animals, and their population would probably continue growing. All the other choices would limit the growth rate of a population.

17. c. The ants seem to have driven away the termites that would have eventually killed the tree. The ants that now have found a home in the tunnels protect the tree from intruders, allowing it to grow and remain healthy. This is an example of mutualism, because both species benefit each other.

18. d. Endothermic reactions require an intake of energy or heat for the reactions to progress forward. Sublimation is the change of state from solid to gas, which requires energy. The other choices give off heat or energy, which is exothermic.

19. a. Because this is a recessive trait, to present the disorder an individual must be homozygous recessive for the disease. Even with a shortened life expectancy the gene is not expected to leave the gene pool, eliminating choice **b**. Choice **c** is not true, because a parent carrying one recessive gene will not show symptoms. Choice **d** is not true, because carriers are resistant to malaria, which is extremely useful in parts of the world where malaria is a risk.

20. a. Structural isomers are molecules with the same molecular formula but different structures. The different structures result in different properties for the compounds. Isomers are very common in organic molecules.

21. d. Transfer RNA (tRNA) is responsible for delivering amino acids to the ribosome according to the sequence on mRNA. If the mutation affects tRNA, its anticodons may not be able to read the sequence of codons or it may not be able to attach to the appropriate amino acid.

22. b. Enough sugar needs to be added to 500 mL so that the ratio of the weight to volume is 5%, $5\% = \frac{1}{20} = \frac{?\text{ g sugar}}{500\text{ mL}} = 25$ g.

23. d. Comets are loose collections of ice, dust, and small rock particles that regularly orbit the solar system. They are seen from Earth as patches of light with long tails.

24. a. Angiosperms use flowers for reproduction.

25. d. According to the ideal gas law, temperature is directly proportional to pressure and volume. Because the piston is sealed, the moles of the gas cannot change. Therefore, the only possibility is for volume to increase.

Part 2: Arithmetic Reasoning

1. d. You are looking for n, and $\frac{n}{200,000} = \frac{2}{5}$ or $n = \frac{2}{5} \times 200,000$. $\frac{2}{5}$ of the 200,000 sample population bicycle to work. $\frac{2}{5} \times 200,000 = 80,000$.

2. c. Each job will pay $21,200 after 4 years. You can see this by making a chart:

	1	2	3	4
Books R Us	$18,800	$19,600	$20,400	$21,200
Readers Galore	$17,600	$18,800	$20,000	$21,200

3. a. Ricardo spends 11% for his car, half of the 22% he saves. (You can use % for the pie chart values without doing any additional math, since the values are already out of 100.)

4. a. Savings and housing together make up 50% of Ricardo's budget: 22% + 28%.

5. c. Ricardo spent 6 cents more per dollar on housing than on food: 28 − 22 = 6. Six cents is 6% of each budgeted dollar. $46,500 × 0.06 = $2,790, which is about $2,800.

6. a. The unreduced ratio is 8,000:5,000,000; reduced, the ratio is 8:5,000. Now divide: 5,000 ÷ 8 = 625, for a ratio of 1:625.

7. d. It takes 9 square feet to make a square yard. To find out how many square yards are in 182 square feet, divide: $182 \text{ ft.}^2 \div 9 \frac{\text{ft.}^2}{\text{yd.}^2} = 20.22$ square yards. Since Donna cannot purchase part of a square yard, she has to round up. She must purchase 21 square yards to have enough to carpet the room.

8. b. Jack is likely to make $\frac{2}{5} \times 25 = 10$ of his next 25 free-throw attempts.

9. b. Let x equal the number of people remaining in the room. You have: $x = 12 - (\frac{2}{3}(12) + 3)$ or $x = 12 - (8 + 3) = 12 - 11$. Thus, $x = 1$ person.

10. a. $\frac{0.5}{15} = \frac{5.25}{d}$, or map distance in inches/actual distance in miles.

11. c. This is a two-step problem involving both addition and division. First, arrange the three numbers in a column, keeping the decimal points aligned. Add: 113.9 + 106.7 + 122 = 342.6. Next, divide your answer by 3: 342.6 ÷ 3 = 114.2.

12. d. You want to know R = helicopter's speed in miles per hour. To solve this problem, recall that *rate × time = distance*. It is given that $T = 6{:}17 - 6{:}02 = 15$ minutes = 0.25 hour and $D = 20$ miles. Substitute: $r \times 0.25 = 20$. Simplify: $r = 20 \div 0.25$. Thus, $r = 80$ miles per hour.

13. c. Multiply the number of minutes in an hour by the given number of hours. There are 60 minutes in each hour. Therefore, there are 720 minutes in 12 hours: 12 hours × 60 minutes = 720 minutes.

14. d. Figure the amounts by setting up the following equations: First, S = $3 + $23 = $26. Now, B = ($1 × 5) + ($2 × 2) or $5 + $4 = $9. MR = $1 × 2 = $2; and D = $4 × 1 = $4. Now, add: $9 + $2 + $4 = $15. Now subtract: $26 − $15 = $11.

15. b. You want to find S, the rate Sharon charges to mow a lawn in dollars per hour. You are given Kathy's rate, which is K = 7.50, and you are told that S = 1.5K. Substitute: S = 1.5(7.50). Thus, S = $11.25 per hour.

16. d. A scale is a ratio of model to real, keeping the units consistent. The tower is 986 feet tall, and the replica is 4 inches; 986 feet must be converted to inches, by multiplying by 12: 986 times 12 is 11,832 inches. Set up the ratio of replica to real and simplify: $\frac{4}{11,832} \div \frac{4}{4} = \frac{1}{2958}$.

17. a. 10:30 A.M. to 5:30 P.M. is a seven-hour period. Mike can give 13 lessons, each lasting 30 minutes, if he takes 30 minutes for lunch. $20 × 13 = $260.

18. c. First, determine the distance to drive to work, using the formula $D = R \times T$. Substitute known values and then multiply: $D = 60 \times \frac{1}{2}$, so $D = 30$. The distance to work is 30 miles.

Now, determine the time to drive to work at a rate of 40 miles per hour, again using the formula $D = R \times T$. Substitute known values and then divide by 40: $30 = 40 \times T$, so $0.75 = T$. The new time is 0.75 hour, or three-quarters of an hour. The problem asks how much *extra* time it will take to drive. This is the difference between one-half hour and three-quarters of an hour. Subtract the fractions, after changing one-half to two-quarters: $\frac{3}{4} - \frac{2}{4} = \frac{1}{4}$. One-quarter of an hour is 15 minutes.

19. a. Set up a ratio of length to height. The proportion is $\frac{10}{8} = \frac{l}{5.6}$. Cross multiply to get $8 \times l = 10 \times 5.6$. Multiply 10 times 5.6 to get $8 \times l = 56$. Divide 56 by 8 to get 7 feet long.

20. b. There has been an increase in price of $3; $3 ÷ $50 = 0.06. This is an increase of 0.06, or 6%.

21. c. Take the words in order and substitute the letters and numbers. Patricia has (P =), four times (4 ×) the number of marbles Sean has (S). The statement becomes $P = 4 \times S$, which is equal to $P = 4S$.

22. b. Let x equal the unknown quantity of each denomination. You know that all the coins total $8.20 and that each denomination is multiplied by the same number, x. Therefore, $0.25x + 0.10x + 0.05x + 0.01x = 8.20$. This reduces to $(0.25 + 0.10 + 0.05 + 0.01)x = 8.20$, or $0.41x = 8.20$. Thus, $x = 20$ coins in each denomination.

23. c. $12 \times 5\% + 4 \times 4\% = x$ times 16; $x = 4.75\%$.

24. a. You are asked to find F, Fluffy's age. Begin the solution by breaking the problem into parts: Fluffy is half the age of Muffy becomes $F = (\frac{1}{2})(M)$, Muffy is one-third as old as Spot becomes $M = (\frac{1}{3})(S)$, and Spot is half the neighbor's age becomes $S = (\frac{1}{2})(N)$. You know the neighbor's age is 24 or $N = 24$. Substitute and work backward through the problem: $S = \frac{1}{2}(24) = 12$, $M = \frac{1}{3}(12) = 4$, $F = \frac{1}{2}(4)$. Thus, Fluffy is two years old.

25. a. Mario has finished $\frac{35}{45}$ of his test, which reduces to $\frac{7}{9}$, so he has $\frac{2}{9}$ of the test to go.

26. b. Let x equal D'Andre's rate. D'Andre's rate multiplied by his travel time equals the distance he travels; this equals Adam's rate multiplied by his travel time: $2x = D = 3(x - 5)$. Therefore, $2x = 3x - 15$, or $x = 15$ miles per hour.

27. b. There are three steps involved in solving this problem. First, convert 4.5% to a decimal: 0.045. Multiply that by $26,000 to find out how much the salary increases. Finally, add the result ($1,170) to the original salary of $26,000 to find out the new salary, $27,170.

28. b. Let L equal the number of gallons of gas lost, which is equal to the rate of loss times the time over which it occurs, or $L = RT$. Substitute: $L = (7)(\frac{1}{3}) = 2(\frac{1}{3})$ gallons. Notice that the 14-gallon tank size is irrelevant information in this problem.

29. a. Let R equal Veronica's average speed. Recall that for uniform motion, *distance = rate × time* or $D = RT$. Substitute: $220 = R(5)$ or $R = \frac{220}{5}$. Thus, $R = 44$ miles per hour.

30. b. 860 feet × 560 feet ÷ 43,560 square feet per acre = 11.06 acres.

Part 3: Word Knowledge

1. c. Something that is *lucid* is clear, comprehensible, or understandable.

2. b. *Mourning*, not to be confused with morning, is the act of expressing grief or sadness, or sorrowing.

3. d. Someone who is *resolute* is steadfast, resolved, or determined.

4. c. *Ambivalent* means conflicted, fluctuating, or uncertain. If you chose choice **a** or **b**, you were probably thinking of ambidextrous, which means able to use both hands equally well.

5. b. *Dissent* and disagreement occur when there is a difference of opinion. You were probably thinking of descent if you chose choice **a**. Choice **c** would be a good answer for *decent*.

6. b. As an adjective, *grave* means somber, solemn, or serious.

7. a. *Hapless* means unfortunate or unlucky.

8. a. *Dreary* means dull or boring. Something dreary can cause sleepiness, but does not itself mean sleepy.

9. d. *Arid* means parched, dry, or barren due to a lack of rainfall.

10. c. To *deter* means to dissuade, prevent, or discourage. If you chose choice **a**, you may have been thinking of detour.

11. b. *Covert* means disguised or concealed.

12. a. An *allusion* is a direct or implied reference to something. Choice **b** is a synonym for illusion. If you chose choice **c**, you were probably thinking of elude, which means to avoid.

13. b. Both *desist* and stop mean to cease.

14. c. A *pariah* is a person who has been shunned from the community, or an outcast. A piranha is a fish (choice **b**).

15. a. To *precede* means to come before, or lead. If you chose choice **b** or **c**, you probably mistook precede for proceed, and if you chose choice **d**, you may have been thinking of proceeds.

16. c. To *forgive* means to excuse, allow, or pardon.

17. d. *Potent* means strong, influential, or powerful.

18. d. Something *succinct* is brief or concise.

19. b. To *console* means to provide comfort. If you chose choice **a**, you may have been thinking of consult.

20. c. To *surmise* or guess means to come to a conclusion without evidence.

21. c. *Mimic* means to copy the behavior or qualities of something. The key phrase "to avoid detection" suggests that the predators somehow blend in; the only answer choice that would make this possible is choice **c**.

22. a. *Tantamount* means equivalent to. You know it is not choice **d**, because the second sentence tells you they are comparable actions.

23. d. *Aimlessly* means without aim or objective. The key phrase is "Without a goal in mind," which suggests he is walking without direction, or randomly. The sentence does not mention anything about Greg's mood, so choice **b** is incorrect even though it might appear logical.

24. d. In order to find the answer, ask yourself for what kind of a writer would it be a surprise if they made many typos. That should eliminate choices **a** and **b**. Choice **c** might make sense, but a very intelligent writer who is not thorough could still make many typos.

25. c. Any of these choices could fit, but the second sentence conveys a sense of urgency that only choice **c** makes clear.

26. a. You might narrow this question down to choices **a** and **b** because they both provide logical reasons why the boy would be on the couch all day. Because the sentence tells you that the boy got no sleep, however, choice **a** makes the most sense.

27. b. Someone who approves only his own ideas can be described as *arrogant*.

28. b. The second sentence clarifies the importance of not making mistakes, which might occur if you don't follow or if you stray from the instructions.

29. c. Choice **c** is the only logical choice to describe someone who is also scared.

30. b. The gopher's behavior, ruining the grass, suggests it is troublesome. The only answer that conveys this idea is choice **b**.

31. d. *Riveting* means extremely interesting. The only choice here that logically fits is choice **d**.

32. a. Only choices **a** and **b** fit logically in this sentence. Choice **a** is best because there is no indication why the writing is unreadable; it could be too tiny, too sloppy, or in an unfamiliar language.

33. b. Consider the context of the sentence. Someone who makes many mistakes and who is just starting a career is likely inexperienced.

34. c. The second sentence implies that trivial details are unimportant. Choice **c** is the only choice that fits this definition.

35. b. The sentence implies that the parents originally did not want to buy the boy a puppy but eventually changed their minds. Choice **b** reflects this change of opinion.

Part 4: Paragraph Comprehension

1. b. The taxpayers' association pointed to the school budget as an example of their complaint, but their overall concern was with rising taxes.

2. a. Something that is *persistent* is ongoing, continuing over a period of time. A persistent person keeps trying despite repeated failure, and a persistent problem continually reappears.

3. c. Bob Smith mentioned the school budget because it was an example of waste of taxpayers' money, not because he was anti-education or unathletic.

4. d. The passage states in the last paragraph that some members of the taxpayers' association would run for town council to replace members who kept raising taxes.

5. b. The passage states that the hardware store wanted to ensure that each customer was able to buy a pump, so they used tickets to enforce that.

6. c. The word *deluge* means a flood, an overwhelming rush of water.

7. a. The central idea in this passage is that one should not complain, because there is always someone else whose suffering is worse. The hardware store owners were not heartless, because they were trying to help as many people as possible.

8. c. The author refers to the complaining customers as childish because their problems were not as severe as their neighbors' problems, yet they were very angry at a small inconvenience.

9. d. See the final sentence of the passage.

10. b. The final sentence states that a sense of wonder is important to the human spirit. Choice **d** does mention looking at the stars, but it is the sense of wonder that is important; the stars merely excite one's wonder. Dark skies and clean environment (choices **a** and **c**) might be important, but the author addresses wonder as specifically important to one's spirit.

11. a. George's reaction to his boss's words was anger. We can infer that he left his job because of that anger, since he took a new job earning less money.

12. c. The word *reprimand* means to scold or rebuke. George was scolded for his appearance at work.

13. b. George's boss was angry because George did not dress properly, and his appearance was unprofessional.

14. d. The word *slovenly* means untidy or messy. George's appearance looked sloppy in the office.

15. c. The first sentence points out that it is not practical to use the first-person point of view in business correspondence. Choices **a** and **b** are not in the paragraph. Although choice **d** is in the paragraph and it does tell us something about the first-person point of view, it is too narrow to represent the main idea, which has to do with the first-person point of view as it is related to writing in a business environment.

Part 5: Mathematics Knowledge

1. a. To solve this problem, you must first convert all the fractions to the lowest common denominator, which is 24; $\frac{7}{8} = \frac{21}{24}$; $\frac{3}{4} = \frac{18}{24}$, $\frac{2}{3} = \frac{16}{24}$, $\frac{5}{6} = \frac{20}{24}$. The fraction with the largest numerator, $\frac{21}{24}$, has the greatest value.

2. b. This is a special expression called a *perfect square*. The x terms cancel each other out, leaving just two terms in the expression; therefore, $(x + 5)(x - 5)$ is the correct factoring of the expression.

3. d. Square each side of the equal sign to eliminate the radical: $(\sqrt{b-4})^2 = 5^2$ becomes $b - 4 = 25$. Add 4 to both sides of the equation: $b = 29$.

4. d. The three angles of a triangle add up to 180°. When you subtract 42 and 59 from 180, the result is 79°.

5. c. The perimeter is the sum of the triangle's two legs plus the hypotenuse. Knowing two of the sides, you can find the third side, or hypotenuse (h), using the Pythagorean theorem: $a^2 + a^2 = h^2$, which simplifies to $2a^2 = h^2$. So $h = \sqrt{2a^2}$. This means the perimeter is $2a + \sqrt{2a^2}$.

6. a. The formula for finding the area of triangle is $\frac{1}{2} \times$ the base $\times$ the height; therefore, if you divide the given area, 60, by the height, 15, it will give half the base, 4. The base is 8 centimeters.

7. a. The symbol > means "greater than," and the symbol < means "less than." The only sentence that is correct is choice **a**: four feet is greater than three feet. The other choices are untrue.

8. b. To solve this division problem, subtract the exponents only: $5 - 2 = 3$, so the answer is 10^3.

9. d. Divide the numerator by the denominator to get the correct answer of 0.4.

10. c. To find the perimeter, you can double each of the sides and add the sums: $2(834) + 2(1,288) = 1,668 + 2,576 = 4,244$ feet.

11. b. There are 60 minutes in one hour. Multiply $60 \times 7\frac{1}{6}$ by multiplying $60 \times 7 = 420$ and $60 \times \frac{1}{6} = 10$. Then add $420 + 10$ to get 430 minutes.

12. d. First, the radius needs to be found, which is $\frac{1}{2}$ of the diameter: $r = 47$ centimeters; then, to find the area, square the radius and multiply by π. The correct answer is $2,209\pi$.

13. d. Since both dimensions are tripled, there are two additional factors of 3. Therefore, the new are is $3 \times 3 = 9$ times as large as the original.

14. a. The distance between Plattville and Quincy is the hypotenuse of a right triangle with sides of length 80 and 60. The length of the hypotenuse equals $\sqrt{80^2 + 60^2}$, which equals $\sqrt{6,400 + 3,600}$, which equals $\sqrt{10,000}$, which equals 100 miles.

15. c. In order for a number to be divisible by six, it must be able to be divided by six without a remainder. A shortcut to check divisibility by six is to see if the number is divisible by both two and three. Since 546 is even (ends in 6), the number is divisible by two. Since the sum of the digits is 5 + 4 + 6 = 15 and 15 is divisible by three, 546 is also divisible by three. Since 546 is divisible by both two and three, it is also divisible by six.

16. a. A triangle with two congruent sides could either be isosceles or equilateral. However, because one angle is 40°, it cannot be equilateral (the angles would be 60°).

17. c. Use the FOIL method to find the answer. This stands for the order by which the terms are multiplied: First + Outside + Inside + Last: $(3x \times x) + (3x \times -6) + (4x) + (4 \times -6)$; $3x^2 - 18x + 4x - 24$. The correct answer is $3x^2 - 14x - 24$.

18. d. An acute angle is less than 90°.

19. b. The vertical bars on either side of the expression tell you to find the *absolute value* of 4 – 15. To complete the question, find 4 – 15 to get –11. Then find the absolute value (the distance the number is away from zero on a number line) of –11, which is 11.

20. a. Since 4 and 6 are factors of 24, and 4 is a perfect square, $\sqrt{24} = \sqrt{4} \times \sqrt{6} = 2 \times \sqrt{6}$ or $2\sqrt{6}$.

21. a. In this question, 10 is the base and 4 is the exponent; 10^4 means 10 is used as a factor four times, or $10 \times 10 \times 10 \times 10$.

22. d. The hundredth is the second digit to the right of the decimal point. Because the third decimal is 6, the second is rounded up to 4.

23. b. The correct answer is 1.

24. d. Factor the left side of the equation and set each factor equal to zero: $x^2 - 25 = (x - 5)(x + 5)$; $x - 5 = 0$ or $x + 5 = 0$. Therefore, $x = 5$ or -5.

25. c. This is a division problem with mixed numbers. First, convert the mixed numbers to fractions: $33\frac{1}{2} = \frac{67}{2}$ and $5\frac{1}{4} = \frac{21}{4}$. Next, invert the second fraction and multiply: $\frac{67}{2} \times \frac{4}{21} = \frac{134}{21}$. Reduce to a mixed number: $\frac{134}{21} = 6\frac{8}{21}$. With this result, you know that only six glasses can be completely filled.

Part 6: Electronics Information

1. d. A quartz crystal is typically found in an oscillator and uses the piezoelectric effect to create an electrical signal. This capability is commonly used to keep track of time (as in quartz wristwatches).

2. b. A typical residential wall outlet in North America uses alternating current (AC) voltage.

3. b. Radio waves have the longest wavelengths of the answers given.

4. a. A step-down transformer would be required to reduce the voltage.

5. b. This is the schematic symbol for a circuit breaker.

6. a. One coulomb is the amount of electric charge transported in one second by a steady current of one ampere.

7. d. A diode allows electrical current to flow through it in one direction. This unidirectional behavior is called *rectification*, making one of the functions performed by a diode a rectifier.

8. a. A photovoltaic cell, or solar cell, takes the energy from solar radiation and produces direct current.

9. d. Choice **a** represents a polarized two-plug wire, choice **b** represents the source of a constant current, and **c** represents a speaker.

10. a. *Low potential* to electricians most closely means 600 watts or lower.

11. d. As the frequency of a signal goes higher, the period becomes shorter: 10,000 Hz has a period of 0.0001 seconds ($\frac{1}{10,000}$ of a second). Therefore, frequency and period are inversely related. All the other answer choices have no bearing on frequency.

12. b. When values are in decibels, the gains and losses in power are simply added together to determine the expected power level. $-10\text{ dBm} - 2\text{ dB} + 30\text{ dB} - 3\text{ dB} + 20\text{ dB} - 5\text{ dB} = 30\text{ dBm}$.

13. d. A capacitor's storage potential, or capacitance, is measured in units called *farads*, named after the English physicist Michael Faraday.

14. a. Random access memory (RAM) chips are known as "volatile," which means the data contained is lost when power is turned off.

15. d. The charge polarity of electrons is negative; the charge polarity of protons is positive.

16. c. Remember that in a series circuit the sum of the individual resistors determines the total resistance: $10 + 55 = 65$.

17. d. The amplification factor (also called gain) is usually expressed in terms of power. The decibel (dB), a logarithmic unit, is the most common way of expressing the amplification factor.

18. d. The prefix "micro" means multiply by 10^{6}, so 287 microamps equals 0.000287 A.

19. d. A minimum of #4 wire gauge is required. The amount of power that is transmitted through the electrical line dictates how large the gauge wire should be. American wire gauge (AWG) standards have the largest wires gauge in the lower numbers.

20. c. Cartridge fuses with a rating of 60 amps or higher will have knife-blade terminals on either end, as illustrated.

Part 7: Auto and Shop Information

1. d. Using water alone can indeed help cool the system down. However, the absence of an additive to raise the boiling point or lower the freezing point could limit the operating environments the car could operate in. In addition, pure water can rust the internal mechanisms of the vehicle.

2. c. With the oil pump supplying oil to the entire engine for lubrication, the oil system can be said to connect directly to the internal combustion engine. The other systems mentioned are all automobile systems that are stand-alone (suspension, braking) or are tied solely to the automobile battery.

3. b. The driver has direct control of the steering system through the inputs to the steering mechanism. The other systems mentioned are all stand-alone systems where the driver has little or no input.

4. c. A knock or ping sound from your engine generally means the air/fuel mixture is igniting too soon inside the engine cylinders.

5. a. Using a higher octane gasoline will solve this problem. The octane rating of gasoline is related to its ability to resist the "knock," or the ignition of air/fuel mixture outside the envelope of the normal combustion region.

6. c. Since hydraulic fluid is not compressible, there should be no "spongy" feeling in the brakes. This sort of brake performance could mean there is air in the brake lines. Bleeding the air out of the system through bleeder valves should solve the problem.

7. b. The Society of Automotive Engineers (S.A.E.) established a numerical code system for grading motor oils according to their viscosity characteristics. This S.A.E. rating is used depending on what sort of driving environment the engine will be operating in.

8. c. Depending on driving conditions, tires will usually last 30,000 to 80,000 miles.

9. d. Specific structures are built into the tire tread called *wear bars*. When these wear bars have been worn down to where they are flush with the surrounding tread, the tire is in need of replacement.

10. c. A worn or loose fan belt will make a squealing noise as the rotating pulley spins around without moving the loose fan belt.

11. d. A spark plug not firing properly will result in an engine running rough since one of the cylinders is not firing in proper order and contributing its power cycle to the overall operation.

12. d. You should run for at least 10 minutes to warm the oil up, increasing viscosity. Heating the oil up by running the engine for a short period will increase its viscosity, making it easier to drain.

13. b. When making a circular cut in a piece of metal, the best chisel to use is a round chisel. The butt chisel and the framing chisel are both wood chisels. A socket chisel is a type of framing chisel.

14. b. Paint should always be thinned with turpentine. Any of the other compounds will change the chemical makeup of the paint.

15. c. The tool shown is an electric soldering gun.

16. b. Wood, cinder blocks, and brick and mortar are all materials that could be used to build a permanent foundation, but concrete would be the strongest.

17. b. A Forstner bit has a wide circular cutting edge with a spur in the middle for precise placement.

18. c. A brad is often used in picture frames and light assembly.

19. b. A torque wrench is used to apply a specific amount of tightness to nuts or bolts. It is used where exact tolerances are needed and large amounts of stress or pressure could be expected on the nuts or bolts.

20. c. A table saw is not considered a carpenter's hand tool.

21. a. A posthole digger would be the best tool to dig a small, circular hole a foot or two deep, such as for a mailbox post or a fence post. The other tools listed could be used to dig such a hole, but would require more effort and work.

22. c. The width of the saw cut is called the *kerf* of a saw. On most saws, the kerf is wider than the saw blade because the teeth are flared out sideways.

23. d. A fence guide would be used to help guide a piece of wood through a table saw. The other combinations of tools are not usually used together.

24. d. A bolt cutter is used to cut chains, padlocks, bolts, and other hard, thin metals.

25. b. Aluminum oxide is the material used on most sandpapers. Pumice and emery are also used as abrasives but not on standard sandpaper.

Part 8: Mechanical Comprehension

1. c. A pulley system of this type has a mechanical advantage of 2. So, a 250-pound weight can be lifted with 250 pounds ÷ 2 = 125 pounds.

2. a. The density of mercury is strongly temperature dependent. When placed in hot liquid, mercury expands by a known amount, forcing small amounts of liquid mercury up the thermometer.

3. a. $w_1 \times d_1 = w_2 \times d_2$. 120 pounds × 11 feet = w_2 × 6 feet. Solving for w_2 gives 220 pounds.

4. c. The crank is moving counterclockwise, meaning that when it is pointing downward it is moving away from the piston (to the right). So, the piston will be in a central position. Since the crank is moving to the right, the piston will also be moving to the right.

5. b. 12 miles ÷ 1.5 hours = 8 miles per hour.

6. a. The mechanical advantage (MA) of a ramp is determined by the length of the ramp, l, divided by the height gained, h. In this case, MA = $\frac{l}{h}$ = 25 feet ÷ 10 feet = 2.5. The force required to pull a 300-pound block up a ramp is 300 pounds ÷ 2.5 = 120 pounds.

7. a. The force constant of the spring is 10 pounds ÷ 8 inches = 1.25 pounds per inch. Using the equation, $F = kx$, we have 15 pounds = 1.25 pounds per inch × x. Solving for x gives 12 inches.

8. c. If 18 turns move the nut 1.2 inches, there are 18 turns ÷ 1.2 inches = 15 threads per inch.

9. b. Mechanical advantage = output force ÷ input force. Here, 40 pounds of force is input to lift a 120-pound load. The mechanical advantage is 120 ÷ 40 = 3.

10. a. The mechanical advantage of this pulley system is 4. The force required to lift the 300-pound load is 300 pounds ÷ 4 = 75 pounds.

11. b. Gear 1 turning clockwise will cause gears 2 and 4 to turn counterclockwise. Gear 3 will be the only other gear that turns clockwise.

12. d. When a submarine fills its tanks with water it becomes heavier, which decreases its buoyancy and increases its density. The volume of the submarine remains unchanged through the entire process.

13. d. Because pulley system B has a mechanical advantage of 2, the rope must be pulled twice as far as pulley system A to do the same amount of work: 2 × 10 feet = 20 feet.

14. a. If a vertical line is drawn straight down from the center of gravity, only the line for truck A reaches the ground outside of the truck's tires. This makes the truck unstable.

15. a. Cable A is attached to the arm closest to the crane. Therefore, it has the weakest mechanical advantage and so will be under the most strain to support the weight of the arm.

16. a. The total volume of the block is 2 inches × 2 inches × 5 inches = 20 inches^3. Its density is 0.3 pounds per cubic inch, so its total weight must be 20 inches^3 × 0.3 pounds per inch^3 = 6 pounds.

17. d. $w_1 \times d_1 = w_2 \times d_2$. Talia is 18 feet away from the pivot point. 90 pounds × 8 feet = 10 feet × w_2. Solving for w_2 gives 50 pounds.

18. b. Wood is the best choice. All other objects are very dense and will quickly sink. Wood offers a lower density while still remaining strong enough to function as a raft.

19. d. Each full turn of the pedals will turn the rear wheel 48 ÷ 12 = 4 revolutions. If the pedals are turning at 90 rpm, the rear wheel will move at 4 × 90 rpm = 360 rpm.

20. c. Pulley systems A and B offer a mechanical advantage of 2, whereas pulley system C offers a mechanical advantage of 1. In A and B, the rope used to raise the weight moves 2 feet for every 1 foot the pulley is raised, whereas in C the rope used to raise the weight moves 1 foot for every foot the weight is raised.

21. b. $w_1 \times d_1 = w_2 \times d_2$. 50 pounds × 8 feet = 100 pounds × d_2. Solving for d_2 gives 4 feet.

22. b. In this pulley system, the weight of the load is shared over 2 cables and so the mechanical advantage is 2.

23. b. Since all materials occupy the same volume, the material with the greatest density will be the heaviest. Lead is an extremely dense material and is much denser than all other options.

24. c. Since pulley A is 2.5 times greater in diameter than pulley B, each revolution of A will lead to 2.5 revolutions of B. If A rotates at 50 rpm, then B will rotate at 50 rpm × 2.5 = 125 rpm.

25. b. If gear 3 turns counterclockwise, it will lead to its neighboring gears (2 and 4) to turn clockwise.

Part 9: Assembling Objects

1. a.
2. c.
3. b.
4. b.
5. c.
6. c.
7. d.
8. a.
9. b.
10. c.
11. d.
12. a.
13. b.
14. d.

15. c.
16. a.
17. d.
18. b.
19. c.
20. b.
21. c.
22. d.
23. c.
24. c.
25. b.

Scoring

Write your raw score (the number you got right) for each test in the blanks below. Then turn to Chapter 2 to find out how to convert these raw scores into the scores the armed services use.

1. General Science: _____ right out of 25

2. Arithmetic Reasoning: _____ right out of 30

3. Word Knowledge: _____ right out of 35

4. Paragraph Comprehension: _____ right out of 15

5. Mathematics Knowledge: _____ right out of 25

6. Electronics Information: _____ right out of 20

7. Auto and Shop Information: _____ right out of 25

8. Mechanical Comprehension: _____ right out of 25

9. Assembling Objects: _____ right out of 25

9 ▶ ASVAB PRACTICE TEST 5

CHAPTER SUMMARY

This is the final sample ASVAB test for you to practice with.

F or this test, simulate the actual test-taking experience as closely as you can. Find a quiet place to work where you won't be disturbed. If you own this book, tear out the answer sheet on the following pages and find some #2 pencils to fill in the circles with. Use a timer or stopwatch to time each section. The times are marked at the beginning of each section. After you take the test, use the detailed answer explanations that follow to review any questions you missed.

Part 1: General Science (GS)

1.	ⓐ	ⓑ	ⓒ	ⓓ	10.	ⓐ	ⓑ	ⓒ	ⓓ	18.	ⓐ	ⓑ	ⓒ	ⓓ
2.	ⓐ	ⓑ	ⓒ	ⓓ	11.	ⓐ	ⓑ	ⓒ	ⓓ	19.	ⓐ	ⓑ	ⓒ	ⓓ
3.	ⓐ	ⓑ	ⓒ	ⓓ	12.	ⓐ	ⓑ	ⓒ	ⓓ	20.	ⓐ	ⓑ	ⓒ	ⓓ
4.	ⓐ	ⓑ	ⓒ	ⓓ	13.	ⓐ	ⓑ	ⓒ	ⓓ	21.	ⓐ	ⓑ	ⓒ	ⓓ
5.	ⓐ	ⓑ	ⓒ	ⓓ	14.	ⓐ	ⓑ	ⓒ	ⓓ	22.	ⓐ	ⓑ	ⓒ	ⓓ
6.	ⓐ	ⓑ	ⓒ	ⓓ	15.	ⓐ	ⓑ	ⓒ	ⓓ	23.	ⓐ	ⓑ	ⓒ	ⓓ
7.	ⓐ	ⓑ	ⓒ	ⓓ	16.	ⓐ	ⓑ	ⓒ	ⓓ	24.	ⓐ	ⓑ	ⓒ	ⓓ
8.	ⓐ	ⓑ	ⓒ	ⓓ	17.	ⓐ	ⓑ	ⓒ	ⓓ	25.	ⓐ	ⓑ	ⓒ	ⓓ
9.	ⓐ	ⓑ	ⓒ	ⓓ										

Part 2: Arithmetic Reasoning (AR)

1.	ⓐ	ⓑ	ⓒ	ⓓ	11.	ⓐ	ⓑ	ⓒ	ⓓ	21.	ⓐ	ⓑ	ⓒ	ⓓ
2.	ⓐ	ⓑ	ⓒ	ⓓ	12.	ⓐ	ⓑ	ⓒ	ⓓ	22.	ⓐ	ⓑ	ⓒ	ⓓ
3.	ⓐ	ⓑ	ⓒ	ⓓ	13.	ⓐ	ⓑ	ⓒ	ⓓ	23.	ⓐ	ⓑ	ⓒ	ⓓ
4.	ⓐ	ⓑ	ⓒ	ⓓ	14.	ⓐ	ⓑ	ⓒ	ⓓ	24.	ⓐ	ⓑ	ⓒ	ⓓ
5.	ⓐ	ⓑ	ⓒ	ⓓ	15.	ⓐ	ⓑ	ⓒ	ⓓ	25.	ⓐ	ⓑ	ⓒ	ⓓ
6.	ⓐ	ⓑ	ⓒ	ⓓ	16.	ⓐ	ⓑ	ⓒ	ⓓ	26.	ⓐ	ⓑ	ⓒ	ⓓ
7.	ⓐ	ⓑ	ⓒ	ⓓ	17.	ⓐ	ⓑ	ⓒ	ⓓ	27.	ⓐ	ⓑ	ⓒ	ⓓ
8.	ⓐ	ⓑ	ⓒ	ⓓ	18.	ⓐ	ⓑ	ⓒ	ⓓ	28.	ⓐ	ⓑ	ⓒ	ⓓ
9.	ⓐ	ⓑ	ⓒ	ⓓ	19.	ⓐ	ⓑ	ⓒ	ⓓ	29.	ⓐ	ⓑ	ⓒ	ⓓ
10.	ⓐ	ⓑ	ⓒ	ⓓ	20.	ⓐ	ⓑ	ⓒ	ⓓ	30.	ⓐ	ⓑ	ⓒ	ⓓ

Part 3: Word Knowledge (WK)

1.	ⓐ	ⓑ	ⓒ	ⓓ	13.	ⓐ	ⓑ	ⓒ	ⓓ	25.	ⓐ	ⓑ	ⓒ	ⓓ
2.	ⓐ	ⓑ	ⓒ	ⓓ	14.	ⓐ	ⓑ	ⓒ	ⓓ	26.	ⓐ	ⓑ	ⓒ	ⓓ
3.	ⓐ	ⓑ	ⓒ	ⓓ	15.	ⓐ	ⓑ	ⓒ	ⓓ	27.	ⓐ	ⓑ	ⓒ	ⓓ
4.	ⓐ	ⓑ	ⓒ	ⓓ	16.	ⓐ	ⓑ	ⓒ	ⓓ	28.	ⓐ	ⓑ	ⓒ	ⓓ
5.	ⓐ	ⓑ	ⓒ	ⓓ	17.	ⓐ	ⓑ	ⓒ	ⓓ	29.	ⓐ	ⓑ	ⓒ	ⓓ
6.	ⓐ	ⓑ	ⓒ	ⓓ	18.	ⓐ	ⓑ	ⓒ	ⓓ	30.	ⓐ	ⓑ	ⓒ	ⓓ
7.	ⓐ	ⓑ	ⓒ	ⓓ	19.	ⓐ	ⓑ	ⓒ	ⓓ	31.	ⓐ	ⓑ	ⓒ	ⓓ
8.	ⓐ	ⓑ	ⓒ	ⓓ	20.	ⓐ	ⓑ	ⓒ	ⓓ	32.	ⓐ	ⓑ	ⓒ	ⓓ
9.	ⓐ	ⓑ	ⓒ	ⓓ	21.	ⓐ	ⓑ	ⓒ	ⓓ	33.	ⓐ	ⓑ	ⓒ	ⓓ
10.	ⓐ	ⓑ	ⓒ	ⓓ	22.	ⓐ	ⓑ	ⓒ	ⓓ	34.	ⓐ	ⓑ	ⓒ	ⓓ
11.	ⓐ	ⓑ	ⓒ	ⓓ	23.	ⓐ	ⓑ	ⓒ	ⓓ	35.	ⓐ	ⓑ	ⓒ	ⓓ
12.	ⓐ	ⓑ	ⓒ	ⓓ	24.	ⓐ	ⓑ	ⓒ	ⓓ					

Part 4: Paragraph Comprehension (PC)

1.	ⓐ	ⓑ	ⓒ	ⓓ		6.	ⓐ	ⓑ	ⓒ	ⓓ		11.	ⓐ	ⓑ	ⓒ	ⓓ
2.	ⓐ	ⓑ	ⓒ	ⓓ		7.	ⓐ	ⓑ	ⓒ	ⓓ		12.	ⓐ	ⓑ	ⓒ	ⓓ
3.	ⓐ	ⓑ	ⓒ	ⓓ		8.	ⓐ	ⓑ	ⓒ	ⓓ		13.	ⓐ	ⓑ	ⓒ	ⓓ
4.	ⓐ	ⓑ	ⓒ	ⓓ		9.	ⓐ	ⓑ	ⓒ	ⓓ		14.	ⓐ	ⓑ	ⓒ	ⓓ
5.	ⓐ	ⓑ	ⓒ	ⓓ		10.	ⓐ	ⓑ	ⓒ	ⓓ		15.	ⓐ	ⓑ	ⓒ	ⓓ

Part 5: Mathematics Knowledge (MK)

1.	ⓐ	ⓑ	ⓒ	ⓓ		10.	ⓐ	ⓑ	ⓒ	ⓓ		18.	ⓐ	ⓑ	ⓒ	ⓓ
2.	ⓐ	ⓑ	ⓒ	ⓓ		11.	ⓐ	ⓑ	ⓒ	ⓓ		19.	ⓐ	ⓑ	ⓒ	ⓓ
3.	ⓐ	ⓑ	ⓒ	ⓓ		12.	ⓐ	ⓑ	ⓒ	ⓓ		20.	ⓐ	ⓑ	ⓒ	ⓓ
4.	ⓐ	ⓑ	ⓒ	ⓓ		13.	ⓐ	ⓑ	ⓒ	ⓓ		21.	ⓐ	ⓑ	ⓒ	ⓓ
5.	ⓐ	ⓑ	ⓒ	ⓓ		14.	ⓐ	ⓑ	ⓒ	ⓓ		22.	ⓐ	ⓑ	ⓒ	ⓓ
6.	ⓐ	ⓑ	ⓒ	ⓓ		15.	ⓐ	ⓑ	ⓒ	ⓓ		23.	ⓐ	ⓑ	ⓒ	ⓓ
7.	ⓐ	ⓑ	ⓒ	ⓓ		16.	ⓐ	ⓑ	ⓒ	ⓓ		24.	ⓐ	ⓑ	ⓒ	ⓓ
8.	ⓐ	ⓑ	ⓒ	ⓓ		17.	ⓐ	ⓑ	ⓒ	ⓓ		25.	ⓐ	ⓑ	ⓒ	ⓓ
9.	ⓐ	ⓑ	ⓒ	ⓓ												

Part 6: Electronics Information (EI)

1.	ⓐ	ⓑ	ⓒ	ⓓ		8.	ⓐ	ⓑ	ⓒ	ⓓ		15.	ⓐ	ⓑ	ⓒ	ⓓ
2.	ⓐ	ⓑ	ⓒ	ⓓ		9.	ⓐ	ⓑ	ⓒ	ⓓ		16.	ⓐ	ⓑ	ⓒ	ⓓ
3.	ⓐ	ⓑ	ⓒ	ⓓ		10.	ⓐ	ⓑ	ⓒ	ⓓ		17.	ⓐ	ⓑ	ⓒ	ⓓ
4.	ⓐ	ⓑ	ⓒ	ⓓ		11.	ⓐ	ⓑ	ⓒ	ⓓ		18.	ⓐ	ⓑ	ⓒ	ⓓ
5.	ⓐ	ⓑ	ⓒ	ⓓ		12.	ⓐ	ⓑ	ⓒ	ⓓ		19.	ⓐ	ⓑ	ⓒ	ⓓ
6.	ⓐ	ⓑ	ⓒ	ⓓ		13.	ⓐ	ⓑ	ⓒ	ⓓ		20.	ⓐ	ⓑ	ⓒ	ⓓ
7.	ⓐ	ⓑ	ⓒ	ⓓ		14.	ⓐ	ⓑ	ⓒ	ⓓ						

Part 7: Auto and Shop Information (AS)

1.	ⓐ	ⓑ	ⓒ	ⓓ		10.	ⓐ	ⓑ	ⓒ	ⓓ		18.	ⓐ	ⓑ	ⓒ	ⓓ
2.	ⓐ	ⓑ	ⓒ	ⓓ		11.	ⓐ	ⓑ	ⓒ	ⓓ		19.	ⓐ	ⓑ	ⓒ	ⓓ
3.	ⓐ	ⓑ	ⓒ	ⓓ		12.	ⓐ	ⓑ	ⓒ	ⓓ		20.	ⓐ	ⓑ	ⓒ	ⓓ
4.	ⓐ	ⓑ	ⓒ	ⓓ		13.	ⓐ	ⓑ	ⓒ	ⓓ		21.	ⓐ	ⓑ	ⓒ	ⓓ
5.	ⓐ	ⓑ	ⓒ	ⓓ		14.	ⓐ	ⓑ	ⓒ	ⓓ		22.	ⓐ	ⓑ	ⓒ	ⓓ
6.	ⓐ	ⓑ	ⓒ	ⓓ		15.	ⓐ	ⓑ	ⓒ	ⓓ		23.	ⓐ	ⓑ	ⓒ	ⓓ
7.	ⓐ	ⓑ	ⓒ	ⓓ		16.	ⓐ	ⓑ	ⓒ	ⓓ		24.	ⓐ	ⓑ	ⓒ	ⓓ
8.	ⓐ	ⓑ	ⓒ	ⓓ		17.	ⓐ	ⓑ	ⓒ	ⓓ		25.	ⓐ	ⓑ	ⓒ	ⓓ
9.	ⓐ	ⓑ	ⓒ	ⓓ												

Part 8: Mechanical Comprehension (MC)

1.	(a)	(b)	(c)	(d)
2.	(a)	(b)	(c)	(d)
3.	(a)	(b)	(c)	(d)
4.	(a)	(b)	(c)	(d)
5.	(a)	(b)	(c)	(d)
6.	(a)	(b)	(c)	(d)
7.	(a)	(b)	(c)	(d)
8.	(a)	(b)	(c)	(d)
9.	(a)	(b)	(c)	(d)

10.	(a)	(b)	(c)	(d)
11.	(a)	(b)	(c)	(d)
12.	(a)	(b)	(c)	(d)
13.	(a)	(b)	(c)	(d)
14.	(a)	(b)	(c)	(d)
15.	(a)	(b)	(c)	(d)
16.	(a)	(b)	(c)	(d)
17.	(a)	(b)	(c)	(d)

18.	(a)	(b)	(c)	(d)
19.	(a)	(b)	(c)	(d)
20.	(a)	(b)	(c)	(d)
21.	(a)	(b)	(c)	(d)
22.	(a)	(b)	(c)	(d)
23.	(a)	(b)	(c)	(d)
24.	(a)	(b)	(c)	(d)
25.	(a)	(b)	(c)	(d)

Part 9: Assembling Objects (AO)

1.	(a)	(b)	(c)	(d)
2.	(a)	(b)	(c)	(d)
3.	(a)	(b)	(c)	(d)
4.	(a)	(b)	(c)	(d)
5.	(a)	(b)	(c)	(d)
6.	(a)	(b)	(c)	(d)
7.	(a)	(b)	(c)	(d)
8.	(a)	(b)	(c)	(d)
9.	(a)	(b)	(c)	(d)

10.	(a)	(b)	(c)	(d)
11.	(a)	(b)	(c)	(d)
12.	(a)	(b)	(c)	(d)
13.	(a)	(b)	(c)	(d)
14.	(a)	(b)	(c)	(d)
15.	(a)	(b)	(c)	(d)
16.	(a)	(b)	(c)	(d)
17.	(a)	(b)	(c)	(d)

18.	(a)	(b)	(c)	(d)
19.	(a)	(b)	(c)	(d)
20.	(a)	(b)	(c)	(d)
21.	(a)	(b)	(c)	(d)
22.	(a)	(b)	(c)	(d)
23.	(a)	(b)	(c)	(d)
24.	(a)	(b)	(c)	(d)
25.	(a)	(b)	(c)	(d)

Part 1: General Science

Time: 11 minutes

1. Elements on the right side of the periodic table have the following characteristics EXCEPT
   a. being gaseous at room temperature.
   b. accepting electrons.
   c. having smaller electronegativity.
   d. being poor conductors.

2. Which of the following plant groups produces seeds in cones?
   a. angiosperms
   b. bryophytes
   c. all vascular plants
   d. gymnosperms

3. When two atoms form a molecule and there is an unequal sharing of electrons within their bond, this is called
   a. a covalent bond.
   b. an ionic bond.
   c. hydrogen bonding.
   d. Van der Waals forces.

4. A predator-prey relationship is balanced in a specific area. If another predator is introduced to this area, what is expected to happen?
   a. The balance would not change.
   b. Only the population of the prey would decrease.
   c. Only the population of the predators would decrease.
   d. Both the populations of the prey and the predators would decrease.

5. If during an experiment you wanted to measure the kinetic energy of a system, what would be the best instrument to use?
   a. a thermometer
   b. a volt meter
   c. a pH monitor
   d. a stopwatch

6. Compared to magma, lava is
   a. deeper and cooler.
   b. shallower and cooler.
   c. deeper and hotter.
   d. shallower and hotter.

7. Mutations are favored when they lead to adaptations. However, which of the following does not cause a beneficial mutation?
   a. RNA
   b. a carcinogen
   c. gene linkage
   d. codons

8. The pH of an alkaline solution is
   a. less than 0.
   b. less than 7.
   c. more than 14.
   d. more than 7.

9. What coefficients are needed to balance the reaction?

   $?Fe_2O_3 + 3C \rightarrow ?Fe + 3CO_2$
   a. $2Fe_2O_3$ and $2Fe$
   b. $2Fe_2O_3$ and $4Fe$
   c. $3Fe_2O_3$ and $2Fe$
   d. $3Fe_2O_3$ and $3Fe$

10. A watershed is
  a. a zone of water whose salt content is between that of fresh water and that of the ocean.
  b. an underground layer of porous rock that conducts water.
  c. a place where groundwater seeps out to the surface.
  d. the area of land that collects water that is eventually drained by a river.

11. Two parents do not show a genetic trait that shows up in their offspring. Which of the following explains this phenomenon?
  a. The environment of the offspring brought out the trait.
  b. Both parents were carriers of a recessive trait.
  c. The offspring was actually adopted.
  d. One parent was a carrier of a recessive trait.

12. In order to be considered organic, a compound must contain which of the following elements?
  a. hydrogen
  b. sodium
  c. nitrogen
  d. carbon

13. The mass number of an atom consists of
  a. protons and electrons.
  b. neutrons and electrons.
  c. protons, neutrons, and electrons.
  d. protons and neutrons.

14. What should a population of humans do to maintain an increasing population?
  a. improve their farming
  b. increase their grazing animals
  c. expand their population's boundaries
  d. defend against predators

15. Deserts are usually defined by the criterion that the rainfall is less than
  a. 2 inches per year.
  b. 5 inches per year.
  c. 10 inches per year.
  d. 20 inches per year.

16. What factor would be most helpful to increasing the reaction rate of an endothermic reaction?
  a. increasing its activation energy
  b. increasing the reactor size
  c. using a catalyst
  d. increasing concentration of products

17. The principal function of blood platelets is to
  a. help clot blood.
  b. carry oxygen.
  c. produce antibodies.
  d. consume bacteria.

18. The surface tension of water is relatively strong due to the intermolecular force of
  a. hydrogen bonds.
  b. ionic bonds.
  c. polar covalent bonds.
  d. covalent bonds.

19. A father presents an X-linked trait and a mother does not. What is the probability the mother is a carrier of this trait if they produce a son who also presents the X-linked trait?
  a. 0%
  b. 25%
  c. 50%
  d. 100%

20. The third-largest reservoir of water on Earth is
  a. the ocean.
  b. glaciers and ice caps.
  c. groundwater.
  d. lakes.

21. What needs to be added to the below equation to get the fission reaction started?

$$_{92}^{235}\text{U} + ? \rightarrow {}_{142}^{142}\text{Ba} + {}_{36}^{91}\text{Kr} + 3{}_{0}^{1}\text{n}$$

   a. an electron
   b. a neutron
   c. a proton
   d. nothing, U-235 is unstable enough

22. Complete the two missing parts of the following food chain: X → plant → X → snake
   a. water, owl
   b. water, mouse
   c. sunlight, deer
   d. sunlight, mouse

23. What adaptation would you NOT expect an animal native to tundra to have?
   a. migratory patterns
   b. long times between feedings
   c. insulation
   d. hairless skin

24. What is true about the elements when moving from top to bottom in a family on the periodic table?
   a. They are more reactive.
   b. Their atomic numbers decrease.
   c. They are more stable.
   d. They have smaller mass numbers.

25. What type of bond is formed when *electrons are shared* between two atoms?
   a. a shared bond
   b. an ionic bond
   c. a covalent bond
   d. a multiple bond

Part 2: Arithmetic Reasoning

Time: 36 minutes

1. A survey has shown that a family of four can save about $40 a week by purchasing generic items rather than brand-name ones. How much can a particular family save over six months? (one month = 4.3 weeks)
   a. $1,032
   b. $1,320
   c. $1,310
   d. $1,300

2. Bart's eight-ounce glass is $\frac{4}{5}$ full of water. How many ounces of water does he have?
   a. $4\frac{5}{8}$ ounces
   b. 5 ounces
   c. 6 ounces
   d. $6\frac{2}{5}$ ounces

Use the following pie chart to answer questions 3 and 4.

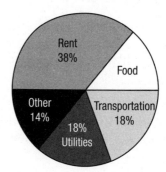

Harold's Monthly Budget

3. What should be the percent label for food?
   a. 12%
   b. 18%
   c. 28%
   d. 38%

4. If Harold's monthly income is $2,450, how much does he spend on rent each month?
   a. $686
   b. $735
   c. $882
   d. $931

RECYCLER	ALUMINUM	CARDBOARD	GLASS	PLASTIC
X	.06/pound	.03/pound	.08/pound	.02/pound
Y	.07/pound	.04/pound	.07/pound	.03/pound

5. If you take recyclables to whichever recycler will pay the most, what is the greatest amount of money you could get for 2,200 pounds of aluminum, 1,400 pounds of cardboard, 3,100 pounds of glass, and 900 pounds of plastic?
   a. $409
   b. $440
   c. $447
   d. $485

6. Five oranges, when removed from a basket containing three more than seven times as many oranges, leaves how many in the basket?
   a. 21
   b. 28
   c. 33
   d. 38

7. Ribbon in a craft store costs $0.75 per yard. Vernon needs to buy $7\frac{1}{3}$ yards. How much will it cost?
   a. $7.33
   b. $6.95
   c. $5.50
   d. $4.25

8. R.J. found a lamp on sale for 0.25 off its original price. What fraction of its original price will R.J. have to pay for the lamp?
   a. $\frac{1}{4}$
   b. $\frac{3}{4}$
   c. $\frac{1}{2}$
   d. $\frac{2}{3}$

9. How many $\frac{1}{4}$-pound hamburgers can be made from six pounds of ground beef?
   a. 18 hamburgers
   b. $20\frac{1}{2}$ hamburgers
   c. 24 hamburgers
   d. $26\frac{1}{4}$ hamburgers

10. The markup on a pair of sneakers is 150%. If the sneakers originally cost $45, what is the price after the markup?
   a. $22.50
   b. $57.50
   c. $67.50
   d. $112.50

11. Matthew had 200 baseball cards. He sold 5% of the cards on Saturday and 10% of the remaining cards on Sunday. How many cards are left?
   a. 170
   b. 171
   c. 175
   d. 185

12. A teacher purchased a number of supplies to start the new school year. The costs are listed as follows: $12.98, $5.68, $20.64, and $6.76. What is the total cost?

   a. $45.96

   b. $46.06

   c. $46.16

   d. $47.16

13. How many hours are in five days?

   a. 60 hours

   b. 100 hours

   c. 120 hours

   d. 240 hours

14. A truck is carrying 1,000 television sets; each set weighs 21.48 pounds. What is the total weight, in pounds, of the entire load?

   a. 214.8 pounds

   b. 2,148 pounds

   c. 21,480 pounds

   d. 214,800 pounds

15. Hilga and Jerome leave from different points walking directly toward each other. Hilga walks $2\frac{1}{2}$ miles per hour, and Jerome walks 4 miles per hour. If they meet in $2\frac{1}{2}$ hours, how far apart were they?

   a. 9 miles

   b. 13 miles

   c. $16\frac{1}{4}$ miles

   d. $18\frac{1}{2}$ miles

16. Des Moines recently received a snowstorm that left a total of eight inches of snow. If it snowed at a consistent rate of three inches every two hours, how much snow had fallen in the first five hours of the storm?

   a. 3 inches

   b. 3.3 inches

   c. 5 inches

   d. 7.5 inches

Use the following graph to answer question 17.

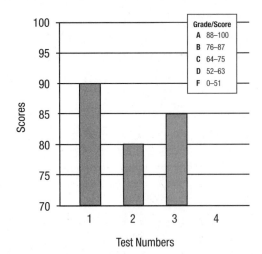

17. Avi's final math grade is based on his scores on four tests. To get an A, Avi needs an average test score of 88 or higher. The graph shown here represents Avi's first three test scores. What is the lowest score Avi can get on the fourth test and still earn an A?

   a. 99

   b. 97

   c. 95

   d. 93

18. Joan will be twice Tom's age in three years when Tom will be 40. How old is Joan now?

   a. 20

   b. 80

   c. 77

   d. 37

19. Kari is running for student council. The rules restrict the candidates to four two-foot-by-three-foot posters. Kari has dozens of four-inch-by-six-inch pictures that she would like to cover the posters with. What is the maximum number of pictures she will be able to use on the four posters?

a. 144
b. 130
c. 125
d. 111

20. It takes five-year-old Carlos 1.6 minutes to tie the lace on his right shoe and 1.5 minutes to tie the lace on his left shoe. How many minutes does it take Carlos to tie both shoes?

a. 2.1 minutes
b. 3.0 minutes
c. 3.1 minutes
d. 4.1 minutes

21. Tamika is restoring an antique storage chest that is in the shape of a rectangular box. She is painting only the outside of the trunk. The trunk is four feet long, 18 inches wide, and two feet tall. There is a one-square-foot brass ornament on the outside of the trunk that will not get painted. How much paint does she need, in square feet, to cover the outside of the trunk?

a. 33 square feet
b. 34 square feet
c. 143 square feet
d. 231 square feet

22. 2,520 seconds is equivalent to how many minutes?

a. 84 minutes
b. 42 minutes
c. 151,200 minutes
d. 126 minutes

23. Belinda is building a garden shed. When she helped her neighbor build an identical shed, it took them 22 hours to complete the job together. If it would have taken her neighbor, working alone, 38 hours to build the shed, how long will it take Belinda, working alone, to build her shed?

a. 33.75 hours
b. 41.00 hours
c. 41.25 hours
d. 52.25 hours

24. An empty crate weighs 8.16 kg and an orange weighs 220 g. If Jon can lift 11,000 g, how many oranges can he pack in the crate before lifting it onto his truck?

a. 12
b. 13
c. 37
d. 46

25. Jeff was 10 minutes early for class. Dee came in four minutes after Mae, who was half as early as Jeff. How many minutes early was Dee?

a. 1 minute
b. 2 minutes
c. 2.5 minutes
d. 6 minutes

26. A certain radio station plays classical music during 20% of its airtime. If the station is on the air 24 hours a day, how many hours each day is the station NOT playing classical music?

a. 8.0 hours
b. 15.6 hours
c. 18.2 hours
d. 19.2 hours

27. Change $\frac{55}{6}$ to a mixed number.

a. $8\frac{1}{6}$
b. $9\frac{1}{6}$
c. $9\frac{1}{55}$
d. $9\frac{6}{55}$

28. The animal shelter is developing a new outdoor grass area for dogs. A fence needs to be purchased that will surround the entire grassy section. The dimensions of the area are 120 feet by 250 feet. How much fencing needs to be purchased?

    a. 740 feet

    b. 30,000 square feet

    c. 740 square feet

    d. 30,000 feet

29. If it takes Danielle 22.4 minutes to walk 1.25 miles, how many minutes will it take her to walk one mile?

    a. 17.92 minutes

    b. 18 minutes

    c. 19.9 minutes

    d. 21.15 minutes

30. Luis is mailing two packages. One weighs 12.9 pounds, and the other weighs half as much. What is the total weight, in pounds, of the two packages?

    a. 6.45 pounds

    b. 12.8 pounds

    c. 18.5 pounds

    d. 19.35 pounds

Part 3: Word Knowledge

Time: 11 minutes

1. *Noisome* most nearly means

    a. loud.

    b. harmful.

    c. full.

    d. clean.

2. *Capsize* most nearly means

    a. enlarge.

    b. profit.

    c. overturn.

    d. shrink.

3. *Arsenal* most nearly means

    a. stockpile.

    b. fire.

    c. crime.

    d. warfare.

4. *Inert* most nearly means

    a. revered.

    b. energetic.

    c. motionless.

    d. buried.

5. *Affix* most nearly means

    a. repair.

    b. suffer.

    c. fasten.

    d. send.

6. *Aptitude* most nearly means

    a. capability.

    b. mood.

    c. height.

    d. attention.

7. *Fractious* most nearly means

    a. make-believe.

    b. true.

    c. friendly.

    d. quarrelsome.

8. *Serene* most nearly means

    a. loud.

    b. calm.

    c. melodious.

    d. stern.

9. *Improbable* most nearly means
 a. unlikeable.
 b. unlikely.
 c. unsuitable.
 d. unmistakable.

10. *Practical* most nearly means
 a. expert.
 b. healthy.
 c. useless.
 d. convenient.

11. *Elementary* most nearly means
 a. basic.
 b. school.
 c. fancy.
 d. specific.

12. *Impart* most nearly means
 a. separate.
 b. incomplete.
 c. give.
 d. finish.

13. *Cower* most nearly means
 a. farm.
 b. creep.
 c. recoil.
 d. frighten.

14. *Spartan* most nearly means
 a. strong.
 b. simple.
 c. complicated.
 d. experienced.

15. *Adept* most nearly means
 a. skilled.
 b. unrelated.
 c. included.
 d. accepted.

16. *Agility* most nearly means
 a. weakness.
 b. harmony.
 c. irritability.
 d. dexterity.

17. *Harry* most nearly means
 a. bother.
 b. accelerate.
 c. furry.
 d. congratulate.

18. *Remorse* most nearly means
 a. solitude.
 b. punishment.
 c. regret.
 d. frailty.

19. *Haggard* most nearly means
 a. tiny.
 b. rough.
 c. exhausted.
 d. strong.

20. *Prominent* most nearly means
 a. appropriate.
 b. important.
 c. supportive.
 d. unnoticeable.

21. Never one to ignore a suggestion, Max was _____ to his student's ideas.
 a. dismissive
 b. apathetic
 c. attentive
 d. reciprocal

22. Unsure of what lay ahead, the careful explorer went forward _____.
 a. brazenly
 b. cautiously
 c. hurriedly
 d. progressively

23. Suspecting the salesperson of being less than truthful, Lindsay did not buy the chair, because of its _____ quality.
a. comfortable
b. excellent
c. expensive
d. dubious

24. _____ by the reputation of her more experienced opponent, Nancy took the field with confidence.
a. Daunted
b. Unfazed
c. Informed
d. Terrified

25. The two generals differed markedly in their strategies; Percy was calculating and cautious while Norton was hasty and _____.
a. guarded
b. brave
c. reckless
d. prudent

26. Because so much of academia is _____ to many people, its theories are often dismissed as highbrow and farfetched.
a. inaccessible
b. important
c. understandable
d. controversial

27. _____ the upscale dress code, Wes came to work in jeans and a T-shirt every day.
a. Obeying
b. Flouting
c. Wearing
d. Knowing

28. The _____ of the mansion stood in stark contrast to the nondescript, ramshackle buildings surrounding the square.
a. drabness
b. grandeur
c. importance
d. location

29. Jodi's parents were surprised when she went to bed when they asked; she was usually very _____.
a. agreeable
b. tired
c. hopeful
d. stubborn

30. As he aged, he became increasingly _____, repeating himself and forgetting where he put things.
a. weak
b. tired
c. senile
d. thoughtless

31. It seems strange that a poem about such a _____ subject as waiting for the bus could be so fascinating and beautiful.
a. random
b. mundane
c. remarkable
d. controversial

32. Under fire from the press for taking so long to find the culprit, the police _____ their search.
a. intensified
b. canceled
c. doubted
d. undertook

33. The final scene of the film is so touching that even the most _____ crowd would be moved to tears.
- **a.** sullen
- **b.** impassive
- **c.** emotional
- **d.** peaceable

34. Upon their return home, the soldiers were lauded as _____.
- **a.** victims
- **b.** heroes
- **c.** veterans
- **d.** reinforcements

35. The short-tempered clerk was so _____ to customers that soon the store had no more business.
- **a.** helpful
- **b.** serious
- **c.** rude
- **d.** outgoing

Part 4:
Paragraph Comprehension

Time: 13 minutes

Every 10 years in America, the federal government conducts a national census to *enumerate* the national population. The United States Constitution actually requires that all American citizens, non-citizen long-term visitors, and both legal and illegal immigrants be counted on a *decennial* basis, with specific information gathered regarding population density in all voting districts. This information is what determines how many seats each state is permitted within the House of Representatives.

The census has been conducted every 10 years since 1790. Specific questions have varied from one census to another, but the basic information gathered has been the same since the beginning: how many people live in a particular voting district. This infor-

mation is vitally important, since it determines the extent of political representation the voters have in Washington, DC.

1. According to the passage, the basic purpose of the census is to
- **a.** learn information about American voters.
- **b.** see how population densities influence political trends.
- **c.** determine a voting district's political representation.
- **d.** keep the Postal Service in business.

2. As used in the passage, *enumerate* most nearly means to
- **a.** expound on.
- **b.** count.
- **c.** make amends.
- **d.** steal from the treasury.

3. The census is conducted every 10 years because
- **a.** population trends can best be tracked in 10-year intervals.
- **b.** seats in the House of Representatives expire every 10 years.
- **c.** the American people get angry if it is more frequent.
- **d.** the Constitution requires it.

4. As used in the passage, *decennial* most nearly means
- **a.** Constitutional.
- **b.** every 10 years.
- **c.** decaying.
- **d.** irritating.

The stories about King Arthur are an *enduring* legend in Western literature. Most people are familiar with the Round Table and famous characters such as Merlin, Sir Lancelot, Guinevere, and King Arthur himself. The stories date back to the Middle Ages, with such classic works as Sir Thomas Malory's famous *Le Morte d'Arthur* (*The Death of Arthur*), Alfred Lord Tennyson's *Idylls of the King*, and T. H. White's *The Once and Future King*. The legend is so enjoyable that writers even today use it to create new works of fiction.

But many people are not aware that there was a real King Arthur, a real Merlin, and even a real castle of Camelot! The actual details of these historical facts and personalities are very sketchy, but historical documents record a warrior named Arthur who led an army against Anglo-Saxon invasions during the sixth century. A man named *Merlinus Ambrosius* was instrumental in establishing a lasting British independence, and he was probably the *prototype* of Merlin. Perhaps someday historians will unveil more about this legendary topic.

5. The author of this passage would most likely agree with which statement?
  a. King Arthur is an old-fashioned story.
  b. Alfred Lord Tennyson wrote many poems.
  c. The legend of King Arthur is based loosely on historical facts.
  d. The future of the Arthurian legend is in question.

6. As used in the passage, *enduring* most nearly means
  a. lasting a long time.
  b. ending quickly.
  c. interesting and lively.
  d. historically accurate.

7. According to the passage, Merlin should be best remembered for
  a. being a powerful magician.
  b. inventing the round table.
  c. helping to establish British independence.
  d. wearing funny hats.

8. As used in the passage, *prototype* most nearly means
  a. clearly written.
  b. the historical basis.
  c. fictional character.
  d. well-fed.

In 1440, a German named Johannes Gutenberg created a new invention which revolutionized Western society—the printing press. In modern times, most of us take printing for granted, being able to create printed documents with the push of a button and the click of a mouse, but 600 years ago no such technology existed. Books were produced by hand, people working long hours to write out each page using pens made from feathers! The closest thing to a printing press was the art of *xylography*, which involved engraving an entire page of text into a wooden block, which was then covered with ink and pressed against paper.

Gutenberg invented something called "moveable type," which consisted of individual letters made of lead that could be placed together to form words and sentences. His press allowed a printer to set those lead letters together to produce an entire page of text, which was then inked and printed onto paper. Books could be reproduced on a large scale very quickly, which allowed printers to *disseminate* ideas around the world without much effort and expense.

9. The printing press revolutionized Western society because
  a. it allowed people to make money.
  b. it was fast.
  c. it enabled people to share ideas worldwide.
  d. there had never been one before.

10. As used in the passage, *disseminate* most nearly means to
  a. spread around.
  b. heat up quickly.
  c. cool down quickly.
  d. cause pain.

11. Moveable type is made of
  a. ink.
  b. paper.
  c. lead.
  d. feathers.

12. The art of *xylography* involves
  a. playing music.
  b. engraving lead.
  c. making paper.
  d. engraving on wood.

Reality TV shows will have an adverse effect on traditional dramas and comedies. As reality TV increases in popularity, network executives will begin canceling more traditional programs and replacing them with the latest in reality TV.

13. This paragraph best supports the statement that
  a. Reality TV is low quality.
  b. Reality TV shows get the highest ratings.
  c. More and more people love to watch and participate in reality TV.
  d. As reality TV gets more popular, more traditional television shows may be threatened.

In cities throughout the country, there is a new direction in local campaign coverage. Frequently in local elections, journalists are not giving voters enough information to understand the issues and evaluate the candidates. The local news media devotes too much time to scandal and not enough time to policy.

14. This paragraph best supports the statement that the local news media
  a. is not doing an adequate job when it comes to covering local campaigns.
  b. does not understand either campaign issues or politics.
  c. should learn how to cover politics by watching the national news media.
  d. has no interest in covering stories about local political events.

The entire low-carbohydrate versus low-fat diet argument is so prevalent that one would think that these are the only two options available for losing weight and staying healthy. Some experts even feel that the low-carb and low-fat debate distracts us from an even more important issue—our culture's reliance on processed and manufactured foods.

15. The paragraph best supports the statement that
  a. experts state that not all fats are equal, so we need not reduce our intake of all fats—just those that contain partially hydrogenated oils.
  b. important health concerns get overlooked when we focus exclusively on the low-fat versus low-carb question.
  c. low-carbohydrate diets lead to significant and sustained weight loss.
  d. processed foods can lead to many adverse health problems including heart disease, cancer, diabetes, and obesity.

Part 5: Mathematics Knowledge

Time: 24 minutes

1. Which of the following is equivalent to $(x - 3)(x + 7)$?
  a. $x^2 - 3x - 21$
  b. $x^2 - 4x - 21$
  c. $x^2 + 4x - 21$
  d. $x^2 - 21$

2. Which of the following represents a composite number?
  a. 11
  b. 29
  c. 41
  d. 91

3. Choose the answer to the following problem:
$\frac{5}{12} \times \frac{1}{6} \times \frac{2}{3} =$
  a. $\frac{10}{12}$
  b. $\frac{5}{6}$
  c. $\frac{5}{108}$
  d. $\frac{5}{216}$

4. Find the median of the following group of numbers: 14 12 20 22 14 16
  a. 12
  b. 14
  c. 15
  d. 16

5. What is the value of X in the following figure?

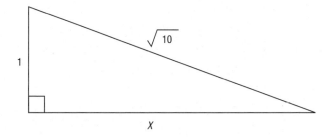

  a. 3
  b. 4
  c. 5
  d. 9

6. In which of the following are the diagonals of the figure always congruent and perpendicular?
  a. isosceles trapezoid
  b. square
  c. isosceles triangle
  d. rhombus

7. In the following diagram, a circle of area 100π square inches is inscribed in a square. What is the length of side AB?

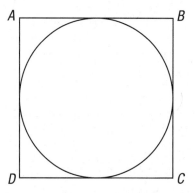

  a. 10 inches
  b. 20 inches
  c. 100 inches
  d. 400 inches

8. Which of the following expressions is equal to 40,503?
  a. $400 + 50 + 3$
  b. $4,000 + 500 + 3$
  c. $40,000 + 50 + 3$
  d. $40,000 + 500 + 3$

9. If the perimeter of a rectangle is 40 centimeters and the shorter sides are 4 centimeters, what is the length of the longer sides?
  a. 12 centimeters
  b. 10 centimeters
  c. 18 centimeters
  d. 16 centimeters

10. A straight angle is
  a. exactly 180°.
  b. between 90° and 180°.
  c. 90°.
  d. less than 90°.

11. If $\frac{1}{19} = \frac{x}{76}$, what is x?
   a. 3
   b. 3.5
   c. 4
   d. 5

12. Which value of x will make the following inequality true: $12x - 1 < 35$
   a. 2
   b. 3
   c. 4
   d. 5

13. Which of the following could describe a quadrilateral with two pairs of parallel sides and two interior angles that measure 65°?
   a. square
   b. triangle
   c. rectangle
   d. rhombus

14. Simplify the radical completely: $\sqrt{64x^5 y^8}$.
   a. $8x^2 y^4 \sqrt{x}$
   b. $8x^4 y^8 \sqrt{x}$
   c. $64x^2 y^4$
   d. $8x^5 y^8$

15. Write ten thousand, four hundred forty-seven in numerals.
   a. 10,499,047
   b. 104,447
   c. 10,447
   d. 1,047

16. Which of the following numbers is represented by the prime factors $2 \times 3 \times 7$?
   a. 21
   b. 42
   c. 84
   d. 237

17. Solve the equation for a: $\sqrt{2a+6} - 4 = 6$.
   a. 2
   b. 17
   c. 23
   d. 47

18. Find the sum of $4x - 7y$ and $7x + 7y$.
   a. $11x$
   b. $14y$
   c. $11x + 14y$
   d. $11x - 14y$

19. 3 hours 20 minutes − 1 hour 48 minutes =
   a. 5 hours 8 minutes
   b. 4 hours 8 minutes
   c. 2 hours 28 minutes
   d. 1 hour 32 minutes

20. Name the fraction that indicates the shaded part of the following figure.

   a. $\frac{2}{5}$
   b. $\frac{3}{5}$
   c. $\frac{5}{3}$
   d. $\frac{5}{2}$

21. Which expression best describes the sum of three numbers multiplied by the sum of their reciprocals?
   a. $(a + b + c)(\frac{1}{a} + \frac{1}{b} + \frac{1}{c})$
   b. $(a)(\frac{1}{a}) + (b)(\frac{1}{b}) + (c)(\frac{1}{c})$
   c. $(a + b + c) \div (\frac{1}{a})(\frac{1}{b})(\frac{1}{c})$
   d. $(a)(b)(c) + (\frac{1}{a})(\frac{1}{b})(\frac{1}{c})$

22. Find three consecutive odd integers whose sum is 117.
   a. 39, 39, 39
   b. 38, 39, 40
   c. 37, 39, 41
   d. 39, 41, 43

23. Which of the following points is the solution to the system of equations?

$y = -x + 10$

$y = x - 2$

a. (2,10)

b. (2,0)

c. (3,6)

d. (6,4)

24. Find the sum: $\frac{2w}{z} + \frac{5w}{z}$.

a. $\frac{7w}{2z}$

b. $\frac{7w}{z^2}$

c. $\frac{7w}{z}$

d. $7w$

25. Divide: $\frac{6a2b}{2c} \div \frac{ab^2}{4c^4}$

a. $\frac{24ac}{b}$

b. $\frac{12ac^3}{b}$

c. $\frac{24ac^3}{b}$

d. $12abc^3$

Part 6: Electronics Information

Time: 9 minutes

1. For safety purposes, electrical devices need to be

a. inspected daily.

b. limited in volt and amperage.

c. grounded to prevent electrical shock.

d. designed under international guidelines.

2. What is the frequency of the alternating voltage and current typically used in the United States?

a. 20 Hz

b. 40 Hz

c. 60 Hz

d. 110 Hz

3. If resistors R_1, R_2, and R_3 are all rated at 500 ohms, what is the total resistance?

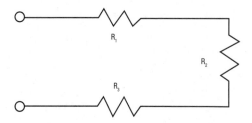

a. 500 watts

b. 500 ohms

c. 1,500 ohms

d. 1,500 watts

4. Putting metal in a microwave while it is operating should be avoided because

a. it can melt.

b. parts of the microwave can be damaged by reflected energy.

c. it could cause a reverse polarity of the structural wiring system.

d. none of the above

5. What is the total current in a parallel resistance circuit with three parallel paths that each have four amperes flowing through them?

a. 2 A

b. 12 A

c. 4 A

d. 8 A

6. The abbreviation FM stands for

a. frequency modulation.

b. frequency multiplier.

c. feedback multiplex.

d. farad magnet.

7. What does this electronic circuit symbol depict?

   a. a conversion from AC to DC power
   b. an electrical surge
   c. a wire that does not join another
   d. a wire that intersects another

8. A volt is a unit of electric(al)
   a. potential.
   b. energy.
   c. pressure.
   d. current.

9. Coulomb's law describes
   a. electromagnetic fields and their association with the electric grid.
   b. the relationship between direct current (DC) and alternating current (AC).
   c. the electrostatic force between electric charges.
   d. the electrical differential between resistors.

10. Total resistance in this schematic is 25 Ω. What is the voltage drop across R1?

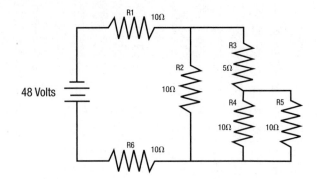

   a. 6.2 V
   b. 12.4 V
   c. 19.2 V
   d. 48 V

11. If a vacuum cleaner is rated at 1,200 watts and operates at 120 volts, how much current will it draw?
   a. 10 amps
   b. 100 amps
   c. 120 amps
   d. 144,000 amps

12. The term given to a unit of electromotive force is a(n)
   a. ohm.
   b. amp.
   c. megawatt.
   d. volt.

13. The best antenna to use when working with frequencies below 300kHz would be a
   a. parabolic antenna.
   b. loopstick antenna.
   c. dish antenna.
   d. wire hanger antenna.

14. Which of the following is an advantage of a corner reflector antenna?
   a. broad spectrum capability
   b. its wireless design
   c. low power out
   d. increased directivity

15. In a directional antenna, what is the correlation between the diameter of a reflector in wave lengths and the gain?
   a. the smaller the diameter, the narrower the lobe
   b. the smaller the diameter, the greater the gain
   c. the larger the diameter, the greater the gain
   d. none of the above

16. In series circuit A, a 10Ω load dissipates 1 watt. In series circuit B, a 10Ω load dissipates 2 watts. What can be said about the current through the load in circuit A if the voltages in both circuits are equal?
   a. The current through load A is equal to the current through load B.
   b. The current through load A is twice the current through load B.
   c. The current through load A is half the current through load B.
   d. The current through load A is zero.

17. What type of antenna is this?

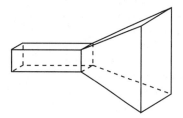

   a. a corner reflector
   b. a horn
   c. a dish
   d. a helical

18. FM radio broadcasting, amateur radio, broadcast television, and commercial aircraft transmit on what radio frequency?
   a. low frequency (LF)
   b. medium frequency (MF)
   c. very high frequency (VHF)
   d. ultra high frequency (UHF)

19. What is the purpose of a tuning capacitor?
   a. It allows an antenna to transmit.
   b. It is used to vary the time period.
   c. It adjusts the resonant frequency.
   d. none of the above

20. A transformer changes which of the following?
   a. power and pressure
   b. voltage and amperage
   c. voltage and current
   d. chemical energy

Part 7:
Auto and Shop Information

Time: 11 minutes

1. One way to ensure optimum gas mileage is to
   a. keep the engine coolant system replenished every 3,000 to 5,000 miles.
   b. keep the fuel tank topped off.
   c. keep the tires properly inflated.
   d. minimize the use of cruise control.

2. A flow meter measures the
   a. projected rate that fuel is being burned.
   b. remaining volume of liquid in a container.
   c. specific gravity of a given fluid.
   d. rate at which a fluid is flowing through a piping system.

3. Which of the following is an example of a flow meter?
   a. speedometer
   b. oil pressure gauge
   c. gas pump gauge
   d. none of the above

4. The abbreviation PCV, when associated with an automobile, stands for
   a. positive crankcase ventilation.
   b. pollution control valve.
   c. primary catalytic volume.
   d. post critical valance.

5. After an oil change, the used oil should be
   a. disposed of in the most convenient manner.
   b. re-used immediately to take advantage of its viscosity.
   c. recycled for re-use.
   d. tested for metal parts from excessive engine wear.

6. An automobile's fuel gauge typically measures its contents in
   a. gallons or liters.
   b. pounds per square inch.
   c. degrees Fahrenheit or Celsius.
   d. miles per hour.

7. An automobile alternator performs which of the following functions?
   a. It provides the spark to ignite the air-fuel mixture.
   b. It recycles the coolant.
   c. It recharges the battery.
   d. It powers the brake system.

8. An acoustical chamber in the exhaust system that reduces engine noise is the
   a. radiator.
   b. muffler.
   c. catalytic converter.
   d. none of the above

9. Which of the following types of springs are found in a suspension system?
   a. leaf springs
   b. universal springs
   c. coil compression springs
   d. both a and c

10. To determine the strength of a solution of antifreeze, you would use a
    a. voltmeter.
    b. hydrometer.
    c. thermometer.
    d. dosimeter.

11. The burning of gasoline during the operation of an internal combustion engine generates what three major pollutants?
a. oxygen, nitrogen, and carbon dioxide
b. oxygen, nitrogen, and carbon monoxide
c. carbon monoxide, nitrogen oxides, and helium
d. hydrocarbons, carbon monoxide, and nitrogen oxides

12. The oil pump ensures that
a. oil is pumped throughout all the engine oil passages.
b. the correct oil-fuel mixture is maintained.
c. oil is supplied to the cooling system.
d. used oil is cleaned and recycled within the oil system.

13. Front-wheel drive vehicles have their transmission and differential combined in a
a. crossaxle.
b. through-put drive.
c. transaxle.
d. universal joint.

14. A "hinge mortise" would typically be found
a. on soffit facing
b. on a floor joist
c. on a door or door jamb
d. on a stair stringer

15. All the cuts listed are one of the six basic woodworking cuts EXCEPT
a. a crosscut.
b. a rip.
c. a miter.
d. a lateral.

16. Which of the following will provide the strongest joint?
a. a nail
b. a screw
c. a solder
d. a weld

17. The chemical process that results in the hardening of concrete is called
a. evaporation.
b. condensation.
c. hydration.
d. dissipation.

18. The tool used to smooth out the surface of poured concrete is called a
a. float.
b. screed.
c. tamp.
d. form.

19. What sort of washer would you use to ensure a bolt does not come loose?
a. flat
b. fender
c. ogee
d. split lock

20. Concrete is typically used in conjunction with which of the following building materials in order to provide a stronger product?
a. bronze reinforcement
b. aluminum reinforcement
c. steel reinforcement
d. plastic reinforcement

21. Concrete is made up of which of the following components?
a. cement, water, and steel
b. gravel and sand
c. gravel, water, and glass
d. cement, sand, gravel, and water

22. Which material may be used as the outer material on a roof in order to keep out rain?
a. tile
b. wood
c. asphalt
d. all the above

23. This hand tool is known as a
a. screwdriver.
b. hammer.
c. crescent wrench.
d. pair of pliers.

24. Which of the following is NOT a type of hammer?
a. ball-peen
b. sledge
c. claw
d. box

25. If a line is *plumb*, what would be its defining characteristic?
a. It would be as tightly drawn as possible.
b. It would form a perfect square.
c. It would be perfectly vertical.
d. It would form a precise 45-degree angle.

Part 8: Mechanical Comprehension

Time: 19 minutes

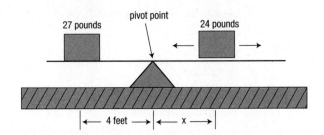

1. In the diagram, Kenneth wants to balance two blocks on either side of a lever. One block weighs 27 pounds and the other weighs 24 pounds. If the 27-pound block is 4 feet to the left of the pivot point, how far to the right of the pivot point should the 24-pound block be placed?
a. 4.5 feet
b. 7 feet
c. 4 feet
d. 8.5 feet

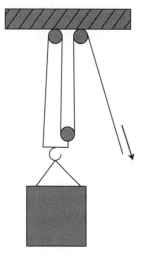

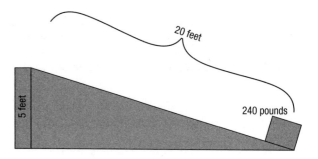

2. If the rope on the end of this pulley system is pulled with 160 pounds of force, what is the maximum weight that can be lifted?

a. 640 pounds

b. 480 pounds

c. 320 pounds

d. 80 pounds

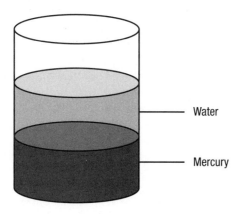

3. A beaker is filled with mercury and water. Mercury is a liquid with a density of 8 g/cm^3 and water has a density of 1 g/cm^3. If a penny with a density of 5 g/cm^3 is dropped into the beaker, where will it settle?

a. at the bottom of the beaker

b. in the middle of the mercury layer

c. in between the mercury and water layers

d. on top of the water layer

4. A 240-pound block is being pulled up an incline by a pulley. The incline is 20 feet long and rises 5 feet. Neglecting friction, how much force is necessary to move the block up the incline?

a. 60 pounds

b. 100 pounds

c. 260 pounds

d. 240 pounds

5. A jack is able to lift a 3,000-pound car using only 50 pounds of force. What is the mechanical advantage of the jack?

a. 4

b. 60

c. 600

d. 2,950

6. The tires of a car are filled in a garage to a pressure of 35 pounds per square inch. Driving the car to a hot desert will have what effect on the tires?

a. Their pressure will increase.

b. Their pressure will decrease.

c. Their weight will increase.

d. Their weight will decrease.

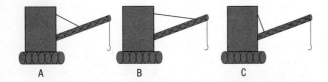

A   B   C

7. A crane raises its arm using a powerful cable attached to the main body. Which cable position offers the greatest mechanical advantage?

a. A
b. B
c. C
d. They all offer the same advantage.

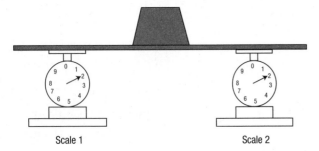

Scale 1   Scale 2

8. Two scales are connected by a plank weighing 2 pounds. A 12-pound block is placed directly in between the two scales. How many pounds will Scale 1 read?

a. 7 pounds
b. 10 pounds
c. 12 pounds
d. 14 pounds

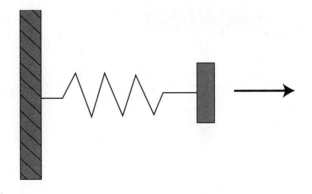

9. A force of 9 pounds stretches a spring 3 inches. How far will the spring move under 12 pounds of force?

a. 3 inches
b. 4 inches
c. 6 inches
d. 36 inches

10. A solid object will float on water when

a. it is less dense than water.
b. it is more dense than water.
c. it has a large surface area.
d. it has a small surface area.

11. A nut travels 1.25 inches after 15 turns of the screw. How many threads per inch does the screw have?

a. 10
b. 12
c. 15
d. 20

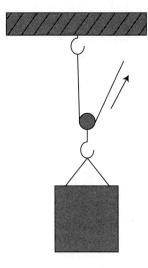

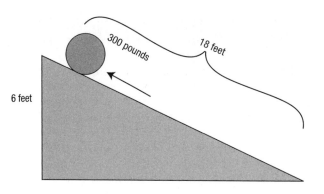

12. Using the pulley system shown above, how much force is required to lift a 200-pound load?
   a. 50 pounds
   b. 100 pounds
   c. 200 pounds
   d. 400 pounds

13. Which material expands most when heated?
   a. wood
   b. steel
   c. glass
   d. rubber

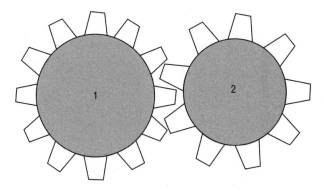

14. Gear 1 has 12 teeth and gear 2 has 9. If the gear 1 turns at 30 rpm, how fast will gear 2 turn?
   a. 20 rpm
   b. 30 rpm
   c. 40 rpm
   d. 60 rpm

15. A 300-pound barrel is being supported on an incline. The incline is 18 feet long and rises 6 feet. How much force is necessary to prevent the barrel from rolling down?
   a. 50 pounds
   b. 100 pounds
   c. 150 pounds
   d. 300 pounds

16. A single-speed bicycle has a front chain ring with 55 teeth. The back gear has 11 teeth. If the bicycle is pedaled for 80 rpm, how many complete revolutions will the rear wheel make in 30 seconds?
   a. 40 revolutions
   b. 80 revolutions
   c. 200 revolutions
   d. 400 revolutions

17. Why do helium-filled balloons float?
   a. Helium is less dense than air.
   b. Helium is a noble gas.
   c. Helium is hotter than air.
   d. Helium is colder than air.

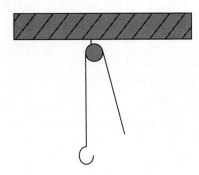

18. The pulley system shown in the figure offers what advantage?

    a. a two-fold mechanical advantage

    b. a three-fold mechanical advantage

    c. a change in the direction of force

    d. no advantage

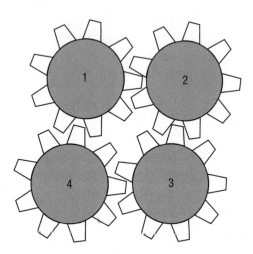

19. If gear 4 turns clockwise, which other gear(s) will also turn counterclockwise?

    a. 1 only

    b. 2 only

    c. 3 only

    d. 1 and 3

20. Two cylindrical pipes are used to drain a tank. Pipe A has a diameter of 2 inches and pipe B has a diameter of 6 inches. If there is equal water pressure inside the tank, how much more water will flow out of pipe B than pipe A?

    a. The same amount will flow out of both pipes.

    b. Three times more will flow out of pipe B.

    c. Six times more will flow out of pipe B.

    d. Nine times more will flow out of pipe B.

21. Steve goes on a run at 8 mph and travels 14 miles. How long did Steve run?

    a. 1 hour 15 minutes

    b. 1 hour 30 minutes

    c. 1 hour 45 minutes

    d. 2 hours

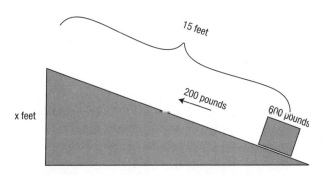

22. A 600-pound block is being pulled up a 15-foot incline. Neglecting friction, if 200 pounds of force is necessary to move the block up the incline, how tall is the incline?

    a. 4 feet

    b. 10 feet

    c. 5 feet

    d. 15 feet

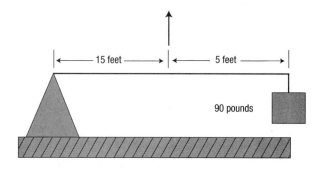

23. In the diagram, Paul wants to lift a 90-pound block using a lever. If the block is 20 feet from the pivot point and Paul is 15 feet from the pivot point, how much force must he apply to lift the block?

a. 120 pounds

b. 450 pounds

c. 20 pounds

d. 90 pounds

24. A helium balloon is released from the ground and quickly rises 2,000 feet. What will happen to the balloon?

a. The balloon will become heavier.

b. The balloon will become lighter.

c. The size of the balloon will increase.

d. The size of the balloon will decrease.

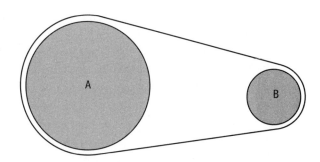

25. Pulley A has 1.5 times the circumference of pulley B. If pulley A rotates counterclockwise at 30 revolutions per minute (rpm), how fast and in what direction will pulley B rotate?

a. 30 rpm clockwise

b. 30 rpm counterclockwise

c. 45 rpm clockwise

d. 45 rpm counterclockwise

Part 9: Assembling Objects

Time: 15 minutes

Each question is composed of five separate drawings. The problem is presented in the first drawing, and the remaining four drawings are possible solutions. Determine which of the four choices contains all of the pieces assembled properly that are shown in the first picture. Note: images are not drawn to scale.

1.

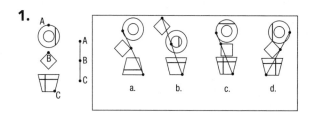

2.

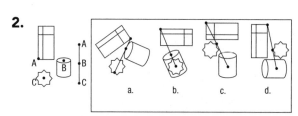

3.

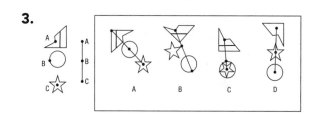

4.

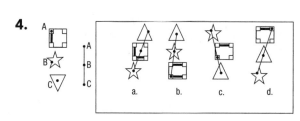

5.

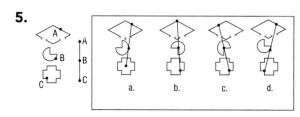

6.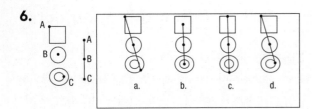

7.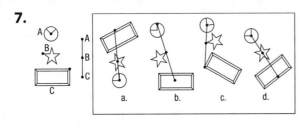

8.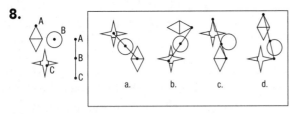

9.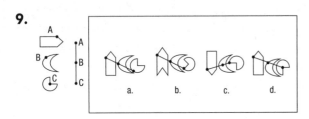

10.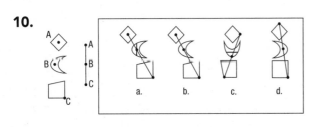

11.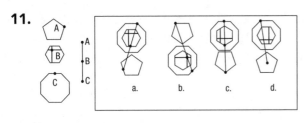

12.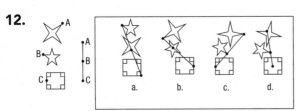

13.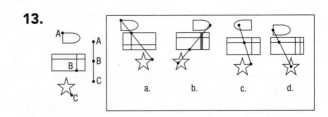

14.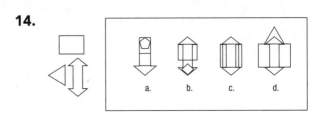

15.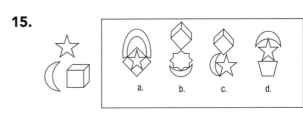

16.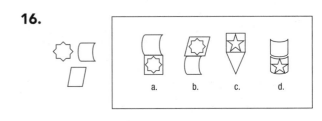

17.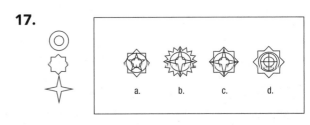

18.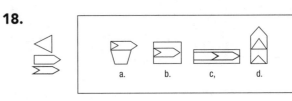

19.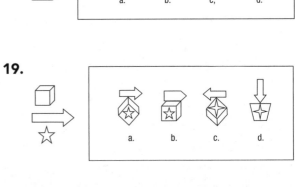

20.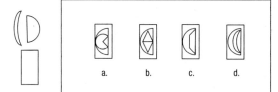

21.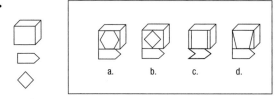

22.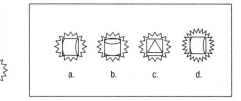

23.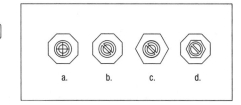

24.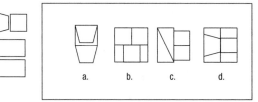

25.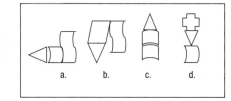

Answers

Part 1: General Science

1. **c.** Elements on the right of the periodic table tend to be nonmetal gases. Moving to the right in the periodic table, elements increase their electronegativity (tendency to accept electrons).

2. **d.** Gymnosperms are conifer plants that store their seeds in cones instead of in fruit like angiosperms.

3. **b.** When there is an unequal sharing of electrons between atoms, one atom becomes negatively charged and the other positively charged. These ions are held together through an ionic bond.

4. **d.** The addition of another predator introduces competition for a limited resource, the prey. As a result, the prey population will decrease and the predator populations will have less food and their populations will decrease.

5. **a.** Temperature is the measure of the average kinetic energy of molecules, which is measured by a thermometer.

6. **b.** Magma is deep in the earth and extremely hot. When magma reaches the surface of the earth it cools and is considered lava.

7. **b.** Carcinogens cause mutations that lead to cancerous growth, which in most cases is unhealthy.

8. **d.** Alkaline solutions are basic so they have a pH between 8 and 14.

9. **b.** Start by balancing the reactants first. From the products it is determined that there are six oxygen atoms, so six are needed in the reactants. This would lead to $2Fe_2O_3$. Now, determine the total iron (Fe) on the product side by looking at what is present as reactants. There are four iron atoms, therefore 4Fe is needed in the products.

10. d. A watershed collects water and drains it into a river.

11. b. Most likely the parents expressed the dominant trait and carried the recessive allele, which was not expressed, as well. There is a 25% chance that each parent gives the offspring the recessive allele and the offspring expresses the recessive trait not expressed in its parents.

12. d. All organic compounds and organisms contain carbon in addition to other elements.

13. d. Electrons have negligible mass and are not included in the mass number.

14. a. Energy only enters the food chain through primary consumers. Improved farms would provide more energy from primary producers. Choice **b** would benefit the population, but not without choice **a**. Choice **d** is helpful, but humans are secondary consumers and have fewer predators than primary consumers.

15. c. Although some deserts get less than 2 inches per year, any place that gets less than 10 inches of rain per year is considered a desert.

16. c. An endothermic reaction most likely has a high activation energy. Catalysts reduce the activation energy of a reaction, which increases the rate of reaction. Choice **d** would cause the reaction to run in the reverse direction. Choice b would likely lead to more space between reactants and less collisions, decreasing the reaction rate.

17. a. Platelets are responsible for clotting blood.

18. a. Intermolecular forces refer to forces between molecules. Water is formed by covalent bonds between hydrogen and oxygen. There is an unequal sharing of electrons in the bonds, which creates a dipole in the molecule—one end has a positive charge and the other a negative. The dipoles of water molecules attract other water molecules and hold the solution strongly together (surface tension).

19. d. The father gives only his Y chromosome to the son, so the mother must have given the son the X-linked trait. Because the mother does not show the X-linked trait, she is considered a carrier of the trait.

20. c. The first and second largest reservoirs are the ocean and the glaciers and ice caps.

21. b. Fission reactions occur when a heavy nucleus, like uranium U-235, is bombarded by a neutron, and splits into two lighter nuclei, in this case barium and krypton, releasing enormous amounts of energy.

22. d. The food chain is the exchange of energy and starts with producers (plants) making energy from sunlight, then primary consumers eating the producers, and finally secondary consumers eating the primary consumers.

23. d. Tundra is cold and windy permafrost areas in polar regions and alpine locations. Adaptations favored in this biome would resist cold and adjust to scarce food supply. Choice **a** benefits animals by moving to warmer locations and searching for food.

24. a. A family represents a column on the periodic table. The atomic radius of elements increases toward the bottom of a family, leaving electrons farther away from the nucleus. Elements toward the bottom are less stable and more reactive.

25. c. When elements share their electrons they form a covalent bond.

Part 2: Arithmetic Reasoning

1. a. This is a two-step multiplication problem. First, multiply to find out how many weeks there are in six months: $6 \times 4.3 = 25.8$. Then, multiply to find out how much is saved: $\$40 \times 25.8 = \$1,032$.

2. d. In this problem, you must multiply a fraction by a whole number. First, rewrite the whole number as a fraction: $8 = \frac{8}{1}$. Next, multiply: $\frac{8}{1} \times \frac{4}{5} = \frac{32}{5}$. Finally, convert to a mixed number: $\frac{32}{5} = 6\frac{2}{5}$.

3. a. Add each of the known sectors, and subtract the sum from 100% to get 12%.

4. d. Since the rent sector is labeled 38%, find 38% of $2,450$: $0.38 \times 2,450 = \$931$.

5. d. First, determine which recycler pays the most for each material. Recycler X pays the most for aluminum, cardboard, and plastic; recycler Y pays the most for glass. Next, multiply the amount in pounds of each material by the price per pound you determined in the first step. Then add these totals together to get your answer: $2,200 \times .07 + 1,400 \times .04 + 3,100 \times .08 + 900 \times .03 = 485$.

6. c. Let x equal the number of oranges left in the basket. Three more than seven times as many oranges as five is $7(5) + 3 = 38$. Removing five leaves $x = 38 - 5 = 33$ oranges.

7. c. Convert both the cost and the length to fractions: $\frac{3}{4} \times \frac{22}{3} = \frac{66}{12}$ or $5\frac{1}{2}$, which is $\$5.50$.

8. b. If the lamp is 0.25 off of its original price, then the sale price will be 0.75 ($1.0 - 0.25 = 0.75$). Convert 0.75 into a fraction and reduce; $\frac{75}{100} = \frac{3}{4}$.

9. c. This is a division of fractions problem. First, change the whole number to a fraction: $6 = \frac{6}{1}$. Then, invert the second fraction and multiply: $\frac{6}{1} \times \frac{4}{1} = 24$.

10. d. To find 150% of 45, change the percent to a decimal and multiply: $1.50 \times 45 = 67.50$. Since this is the markup of the price, add $\$67.50$ to $\$45$ to find the new price of $\$112.50$.

11. b. This is a two-step problem involving multiplication and addition. First, determine how many cards were sold on Saturday: $0.05 \times 200 = 10$. That leaves 190 cards. Then, find out how many cards were sold on Sunday: $0.10 \times 190 = 19$. Next, add the cards that were sold: $10 + 19 = 29$. Finally, subtract from the original number: $200 - 29 = 171$.

12. b. This is a simple addition problem. Be sure to align the decimal points: $12.98 + 5.68 + 20.64 + 6.76 = 46.06$.

13. c. Multiply the number of hours in a day by the given number of days. There are 24 hours in each day. There are 120 hours in 5 days; 5 days $\times$ 24 hours $= 120$ hours.

14. c. This is a multiplication problem. To multiply a number by 1,000 quickly, move the decimal point three digits to the right—one digit for each zero. In this situation, because there are only two decimal places, add a zero.

15. c. Hilga and Jerome's initial distance apart equals the sum of the distance each travels in 2.5 hours. Hilga travels a distance of $(2.5)(2.5) = 6.25$ miles, while Jerome travels $(4)(2.5) = 10$ miles. This means that they were $6.25 + 10 = 16.25$ miles apart.

16. d. Three inches every 2 hours $= 1.5$ inches per hour $\times$ 5 hours $= 7.5$ inches.

17. b. For the lowest score Avi needs to get an A, assume his final average is 88. Average $= (90 + 80 + 85 + a) \div 4 = 88$. To find a, multiply 88 by 4. Then subtract Avi's first three scores: $88 \times 4 = 352$; $352 - (90 + 80 + 85) = 352 - 255 = 97$.

18. c. The problem is to find J, Joan's present age, in years. Begin by breaking the problem up into smaller parts: Joan will be twice Tom's age in three years becomes $J + 3 = 2T$; Tom will be 40 becomes $T = 40$. Substitute: $J + 3 = 2(40)$. Simplify: $J = 80 - 3$, or $J = 77$ years old.

19. a. The area of each poster is 864 square inches (24 inches × 36 inches). Kari may use four posters, for a total of 3,456 square inches (864×4). Each picture has an area of 24 square inches (4×6); the total area of the posters should be divided by the area of each picture, or $3,456 \div 24 = 144$.

20. c. This is a simple addition problem. Add 1.6 and 1.5, keeping the decimal points aligned: $1.6 + 1.5 = 3.1$.

21. a. The surface area of the trunk can be found by finding the sum of the areas of each of the six faces of the trunk. Since the answer is in square feet, change 18 inches to 1.5 feet: $2(4 \times 2) + 2(4 \times 1.5) + 2(2 \times 1.5) = 2(8) + 2(6) + 2(3) = 16 + 12 + 6 = 34$. Subtract the area of the brass ornament: $34 - 1 = 33$ square feet.

22. b. Divide the total number of seconds by the number of seconds in a minute. There are 60 seconds in a minute; 2,520 seconds is 42 minutes; 2,520 seconds ÷ 60 seconds = 42 minutes.

23. d. Let x equal the number of hours it takes Belinda to complete the job. In one hour, the neighbor can do $\frac{1}{38}$ of the job, while Belinda can do $\frac{1}{x}$. Working together, they take 22 hours to complete 100% of the job or: $\frac{1}{38}(22) + \frac{1}{x}(22) = 1$ (where 1 represents 100% of the job). Simplify: $\frac{22}{38} + \frac{22}{x} = 1$ or $\frac{22}{x} = 1 - \frac{22}{38}$, which reduces to $\frac{22}{x} = \frac{16}{38}$. Cross multiply: $16x = (22)(38)$, or $x = 52.25$ hours.

24. a. The empty crate weighs 8.16 kg, or 8,160 g. If Jon can lift 11,000 g and one orange weighs 220 g, then the number of oranges that he can pack into the crate is equal to $\frac{(11,000 - 8,160)}{220} = \frac{2,840}{220} \approx 12.9$. Jon cannot pack a fraction of an orange. He can pack 12 whole oranges into the crate.

25. a. Let D equal the time Dee arrived before class. Choosing to represent time before class as a negative number, you have: Jeff arrived 10 minutes early means $J = -10$, Dee came in four minutes after Mae means $D = M + 4$, Mae, who was half as early as Jeff means $M = (\frac{1}{2})J$. Substitute: $M = -5$, so $D = -5 + 4 = -1$. Thus, $D = 1$ minute before class.

26. d. First, determine the percent of time that the station is NOT playing classical music. Subtract from 100%: $100 - 20 = 80$. Eighty percent of the time the station does NOT play classical music. Then change the percent to a decimal and multiply: $0.8 \times 24 = 19.2$.

27. b. Divide the numerator by the denominator to find the whole number of the mixed number. The remainder, if any, becomes the numerator of the fraction: $55 \div 6 = 9$, remainder 1. The denominator stays the same. Therefore, the mixed number is $9\frac{1}{6}$.

28. a. In order to find the amount of fencing, the perimeter needs to be determined: $120 + 120 + 250 + 250 = 740$ feet.

29. a. This is a division problem. Because there are two decimal points in 1.25, move the decimal point two places in both numbers: $\frac{2,240}{125} = 17.92$.

30. d. This is a two-step problem. Divide 12.9 by 2 to get 6.45, and then add both numbers: $12.90 + 6.45 = 19.35$.

Part 3: Word Knowledge

1. b. *Noisome* means offensive, noxious, or harmful. Choice **a** might seem like a good choice, but noisome does not mean noisy.

2. c. To *capsize* means to flip or turn over. You were probably thinking of capitalize if you chose choice **a** or **b**.

3. a. An *arsenal* is a collection of weapons and munitions; a stockpile is a supply of items. Do not confuse *arsenal* with *arson*, which is a crime related to setting fires.

4. c. *Inert* means inactive, powerless, or motionless. If you chose choice **a** or **d** you may have been thinking of *inverted* or *interred*, respectively.

5. c. *Affix* and fasten both mean to join, attach, or secure.

6. a. *Aptitude* means ability, fitness in a task, or capability. Aptitude is not the same as attitude, which means mood or manner.

7. d. *Fractious* means mutinous, contentious, or quarrelsome. If you chose choice **a**, you might have been thinking of fictional. The word *fractious* is related to the word fraction, which means a piece broken off.

8. c. *Serene* means peaceful or calm. You might have been thinking of siren if you chose choice **a**.

9. b. *Improbable* means doubtful or unlikely. You might have chosen choice **a**, unlikeable, but that means not liked, or displeasing.

10. d. *Practical* can be used to describe something that is worth doing, useful, or convenient.

11. a. Something that is *elementary* is simple, rudimentary, or basic. Elementary school is where children learn basic concepts, but by themselves the terms elementary and school are not synonyms.

12. c. To *impart* means to tell, reveal, or give. Even though its root word is part, the word impart does not relate to separation or lack.

13. c. To *cower* means to cringe or crouch in fear. Be careful not to confuse frighten, a verb meaning to scare, with frightened, an adjective meaning to be scared.

14. b. *Spartan* means disciplined, frugal or simple.

15. a. Someone who is *adept* is highly proficient or skilled; an expert. Do not confuse adept with adopt, a verb that means to incorporate or include.

16. d. Both *agility* and dexterity are qualities meaning quick or nimble, or clever.

17. a. *Harry* means to assault, pester, or bother. Be careful not to confuse harry with hurry, hairy, or hurray.

18. c. *Remorse* is a feeling of compunction or regret.

19. c. *Haggard* means worn-out, weak, or exhausted.

20. b. *Prominent* means well-known, celebrated, or important.

21. c. The key phrase is "Never one to ignore a suggestion." This tells you that Max considers suggestions, or pays attention to them, which eliminates choices **a** and **b**. Choice **c**, attentive, means considerate or receptive.

22. b. If a careful explorer is unsure, he or she would probably act with caution, or cautiously. Choices **a**, **c**, and **d** do not reflect a careful approach.

23. d. The sentence tells us that Lindsay is suspicious of the salesperson, that she believes there is something wrong with the chair. While choice **c** is a likely reason why someone might decide not to buy a chair, only choice **d** agrees with Lindsay's suspicion.

24. b. The clues in this sentence are the words *experienced* and *confidence*; they tell you that Nancy is facing a challenging opponent, but she is not worried. Therefore, you should eliminate choices **a** and **d**. Choice **c**, though it might make sense, is not as strong a choice as **b**.

25. c. Choices **a** and **d** better describe Percy. *Brave* is not necessarily the opposite of cautious, but *reckless* certainly is.

26. a. The key phrase in this sentence is "dismissed as highbrow and farfetched"; it tells you that the missing word should be negatively connoted, which rules out choices **b** and **c**. Choice **d** does not provide an adequate reason why the theories would be dismissed, but *inaccessible* means "unfamiliar" or "obscure," which explains people's rejection.

27. b. Jeans and a T-shirt probably do not comply with an upscale dress code, so choice **a** is incorrect. Choice **c** does not make any sense. Choice **b** better connects and explains the second half of the sentence than choice **d**, even though both might be true.

28. b. The sentence asks for the opposite of nondescript and ramshackle. Choice **b** is the only logical answer.

29. d. The sentence implies that Jodi usually does not go to bed when asked; choice **d** is the only choice that reflects this idea.

30. c. Someone who is senile has difficulty remembering things. *Thoughtless* does not mean forgetful, but rather, inconsiderate or rude.

31. b. The missing word should mean the opposite of fascinating and beautiful; *mundane* means ordinary.

32. a. If the police are being criticized for taking too much time, then a logical response would be something to speed up the process and increase the chance of catching the culprit, to intensify efforts.

33. b. From the sentence you know that the missing word should describe a crowd that is insensitive. *Impassive*, meaning without emotion or apathetic, is the only word that fits.

34. b. The verb *laud* means to praise or honor; the only word that fits logically with that behavior is heroes.

35. c. A short-tempered person is likely to be rude, and such behavior would certainly have a negative impact on the customers. The other answer choices do not convey this meaning.

Part 4: Paragraph Comprehension

1. c. The passage states that the census is used to determine how many representatives each voting district can have in Washington, DC. None of the other choices is addressed.

2. b. The word *enumerate* means to count. The census counts the number of people who live in any voting district; thus, the people who work for the census are called enumerators or counters.

3. d. The passage states in the first paragraph that the 10-year census is required by the U.S. Constitution. None of the other choices is addressed.

4. b. The word *decennial* means occurring every 10 years. The prefix dec- means 10, and the root -ennial is the same as our word annual.

5. c. The passage states that many details of the Arthurian legend are based on historical facts. The author does touch on Tennyson's works, and mentions the legend's existence from the past into the future, but only choice **c** can be fully supported from the passage.

6. a. Something that *endures* lasts a long time despite difficulties and opposition. The legend of King Arthur is enduring because it has been written and read about for hundreds of years.

7. c. The second paragraph states that the real-life Merlin was influential in helping to establish British independence. None of the other choices is mentioned in the text.

8. b. The prefix proto- means first in time or earliest, so a *prototype* would be the first historical appearance of a person or thing.

9. c. The printing press revolutionized Western society because it allowed people to share ideas easily, as stated in the last sentence. The other choices might or might not be true, but they are not addressed in the passage.

10. a. To *disseminate* means to spread or to scatter in different directions. Farmers will disseminate seeds when they scatter them in a garden.

11. c. The passage states that moveable type consisted of letters molded in lead.

12. d. The first paragraph defines *xylography* as the art of engraving a page of text into a wooden block.

13. d. Both sentences in the paragraph support this choice. Choice **a** is an opinion and is not in the paragraph. Choices **b** and **c** may be true, but they are also not supported by the paragraph.

14. a. Choice **d** may seem attractive at first, but the passage simply says that the local media does not adequately cover local politics.

15. b. Both sentences in this passage support the idea that the emphasis on the low-carb and low-fat debate is misleading and might distract us from other important ideas. The other choices are not supported by or developed in this passage.

Part 5: Mathematics Knowledge

1. c. Multiply the two binomials using the distributive property so that each term from the first set of parentheses gets multiplied by each term of the second set of parentheses: $(x - 3)(x + 7) = x(x + 7) + -3(x + 7)$. Simplify the multiplication next: $x^2 + 7x - 3x - 21$. Combine like terms: $x^2 + 4x - 21$.

2. d. A composite number is a whole number greater than one that has other factors besides one and itself; in other words, it is not prime. Each of the answer choices is a prime number except 91, which has factors of 1, 7, 13, and 91.

3. c. Multiply across: $\frac{10}{216}$. Then reduce to lowest terms to get the answer: $\frac{5}{108}$.

4. c. The median of a group of numbers is found by arranging the numbers in ascending or descending order, and then finding the number in the middle of the set. First, arrange the numbers in order: 12, 14, 14, 16, 20, 22. Since there is an even number of numbers in the list, find the average of the two numbers that share the middle. In this case, the numbers in the middle are 14 and 16, and the average between them is 15.

5. a. The Pythagorean theorem states that the square of the length of the hypotenuse of a right triangle is equal to the sum of the squares of the other two sides, so you know that the following equation applies: $1^2 + x^2 = 10$, so $x^2 = 10 - 1 = 9$, so $x = 3$.

6. b. Both the isosceles trapezoid and the square have congruent diagonals, but only the square has diagonals that are both congruent and perpendicular.

7. b. If the circle is 100π square inches, its radius must be 10 inches, using the formula $A = \pi r^2$. Side AB is twice the radius, so it is 20 inches.

8. d. Use the place value of each of the nonzero numbers. The four is in the ten thousands place, so it is equal to 40,000, the five is in the hundreds place, so it is equal to 500, and the three is in the ones place, so it is equal to 3; $40,000 + 500 + 3 = 40,503$.

9. d. If the shorter sides are each 4 centimeters, then the longer sides must each equal $40 - 8 \div 2$; therefore, the length of each of the longer sides is 16 centimeters.

10. a. A straight angle is exactly 180°.

11. c. In order to find an equivalent fraction, you need to perform the same action on both the numerator and the denominator. One way to solve for x is to ask the question, "What is multiplied by 19 (the denominator) to get a product of 76?" Divide: $76 \div 19 = 4$. Then, multiply the numerator by 4 in order to find the value of x: $4 \times 1 = 4$.

12. a. To solve the inequality $12x - 1 < 35$, first solve the equation $12x - 1 = 35$. In this case, the solution is $x = 3$. Replace the equal sign with the *less than* symbol ($<$): $x < 3$. Since values of x *less than* 3 satisfy this inequality, 2 is the only answer choice that would make the inequality true.

13. d. Squares, rectangles, and rhombuses are quadrilateral (have four sides), and each has two pairs of parallel sides. However, all angles in both squares and rectangles are 90°. Therefore, only a rhombus could contain two angles that measure 65°.

14. a. To simplify the radical, first find the square root of 64, which is 8. Then divide each exponent on the variables by 2 to find the square root of the variables. If the exponent is odd, the remainder stays inside the radical: $\sqrt{x^5} = x^2\sqrt{x}$ and $\sqrt{y^8} = y^4$. Thus, the result is $8x^2y^4\sqrt{x}$.

15. c. The correct answer is 10,447. It helps, if you are in a place where you can do so, to read the answer aloud; that way, you will likely catch any mistake. When writing numbers with four or more digits, begin at the right and separate the digits into groups of three with commas.

16. b. A prime number is a whole number whose only factors are one and itself. Two, three, and seven are all prime numbers. The prime factors of a number are the prime numbers that multiply to equal that number: $2 \times 3 \times 7 = 42$.

17. d. First, add 4 to both sides of the equation: $\sqrt{2a+6} - 4 + 4 = 6 + 4$. The equation simplifies to $\sqrt{2a+6} = 10$. Square each side to eliminate the radical sign: $(\sqrt{2a+6})^2 = 10^2$. The equation becomes $2a + 6 = 100$. Subtract 6 from each side of the equal sign and simplify: $2a + 6 - 6 = 100 - 6$; $2a = 94$. Divide each side by 2: $\frac{2a}{2} = \frac{94}{2}$. Therefore, $a = 47$.

18. a. Only like terms can be added: $4x - 7y + 7x + 7y$; $4x + 7x$ and $-7y + 7y$. The y terms cancel each other out, leaving $11x$ as the correct answer.

19. d. You must "borrow" 60 minutes from the three hours in order to be able to subtract.

20. b. Since there are three sections shaded out of a total of five sections, the part shaded is $\frac{3}{5}$.

21. a. The sum of three numbers means $(a + b + c)$, the sum of their reciprocals means $(\frac{1}{a} + \frac{1}{b} + \frac{1}{c})$. Combine terms: $(a + b + c)(\frac{1}{a} + \frac{1}{b} + \frac{1}{c})$. Thus, choice **a** is the correct answer.

22. c. Consecutive odd integers are positive or negative whole numbers in a row that are two apart, such as 1, 3, 5 or −23, −21, −19. To find three consecutive odd integers whose sum is 117, divide 117 by 3 to get 39; $39 - 2 = 37$ and $39 + 2 = 41$. To check, add the three integers: $37 + 39 + 41 = 117$.

23. d. By adding the two equations vertically, you end up with $2y = 8$, so y must equal 4. Substitute 4 for y in either original equation to get $x = 6$. Therefore, the point of intersection where the two lines are equal is $(6,4)$.

24. c. Since there is a common denominator, add the numerators and keep the denominator: $\frac{7w}{z}$.

25. b. Take the reciprocal of the fraction being divided by, change the operation to multiplication, and cancel common factors between the numerators and denominators: $\frac{6a^2b}{2c} \div \frac{ab^2}{4c^4}$ becomes $\frac{6a^2b}{2c} \times \frac{4c^4}{ab^2} = \frac{12ac^3}{b}$.

Part 6: Electronics Information

1. c. Not grounding an electrical device runs the risk of electrocution.

2. c. 60 Hz is the frequency of the alternating voltage, which is the type of voltage used in the United States.

3. c. To determine the total resistance in a series circuit similar to the one presented, total resistance is equal to the sum of the individual resistors. Hence, the total resistance in this schematic would be $R_1 + R_2 + R_3 = 1,500$ ohms.

4. b. Metal in a microwave oven reflecting the microwave energy generated by the microwave's magnetron can be reflected back. The metal can also cause arcing and sparks from interaction with the microwaves.

5. b. The total current is equal to the sum of the currents through each resistor. Therefore, $4A + 4A + 4A = 12A$.

6. a. FM stands for frequency modulation.

7. c. This symbol in a schematic depicts a wire that does not join another.

8. c. Electrical pressure results from a difference of electrical force between two points. Hence, voltage is what pushes electricity through a circuit.

9. c. Coulomb's law describes the electrostatic force between electric charges.

10. c. The total resistance (25Ω) is already known. Using Ohm's law to determine the voltage drop, we first solve for I, which gives the total current flowing through the circuit. Since the resistors are in series, the same amount of current flows through each resistor. Once I is known, Ohm's law again lets us solve for E across R1:
$I = E/R = 48/25 = 1.92$ A
$E = IR = 1.92 \times 10 = 19.2$ V

11. a. If a vacuum cleaner is rated at 1,200 watts and operates at 120 volts, it will draw 10 amps of current. The Power Law can be applied:
$P = I \times E; I = P \div E; I = 1,200$ watts $\div 120$ volts; $I = 10$ amperes.

12. d. The electronic term given to a unit of electromotive force is a *volt*.

13. b. A loopstick antenna is optimized for frequencies below 300kHz. Parabolic-shaped or dish antennas typically operate in the gigahertz range.

14. d. The design of a corner reflector antenna includes a conductive sheet behind it to direct radiation in the forward direction, enhancing reception by increasing the directivity of the RF signals.

15. c. In antenna design, the larger the diameter of the reflector, the greater the reception effectiveness of a directional antenna, also known as gain.

16. c. The power in circuit A is one-half the power in B, so the current through A must be one-half the current through B. If either circuit had no current flowing, there would be zero power dissipated.

17. b. The image shown is a horn antenna.

18. c. FM radio broadcasting, amateur radio, broadcast television, and commercial aircraft transmit on very high frequency (VHF). VHF bands use the 30–300 MHz frequency band.

19. c. A tuning capacitor is used in a radio device to adjust the resonant frequency or tune a radio frequency.

20. b. A transformer changes voltage and amperage.

Part 7: Auto and Shop Information

1. c. Properly inflated tires, along with a tuned-up engine, will help to ensure you are getting the best gas mileage possible out of your vehicle.

2. d. A flow meter will measure the rate at which a fluid is flowing through the piping system.

3. c. An example of a flow meter would be a gas pump gauge. The pump gauge measures how much fuel is passing from the pump, through the nozzle, and into your tank.

4. a. The positive crankcase ventilation (PCV) system recirculates harmful emissions from the engine that would otherwise be vented out into the atmosphere.

5. c. Recycled oil can have any number of uses from refinement into lubricating oil, recycling into oil to be burned for energy consumption, or for use in smaller oil-burning heaters. Discarding the used oil into the ecosystem via a wastewater drain will result in oil pollution of our waterways and our groundwater systems.

6. a. Fuel gauges will typically read in gallons or liters.

7. c. The automobile battery stores electricity and supplies power for a number of vehicle functions, including starting and ignition requirements. When the battery is drained of power, the alternator recharges the battery while the engine is running, in essence making electricity through rotary motion from a belt assembly powered by the engine.

8. b. The muffler is a component mounted midway between the engine and the exhaust where baffles and other sound-deadening materials are positioned to quiet and block the noise of the engine cylinder explosions and power cycles.

9. d. Leaf springs and coil compression springs are both suspension devices used to provide a smoother ride.

10. b. A hydrometer is an instrument used to measure the specific gravity (or relative density) of liquids. It examines the ratio of the density of the solution of antifreeze to the density of water.

11. d. Carbon monoxide (CO) results from the incomplete combustion of vehicle fuels. Gasoline engines emit a higher proportion of CO than diesel engines, due to the lower combustion temperature. Nitrogen oxides (NOx) are precursors for the formation of smog components such as ground-level ozone. Hydrocarbons contribute to the formation of tropospheric ozone and greenhouse gases.

12. a. Engines need a thin film of lubricant to ensure the various metal-on-metal contact points do not overheat or suffer excessive wear. The oil pump pushes oil through engine oil passages.

13. c. The transaxle combines a transmission, the differential, and associated components into one integrated assembly. Automobile configurations that have the engine at the same end of the car as the driven wheels (e.g., front-wheel drive/front-engine mounted or rear-wheel drive/rear-engine mounted) use a transaxle since space and mechanical restrictions make it difficult to mount a conventional drivetrain.

14. c. A hinge mortise is a recessed notch cut into a piece of wood so that a door hinge will fit flush within the mortise.

15. d. A lateral cut is not one of the six basic woodworking cuts. In addition to crosscut, rip, and miter, the remaining three are bevel crosscut, bevel rip, and bevel miter cuts.

16. d. A weld melts the two materials needing to be joined so when they cool they become one piece through the process of coalescence. A nail and screw merely join two pieces of wood together. A solder uses a fusible metal alloy that joins two pieces together but lacks the strength of a weld.

17. c. Hydration is the process by which the water reacts with the cement and bonds the other components together, eventually creating a stonelike material.

18. a. A float, sometimes called a bull float, is used to put a smooth final finish to floors. A screed is used to level the just-poured concrete. Tamping is a process whereby the materials in concrete are consolidated and it forces coarse aggregates below the surface. Forms are the temporary structure or mold for the support of concrete while it is setting and curing.

19. d. A split lock washer is designed to prevent nuts and bolts from backing out. A flat washer is used to distribute loads evenly through the connection. A fender washer is an oversize flat washer used to further distribute load, especially on soft materials. An ogee washer is typically used in dock and wood construction.

20. c. Steel is most often used to provide additional strength in concrete slabs and walls due to its high strength and relatively low cost.

21. d. Cement, sand, gravel, and water are the four primary ingredients in concrete.

22. d. Tile shingles are expensive but have a long life. Wooden "shake shingles" are also used as roofing material. The most common outer roofing material is asphalt shingles, since they are low in cost and provide good protection.

23. c. The hand tool depicted is a crescent wrench.

24. d. There is no tool known as a box hammer.

25. c. If a line is plumb, it is perfectly vertical.

Part 8: Mechanical Comprehension

1. a. $w_1 \times d_1 = w_2 \times d_2$. 27 pounds $\times$ 4 feet = 24 pounds $\times d_2$. Solving for d_2 gives 4.5 feet.

2. b. A pulley system of this type has a mechanical advantage of 3. If 160 pounds of force is applied, a maximum weight of 160 pounds $\times$ 3 = 480 pounds can be lifted.

3. c. An object will float on top of a liquid if its density is less than the liquid it is in and sink if its density is greater. In this case, the penny is less dense than mercury and denser than water, so it will float on top of the mercury and sink in water, meaning it will settle directly in between the two layers.

4. a. The mechanical advantage (MA) of a ramp is determined by the length of the ramp, l, divided by the height gained, h. In this case, MA = $\frac{l}{h}$ = 20 feet ÷ 5 feet = 4. The force required to pull a 240-pound block up a ramp is 240 pounds ÷ 4 = 60 pounds.

5. b. Mechanical advantage = output force ÷ input force. Here, 50 pounds of force is input into a jack to lift a 3,000-pound car. The mechanical advantage is 3,000 ÷ 50 = 60.

6. a. Heating leads to an increase in pressure of a contained gas. Since no air is added or removed from the tires, their overall weight remains constant.

7. b. The arm acts as a lever with the pivot point being where it intersects the crane body. By attaching the cable as far along the arm as possible, the greatest mechanical advantage is achieved.

8. a. The total weight of the block and the plank is 14 pounds. The weight is distributed evenly between the two scales, meaning that Scale 1 will read 7 pounds.

9. b. The force constant of the spring is 9 pounds ÷ 3 inches = 3 pounds per inch. Using the equation, $F = kx$, we have 12 pounds = 3 pounds per inch × x. Solving for x gives 4 inches.

10. a. An object's density determines whether it will float or sink. To float, it must have a lower density than water. Surface area will not affect whether an object ultimately floats or sinks.

11. b. If 15 turns move the nut 1.25 inches, there are 15 turns ÷ 1.25 inches = 12 threads per inch.

12. b. The mechanical advantage of this pulley system is 2. The force required to lift the 200-pound load is 200 pounds ÷ 2 = 100 pounds.

13. b. Metals such as steel tend to expand considerably when heated. The other materials may expand somewhat when heated, but to a lesser extent.

14. c. Each revolution of gear 1 will turn gear 2 12 teeth ÷ 9 teeth = $1\frac{1}{3}$ times. At 30 revolutions per minute, gear 2 will turn at 30 rpm × $1\frac{1}{3}$ = 40 rpm.

15. b. The mechanical advantage (MA) of a ramp is determined by the length of the ramp, l, divided by the height gained, h. In this case, MA = $\frac{l}{h}$ = 18 feet ÷ 6 feet = 3. Since the barrel weighs 300 pounds, a force of 300 ÷ 3 = 100 pounds is required to keep the barrel in place.

16. c. Each turn of the pedals will move the rear wheel 55 ÷ 11 = 5 revolutions. If the bike is pedaled at 80 rpm, the rear wheel will rotate at 80 rpm × 5 revolutions = 400 rpm. Since 30 seconds is half of one minute, the rear wheel will complete 400 rpm ÷ 2 = 200 revolutions

17. a. Helium is less dense than air. Objects will float when they are less dense than air. Helium will float regardless of its temperature.

18. c. While no mechanical advantage is gained, a pulley system such as this one allows one to raise an object while pulling downward, rather than having to climb above the object to pull it.

19. d. If gear 4 turns clockwise, the neighboring gears 1 and 3 will turn counterclockwise.

20. d. The amount of water that flows out through the pipes is proportional to the size of the pipe opening. Since the area of the opening is proportional to the square of the diameter, the ratio of the amount of water that flows out of A and B is $6^2 \div 2^2 = 9$.

21. c. 14 miles ÷ 8 mph = 1.75 hours = 1 hour 45 minutes.

22. c. If the 600-pound block can be lifted with 200 pounds of force, the ramp has a mechanical advantage (MA) of 3. The MA of a ramp is determined by the length of the ramp, l, divided by the height gained, h. In this case, MA $= 3 = \frac{l}{h} = \frac{15 \text{ feet}}{h}$. Solving for h tells us the ramp is 5 feet high.

23. a. $w_1 \times d_1 = w_2 \times d_2$. Paul is 15 feet away from the pivot point and the block is 20 feet away. 90×20 feet $= 15$ feet $\times w_2$. Solving for w_2 gives 120 pounds.

24. c. As the balloon rises, the air pressure surrounding it will decrease and the internal pressure from the helium will press outward on the walls of the balloon, increasing it in size. Since the balloon is a closed system, its weight will be unaffected.

25. d. Since pulley A is 1.5 times greater in circumference than pulley B, each revolution of A will lead to 1.5 revolutions of B. The belt of the pulley will cause pulley B to move in the same direction (counter-clockwise) as pulley A.

Part 9: Assembling Objects

1. c.
2. b.
3. c.
4. d.
5. d.
6. d.
7. c.
8. b.
9. d.
10. b.

11. b.
12. c.
13. a.
14. d.
15. c.
16. b.
17. c.
18. d.
19. a.
20. d.
21. b.
22. d.
23. b.
24. d.
25. a.

Scoring

Write your raw score (the number you got right) for each test in the blanks below. Then turn to Chapter 2 to find out how to convert these raw scores into the scores the armed services use.

1. General Science: _____ right out of 25
2. Arithmetic Reasoning: _____ right out of 30
3. Word Knowledge: _____ right out of 35
4. Paragraph Comprehension: _____ right out of 15
5. Mathematics Knowledge: _____ right out of 25
6. Electronics Information: _____ right out of 20
7. Auto and Shop Information: _____ right out of 25
8. Mechanical Comprehension: _____ right out of 25
9. Assembling Objects: _____ right out of 25

ADDITIONAL ONLINE PRACTICE ▶

Whether you need help building basic skills or preparing for an exam, visit the LearningExpress Practice Center! On this site, you can access additional practice materials. Using the code below, you'll be able to log in and take an additional full-length ASVAB practice exam. This online practice exam will also provide you with:

- **Immediate Scoring**
- **Detailed answer explanations**
- **Personalized recommendations for further practice and study**

Log on to the LearningExpress Practice Center by using the URL: **www.learnatest.com/practice**

This is your Access Code: **7496**

Follow the steps online to redeem your access code. After you've used your access code to register with the site, you will be prompted to create a username and password. For easy reference, record them here.

Username: _____ **Password:** _____

With your username and password, you can log in and answer these practice questions as many times as you like. If you have any questions or problems, please contact LearningExpress customer service at 1-800-295-9556 ext. 2, or e-mail us at **customerservice@learningexpressllc.com**

NOTES

NOTES

NOTES

NOTES

NOTES

NOTES

NOTES

NOTES

NOTES

NOTES